CW00735847

SHIELS TO SHIE

Frontispiece: the promontory at the northern entrance to the River Tyne, seen from the direction of the bay to the north known as The Haven.

Shiels to Shields

The Life Story of
a North Tyneside Town

Danny Lawrence

*To my sister Margaret and wife Helen
for all their love and support*

Shiels to Shields: The Life Story of a North Tyneside Town

Copyright © Danny Lawrence, 2016

First edition

Published by Carnegie Publishing Ltd
Chatsworth Road, Lancaster LA1 4SL
www.carnegiepublishing.com

British Library Cataloguing-in-Publication data
A catalogue record for this book is available from the British Library

ISBN 978-1-85936-228-0

Designed, typeset and originated by Carnegie Publishing
Print managed and manufactured by Jellyfish Solutions

Contents

Preface vii

Acknowledgements xvii

1 The early history of Tynemouth... 1
   Romans, Anglo-Saxons, Danes and Normans 1
   Tynemouth Priory from the Norman Conquest
   to the Dissolution of the Monasteries 10
   Tynemouth Castle from the medieval era to the accession of
   William and Mary 15

2 North Shields v. Newcastle: a struggle for survival 28
   The early pattern of settlement 29
   Conflict and competition with Newcastle 30
   Ralph Gardner's resistance 37
   The end of the Newcastle monopoly 40

3 It's like taking coals to Shields 41
   The initial phase: coal collecting 42
   The evolution of the coal trade 43

4 Free at last: economic change since the eighteenth century 51
   The rise and fall of coal 54
   Shipping 58
   Shipbuilding 70
   Fishing... 74
   The expansion of commercial services and utilities... 77

5 Transformation of the built environment 79
   The long narrow street 84
   The Bank Top 86

6 Beyond Shields 97
   Access by river 97
   Access by road 100
   Access by rail 102

7 Civic pride and independence 108
   Component parts of Tynemouth Borough 109
   Public utilities and services 115

8 Religious institutions 129
   Organised religion from the sixteenth to the mid-nineteenth
   century 130
   Religious institutions in the mid-nineteenth century. 148
   Religion and social class 150
   Consolidation and decline. 155
   Other religious groups 168

9 Leisure time 171
   Constraints and influences 171
   Victorian leisure in the home 177
   Victorian leisure outside the home 178

10 The labouring classes (I): barriers to progress 205
   Political oppression 206
   Economic exploitation 217
   Justice and injustice 222

11 The labouring classes (II): social and economic conditions 228
   Squalor 228
   Disease 239
   Idleness 246
   Ignorance 250
   Want 263

12 The labouring classes (III): responses to poverty 276
   Help from others. 276
   Self-help 287

13 A final word 303

   Notes and references 307

   Bibliography 323

   Index 337

Preface

Background

S*HIELS TO SHIELDS* describes how North Shields developed from a cluster of fishermen's shelters on the north bank of the entrance to the River Tyne into a thriving town and independent borough. It did so despite bitter recurring disputes with its much bigger neighbour Newcastle. This comprehensive account of the town's extraordinary life story is long overdue and in the best Carnegie tradition is written in a style accessible to the widest possible readership.

Although *Shiels to Shields* is concerned with a particular locality, its development is discussed in the context of national events and issues. This is essential both to understand the town's evolution and to enable the book to contribute to our wider understanding of social, economic and political change in Britain. As Ruth Finnegan has noted: 'Historians are increasingly turning to questions raised in social history, and moving outside elite studies to those of ordinary people. ... This has led to a new appreciation of the role of individual lives and of the local and personal variants within what once looked uniform and homogeneous trends such as industrialization or modernization.'[1] *Shiels to Shields* is a contribution to that new appreciation of our history. It is also a *Who Do You Think You Are?* for those with roots in North Shields. It not only describes its development but the conditions in which ordinary people lived their lives and the struggles they endured to establish the opportunities and life styles most of us enjoy today.

Those familiar only with the North Shields of today may find it difficult to recognise the North Shields described in this book. Ironically, after centuries when it struggled merely to survive, it ultimately became a victim of its own success. The huge development of the local economy first stimulated but then encouraged its decline as a residential area. The industries that made their owners wealthy created environmental conditions that they did not find congenial. They began to move into the unspoiled countryside beyond the wealth-creating part of the town. Later, the middle classes moved in increasing numbers into its newly built private suburbs. As the worst of the housing was cleared from the riverside; much of the town's working-class population moved into publicly built suburbs. Now, thanks to modern transportation, the residents of North Shields and the surrounding area can work, shop and seek entertainment wherever they want within the Tyneside conurbation. Unfortunately, that has contributed to a decline in the fortunes of North Shields' town centre.

When I was young and North Shields was still part of the County Borough of Tynemouth, I wondered why the borough took its name from one particular residential area. My first thought was that it was because Tynemouth was 'posher' than North Shields. The late Norman Christenson echoed those thoughts in his *Plodgin' Through the Clarts* when he described the Borough as split into 'Tynemouth … the posh half of the town' and 'North Shields … always the poor relation'.[2] However, my childhood hypothesis was mistaken. Naming the Borough after Tynemouth was a recognition that it existed long before North Shields and that North Shields owed its very existence to the monks of Tynemouth Priory.

North Shields is now part of the Metropolitan Borough of North Tyneside. Prior to that, it contained the heaviest concentration of the population of the County Borough of Tynemouth. North Shields was then and still remains a real place, with a distinctive history, to which people have a sense of belonging. Sadly, much of its heritage was lost during the twentieth century. Fortunately, the more disparate North Tyneside is now making considerable efforts to preserve what is left.

I was born in 1940, just nine years before the Borough of Tynemouth celebrated its 100th anniversary. The town's best years were over by then but I was fortunate to have lived in it before its Georgian heart was ripped out in the 1970s to make room for a never very successful shopping centre. I grew up feeling part of North Shields. I was not only *from* North Shields but also *of* North Shields. I took its physical features and socio-economic contours for granted. To me, it was an established entity. The physical and socio-economic landscape that constituted North Shields appeared like a fixed stage backdrop against which my young life was being played.

That feeling was reinforced by the fact that I grew up close to all those civic elements which symbolise an established and autonomous community. The County Borough of Tynemouth had its own coat of arms and its own mayor. Its municipal offices were only yards from where I lived. Across the street, I could see the police station and magistrates' courts. Just round the corner was the entrance to the Town Hall. All these buildings were built of stone (albeit black stone that in my childhood ignorance I assumed was its natural condition) and seemed to bear testament to the fact that these symbolic buildings were both important and old. The headquarters of the fire and ambulance services were on our street, less than ten doors away. Behind us was the main post office with its imposing brick and red stone façade. Within 100 yards was the impressive corner building, with its projecting four-faced clock, that was the town's main library. The results

of the 1945 election, when Labour secured a unexpected landslide victory; that of 1950, when Labour scraped home with a tiny majority, and that of 1951, which brought Winston Churchill back into power, were all declared within sight and sound of my home before I had reached the age of eleven.

My sense of North Shields as a completed and enduring entity was reinforced in other ways. Its past was there to be seen alongside its present. On a cliff above the entrance to the River Tyne stood the remains of Tynemouth Priory in which three kings (two of Northumbria and one of Scotland) had been buried. A short distance away, a column and statue, comparable in grandeur to Nelson's in Trafalgar Square, towered over the entrance to the River Tyne. It had been erected in honour of Admiral Lord Collingwood, a Northumbrian with a family home in North Shields, who led the British fleet into action at Trafalgar and assumed command after Nelson was fatally wounded. A little further up the Tyne was the then very busy North Shields Fish Quay. It was from the little fishing *shiels* that had once occupied the same riverbank that the town had taken its name. But I also knew that long before I was born North Shields had outgrown those early beginnings and that the town centre that I grew up to take for granted had been created on the plateau high above the riverside.

I assumed all this had happened a long time ago and, relative to my short life, that was the case. North Shields, as I saw it as a child, seemed to be an established given to which I was proud to belong. It was a major fishing port. It could boast being the home to Smith's Dock, then the largest ship repair company in the world. In addition to all manner of other industries, traditional and modern, it had numerous churches, cinemas, banks, building societies and shops of every description; large (by the standards of those days) and small (even by the standards of those days). The town was the hub of a local transport network. At the top of the street where I was born and raised, the red double-deckers of the Tynemouth Bus Company converged on the impressive Georgian Northumberland Square. From there, passengers were transported through residential areas to all parts of the Borough of Tynemouth and beyond, through Wallsend, as far as Newcastle and Gateshead. Brown United buses used the Square to take passengers to the mining areas around Backworth where my father had been born. Yellow Newcastle buses used the recently built dual-carriageway Coast Road to carry passengers to and from North Shields and then along an older road parallel to the river to the terminus by Tynemouth Priory. A little further to the west, green Tyneside buses ran from North Shields to Newcastle but, in this instance, alongside the heavily industrialised riverside. A few minutes walking distance to the west of Northumberland Square was the railway station which created, in my young mind, a sense of substance and permanence. Its arched entrances led into a large cobbled

North Shields General Post Office. The Post Office is on the right foreground of this postcard issued about 1900.

CONTEMPORARY POSTCARD

Saville Street and General Post Office, North Shields

| Shiels to Shields

Collingwood's Monument, erected in 1845. The statue was sculpted by John Graham Lough and stands on a pedestal designed by John Dobson. The cannons from Collingwood's Trafalgar flagship *Royal Sovereign* were added in 1849.

area, covered with a high glass canopy. From there, passengers entered the lofty enclosed waiting area with its ticket kiosks and newsagent's shop. Down a pillared, wrought-iron decorated, glass-roofed staircase, they descended to the platform where electric trains took passengers not only to the more distant parts of Tyneside but also, via the mainline station at Newcastle, the whole of the rest of Britain. North Shields also boasted two hospitals, a semi-professional football team, two Northumberland League cricket clubs, a rugby club, golf club and all manner of other recreational facilities – even its own daily newspaper. Its citizens enjoyed access to several meticulously maintained public parks in which the gardeners competed with one another each year to produce the most elaborate floral displays.

I could go on – and on – but the essential point I wish to convey is that I grew up thinking of North Shields not as a place of on-going change but as a completed and permanent town. The few changes to the physical environment I witnessed were primarily to repair the damage inflicted by the Luftwaffe. Bomb sites were part of the North Shields landscape for a long time: a horrific reminder to those old enough to remember World War Two. Having been born in the closing days of 1940, with the worst of the bombing coming in the next two years, my own memories of the war and its privations have never been strong. My main recollections are of a world which, according to the grown-ups, was at last returning to normal. I can recall unzipping my first banana and both the first and second lifting of rationing on sweets. But, as a child, I remained unaware of the much more significant changes that had followed the end of the war. I was, for example, too young to appreciate the significance of the introduction of the free-at-the-point-of-delivery National Health Service and free secondary education, of which I was to be an early beneficiary.

What I read into the physical features of North Shields I also read into its social contours. The population of North Shields appeared to be as settled as its institutions. I was aware of class distinctions from an early age and became self-conscious about them when I went to Tynemouth Municipal High School. Unlike most of my grammar school contemporaries, I was from a working-class background. Yet, except in respect of class, the population was not obviously heterogeneous. 'The canny folks of Shields' had, like me, been born and bred there. To varying degrees, we spoke with the same distinctive North Shields variant of the Geordie accent. People did differ in terms of their religious affiliations, but it seemed to make no obvious difference to the way in which they related to one another. Indeed, my own father was a Protestant and my mother a Catholic. I knew we had some Jews in the town but only because my father, for no obvious reason, once casually remarked that someone who had just alighted from the bus on which we were travelling was Jewish. With few exceptions, everyone was white. I was aware that a handful of shops were owned by people born in Italy and Poland and I had my hair cut for a time by a German barber. But North Shields was not an obvious multi-ethnic or multi-cultural community. On the contrary, it seemed to me to be notably homogeneous.

The history I was taught at school concentrated almost exclusively on political, military and economic change at a national level. We learned a smattering of economic history, though almost entirely in terms of the technical transformations that took place during the Industrial Revolution. Social history, and particularly local social history, appeared not to warrant serious consideration. I cannot recall any teacher even mentioning the way in which the socio-economic transformations of the industrial revolution affected North Shields. So while I learned, in very general terms, about the ancient Britons, Romans, Anglo-Saxons and Normans and left school with an 'O' level in history, having been introduced to such topics as the Black Hole of Calcutta and the scaling of the Heights of Abraham, I knew virtually nothing about the history of my own town and community.

From school, after a year working in the personnel department of Swan Hunter's world-famous shipyard, I went to university to study the social sciences. After graduating, I became a lecturer in sociology. My first major piece of research resulted in the publication of *Black Migrants, White Natives: A Study of Race Relations in Nottingham*. The research and discussion in that book relates to the exploitation of minorities in British colonies and the subsequent socio-economic processes that brought immigrants from those colonies to this country – in the very period during which I was growing up in North Shields and studying at university. At that point in my life I did not appreciate that there were elements in that research comparable to the origins and development of North Shields. That

| Shiels to Shields

ignorance continued until, later in life, when I had time to study the origins of North Shields and my own family history.

In offering this wide-ranging treatment of the history of North Shields, I am conscious that I am a largely self-taught rather than trained academic historian. I specialised in science at school; took a social science degree at university (which did include a course in social history taught by the late John Saville); completed a Ph.D. on race relations and earned my living for 33 years as a sociologist at the University of Nottingham. However, whatever my personal limitations, *Shiels to Shields* is the most substantial book on North Shields since Craster's major work published in 1907.[3] My hope is that *Shiels to Shields* will serve as a history of the town for the present and near future and prove a useful starting point for further research. That is why *Shiels to Shields* includes detailed references. They are included not only to acknowledge properly the contributions of earlier writers but also to make it easier for others to review the sources on which I have drawn. Writing the book has taken many years of hard work, so I will be disappointed if it becomes another unacknowledged source to be mined by those putting together pieces for internet websites.

Finally, I must add that when using quotations from earlier work I have retained the original spelling and punctuation, often markedly different from that in use today.

Outline of the book

North Shields might never have existed had it not been for the actions of those who controlled the Priory at Tynemouth. This association is critical to understanding the origins and early history of the town. For that reason, Chapter 1 is devoted to the history of the Priory and Castle which stood on the imposing promontory at the entrance to the River Tyne. All one can see of them today are picturesque remains, but their historical significance is important and needs explanation. The chapter outlines the history of the site during several phases, from the Roman through to the Anglo-Saxon and Danish invasions and beyond to its role after the Norman Conquest. Although the role of the Priory may have ended with the dissolution of the monasteries, the site remained important as a castle during successive conflicts with Scotland and during the civil wars of the mid-seventeenth century. The later history of the Castle was less eventful but it continued to play a role in guarding the Tyne against foreign invasions and was in use for that purpose as recently as the twentieth century.*

---

* Tynemouth Priory and Castle have been the setting for several works of fiction including Jane Harvey's gothic novel *The Castle of Tynemouth: A Tale* (1806); Winifred Cawley's *Down the Lonely Stairs*, a civil-war children's story that portrays seventeenth-century society from the point of view of both the wealthy coal merchants and the miners (1964); and Ian Watson's science fiction novel, *The Fire Worm* (1988).

Tynemouth Priory's illustrious history was brought to an abrupt end in the sixteenth century. The small settlement that its monks had established on the riverside survived but, without its ecclesiastical champion, North Shields was in real danger of disappearing from the map. This was not yet the world of free trade and global markets that we know today. It was a world of protectionism, dominated by local privileges conferred on towns and cities by royal charters. North Shields was always – and very much – the underdog in relation to Newcastle. Ever since Newcastle's burgesses had been granted a royal charter in 1213, they insisted that they enjoyed a legal monopoly of trade on the Tyne, and sought to maintain their dominant position through fair means and foul. It was only after a centuries-long, bitter struggle that North Shields eventually emerged in the nineteenth century as a town with a burgeoning economy which made it a magnet for migrants. Chapter 2, *North Shields v. Newcastle – a Battle for Survival*, describes the origins and early development of North Shields; the centuries-long conflict between it and Newcastle, and the end to the Newcastle monopoly, which came slowly as a result of changes in the economic climate at both national and international level.

North Shields suffered in many ways as a result of the ruthless domination of the commercial life of the River Tyne by the burgesses of Newcastle. It probably lost most by not being able to share fully in the lucrative trade in coal which meant so much to Newcastle. Coal and Newcastle came to be so closely identified that in many parts of the world the expression *It's Like Taking Coals to Newcastle* was adopted to signify an activity that was utterly pointless. No one, of course, has encountered the expression *It's Like Taking Coals to Shields*. I have coined it as the title for Chapter 3 to help make the point that without Newcastle's determination to curtail the competition from its neighbouring Tyneside towns, North Shields, given its more convenient position at the mouth of the river, might also have become a major British town.

Stearns emphasised that, 'beginning in the eighteenth century, demographic, economic and political forces arose in Europe that were truly revolutionary'.[4] In the case of North Shields, those changes coincided with the decline in the monopolistic position which Newcastle had enjoyed on the Tyne in previous centuries. The combination of these general and particular developments provided commercial opportunities for North Shields' entrepreneurs beyond the dreams of those who had lived in earlier periods. Many became rich and influential in the process. Chapter 4, *Free at Last: Economic Change since the Eighteenth Century*, provides examples of key developments in the local economy, particularly with respect to the coal trade, shipping, shipbuilding, fishing, commercial services and utilities.

At the beginning of the eighteenth century, North Shields was limited to a narrow strip of land, sandwiched between the high north bank of the Tyne and the river. As the range and scale of its economic activities and population increased, it could expand only on the Bank Top (or Bankhead) some 70 feet (25 m) above. Until that time, the long narrow street and the plateau above were virtually separate worlds. The inhabitants of North Shields, almost all of whom earned their living directly or indirectly from activities related to the river and sea, lived in crowded conditions on the riverside. The Bank Top was used mainly as pasture for cattle. Chapter 5, *Transformation of the Built Environment*, describes the several phases during which a very different North Shields developed on the Bank Top.

At the start of the eighteenth century, large areas of land separated North Shields from its neighbouring townships. Routes of a sort did exist but they were at best inconvenient and at worst dangerous. As a result, residents of the original riverside town were relatively isolated. Chapter 6, *Beyond Shields*, describes the changes that took place locally as the development of steamships improved movement by river and sea and the building of roads and railways transformed movement by land.

The transformation of North Shields in the eighteenth and nineteenth centuries had major implications for the town's pattern of local government. By the early nineteenth century, it was obvious that a different form of administration was needed. Chapter 7, *Civic Pride and Independence*, describes the stages leading up to the establishment of the Borough of Tynemouth in 1849. It also makes brief references to the other townships which together with North Shields made up the new borough and describes some of the early public services it established.

In a now largely secular country, it is difficult to appreciate the intensity with which religious beliefs were held in the past. By the eighteenth and nineteenth centuries there was more tolerance, but religious convictions remained strong. The large number of new churches built was in part a function of factionalism within the non-conformist Protestant churches of the period but, since the splits were usually based on issues of principle, even that is an indication of how passionate people were about their religious beliefs. Chapter 8, *Religious Institutions*, explains what made these different religious groupings distinctive and describes the extraordinary expansion of religious activity in the town and its equally extraordinary decline.

Although working hours were long, the people of North Shields did have some time for recreation and, as the nineteenth century progressed, an increasing range of activities became available to them. As well as leisure time spent at home there was a growth in sporting activities and spectator sports which could be pursued outdoors as well as clubs, institutions, theatres, and other venues which provided indoor diversions and entertainment. Some of those discussed in Chapter 9, *Leisure Time*, are likely to surprise those familiar with the North Shields of today. For example, its residents once enjoyed a flourishing, professional theatrical scene and its fabled, numerous but now fast disappearing public houses provided much more than liquid refreshment to those who visited them.

By the end of the nineteenth century, North Shields had secured its position at the mouth of the Tyne, expanded at a phenomenal rate on the Bank Top and had a thriving local economy. But, despite the improvements in the lives of many working-class people, there remained a gulf between their lives and those of the much smaller number who belonged to the middle and upper classes. Members of the working classes had played a key role in establishing Britain as the workshop of the world and making it the world's most powerful and influential nation, yet they were still treated as second-class citizens. It is the lot of those ordinary people and their struggle to achieve formal equality and a significant improvement in their standard of living that provides the material for the concluding chapters of *Shiels to Shields*.

Chapters 10, 11 and 12, under the umbrella title of *North Shields' Labouring Classes*, focus on the working-class people of North Shields. The three chapters describe the conditions and circumstances that confronted them in the eighteenth and nineteenth centuries in times of peace and war. Chapter 10, *Barriers to progress*, is a discussion of the disadvantageous framework within which those lives were lived: a framework which imposed sometimes punitive constraints on those who attempted to change it. Chapter 11, *Social and economic conditions*, is concerned with the day-to-day conditions experienced by ordinary people in North Shields. The chapter's framework is derived from the pivotal report on social security written by William Beveridge just after I was born, which set out his recommendations on how best to slay what he called 'five giant evils': recommendations which formed the basis of what became known as the Welfare State. As the reports of Booth, Rowntree, Beveridge and others had been obliged to acknowledge, large sections of the population lived below, on or near the poverty line. Chapter 12, *Responses to poverty*, focuses on the changes in the way those in authority responded to the plight of those in need and also what those in need, or who anticipated being in need, did to help themselves.

Chapter 13, *A final word*, is a personal reflection on why it is important to understand our past and why none of us should treat our social history as an optional extra to be pursued only by ivory-towered academics. Social history should no more be the preserve of a few than it should be allowed to degenerate into an exercise in nostalgia. Old photographs of North Shields are not images of a world that is lost. They are images of a past that is still exercising an influence over the present – just as the present will help determine the course of the future. Our past, present and future are indivisible.

Acknowledgements

I MOVED from my home town of North Shields in the mid-1960s when I took up my first academic appointment. Despite that, I continued to feel that I belonged to North Shields and always wanted to know more about *my* town. The opportunity to make a systematic study of it had to wait for my retirement. I made good progress initially but came to a virtual halt when I allowed myself to be side-tracked by a fascination with the great comic actor Stan Laurel and the way in which his North Shields boyhood was echoed in many of the themes and gags he introduced into his films with Oliver Hardy. In reviewing my book *The Making of Stan Laurel*, Chuck Wentzel described it as a deft demonstration that 'you can take the boy out of North Shields but you can't take North Shields out of the boy'. That observation applies equally well to me. I gained a great deal by being brought up in such an interesting place, and the experience has left a lasting mark on me. *Shiels to Shields* is the long, complex life story of the fascinating town I still think of as home, and represents a belated thank you to the numerous people who influenced me in ways I did not always appreciate at the time.

I have learned so much from so many people that it is impossible to acknowledge them even if I could recall all their names. For that reason I must start by recording my thanks and apologies to those who merit but who do not receive a specific mention. Fortunately, I am able to acknowledge those who have helped me most. Let me begin with my wife Helen who was also born in North Shields. I need to thank her for all her love and support; for her specific help with the book but perhaps most of all for her forbearance during those long periods I have been preoccupied with it. My second acknowledgement is to my sister Margaret. Her interest in the development of North Shields communicated itself to me at an early age and we have been exchanging snippets of information about our home town all our adult lives. I am grateful to her for her support in so many direct and indirect ways over the years. I am also fortunate in having a life-long friend who has shared my interest in the development of North Shields. George Thomson and I have spent many hours talking about it, often boring our wives in the process. For that I must apologise – but I have no regrets about those many long conversations with George. I hope that he feels that the book has enough merit for me to associate him with it in this way.

My dear Mam and Dad received only an elementary school education but allowed me to take advantage of the greater opportunities provided by the 1944 Education Act. They registered me for King Edward's Primary School. It involved me in a long walk four times each day, but it was an excellent choice and I would like to acknowledge the critical importance of the years I spent there. Sadly, only Mrs Munro (then Miss Willis) is still alive but I want to put on record my thanks to Mr Reay, Mr Johnson, Miss Graham, Mr Douglas and Mr Hope for giving me such a good educational start in life.

After passing the 11+ examination, I moved on to Tynemouth Municipal High School. It was not as intellectually satisfying as I had hoped. Although I must accept the main responsibility for that, because I was easily distracted from my studies, not all my grammar school teachers commanded my respect and only a few made an obvious impression on me. Foremost among those who did was Mavis Burnett (now Mrs Cumings). She impressed me with her integrity, sincerity and genuine concern for all her pupils, even the wayward ones, like myself, who thought it fun to disrupt her lessons. Most of all, I must thank her for encouraging me to write. In the sixth form, where I studied science, I received a few lessons in 'general education' from the late Mr Liddell. They were stimulating and made me realise there was much more to education than rote learning and the passing of conventional examinations. Finally, I owe a debt to the late Ken Murray who taught me biology in the sixth form. He may not have been the most systematic of teachers. What he did possess was more crucial: the ability to transmit his enthusiasm for his subject to his students.

At the University of Hull, I was particularly fortunate in my teachers, all of whom possessed that ability to convey an interest in their subject to their students. I owe particular debts (in alphabetical order) to Bob Chester (Sociology), Bob Dowse (Politics), Peter Robinson (Psychology), John Saville (Social History), Trevor Smith (Politics) and Axel Stern (Philosophy). Bob Chester and Trevor Smith (now Professor the Lord Smith of Clifton) were particularly supportive. Without their active encouragement, I might not have taken up an academic career. At Nottingham University, I was equally fortunate in my colleagues. I should like to single out three for particular mention. Professor Julius Gould, my first boss, was supportive in many ways in the early stages of my academic career. His successor, Michael King, also helped in any way he could and had an uncanny ability to make penetrating, constructive criticisms on anything I wrote. When information technology arrived on the scene in the 1980s, I embraced it enthusiastically, but without the greater understanding of my colleague Ken Levine I would not have been able to deploy it nearly as effectively.

I am indebted to the staff of the North Tyneside Local Studies Library (located in North Shields) for some of the local materials I have consulted in the preparation of this book. Under the guiding hand of the now retired

Eric Hollerton, they have brought together an excellent collection. No one who uses it should take for granted the enormous dedication that was necessary to collect and organise it over many years.

At various points in the book I convert monetary sums in earlier periods to what they represent at the time of writing. That is more difficult than is often supposed and I must record my thanks to the Economic History Association and its sponsoring organizations for its valuable website EH.net which discusses in detail the advantages and disadvantages of the different conversions available. Unless otherwise stated, the calculations in this book use the *Average Earnings* index which employs an appropriate multiplier based on the difference between average earnings at the two dates being compared.[5]

Alan Armstrong, Emeritus Professor of Social History at the University of Kent, was kind enough to read a first draft of this book. He was then even more generous with his time: directing me to sources I had missed; drawing my attention to alternative interpretations of the material I had discussed and making a multitude of suggestions on how my material was organised. This is a very much better book than it would have been without his help. But, despite his guiding hand, he cannot be associated with any of its remaining weaknesses or limitations.

Finally, I wish to put on record my thanks to Anna Goddard, Alistair Hodge and Rachel Clarke of Carnegie Publishing and North Tyneside Metropolitan Council, especially Chris Bishop and Diane Leggett, for their generous support in bringing *Shiels to Shields* to market.

1

The early history of Tynemouth

Romans, Anglo-Saxons, Danes and Normans

THE relationship between Tynemouth and North Shields is analogous to that between a parent and child. Tynemouth or, to be more precise, the monks who lived there, gave birth to North Shields. They nurtured and protected it during its early life but were unable to see the settlement grow to maturity because in the reign of Henry VIII unforeseen circumstances brought about the Priory's sudden and premature demise. Because of this intimate relationship, the life story of North Shields must naturally begin with the huge promontory at the mouth of the Tyne on which the monks had established their home. This often bleak and forbidding setting had natural assets which made it more obviously suitable for a military fortification and it served that purpose too.

The ninth-century historian Ninnius and the sixteenth-century writer Leland both maintained that during the reign of Severus (AD 193–211) Hadrian's Wall was extended along the north bank of the Tyne as far as Tynemouth. William Camden made a similar point in the seventeenth century.

Some there be who thinke that the rampier and not the wall went as farre as to the very mouth of Tine, which is called Tinmouth and stifly affirme that it was termed *Pen-hal-crag*, that is, *The head of the rampier in the rocke*, whom I will not contradict. But I durst almost avouch that this was in the Romans time Tunnocellum, seeing that *Tunnocellum* soundeth as much as *The Promontorie of Tunn or Tine*, where the first cohort Aelia Classica, enrolled by Aelius Hadrianus the Emperour, was in pay for sea service.[1]

Reed, more specifically, argued that the use of the site dated from AD 117.

It was not until AD 117 that Tynemouth started to play a part in the Roman occupation, although to a much lesser degree than Ostia Verdre [South Shields], Segedunum [Wallsend] and Pons Alius [Newcastle]. It was during this year that a lighthouse was built at Tynemouth. This lighthouse and the one built at Dover are reputed to be the first two ever built in Britain. With the building of this lighthouse, Tynemouth became known to the Romans as Tunnocellum, which signified the promontory of 'Tunna' or 'Tina'; where 'Tina' or 'Tyne' meant flaming torch or beacon.[2]

The 1894–95 *Comprehensive Gazetteer for England and Wales* stated that 'two Roman camps were at Tynemouth and North Shields' and a County Handbook of Northumberland specified that the fortification at Tynemouth was manned by a cohort of Lingone (Romanised Celts from Gaul) until the fourth century.[3] But, despite these several confident statements, an HMSO guidebook is more tentative. It suggests that while 'it would seem probable that the Romans made use of such a formidable site there is little hard evidence to support such conjecture'.[4] The Borough of Tynemouth's own 1949 account of its history makes no claim that it was the site of a permanent Roman settlement.[5]

On the opposite bank of the Tyne, in what is now South Shields, there was a major Roman fort, Arbeia, bigger even than that of Segedunum at

Inscribed Roman stones found in 1782 and 1783. *Left*: an altar dedicated to Jupiter Optimus Maximus. *Right*: an incomplete inscription on which scholars are not agreed. Although unearthed on the site of the Priory, it remains possible that these stones were brought there from elsewhere.

FROM *A HISTORY OF NORTHUMBERLAND*, VOL. VIII, BY COURTESY OF THE FAMILY OF H.H.E. CRASTER

Wallsend. The full scale of it (615 × 315 feet or about 200 × 100 m) was rediscovered in the late nineteenth century. Given its obvious importance, it is perhaps not surprising that North Shields historians, such as Haswell, were keen to claim that there was also a Roman presence on the north bank of the entrance to the Tyne.

Standing out in the face of the broken and restless waters of the North Sea, and almost surrounded by them, the bluff and precipitous promontory is, in virtue of its commanding position, pre-eminently suited for the purposes of watch and ward, and the ubiquitous Roman, with eagle's eye for an eyrie, was not likely to overlook the advantages it offered him. Here, accordingly, only three miles away

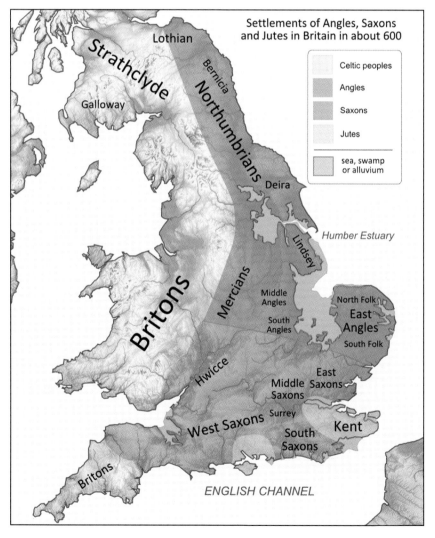

Distribution of Ethnic Groups in Britain, c.600. Note how it was the Angles, rather than the Saxons or Jutes, who were predominant in Bernicia and Deira and the North more generally.

from Segedunum, the terminus of Hadrian's great wall, he pitched the easternmost camp of that great line of defence.[6]

By the end of the fourth century, Rome's hold on Britain had effectively been lost. That allowed pre-Roman tribal identities to be reasserted but what we now know as England also came under attack from the Picts and Scots in the north and the Irish in the west.[7] In time there were also forays from Germanic tribes, the Angles, Saxons and Jutes, and in the first half of the sixth century they began to settle in large numbers. At that point, many native Britons were driven into the west of Scotland, Cumbria, Wales and Cornwall. Some in the south-west chose to cross the Channel to settle in the area of France known to this day as Brittany, where other Britons had been stationed as part of the Roman army. The native Britons offered significant resistance to the invaders who did not succeed in conquering the whole of what had been Roman Britain. Nevertheless, their invasions fundamentally changed the character and composition of British society.

It was the Angles who left their mark on Northumbria and gave the promontory on which Tynemouth Priory would later be built the name Benebalcrag (or Pen Bal Crag).

The original Northumbrians who were the descendants of Anglian settlers … formed a sort of community out of which came a lasting separate variety [of speech].[8]

Although the newcomers were in an increasingly dominant position by the end of the sixth century, there was no equivalent of a *Pax Romanica* (Roman peace). New tribal divisions now co-existed with the older ones and warrior kings spent their lives fighting one another, to the extent that Blair notes that 'the normal expectation of a Northumbrian king in the seventh century was to be killed in battle'.[9]

Northumbria (land north of the River Humber) consisted of two kingdoms. Deira extended from the Humber to the Tyne. Bernicia lay to the north of the Tyne. Although it is not necessary to describe the complex relationship between these two kingdoms, we do need to identify the elements which related to developments at Tynemouth. The pivotal figure, initially, was Edwin, the son of a former king of Deira. He became a political exile when the king of Bernicia, Æthelfrith, invaded and assumed control over Deira in about 604. Edwin appears to have spent time in Wales and Mercia before moving to East Anglia, under the protection of King Rædwald. When Rædwald invaded Northumbria in 616, and Æthelfrith was killed, Edwin was installed as his successor. Not satisfied with being king of a united Northumbria, he ventured farther north and extended his rule into Scotland and as far west as Anglesey and the Isle of Man. When his protector and ally Rædwald died in 625, Edwin also assumed control over

East Anglia and, after further military victories, became the effective ruler of much of what we now know as England. Kent, however, a stronghold of the Jutes, remained outside his sphere of influence. To try to remedy that, he sought to marry Æthelburh, the daughter of Kent's King Æthelbert.[10]

The main obstacle to the marriage was that Æthelbert and his family had been converted to Christianity and regarded Edwin as a pagan. According to Bede:

> When Edwin first sent ambassadors … for her hand in marriage, he received the reply that it was unlawful for a Christian maiden to be married to a heathen. … When the messengers brought back this reply, Edwin promised to put no obstacle of any kind in the way of the Christian faith … He also said that he too would accept the same religion, provided that it was found, when examined by his advisers, to be holier.[11]

Edwin married Æthelburh on those terms in 625. When he returned north with his new bride, she was accompanied by a Roman chaplain, Paulinus. Two years later, Edwin and his court became Christians. According to several scholars, Edwin marked his conversion by building a timber church and convent on Benebalcrag. Gibson, for example, refers to the St Albans monk (from the order which later assumed responsibility for Tynemouth Priory) who, in a treatise, states that Edwin, king of Northumbria, erected a wooden chapel on Benebalcrag in which his daughter Rosella 'took the sacred veil' (that is, became a nun).[12] Consistent with this documentary evidence, a 1963 excavation to the north of the priory nave found evidence of a pre-Norman timber building which seems to have had a religious purpose. If these accounts of a timber church at Benebalcrag are true, it means that that it pre-dated St Aidan's church at Lindisfarne by eight years, making it the first church to be established in Northumbria after the departure of the Romans.*

Edwin was killed in battle in 633. For a brief period Deira and Bernicia became separate kingdoms again but were reunited in 634 under Oswald, the son of Æthelfrith who, like Edwin before him, had been obliged to flee from Northumbria after his father had been killed in battle. The St Albans monk who wrote the history of Benebalcrag states that Oswald then 'caused an edifice of stone to be raised upon the site'. He went on to record 'that an Oratory, dedicated to the Blessed Virgin, existed here soon after the second structure had been built, and that many persons possessing worldly distinction were assembled under a regular ordinance and vow of religious life'.[13]

---

* There is no agreement on this point. Bede made no mention of a church being built during Edwin's reign. Other accounts even suggest the original wooden structure erected by Edwin may have been at York.

Religious life at the original wooden church erected on Benebalcrag would have been within the Roman tradition. Oswald, however, had been exiled in Scotland, where he was converted to Christianity within the Celtic tradition. So it seems probable that this new building at Benebalcrag would have been accompanied by a change in the nature of the Christian tradition pursued on the site, from Roman to Celtic. At the time, Christianity was being re-introduced into Britain and Northumbria from two directions and via two religious traditions. In 597, a Roman mission had arrived in Kent, led by Augustine. Paulinus, who travelled to Northumbria after Edwin's wedding, was a member of that Roman mission. In contrast, the Celtic religious tradition entered England from Ireland via Scotland after St Columba founded his mission on the island of Iona in 563. It was there that Oswald was converted to Christianity and why Aidan was invited to introduce the Celtic Christian tradition into Northumbria in 635.

There has been a tendency to exaggerate the differences between the Celtic and Roman traditions, but they were sufficiently different for there to be a perceived need to reconcile them. Following several failed attempts, a synod was called for that express purpose at Whitby in 664, as a complement to similar synods held in other countries. It was the Roman tradition of a strict hierarchical discipline that prevailed over the looser, more individualistic style of Celtic Christianity. Even more significant, with respect to the future of Tynemouth, was that bishops soon emerged as important political figures in their own right. Marsden sums up the events of Whitby in the following terms: 'The age of ascetic Celtic evangelism, personified in Aidan of Lindisfarne, was transformed within a decade into the age of power-broking prince bishops which dawned at the bitterly-contested council at Whitby in 664.' He added that 'the simple Celtic church of Oswald's restoration was already being overlaid in the 650s with a new superstructure of ecclesiastical grandeur'.[14]

By then, there had been other momentous events in Northumberland. Oswald (later St Oswald) was killed in 642, aged 38, in a battle against the still pagan Mercians. He died what is regarded as the first English martyr's death. His brother Oswy then took command of Bernicia. The throne of Deira was assumed by Oswin, a close relative of Edwin's. Oswy sought to reunite the whole of Northumbria: first by marrying Edwin's daughter and then by raising an army against Oswin. According to Bede, Oswin was hopelessly outnumbered and sought refuge in what is now Gilling in Yorkshire. There, in 651, he was betrayed by a friend and murdered. But, far from bringing about a re-unification of the two kingdoms, the assassination of Oswin did the opposite. It drove Deira into an alliance with Mercia against Bernicia.[15]

Higham suggests that Oswin's death was seen as a criminal act rather than the legitimate outcome of a military conflict.[16] The circumstances of his death appear to have been particularly shocking because he had been an unusually popular leader.

BERNICIA
NORTHUMBRIA
DEIRA
Aethelfrith
593-604
Aethelfrith
604-616
Aelle
569-588
Edwin
son of Aelle
616-633
Eanfrith
633-634
Osric
633-634
Oswald
son of Aethelfrith
634-642
Oswy
brother of Oswald
642-670
Oswin
son of Osric
644-651

Northumbrian kings. The background is from the Lindisfarne Gospels, *c.*700.

> Pleasant in speech and courteous in manner, he was generous to all, to nobles and common people alike. And so it came about that all men loved him for the royal dignity displayed in his character, his appearance and his noble deeds, and from almost every kingdom men of even the noblest birth flocked to serve him. Among all his other gifts of virtue and modesty with which he was, if I may say so, greatly blessed, the greatest is said to have been his humility.[17]

Oswin's reputation and death proved to be of great significance for the monastery at Tynemouth. Although killed within his own kingdom of Deira, he was buried at Tynemouth in Bernicia. This decision was probably made in the hope that it would discourage pilgrimages to his tomb and reduce the political ramifications of his death. If so, the ploy was unsuccessful. Oswin continued to attract great devotion after his death and, subsequently, when miracles were reported at what had become his shrine at Benebalcrag, he was declared a saint. The full significance of his beatification and the implications of his remains being buried at Tynemouth may be difficult for us to grasp today but, as Blair emphasises, it is crucial for us to try to do so.

> Whatever may be the reaction of men today – scorn, ridicule, revulsion – we do well to recognize how great was the part played by the cult of saints, how great was the power of holy bones among those

who lived in the age of Bede. Ridicule is easy. ... But such ridicule would not have been understood by those who revered the bones. ... These were the mortal remains of good men who, though long dead, still lived in an everlasting kingdom whence they might be able to bring help to those in need.[18]

Oswin's remains brought 'vast numbers of pilgrims' to Tynemouth. It became a favoured burial place and made the monastery 'the beneficiary of rich gifts'.[19]*

The next phase in the history of Tynemouth began when the Danes started to raid the English coast. The monastery at the entrance to the Tyne was an obvious target. It was plundered in the years 788, 794 and 800 and attacked again in 832 although, by then, the monks had strengthened their fortifications, and the Danes were driven off. In 865 another attack breached their defences and the monks, and nuns of St Hilda's who had come to Tynemouth for safety, were slaughtered.

The first invasion of the mainland believed to have been aimed at conquest rather than pillage took place in the same year. A Danish army landed in East Anglia and King Edmund, the local ruler, bought peace for his own kingdom by supplying the invaders with food, horses and winter quarters. When they moved north the following year, the Northumbrians were embroiled in yet another local conflict and offered little resistance. The Danes took York, strengthened its defences and made it their stronghold.

In the face of the invasion, the warring Northumbrians set aside their differences and the combined forces of Bernicia and Deira attempted to retake York in 867. They were not only defeated but subjected to a mass slaughter.[20] Both their leaders lost their lives and the remnants of the Northumbrian armies scattered. After taking control of East Anglia in 870, and defeating the Mercians in 874, the Danes focused their attention on Bernicia, north of the Tyne. In 875, under Healfdene, the Danish army over-wintered at Tynemouth before imposing its rule over the whole of Bernicia and conducting raids against the Picts and Britons of Strathclyde.

The *History of the Church at Durham* places Healfdene's residence at Tynemouth, where he was able to marshal both his army and his fleet. The prominent and already embanked monastic promontory was an important focus of local landownership and of government

---

* The most famous people laid to rest there, other than Oswin are Osred, an exiled king of Northumbria, killed in similar circumstances to Oswin in 792; King Malcolm of Scotland in 1093; and St Henry of Coquet in 1127. Malcolm's remains were said to have been returned to his native land at a later stage and re-buried in Dunfermline, but there were suspicions that the body sent to Scotland was that of a Monkseaton farmer and that both Malcolm and his son still lie buried at Tynemouth.

and provided a defensible military camp of the kind favoured by the Danes in Britain.[21]

The Danish presence did not signal the end of Christianity at Benebalcrag. There is evidence of a resurgence of religious activity on the site when an Anglo-Saxon kingship based on Bamburgh re-emerged late in the ninth century. It appears that this particular development was not challenged by the Danes because they were then preoccupied in further struggles with Mercia.[22]

The linguistic record of the area suggests that the Danes had only a limited impact on the population. According to Elmes, 'the linguistic landscape of Northumberland is a little like a grassed-over ancient fortress – it doesn't take much excavation to reveal the basic structure of an ancient language tradition'. He then notes that unlike counties farther south, Northumberland and Tyneside show little of the Scandinavian influence found throughout Yorkshire. He emphasises that in Northumberland and Tyneside, 'the names and the speech come from the Anglian-speaking peoples'.[23]

Subsequently, in the decade before the Norman Conquest, when Harold Godwinson was the dominant figure in Edward the Confessor's council and his most obvious successor, Harold's brother Tostig was made Earl of Northumbria. He made Tynemouth one of his fortresses and planned to re-establish a monastery on the site. His plans were confounded when sections of the Northumbrian population actively opposed him. Conscious of the need for allies if he was to assume the throne on Edward's death, Harold sided with the Northumbrians against his brother. Feeling deserted and betrayed, Tostig fled to the court of Harold Hardrada, the king of Norway who also had a claim on the English throne. Harold's decision to abandon his brother seems to have been a political blunder. While he did assume the throne, he then had to face two challenges. The first, from across the North Sea, came from an alliance between his brother Tostig and Hardrada. The second, from across the Channel, came from Edward the Confessor's illegitimate brother William. In 1066, while gathered on the south coast to meet William's forces, Harold was obliged to rush north to confront a huge invasion led by Tostig and Hardrada. His forces secured a decisive victory at Stamford Bridge, but just nineteen days later, on 14 October 1066, Harold was killed and his army defeated. William's troops had landed while Harold's army was away in the North, and it was an already tired and depleted Anglo-Saxon force that they confronted and defeated at the Battle of Hastings. William the Bastard, Duke of Normandy, assumed the role of ruler of England and a major new phase in English history began.

It is interesting to speculate on what would have happened had Tostig not fallen foul of the Northumbrians, or if Harold had not chosen to support them at the expense of his brother. There would have been no battle to fight at Stamford Bridge. Harold's waiting army would probably have defeated William's forces. There would not have been a Norman England. So the Northumbrians, at least indirectly, can be held responsible for the end of Anglo-Saxon Britain and its replacement by the harsh, dictatorial rule of the Normans.

Tynemouth Priory from the Norman Conquest to the Dissolution of the Monasteries

There were no Northumbrians among the Anglo-Saxon forces at Hastings. That reinforces the point made by Kapelle that, in the Anglo-Saxon world, Northumbria was not so much part of England but a distinct area adjacent to it. Kapelle goes on to suggest that this distinction between Northumbria and England continued for a time after the Conquest. For example, in 1095, Rufus granted charters to the monks at Tynemouth '*in nort de Tyne et in suth de Tyne et in Anglia*' (i.e. to the north and to the south of the Tyne *and* in England) in an acknowledgement of the distinction. Kapelle also maintains it is no coincidence that the Domesday Book stops at the Tees – without any description of Northumbria beyond that point.[24] North of the Tees, it would seem, William was essentially an overlord with no direct powers.

The Northumbrians showed no willingness to acknowledge William as their new king. In February 1067, he appointed Copsig, a former aide of Tostig, as Earl of Northumberland. He was set the unenviable task of raising taxes to help pay for William's mercenaries. By March, Copsig was dead: beheaded by the Northumbrians. In the ensuing years, a great deal more blood was shed before the Normans' position became secure. William next appointed Robert Commines as Earl over the land beyond the River Tees. In January 1069, his troops looted Durham. The Northumbrians were quick to retaliate. The following morning, Commines' 700-strong force was taken by surprise and almost all his men killed. Northumbria beyond the Tees was now in open revolt against William. Edgar Aetheling, another claimant to the English throne, who had been acclaimed by the Witan (the Anglo-Saxon governing body) after King Harold's death, took advantage of the situation and came from Scotland to join the resistance to the Normans. However, the Anglo-Saxons were unable to consolidate their position. William's army moved quickly from the south and routed them.

Despite this defeat, the Northumbrians continued to resist the Normans. In 1069, according to the Anglo-Saxon Chronicles, the Northumbrians were supported by a fleet of 240 Danish ships. This time the Normans were defeated and their York garrison slaughtered – but not before they had set fire to the town. Faced with a winter in the burned-out remains of York, the Danes retreated. William then set about trying to bring Northumbrian resistance to an end. He split his forces into small units and they engaged in a brutally punitive campaign. Peasants were killed or driven out of their homes; their animals were killed and their ricks burned.[25] Despite, or perhaps because of such ruthless tactics, resistance to William continued for some time. Another Danish fleet arrived in 1070 and forged an alliance with those involved with the revolt in the Fens, led by Hereward and refugees from Northumbria. However, William managed to bribe the Danes to return to Scandinavia. Armed resistance to William's brutal acts of suppression and his increasingly strong forces (including large numbers of French mercenaries) eventually died away. By 1095, William's son Rufus (William II) was in a position to grant Hubert Delaval, who had fought alongside William at Hastings, a valuable estate adjacent to Tynemouth Priory.

As William's forces moved north in 1069, a group, camped at Monkchester (later Newcastle upon Tyne) turned its attention to Tynemouth. According to Craster, 'the supplies of the surrounding country had been carried thither [to Benebalcrag] that they might not fall into the hands of the Norman soldiery'. This suggests to Craster that defensive works already protected the western side of the promontory, the only part accessible from the land. However, concentrating supplies in this way proved to be a mistake. Short of food and fodder and attracted by the prospect of supplies at Tynemouth, a Norman foraging party was sent to seize them. In the course of the raid, the Saxon church on Benebalcrag was set on fire and remained in a derelict state for many years.[26]

Over the next 40 years, responsibility for the church passed through several hands, reflecting, among other things, the many internal disputes within William's new kingdom. In 1075, Tynemouth was granted to the Prior of Winchcombe by William's new Earl of Northumberland. When he was executed by William, responsibility for Tynemouth was given to the monks of Jarrow. Then, in 1083, responsibility for both Jarrow and Tynemouth was transferred to Durham Cathedral. Following a dispute between the Bishop of Durham and Robert de Mowbray, the new Earl of Northumberland, Tynemouth became a Benedictine cell of St Albans, at that time the premier abbey in England. The work on a new church, which began after the installation of the new monks from St Albans in 1090, was then delayed by two conflicts. The first was between the Scots and William the Conqueror's successor, William Rufus. The second was between William Rufus and many of the Norman nobles, including the Earl of Northumberland, Robert de Mowbray, who supported the claim to the throne of the Conqueror's elder son Robert, Duke of Normandy.

During the conflict with the Scots, Malcolm III of Scotland who had invaded Northumberland in 1093, was killed in a battle near Alnwick, but taken to Tynemouth for burial. During the second conflict, between William Rufus and Mowbray and others who did not recognise him as king, Tynemouth was besieged by the king's forces and captured after a two month siege in 1095. Mowbray was then besieged at Bamburgh Castle, farther up the Northumbrian coast. He succeeded in escaping and returned to Tynemouth in an attempt to raise an army to cut off the king's position from the south. Instead, a force from Newcastle attacked Tynemouth. It fell after only two days. Mowbray, who had been wounded, was dragged from the church and taken to Bamburgh to ensure its surrender.

In 1100, on the anniversary of the martyrdom of St Oswin, the re-building begun under Robert de Mowbray was ready to receive the saint's relics which had been housed in the pre-Conquest church. The new church, dedicated to the Blessed Virgin Mary, came to be known as The Church of Our Lady and St Oswin. Henry I confirmed the possessions and privileges that had been bestowed on the monastery by Mowbray, the rebel Earl of Northumberland, and, in addition, granted it the right to fisheries and wrecks in the Tyne. The monastery, which had already been lavishly endowed by Robert de Mowbray, and by others, went on to prosper.[27]

Given that all that now remains at Benebalcrag are the ruined remains of its once magnificent buildings, it is crucial to give an indication of the extent of the Tynemouth Priory's possessions and sources of income, to illustrate how influential it used to be. As most of the place-names listed below will be unfamiliar to those who have not lived in the North East, it is important to emphasise that they cover a large area. Those readers familiar with the

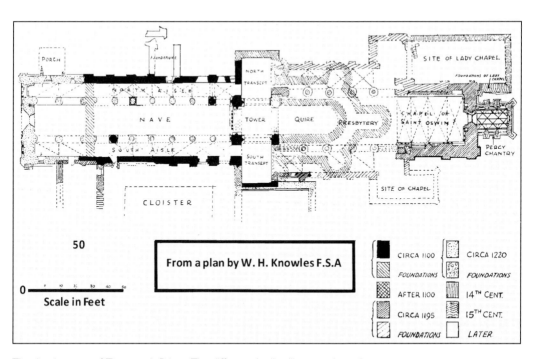

The development of Tynemouth Priory. The different shading illustrates how the Priory looked during successive phases of its development.

FROM A HISTORY OF NORTHUMBERLAND, VOL. VIII, BY COURTESY OF THE FAMILY OF H.H.E. CRASTER place-names will probably be surprised at their wide distribution. Most were acquired in the twelfth century and retained until the dissolution of the monasteries in the sixteenth century.

The Priory's temporal (as distinct from ecclesiastical) possessions in Northumberland included the townships of Tynemouth, Preston, Whitley, Monkseaton, Seghill, Chirton, Earsdon, Backworth, Murton, Flatworth, Amble, Hauxley, Coquet Island, Bewick, Lilburn, Harehope, Wooperton, Eglingham, Bebside, Cowpen, West Harford, Elswick, Westgate, Benwell, Denton, Wolsington, South Dissington, Wylam and Welton. The Priory also enjoyed rent from the Tower at Craster and owned land in Warkworth, Donkin Rigg, Woodhorn, North Seton, Ellington, Mersfen, Newbiggin, Seghill, Holywell and Hartley, as well as several houses in Newcastle and Gateshead. Its ecclesiastical properties included Woodhorn, Whalton, Hartburn, Bolam, Bewick, Eglingham, Edlingham, Bywell St. Peter's and Haltwhistle. It also enjoyed tithes from other churches at Corbridge, Warkworth, Rothbury, Newburn, Wooler, Elswick, Bothal, Wylam, Ovington, Dissington and Black Callerton. The Priory even derived income from some properties across the River Tyne in Durham.[28]

Over the next two centuries Tynemouth Priory was extended and improved in a variety of ways and was of undoubted national importance. Hadcock maintains that it soon became more important than many of England's great abbeys. Nevertheless, and despite the beginning of commercial activities in North Shields, its fortunes did fluctuate.

> There were perpetual demands upon the priory for hospitality by guests of all classes, including kings, especially during the Scottish wars, and the expenses incurred by this, and the obligation of keeping an armed force became a great embarrassment, and several appeals were made to the king on the subject. During the first half of the fourteenth century, the priory had become so impoverished through these causes and through a succession of raids upon the estates by Northumbrians and Scots, that the monks could scarcely live.[29]

Even when times were more peaceful, and the Priory's finances sound, life for the monks at Tynemouth was not without personal hardship. Benebalcrag, as anyone familiar with Tynemouth will confirm, can be a peculiarly inhospitable place. As a letter from a monk at Tynemouth, preserved in St Albans confirms, being based there left a great deal to be desired in terms of creature comforts. The monk in question was more than complimentary about the church, which he described as 'of wondrous beauty', and he plainly considered it an honour that 'within it rests the body of the Blessed martyr Oswin in a silver shrine, magnificently embellished with gold and jewels'. However, what he had to say about day-to-day life in Tynemouth is couched in decidedly unflattering terms.

Our house is confined to the top of a high rock, and is surrounded by the sea on every side but one. Here is the approach to the monastery through a gate cut out of the rock, so narrow that a cart can hardly pass through. Day and night the waves break and roar and undermine the cliff. Thick sea-frets roll in, wrapping everything in gloom. Dim eyes, hoarse voices, sore throats are the consequence. Spring and summer never come here. The north wind is always blowing and brings with it cold and snow; or storms in which the wind tosses the salt sea foam in masses over our buildings and rains it down within the castle. Shipwrecks are frequent. It is great pity to see the numbed crew, whom no power on earth can save, whose vessel, mast swaying and timbers parted, rushes upon rock or reef. No ring-dove or nightingale is here, only grey birds which nest in the rocks and greedily prey upon the drowned, and whose screaming cry is a token of a coming storm. The people who live by the seashore feed upon black malodorous seaweed called 'slauk' that they gather on the rocks. The constant eating of it turns their complexions black. Men, women and children are as dark as Africans or the swarthiest Jews. In the

John Storey's conjectural reconstruction of Tynemouth Priory. From William Sidney Gibson's *A Descriptive and Historical Guide to Tynemouth*, published by Philipson and Hare, Tyne Street, North Shields, in 1849.

| Shiels to Shields

spring the sea-air blights the blossoms of the stunted fruit trees, so that you think yourself lucky to see a wizened apple, though it will set your teeth on edge should you try to eat it. See to it, brother that you do not come to so comfortless a place.[30]

By the start of the sixteenth century, the monastery was at the height of its power and influence. Yet, within just 40 years, it ceased to exist: ultimately because of the marital antics of Henry VIII which led to his excommunication from the Catholic Church. Henry's response was one of defiance. He declared himself head of the Church in England and sweeping changes were introduced which were revolutionary in both their social and economic consequences. Henry's actions met with some resistance, especially in the North, but were put down and savage retribution exacted from those who had opposed him.

The most important change for Tynemouth was the dissolution of the monasteries. Overall, what amounted to a profound redistribution of wealth and influence, affected about 17 per cent of the land in England. Henry was by no means the only beneficiary. The marked shift in the balance of power between the sacred and secular strengthened the gentry and middle classes and, it has been argued, helped bring about a new dynamism in English society. In the case of Tynemouth, on 12 January 1539, over 900 years after Edwin is reputed to have established the first religious settlement on the site, the Prior signed a deed of surrender making over the monastery's possessions to the king. In addition to the extensive holdings in land, he was obliged to hand over 62 ounces of gold and 2,000 ounces of silver to the Crown.[31] Subsequently, in what to the monks must have appeared a shocking act of desecration, the king's supporters broke up the shrine of St Oswin and scattered his bones in all directions.*

Tynemouth Castle from the medieval era to the accession of William and Mary

Whilst the dissolution of the monasteries brought an end to Tynemouth Priory, it did not mean the end of Tynemouth Castle. The fortifications were still needed. Although it is not possible to draw a simple dividing line between what was priory and what was castle, the same Robert de Mowbray who was responsible for rebuilding the monastery, can also be said to have founded Tynemouth Castle. And what he had created by 1095 was enough of a fortress to have withstood the two-month siege by the forces of William Rufus.

---

* The once magnificent church was subsequently allowed to fall into decay, except for the nave, which continued to be used as a parish church. When the church was later abandoned, the lead was stripped from the roof in 1664 and the monastic buildings pulled down to build barracks, a governor's house and a lighthouse.

In 1138, Tynemouth escaped an attack by Scottish marauders by paying a ransom. With a threat of a similar invasion in 1296, Edward I (1272–1307) gave the monks permission to 'fortify their monastery with a wall of stone and lime and to crenelate it'. Massive outer defensive walls with towers and battlements were constructed and, 'luckily for the people of Tynemouth, the work was begun at once and in the following year they sought refuge within it when William Wallace's army over-ran Northumberland'.[32] At that stage, the Crown had no special rights over the Castle. Ralph de Neville is reported to have attempted to treat Tynemouth as a royal fortress in 1346 but was thwarted by the Prior who won an acknowledgement from Edward III (1327–77) that he alone had authority within its walls.[33] It followed that when there was a need to resist further Scottish attacks in the early fourteenth century, it was the Prior who recruited 80 men to defend it.

The fortifications at Tynemouth had fallen into disrepair and were not strong enough to survive another Scottish attack in 1389, after the Battle of Otterburn. This damage, along with the undermining of part of the walls by cliff falls, created an urgent need for extensive repairs. A new four-storey gate-house, a covered barbican, moat and drawbridge were constructed. When the work was completed at the beginning of the fifteenth century, the distance round the outer walls was almost 3,200 feet (975 m), enclosing a greater area than most other English castles. By this time it was under royal control and considered to be one the country's strongest border fortresses. It was of particular importance in the continuing conflict between England and Scotland. When a pro-French Catholic faction in Scotland rejected Henry VIII's overtures for the engagement of his son Edward to Mary Queen of Scots, Henry responded by invading Scotland. In 1544, the Earl of Hertford made Tynemouth a base for the English fleet and over 10,000 men embarked there en route to take on the Scots. Hertford also recommended further enhancements to Tynemouth's fortifications. Following the advice of Italian experts, major improvements were made, involving over 1,000 men, which were completed in 1546.[34] An outwork was constructed in front of the gatehouse and a battery built on the low promontory to the south – with a wall to connect them. Parts of the monastery buildings were dismantled to provide the stone for these enhancements. The Castle was partly garrisoned by Spanish mercenaries and the newly built battery site became known (and continues to be known to this day) as the Spanish Battery.

The cost of maintaining the Castle was a major issue for those responsible for it in the middle of the sixteenth century. That in turn led to a reconsideration of its military role. In earlier centuries, castles had been built on sites like Benebalcrag because the natural contours of the land provided them with much of their defensive capabilities. They needed to be strong and ideally constructed of double or even triple lines of defence to shelter local inhabitants in time of invasion. By the reign of Elizabeth I (1558–1603), with England increasingly concerned with the threat of invasion from other European nations, more thought was being given to the defence of the coastline and river estuaries. The expense of maintaining Tynemouth Castle could no longer be justified just as a place of refuge. It also had to be justified in terms of a defence of the entrance to the Tyne. For that purpose, batteries of artillery pieces were more important than moats, draw-bridges and thick walls. Yet at the very time detailed discussions were taking place about the future of Tynemouth Castle, the internal religious conflicts, which were leading the country inexorably toward civil war, gave the Castle a new lease of life both as a castle in its traditional medieval form and as a prison.

The key events which involved Tynemouth Castle arose from the jockeying for dominance between Catholics and Protestants. Following the death of Henry VIII, Thomas Cranmer had pursued a punitive campaign against Catholics. When the Catholic Mary I came to the throne in 1553, the boot was on the other foot. When Elizabeth I succeeded her in 1558, she overturned the religious changes introduced by her half-sister. England became Protestant again. Initially, Catholics were treated with comparative leniency but, when Catholic missionaries arrived in England, Elizabeth responded by enforcing her religious laws more severely. Catholicism became to all intents and purposes a crime against the state. By the end of her reign, practising Catholics were liable to capital punishment as traitors.

Events in Scotland complicated matters further. When the already widowed 19-year-old Catholic Mary Queen of Scots returned in 1558, it was to a now officially Protestant Scotland. So her return was not welcomed in either England or Scotland. She was unwelcome to Elizabeth because Mary was heir presumptive to the English throne. Moreover, because Catholics in Europe considered Elizabeth illegitimate (having been born to Henry VIII's second wife after the Pope had refused to grant him a divorce) some considered Mary's claim to the English throne to be stronger than that of Elizabeth. North of the border, the concern was that Mary's Catholicism would undermine Scottish Protestantism. When the Earl of Bothwell, one of Mary's closest Scottish advisers, clashed with other Scottish lords, he was imprisoned, first in Edinburgh in 1562 and then in Tynemouth Castle. Lord Keith, son of the Earl Marshal of Scotland and Sir Andrew Kerr of Cessford also spent time incarcerated at Tynemouth.[35]

Northern Catholic nobles gave vent to their reservations about Elizabeth I with the so-called Rising of the North, launched in the closing months of 1569. It was led by Charles, Earl of Westmorland and Thomas Percy, Earl of Northumberland. For some reason, Sir Henry Percy, the brother of Thomas, declined to join them. In a short-lived campaign, English Bibles were destroyed and traditional altars and statues restored. However, the rebels were soon in retreat. To ensure that they did not capture Tynemouth Castle, Sir Henry Percy installed a garrison of 200 soldiers, complemented by another 100 men from Newcastle, and sent out 1,200 horsemen to keep watch for his brother's forces between Tynemouth and Newcastle. The Earl of Westmorland escaped capture but the Earl of Northumberland did not and was eventually beheaded.[36]

It is not obvious why Sir Henry Percy betrayed his brother, especially when subsequent events showed that he too had Catholic sympathies for which he was prepared to risk his life. He may have been motivated by self-interest, because he succeeded his brother as the eighth Earl of Northumberland and was awarded the lease of Tynemouth Castle in perpetuity. But, within a year, he too had fallen out with Elizabeth. After being forced to abdicate, Mary Queen of Scots sought refuge in England only to be imprisoned by Elizabeth. Henry Percy was party to her subsequent escape and a warrant was issued for his arrest. He was also charged with 'criminal negligence in the Queen's service' because of the poor state of Tynemouth Castle. Henry was thrown into the Tower and fined but allowed to retain his responsibility for the castle provided he paid for someone else to accept day-to-day responsibility for it.[37]

In 1583 he was in more trouble. Charged with being the leading English figure in a conspiracy to pave the way for an invasion of England by the Catholic forces of France and Spain, he was incarcerated in the Tower of London. When Tynemouth Castle was then found to be in an even worse state than in the earlier period, and hopelessly ill-equipped to deal with an invasion by France and Spain, this was construed as conspiracy rather than incompetence on Henry's part. He was subsequently found dead with a bullet in his heart. Whether he committed suicide or was murdered is not known.[38]

Concern about the state of the castle was heightened by the continuing pro-Catholic sentiment in Northumberland and intelligence about an impending Spanish Armada. There was real fear that the enemy might attack the Tyne, and the Privy Council gave the Earl of Huntingdon explicit responsibility 'for the better defence of the castle at Tynemouth'. His reply amounted to 'where on earth do I start'. Fortunately for the Protestant cause, the decisive battle with the Spanish Armada was fought elsewhere.

Henry, the ninth Earl of Northumberland, who had been born at Tynemouth Castle, repaired the Percy family's relationship with the Crown by volunteering to fight against the Spanish. He was put in charge of Tynemouth Castle in 1591, but it still remained in urgent need of repair. In the absence of financial help from the government, the Earl appears to have done little more than collect his rent and tithes from Tynemouth's considerable estate. Although Henry was nominally a Protestant, he sent his relative Thomas Percy on a secret mission to James VI of Scotland (the son of the executed Catholic Mary Queen of Scots) to indicate that English Catholics would accept him as king of England provided he would afford them a greater degree of religious tolerance. Percy is said to have written, 'It were a pity to lose a good Kingdom for not tolerating a mass in a corner'.

On Elizabeth's death, James VI became King James I of England but chose to continue with Elizabeth's persecution of Catholics. In desperation,

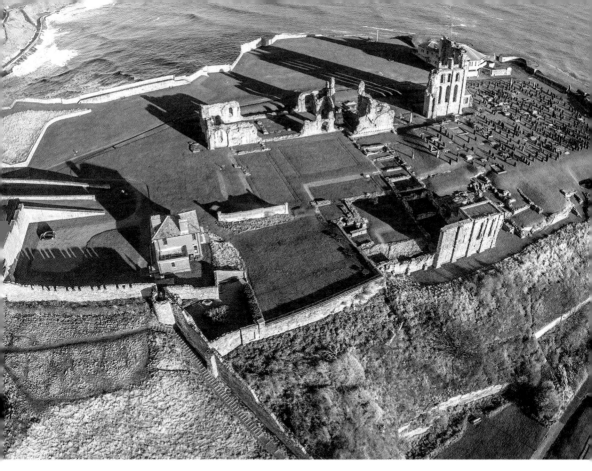

Aerial image of Tynemouth, Priory and Castle, 2015. Note the steep cliff around the promontory and the remains of the Priory, Castle and castle walls.

in 1605, Guy Fawkes, Thomas Percy and others attempted to blow up the Houses of Parliament. Percy's role was central. He hired the cellar in which the 36 barrels of gunpowder were stored. The Gunpowder Plot played right into the hands of the Protestants. Who could now deny that Catholics were subversive traitors? The fact that Thomas was a kinsman of the Earl of Northumberland put him under suspicion too. Although there may have been no direct evidence that he was involved in the plot, the castles belonging to the Percy family at Tynemouth, Alnwick, Prudhoe and Cockermouth were all seized.

A subsequent inspection of Tynemouth Castle did nothing to improve the Earl's position.

> Various buildings had been destroyed and their materials carried off by unauthorised persons. The kiln has been pulled down and its timber and slate used for the 'repayring and lofting' of the house

of the vicar. The coverings and leads were gone from Edmund's Chamber; the little chamber wherein John Harbotle and John Smyth laye, called by their names', had been demolished; the bake house and bolting-house had been pulled down and its timber and slates conveyed into the town of Shields.[39]

The Earl was sent to the Tower, tried, found guilty, and ordered to pay a large fine and left in the Tower 'during his Majesty's pleasure'.

No decision was made to repair Tynemouth Castle until 1626. At that point money was allocated by the government provided the residents of Newcastle made up the difference – because it was the Newcastle burgesses who had been protesting that the state of Tynemouth Castle made Newcastle vulnerable. It seems that the repairs were never made. An alternative plan was drawn up to build a new fort. That scheme too was dropped. Lord Clifford, lord-lieutenant of the northern counties, recommended that a cheaper solution would be to capitalise on the existing Spanish Battery. That advice too was ignored. When improvements to the fortifications were eventually carried out 15 years later, they were made under very different circumstances. By then, the threat to the monarchy came not from the Catholic minority, who were now forced to worship in secret, but from the Puritans, Protestant extremists who wanted the Reformation to go much further. Charles I played into their hands just as Guy Fawkes and his co-conspirators had played into the hands of the anti-Catholics twenty years before: first by marrying the Catholic sister of Louis XIII of France and then appointing a bishop with Catholic sympathies. Even so, when in 1633, along with a formidable retinue, he sailed into the Tyne and rested at Tynemouth Castle on the way to his coronation as king of Scotland, no one could have anticipated what was to follow. Within four years his relationship with the Scots was in ruins. His attempt to impose the Anglican Book of Common Prayer on them was seen as an affront to their religious beliefs and a threat to their independence. A Covenanting Assembly formally rejected the episcopalian liturgy in what was a direct challenge to the king. With war looking inevitable, and no time to make good the years of neglect at Tynemouth, the English chose to leave the river estuary unguarded and pieces of artillery were actually removed from Tynemouth to reinforce the defences at Newcastle.[40]

The first so-called Bishops' War with Scotland did not result in bloodshed. The Covenanters assembled what the English believed was an overwhelming army and Charles capitulated. When he refused to endorse the agreement he had reached, the Covenanters again took up arms against him, in 1640. The king's forces evacuated Newcastle and it was taken by the Scots without a struggle. The Scots then occupied Tynemouth Castle. That not only provided them with easy communications with Scotland by sea and land but control over the vital coal trade from the Tyne. They then did what the English had failed to do despite decades of discussion: arm the Castle properly. The Scots held Tynemouth for a year and returned home only when Charles had backed down again.

Charles' difficulties continued not only with respect to Scotland but also, within England, with his relations with Parliament and the Puritans. Parliament had not been prepared to finance Charles during his second confrontation with the Covenanters without imposing conditions that he refused to accept. He retaliated by dissolving Parliament and making the political blunder of raising an Irish Catholic army to fight the Protestant Scots. To those already suspicious of the King's Catholic sympathies, this must have seemed to be proof that he was a threat to the Reformation. Many Protestants at the time appeared to view religion in simplistic terms, as a fight between good and evil. It could now be equated with a fight between monarchy and Catholicism on the one hand and Parliament and Protestantism on the other.

It is not possible to generalise on how the north-east of England stood on these issues. A correspondent with the Lord Treasurer claimed in 1575 that while the people of Gateshead were good Protestants 'the towne of Newcastell are all Papistes'.[41] I have been unable to find any systematic analysis of how the population of Tynemouth and North Shields divided in the face of this stark conflict. Events suggest that while some supported a monarch predisposed to Catholicism, others sided with a Parliament predisposed to Puritanism. There were undoubtedly others who were indifferent to the underlying issues. However, the option to remain detached became difficult when, following the defeat of an English army at Newburn, the Presbyterian Scots occupied Newcastle the following year. Even after their withdrawal, local people were unable to remain aloof from national politics because, after an open breach between King and Parliament in 1641, Charles responded quickly to secure his position on Tyneside.

In 1641 he gave William Cavendish, Earl of Newcastle, instructions to fortify Newcastle and secure the river. Troops were sent to Tynemouth Castle along with heavy artillery. The fortifications were repaired; the Spanish Battery was given an additional brick superstructure, and two make-shift forts (one at the Low Light) were constructed with a commanding view over the entrance to the river. These royalist preparations alarmed the local puritans sympathetic to Parliament. There was concern that 'the whole trade of Newcastle, for coal or otherwise, will be subject to be interrupted whensoever his majesty shall please'. One of the local puritans then sent the following message to the House of Commons.

> The Earl of Newcastle came here on Friday last, to be governor of Newcastle. ... Three hundred soldiers is sent down to Tynemouth Castle to guard it, and they have all arms given them out of the magazine here in this town. There is great guns going down to them,

six pieces. They are casting up trenches as fast as may be. There is a fort making at the haven mouth that no ships can go in or out without their leave. We never lived in the like fear which we now live in. ... They have got engineers out of Germany and gunners for the great guns. ... The earl is making forts at Sheeles [North and South Shields], one on each side. There is divers of great ordnance removed to the keyside [quayside] to be sent down. There is here an expectation of some directions from Parliament to countermand them; and, if speedy course were yet taken, it might reduce all that is done.[42]

Parliament responded by sending two ships to the Tyne and petitioned the king to stop his provocative actions. Instead of backing down, on 22 August, Charles raised his standard in Nottingham and England went to

Tynemouth Castle in the eighteenth century. An unknown artist's portrayal of Tynemouth Castle and Lighthouse and the ruins of the Priory in the eighteenth century.

FROM A HISTORY OF NORTHUMBERLAND, VOL. VIII, BY COURTESY OF THE FAMILY OF H.H.E. CRASTER

| Shiels to Shields

war – with itself. Charles' close aide Prince Rupert sailed into the Tyne and prepared Tynemouth Castle to resist an attack.[43] Parliament responded with a blockade of the river.[44] Parliamentary forces then secured Sunderland and began to ship its coals at the expense of the coal merchants of Newcastle. The situation was made worse in 1644, when a Scottish army, allied with Parliament, crossed the border and confronted the king's forces in Newcastle and Tynemouth. After the victory of parliamentary forces over the royalists at Marston Moor in July 1644, a second Scottish army was free to join the sieges and blockade of the river. Nevertheless, Newcastle held out from February to October and Tynemouth resisted for even longer. That mattered because until the Castle was captured, ships could still not pass freely to and from Newcastle. Indeed, as the following extract makes clear, taking Tynemouth Castle was judged to be more of a priority than the fall of Newcastle.

> If the Scots are now besieging Tinmouth castle, while some other forces are diverting the enemy from relieving it, it will be an excellent service, for by taking of the said castle, we shall be master of the sea, and be inabled not only to bring in provision by our ships for the army of Scots, but to send out coale and accommodate the city of London with them. … And the said castle of Tinmouth being once taken, the towne of Newcastle would never long be able to hold out.[45]

The newly built fort at the Low Light fell in October just days before Newcastle. Tynemouth Castle would have held out longer had it not been for what the Puritans described as the Hand of God. The garrison of the Castle succumbed to what was described as 'plague', and the spread of the infection brought about the defeat of the royalist forces more quickly than the Scottish artillery would have done. In the words of a letter written at the time: 'Though we cannot reach them in that high hill, yet can, you see, and indeed it is very wonderful to observe how wonderfully God hath wrought for us in these troubles, without and beyond the help of man.'[46] So, on 27 October 1644, the surviving royalists left the Castle. Tynemouth was again in Scottish hands. Trade with Newcastle resumed and the price of coal fell, to the relief of the population of London who had come to rely on it.

In 1645 the royalists lost the critical battle of the Civil War at Naseby. Charles I eventually surrendered in 1646 – but not to the Parliamentarians. He gave himself up to the Scots at Newark. At the time, the Scots were still occupying Tynemouth Castle but were unwilling to yield it to the parliamentarians. The Castle then became the scene of negotiations between the King and the Scots. In May 1646, just two weeks after his surrender, Charles I travelled on a barge from Newcastle to North Shields and dined with the Scottish governor of the Castle. The King revisited the Castle again on 2 September and discussions continued for another month with Scotland's negotiators. After the talks broke down, plans were drawn up for Charles to escape on a Dutch warship, sent to the Tyne by his son-in-law the Prince of Orange. The rendezvous was planned for Christmas 1646 but the plan came to nothing because, for some reason, the king failed to make his way to Tynemouth from Newcastle. In the following month, he, Tynemouth Castle and Newcastle were all handed over to Parliament. Craster notes that two regiments of foot were stationed at Newcastle and from among them four companies were used to garrison Tynemouth Castle. Later in 1648, a significant sum of money was provided to repair the fortifications.[47]

But the civil strife had still not come to an end. The king refused to accept the army council's proposals for peace and escaped to the Isle of Wight from where he negotiated both with Parliament and the Scots. In December 1647, he reached an agreement with the Scots in which he undertook to accept presbyterianism in return for military support. A second civil war then began in the spring of 1648 but proved short-lived when Charles's hopes of aid from France and Ireland were not realised. Cromwell defeated the Scots at Preston and put down the royalist risings that had erupted in a number of places – though nowhere more quickly than Tynemouth where the Castle changed hands from parliament, to royalist and back to parliament in a single day.

For some reason, Lt. Col. Henry Lilburn, who had been left in charge of the Castle, defected to the royalist cause. He ordered his men out of the Castle, freed and armed the prisoners and pulled up the drawbridge. He then sent out an appeal to other royalists in the area. Many local seamen and others came to join him. However, troops despatched from Newcastle with scaling ladders forced an entry into the Castle and Lilburn's act of defiance soon came to an end. His severed head was stuck up on the walls for all to see. Following the incident, four companies of foot were sent to replace Lilburn's now suspect soldiers.[48] Subsequently, in and around Tynemouth, a series of attempts were made by royalist sympathisers either to re-take the Castle or persuade the garrison to go over to the king's side. There was even a bizarre plan to 'contrive a way from the coal-pits, about two miles distant, underground into the Castle, and so to supply the garrison with provisions in the event of its declaration for the king and having to stand a siege'.[49]

The local population of Tynemouth and North Shields had suffered greatly at the hands of the warring faction during the civil wars. Irrespective of their own personal sympathies, they had been obliged to provide food and shelter for the different sets of troops who had occupied their township. Ralph Gardner of the nearby township of Chirton, claimed that the royalists had cost him £500, the Scots £400 and the Parliamentarians £200 (the equivalent of about £2 million in total in 2014). Local coal owners had been obliged to provide the various garrisons with free coal. Parishioners had not only been denied the use of their parish church, because it was a remnant of the Priory within the Castle walls, but by the end of the conflict found it in ruins.[50]

Cromwell, the leader of the Puritans who controlled the country after the execution of Charles I, died in 1658. He was succeeded by his son Richard but by 1659 it was impossible to reconcile the conflict between the military and constitutional authorities within the so-called Commonwealth. The garrison at Tynemouth initially supported the army. However, when General Monck accepted the commission of commander-in-chief of the parliamentary forces and left his station on the Scottish border and began to move in the direction of Tynemouth, the garrison changed sides. It was Monck's successful march south which led directly to the restoration of the power of Parliament and indirectly to the restoration of the monarchy.

Charles II accession to the throne in 1660 marked an end to Puritanism as the dominant way of life in England. Social festivities which had been banned were resumed. Theatres which had been closed were re-opened. Christmas was restored to the calendar. The Church of England was re-established. However, although sympathetic to Catholicism and nominally committed to religious tolerance, Charles bowed to anti-Catholic feeling rather than risk his throne. He also had more to contend with than religious conflict. An outbreak of plague in 1665 left around 70,000 dead in London alone and a huge swathe of the city was destroyed by fire in 1666. England and Holland were already at war and France and Denmark soon allied themselves with the Dutch against England. Concerned that the Tyne might be attacked, the king asked the burgesses of Newcastle to contribute towards the cost of repairing the fortifications of Tynemouth Castle. The request came at a time when there were rumours of a plot among the garrisons of both Tynemouth and Berwick castles. A letter in the surviving State Papers of the period refers to 'the fanatics at Shields, where there is a nest of them pray and hope for deliverance by the Dutch and French'.[51]

When in 1677 a Dutch fleet sailed up the Medway and destroyed three anchored English warships, it induced a widespread panic on Tyneside. The same State Papers make reference to a Newcastle correspondent who had written that: 'People are distracted and at their wits' end with the sad news. The people generally give up the place for lost, and daily apprehend the enemy's landing; they cry that all is lost for want of care.'[52]

Despite such apprehension, preparations were underway to protect the Tyne. Under Col. Villiers' governorship, a new battery was completed and there were sufficient regular troops and volunteers to garrison the Castle. Ships were available to be sunk in the entrance to the river if necessary and two fire-ships and other 'guard-ships' were also anchored at the harbour mouth. The 1670 cessation of hostilities proved short-lived and another, more widespread war involving the Dutch broke out in 1672, but by then Clifford's Fort had been completed at the 'Narrows' in North Shields with batteries of 10- and 20-pound guns to provide the river with further protection.[53] It remained in use until 1927, after which the Borough Council purchased it from the War Office to allow for extensions to the Fish Quay.

Charles II's attempt to relax anti-Catholic legislation in 1672 produced such a strong reaction from Parliament that the regulations were actually reinforced. The 1673 Test Act required all civil and military officers of the Crown to renounce Catholic doctrines and a second Act in 1678 denied Catholics the right to sit in either chamber of Parliament. On his death in 1685, Charles II was succeeded by James II. He chose to ignore the Test Acts, appointed Catholics to public office, and in 1687 issued a Declaration of Liberty of Conscience. These actions also proved counter-productive. Given that he already had a son and heir, the prospect of a Catholic dynasty alarmed Anglicans and Dissenters alike. It was at this point that Tory and Whig parliamentarians encouraged William of Orange (from the Netherlands), who had married Mary (an heir to the English throne) to invade England. The object may have been to save England from Catholicism but, given that England had been at war with the Dutch

Clifford's Fort, c.1750, by an unknown artist.

| Shiels to Shields

Tynemouth Castle, Priory and Lighthouse, c.1845: a painting by James (also known as John) Wilson Carmichael (1800–68). Carmichael was born in Newcastle, the son of a carpenter, and spent three years at sea before completing his apprenticeship as a carpenter. He went on to become a celebrated marine artist.

just a few years earlier, this extraordinary turn of events must have been bewildering to those not involved in the affairs of state.

Col. Villiers, who opposed the invitation to William and Mary, left Tynemouth Castle with two companies of soldiers determined to join any resistance to the scheme. However, he was captured at York and the rest of the Tynemouth garrison surrendered shortly afterwards. Since Carlisle and Berwick castles had already surrendered, James II was left with no strongholds in the North.[54] His reign came to an end after only two minor clashes between the opposing armies.

The later history of Tynemouth Castle was to prove less eventful but it continued to guard the river against potential foreign invasion for successive centuries and was in use as recently as the twentieth century. A major modern artillery piece still occupies a position on the edge of the cliff as a stark reminder of how recently the shores of Britain were in danger of invasion.

2

North Shields v. Newcastle:
a struggle for survival

While Tynemouth monastery may have come to an abrupt end in the sixteenth century and Tynemouth Castle reduced in significance by the end of the seventeenth, the adjacent settlement of North Shields continued to develop, albeit haltingly. Indeed, had the burgesses of Newcastle had their way, there would have been no need for this book: there would have been no North Shields for my ancestors to come to in the nineteenth century. It was only after a centuries-long, bitter struggle against its hostile Newcastle neighbour that North Shields not only survived but emerged in the nineteenth century as a magnet for migrants.

Despite coming from North Shields, when at university and asked where I was from, I almost invariably answered 'near Newcastle'. I did so because to answer 'North Shields' usually produced a blank expression on the part of the inquirer. I resented having to do it because I was not only *not* from Newcastle but felt little sense of identity with it. To outsiders who look at a map of Tyneside it may seem that North Shields is just part of the Newcastle conurbation. To those of us born and raised in North Shields it is an entirely separate place, eight miles from Newcastle. Not identifying with Newcastle did not prevent me from 'jumping on the bandwagon' when Newcastle United won the FA Cup three times in the early 1950s. It remained the case that my boyhood team was not Newcastle United. It was North Shields AFC, who played in the North-Eastern League alongside Sunderland and Middlesbrough Reserves – but not Newcastle United Reserves. They played in the Central League: something I regretted because it meant that North Shields did not have the opportunity to compete against even Newcastle United's second team.

The situation with respect to football in the 1950s epitomised the nature of the relationship between Newcastle and North Shields in earlier centuries. By being in a different league, Newcastle United was never in direct competition with North Shields AFC. And so it had been for centuries with respect to commercial competition between the two towns. The burgesses of Newcastle had deliberately, and by fair means and foul, created a situation in which North Shields was denied the opportunity to compete against Newcastle. That bitter conflict may now be forgotten but it needs to be understood to comprehend the nature and significance of the expansion of North Shields in the nineteenth century.

The right to buy and sell land and trade freely is taken for granted today. In medieval England it was different. Land allocated by a monarch to the lord of a manor could usually be treated as private property, but ultimately the lord was a tenant rather than the owner of an estate. Should the lord of a manor be found guilty of treason, or die without a legal heir, the land would revert to the Crown. Land, other than that which remained within the royal domain, was divided into areas known as manors. Most were in secular hands but a large number had been granted to the Church. In these instances, a bishop, prior or similar ecclesiastical dignitary was the equivalent of the lord of the manor.

Within rural manors, economic self-sufficiency was deemed desirable and, while no manor ever was self-contained, the notion did have implications for commerce. To have only a limited need for trade with the world outside the manor was regarded as a sign of good management. These generalisations did not extend to manors containing towns. Trade was the primary function of towns and one important consequence of this commercial focus was that it weakened the lord of the manor's position in relation to those below him in the feudal hierarchy. The burgesses of towns were able to exercise more control over their situations than their serf equivalents in rural manors by obtaining royal charters which gave them exclusive rights to particular commercial activities. Such monopolies were plainly disadvantageous to other would-be entrepreneurs in the area, and it was the granting of such charters to the burgesses of Newcastle, beginning in 1213, that set the scene for the long and bitter quarrel between North Shields and its larger neighbour upstream.

The Prior and monks at Tynemouth, like the lords of any other manor, enjoyed the benefits which derived from their extensive land-holdings. But, by the thirteenth century, the Prior and his monks were also involved in a variety of commercial pursuits, and it was the attempt to establish a centre for trade at the entrance to the Tyne which provoked the first of many clashes with the burgesses of Newcastle.

The early pattern of settlement

The origin of North Shields can be traced back to a small number of probably turf huts (described variously as 'shiels', 'sheeles' or 'sheales'), which were erected on the riverbank close to where the Pow Burn entered the Tyne. At that time and for centuries later the now culverted and almost forgotten Pow Burn provided the first safe haven on the north bank of the River Tyne. Coates provides evidence that at least until 1760 it was a tidal tributary, navigable at least by small craft for half a mile upstream into what is now Northumberland Park. Running from two sources in the area of the present-day Preston Grange and Marden estates, the Burn ran through what is now Tynemouth Golf Course and the Park and then into the sheltered valley below Tynemouth Road.[1]

Shiels were not unique to the area. As far back as the seventh century, similar shelters had been used by Northumbrian shepherds during summer months. But at Tynemouth they served a different purpose. A small population of fishermen, in return for the privilege of being allowed their own fishing boats, provided fish for the monastery. It was from their shiels and the adjacent wharf that these local fishermen went out to sea.[2] And it was from the north shiels and their counterparts on the south of the river that the two communities of North and South Shields were later to take their names.*

In 1225, Prior Germanus took the decision to reclaim a substantial area of marshy ground to the east of the shiels but still within the demesne of Tynemouth Priory.† The land was drained; seven houses were built on it, and a further 20 houses constructed beyond that site. Each had its own quay. A variety of commercial activities soon developed. As well as baking, brewing and fishing for local needs, there was a trade in coal and fish, from locally caught salmon and fish brought back by the 16 vessels which sailed from Shields, sometimes as far north as Iceland.‡ There was also a trade in dressed hides from a tannery at the nearby township of Preston.[3]

Conflict and competition with Newcastle

This development of a potential commercial rival downstream led to concern among the burgesses of Newcastle. In 1267, the Mayor, Nicholas Scot, came to Shields with what Craster describes as an armed rabble.§

---

* Taggart, however, suggests the word Shield (or Shields) may derive from the term for a Roman camp and notes the many references to Shield or Shields in the proximity of the Roman Wall e.g. Sewing Shields, Shield-Field, Winshields, Car Shield and Shield-on-the-Wall.

† The demesne was the part of manorial lands reserved for the lord's (or in this case the Prior's) own use. Serfs were required to work in the demesne for a specified time each week.

‡ Salmon used the river until the nineteenth century and to such an extent that Thomas Bewick, the celebrated artist and engraver, suggested that something needed to be done about the porpoises which gathered at the entrance to the Tyne to feed on them. In 1862, on page 224 of his memoirs, he wrote: 'I have seen a shoal of porpoises, off Tynemouth, swimming abreast of each other, and thus occupying a space of apparently more than a hundred yards from the shore, seawards, and crossing the mouth of the river, so that no salmon could enter it. They went backward and forward for more than a mile, along shore, and with such surprising rapidity that in their course, they caused a foam to arise, like the breakers on the sea in a storm.'

§ A medieval mayor was not a mere figurehead. The mayor presided over a town's borough court, which dealt with legal affairs and the general conduct of the town.

They beat and maltreated the monks and servants of the Priory on whom they could lay their hands; they set fire to the mills and houses, and carried off a vessel loaded with coal which they found lying there.[4]

In retaliation, the Prior brought a law suit against Newcastle, which resulted in the burgesses agreeing not to repeat their unruly behaviour. Although the agreement seems to have been honoured, it did not mean that the Newcastle burgesses gave up their fight against the fledgling town at the mouth of the Tyne. They merely adopted a different strategy. In 1275, they petitioned Edward I and, in a shrewd political move, asserted that the decrease in the king's income from the city could be directly attributed to the development of North Shields. They asserted that, by competing with Newcastle, the Prior at Tynemouth was siphoning off income that would otherwise be going to the king. The crime of the Prior, and his counterpart, the Prior of Durham, was that they had 'raised towns where no towns ought to be, but only huts for sheltering fishermen'.[5] A decision on the petition was delayed until 1291, by which time the initial settlement at North Shields had grown into a port and township of about 100 houses.

The Prior had not only to answer the charges of the Newcastle burgesses but also those made by the King's attorney. The Prior's defence was that the commercial activity taking place in Shields was legitimate because of the charters granted to the monastery by King Stephen (1135–54) and Richard I (1189–99), both of which came before the conflicting privileges granted to the burgesses of Newcastle by King John (1199–1216). The charter of Richard I was as generous and open-ended as it could be. It included the words: 'We have granted to God and to the Church of St Oswin of Tynemouth, and to the monks of St Alban's there serving God, all liberties and free customs which the royal power can confer upon any church, in as ample a manner as can be done.'[6]

Despite this defence, the judgement was given in favour of the King and Newcastle.

Owners of vessels were forbidden in future to unload or take in cargoes at Shields, or to sell their merchandise in that town. No provisions were to be sold there to merchantmen. All wharves which extended below high-water mark were ordered to be removed.[7]

The Crown, as well as Newcastle, gained from the judgement – and not only in terms of trade. Henry I (1068–1100) had granted the Priory the right to shipwrecks, which were not uncommon in the treacherous waters at the entrance to the River Tyne. Under the new ruling they became the property of Edward I and his heirs. The gains made by the burgesses of Newcastle were comprehensive. They were given exclusive jurisdiction on the river from Sparhawk (a sandbank about quarter of a mile off Benebalcrag) as far as the Hedwin Streams (shallow rapids) in the parish of Ryton, several miles beyond Newcastle.

Edward's ruling did more that confer a commercial advantage on Newcastle: it brought North Shields to its knees. The population drifted away. Houses fell into disrepair. Coal was still mined on the corner of what became Union Street and Howard Street, but could no longer be loaded at Shields. Even though the pit was only yards from the river, coal had to be sent in carts to Newcastle. When it reached there, it was loaded onto ships that had been obliged to travel nine unnecessary miles up a river with difficult to navigate sandbanks. They then had to negotiate the same journey back to the open sea.

In commenting on this judgement in favour of Newcastle, Haswell suggested that Edward, like his predecessors and successors, had awarded charters in the self-interest of the Crown rather than the merits of the case. That, he suggests, is obvious if one looks at some of the other decisions made in relation to Tynemouth and North Shields during this period. For example, in 1292, the bakeries at North Shields had been closed after protests from Newcastle. In 1303, Edward II's wife stayed at the Priory while he went on into Scotland. In the same year, the king granted Tynemouth the right to hold a fair. In the following year, after a Newcastle petition, he revoked that right. So despite the fact that earlier kings had granted charters to successive priors, giving them the right to 'sell their merchandise as they please', and had protected them from the claims of Newcastle, Edward I, while happy to accept the hospitality of the Priory, 'never hesitated to set aside such charters in the interest of the party with the longer purse'.[8]

Newcastle was less successful in suppressing trade on the south bank of the river. The Bishop of Durham proved a more formidable adversary than the Prior of Tynemouth and won several legal tussles with Newcastle, for example from Richard II in 1383 which granted the bishopric a charter which allowed it to ship coal from the south bank of the Tyne 'without impediment from the men of Newcastle'.[9]

It is not clear how long or how completely the judgements in favour of Newcastle were respected by the monks at Tynemouth. What is apparent is that towards the end of the fourteenth century considerable commercial activity was again evident in North Shields.

Four acres of land below high-water mark were reclaimed and covered by about 200 houses – inns and stables, wine taverns, butchers' stalls, shambles, shopping, herring and fish houses. A new market was started. An assize [record of weights and measures] of bread and wine and ale was kept. The prior made himself thirteen bake-houses, where a thousand quarters of corn were yearly baked into bread; and brew-houses, at which he found a vent, every year, for two thousand quarters of his barley-malt. He claimed and took wreck of the sea, flotsam and jetsam, and deodands found upon the water.* Twenty years later, as trade increased, he commenced building staithes along the shore, where ships could lie to and load at all stages of the tide.[10]

There is also evidence that 14 staithes (wooden frameworks projecting into the river) had been erected between 1386 and 1429, varying in size from 20 feet × 15 feet (6 m × 4 m) to 60 feet × 40 feet (18 m × 12 m). Most had mussel-scalps attached. Others housed curing houses. North Shields also had 20 cobles and seven larger craft owned by four ship-owners.

Despite complaints, the monks continued with their commercial activities. Around 1433, they bought two vessels of their own and carried out a trade in fish, salt and coal. They became fishmongers on a substantial scale: salting and smoking herring; selling cod and ling caught in the water of the Shetlands and in salmon caught locally in three long weirs or 'salmon-yares'. What is noteworthy is that, during this period, their activities seem to have met with royal approval. Henry VI (1422–61) granted to the then Prior, Langton, 'the custom and toll received for grain, salt, salt-fish, leather, merchandise, and coal loaded by him and his tenants within the port of Tyne'.[11] The Priory also received 'all fines and amercements of tenants and farmers within the lordship of Tynemouth and at Shields for bread baked, ale brewed, and victuals sold to mariners within the liberty and jurisdiction of the town of Newcastle'.†

This renewed commercial activity at Shields and the royal approval given to it, led to further protests from Newcastle. The privileges granted to Prior Langton by Henry VI were withdrawn in 1450, only be re-affirmed 12 years later by Edward IV (1461–70). Further clashes with Newcastle became inevitable, although the first recorded violence in this period did not take place until 1510.

The Priors of Tynemouth were always the mortal enemies of Newcastle, and jealous of its glories, so much so that in 1510 a great number of the people of Newcastle, headed by some of the aldermen and principal townsmen, assembled at Jesmond with intent to kill the Prior; fortunately he escaped from their hands.[12]

---

* Deodand was a legal term in use until the nineteenth century for an object (or animal) that had caused someone's death. In medieval Europe, the object, or its equivalent value, passed to the Church or the Crown. The term comes from the Latin *Deo dandum* which means 'to be given to God'.

† A fine in this period was a sum of money paid to obtain a grant, concession, or privilege. It was not a financial penalty as we use the term today. An amercement was a financial penalty imposed for minor offences. As an example, a failure to pay a fine for a granted privilege would lead to the imposition of an amercement.

As before, Newcastle sought the help of the King. In 1530 it obtained an Act from Henry VIII (1509–47) re-affirming the rights of Newcastle over North Shields (and South Shields). This crucial legislation, which was not formally repealed until 1850, did allow fishing and the manufacture of salt to continue at North Shields but laid down

> … that from henseforth any marchant or marchantes, or any other person or persons, shall not ship, lode, or unlode, charge or discharge any manner of goodes, wares or marchandises to be solde here within this your realme or elsewhere, in to or from any ship or shippes, or other vessels, in or at any other place or places within the said port, river and haven, between the said place called the Sparhauke, and the said place called Hedwinstremes, but only at the said towne of Newcastell, and no where els, upon peine of fortfaiture of all suche goodes, wares and marchaundises to the king, our said soveraigne lorde, and to his heires, kings of England.[13]

So, even with the active support of an influential monastery, North Shields was again forbidden by law to enter into competition with Newcastle. Within the next decade, the situation deteriorated still further when the struggling town lost it ecclesiastical champion. As already noted, in 1539, the Priory and all its accumulated wealth and belongings were transferred to Henry VIII – including the land on which the struggling North Shields was built. This allowed for a more ruthless enforcement of the 1530 Act than might otherwise have been the case and North Shields passed into yet another period of marked decline. Houses previously maintained by the monastery fell into disrepair. The number of fishermen declined and many of those engaged in other, now prohibited trades left the town.

The fortunes of North Shields did not begin to improve significantly until the seventeenth century. The revival was based on salt making: a process described by Brereton in 1635. At high tide, salt water was fed into a pit and from there fed into iron pans heated by coal-fired brick furnaces. The water was boiled and topped up three times before the then strong brine solution was run off into another set of pans where the salt precipitated after further boiling.[14] In 1638, there were 32 such pans in North Shields (and more in South Shields). Although the material to build saltpans still had to be taken up-river to Newcastle to be unloaded, the salt-makers of North and South Shields still succeeded in expanding their trade and even secured a near-monopoly for it. In 1634, they became incorporated under the name of the Society of Salt-makers at the North and South Shields. A payment was made to the king for the right to erect salt works on the coast and on the rivers Tyne and Wear and the Society also secured a crucial agreement that no new salt works would be allowed on the coast between Berwick and Southampton.

Despite the expansion in salt making, the disadvantaged position of North Shields in relation to Newcastle remained much the same with respect to other trades. Although new collieries were opening in the townships adjacent to North Shields, coal could still only be loaded at Newcastle. Ships' masters were obliged to use Newcastle to unload and load their cargoes; take on or off-load their ballast or have their vessels repaired. This imposition proved an even greater problem for mariners in the seventeenth century when larger tonnage ships were in use. That made navigating the Tyne to and from Newcastle increasingly slow and dangerous. Two further matters made the situation even more aggravating for the residents of both North and South Shields. The first was that, after 1613, Newcastle had been given responsibility for the river but allowed it to silt up. The second was that freemen of Newcastle were able to exploit their monopoly by doing what they refused to allow others to do, that is discharge their ballast and load their cargoes in the harbours of North or South Shields. By avoiding the difficult and potentially dangerous journey to and from Newcastle they could even sometimes complete a voyage to and from London before other ships were ready to set sail again.[15]

As in earlier periods, commercial activity that appeared to breach the Newcastle monopoly was challenged. For example, in 1627, the mayor and burgesses of Newcastle prosecuted Humphrey Johnson for maintaining a brewery and obtained an order to have it closed down.[16] In 1646, a North Shields shipwright and his wife and daughter, suffered a worse fate. Thomas Cliffe and three of his men freed a ship from the rocks under Tynemouth Castle and then repaired it. When that became known in Newcastle, a group came down to North Shields, arrested Cliffe and put him in prison. His wife and daughter 'railed against' these actions and in the struggle that followed his daughter's arm was broken and his

Contemporary stylised representation of the attack on Mrs Cliffe, from the 1849 reprint of Gardner's *Book and Petitions* to mark the occasion of the establishment of the Borough of Tynemouth.

North Shields v. Newcastle |

wife was 'clubbed about the head and body'. She died of her injuries two weeks later.[17]

Subsequently, Cliffe was involved in a protracted legal battle with the Shipwrights' Company of Newcastle who claimed to have the sole right to practise their trade on the Tyne. The ultimate outcome was that after about six years of legal wrangling, with the case still unresolved, Cliffe was forced to leave Tyneside. He is reported to have said: 'I dare not go home by reason of their threats to put me where I shall never see sun or moone more if they light on me.'[18]

A successful challenge to the Newcastle monopoly was mounted in 1631 by the influential Sir Robert Heath, a Lord Chief Justice of Common Pleas, who owned land in North Shields. When he began building a ballast wharf and saltpans, the burgesses of Newcastle tried to stop the development by the use of force. When that failed, like their predecessors in earlier centuries, they appealed to the king and council. This time they were unsuccessful. After several hearings, the judgement was that: 'Sir Robert Heath's ballast wharf now a–building shall be built, go forward and be quite finished and backed with ballast to make it fit for the salt works which, for his Majesty's service are begun and intended to be performed.'[19]

This, however, was an isolated relaxation of the Newcastle monopoly and had no general implications for Newcastle's dominant position on the Tyne. No one but a freeman of Newcastle was allowed to build or repair ships on the Tyne. The master of a ship entering the Tyne was not allowed to use the services of any carpenter or shipwright who was not a freeman of Newcastle, even to save the vessel from sinking. No one who was not a brother of Trinity House, and consequently a freeman of Newcastle, was allowed to pilot a ship in or out of the Tyne and no one but such a freeman was permitted to load or discharge vessels in the port. To enforce the claims of Newcastle, those who controlled the coal trade were bound by oath not to supply coal to any vessel which failed to comply with all the demands of the mayor and burgesses of Newcastle. No provisions or goods brought into the Tyne could be discharged from any vessel except in the market at Newcastle. Consequently, 'many were the Shieldsmen fined and imprisoned for buying from vessels arriving in the harbour'.[20]

Ralph Gardner's resistance

The next sustained challenge to the Newcastle monopoly came from Ralph Gardner who, ironically, was born in Newcastle.* In 1650, at the age of 25, he set up a small brewery in Chirton, then a township adjacent to North Shields. He was warned to cease his activities by the brewers of Newcastle and fined when he failed to do so. When he refused to pay the fine, he was arrested and imprisoned in August 1652. He was refused bail and not allowed visitors. Several writs based on the Habeus Corpus Act of 1640 were deliberately destroyed. Gardner was never brought to trial but managed to escape to Scotland in February 1653. On returning to Chirton, he began gathering evidence for a legal action to try to end the Newcastle monopoly once and for all.

Within three months of his escape, an armed gang from Newcastle attacked him at his home in Chirton and attempted to re-arrest him.

> A great number of men belonging to Newcastle, with swords drawn and pistols ... shot at some of the said gentleman's servants, and beat his wife, and much blood was spilt, they pretending they came by warrant, and produced a warrant from the Mayor and Sheriff of Newcastle to take him and carry him away to prison, under pretence of debt; but the seamen got ashoar, fell upon the said Newcastle men, wounded and disarmed them, and relieved the said gentleman.[21]

In anticipation of a further attack, which did take place a few days later, Gardner left for London to take his case to a wider audience.[22] Like Cliffe before him, he had the support of many of those who traded with Newcastle but, unlike Cliffe, he also enjoyed the support of powerful local figures such as Sir Ralph Delaval.† In addition to drawing attention to Newcastle's abuse of its monopolistic position, and the inhumane prison conditions to which he had been subjected despite never having been brought to trial, Gardner also publicised the problems of navigation on the Tyne and the disadvantages caused by the lack of a market at North Shields.

On 29 September 1653, Gardner petitioned Parliament for what was, in essence, free trade on the Tyne. He also asked for the river to be placed in the hands of independent commissioners. Unfortunately for Gardner and North Shields, the fate of his petition was decided by an extraordinary

---

* Gardner's Chirton home was pulled down in 1856 and a monument erected nearby in 1882 as a public acknowledgement of his efforts on behalf of the town. Ralph Gardner Secondary School which was built in Chirton close to the site of his home was pulled down in the late twentieth century to make way for a housing development.

† Sir Ralph Delaval (1622–91) was the son of Robert Delaval of Seaton Delaval. An Oxford graduate who was admitted to Lincoln's Inn, he became high sheriff of Northumberland in 1649; was an MP for over 20 years and created a baronet in 1659.

twist of fate in national politics. On 5 October 1653 his petition was referred to the Committee for Trade and Corporations. The committee pressed ahead with its deliberations despite Newcastle's efforts to thwart its work by seeking lengthy postponements.* It reported in favour of North Shields and the other towns downstream of Newcastle, and recommended a series of important reforms. An Act of Parliament to give effect to the recommendations was scheduled for debate on 13 December 1653. But, on the day before, by what must have seemed the cruellest stroke of fate, Parliament was dissolved by Cromwell's soldiers. The end of the 'Barebones' Parliament also meant the end of Gardner's petition.[23]

Had it passed, the Act would have contained provisions which were more far-reaching than those eventually granted to the Tyne Commissioners in the mid-nineteenth century. All the former powers, privileges and grants accorded Newcastle would have been repealed. In their place, Commissioners of the Admiralty would have appointed paid conservators 'to do all matters and things necessary for the conservancy of so famous and commodious a river'. Ships' masters would have been free to discharge and load where they chose; to employ whatever craftsmen or river pilot they preferred. They would also have enjoyed the freedom to buy provisions from anywhere on the river. All goods and provisions which came in by sea for the use of the salt-works, collieries, and other buildings at or near Shields could have been discharged at Shields. Only merchandise and grain specifically destined for the use of Newcastle would have had to be discharged at Newcastle or in its near vicinity. The Newcastle monopoly of the coal trade would have been abolished and coal-owners free to sell it to whomever they chose. Ballast shores would have been erected at Shields or other convenient places and the casting of ballast at sea, or in the river, would have been outlawed. Finally, North Shields would have at last enjoyed the right to hold a market, twice a week.[24]

Despite this devastating disappointment, Gardner did not give up. In 1654 he attempted something more modest. He petitioned Cromwell directly, in his capacity as Lord Protector, for North Shields to be given the right to hold a regular market. That was much more significant than those of us with ready access to supermarkets and out-of-town shopping centres can appreciate, now that street markets tend to be seen as quaint legacies of a bygone age. There was much more to a weekly medieval market than its modern-day equivalent. At a time when there was little other opportunity

---

* Haswell suggests that the representatives of Newcastle may have been playing for time because they could not produce the charter on which their whole case was based. On page 30 of *The Maister*, he maintains that: 'Not until some two hundred year later was it definitely ascertained that the original charter upon which all this mischievous work was founded did not exist. ... The charter of Henry II, it was admitted on behalf of Newcastle in 1850, did not exist, and as to John's, which merely confirmed Henry's, there was but an office copy! The Tynemouth charters, on the contrary, were original, extant and legible.'

Ralph Gardner's Chirton house and memorial. The house was drawn and etched by John Storey. The insert is the Gardner memorial.
AUTHOR COLLECTION

for the exchange of goods, they were of crucial commercial importance. They made possible the long-established practice of concluding bargains in the presence of witnesses. In the event of a subsequent dispute, those witnesses could attest to the terms of the original transaction. Towns which enjoyed the right to hold markets were at a commercial advantage to their local neighbours. The corollary was that people who did not live in market towns were disadvantaged – not only because they lacked somewhere to sell their goods locally but because they had to travel a distance even to buy them. As Gardner pointed out in his petition, for the inhabitants of North Shields to have to make such journeys was more than a mere inconvenience.

> In tymes of deep snowes … people dare not adventure by land in the winter season to Newcastle Markett [and] in extremity of weather many boates are cast away and many people are drowned in goeing to and from that markett at Newcastle.[25]

Gardner's seemingly reasonable request was unsuccessful. Faced with this second defeat, Gardner completed and published *England's Grievances Discovered*, the large, carefully argued book he had started in prison. It is a lengthy indictment of the abuses to which the corporation and companies of Newcastle were subjecting North Shields and other Tyneside communities.

The end of the Newcastle monopoly

After the restoration of the monarchy, Newcastle continued to dominate economic activity on the Tyne and to stifle commercial activity in North Shields. For example, in 1672, Newcastle closed down John Overing's brewery. In 1690 the council of Newcastle referred to a committee, 'the consideration of what means were necessary to be used for preventing the great growth of trade at Shields' and, in 1691, orders were made for the seizure of all coal shipped at North Shields.[26] But the days of Newcastle's monopoly of the Tyne were drawing to a close. North Shields was to enter the eighteenth century with a greater freedom than at any stage in its history.

The end to the Newcastle monopoly did not come suddenly after another legal battle but slowly as a result of changes in economic thinking. That led initially to mercantilism, which focused on ways the state could promote the national economy, at the expense of other countries, and shifted the focus away from the kind of local jealousies which existed between Newcastle and its Tyneside neighbours. The economics of supply and demand which replaced mercantilism directly challenged such rights and privileges. It maintained that all individuals should be free to pursue their economic self-interest. Market mechanisms alone should determine success or failure in business and commerce: 'all franchises, liberties, and privileges which distinguished particular groups, areas or communities were to be deplored.'[27]

With this evolving economic thinking North Shields was at last able to develop without the oppressive restrictions that had been imposed on it by Newcastle in earlier centuries. It was able to exploit its natural advantages and become a flourishing town. The landmark dates which most clearly mark the end of the long struggle with Newcastle are 1848 and 1850. On 30 March 1848 an independent port of Shields was created. Its boundary was defined by a straight line drawn across the river from Whitehill Point on the north bank to Jarrow Quay on the south bank. The port was sub-divided in 1865 when North and South Shields were given independent status, with the boundary between them in the middle of the river. The conservancy of the Tyne remained in the hands of Newcastle Corporation until the 1850 River Tyne Improvement Act when the management of the river was transferred to independent commissioners. Newcastle had spent only about a third of the shipping dues it had collected to maintain the river.[28] The new commissioners acted quickly to remedy that with a programme to dredge the river to allow larger ships to use the Tyne.

I will return to such important developments in Chapter 4 but in the next chapter it is important to describe something of the scale and range of benefits gained by Newcastle and lost by North Shields, and other riverside towns, as a consequence of Newcastle's monopoly of trade in general and the coal trade in particular.

3

It's like taking coals to Shields

NORTH SHIELDS suffered in many ways as a result of the ruthless domination of the commercial life of the River Tyne by the burgesses of Newcastle. It probably lost most by not being able to share fully in the lucrative trade in coal. Coal and Newcastle became so closely identified that, in many parts of the world, the expression '*It's like taking coals to Newcastle*', was adopted to signify an activity that was utterly pointless.[*] No one, of course, has encountered the expression '*It's like taking coals to Shields*'. I have coined it as the title of this chapter to help make a simple but key point. Without Newcastle's determination to curtail the competition from its neighbouring Tyneside towns, North Shields, given its much more convenient position at the mouth of the river, might have achieved the same kind of worldwide association with the coal trade as Newcastle. Even with continuing resistance from Newcastle, large fleets of colliers came to use North Shields in the eighteenth century. It became 'a haven sufficient to contain a thousand ships of the largest burden'.[1]

Newcastle's dominance was not due only to its monopolistic position on the river. It occupied a strategic location on the main north–south route from England to Scotland and was at the intersection of an east–west route from the Tyne to Carlisle. Newcastle also stood at the site of the easiest crossing point on the river.[2] Even so, if North Shields had been able to secure an equitable share in the coal trade at an earlier period, its economic fortunes would have been very different. In being prevented from becoming a full player in the vital trade in coal, North Shields was denied the opportunity of becoming a major British town. That will become apparent in this chapter as I outline how the British population came to rely on coal from Tyneside to warm their homes and how craftsmen and manufacturers came to rely on coal as their primary source of energy. Britain may have turned its back on coal in the late twentieth century but without coal and the thousands of miners who risked and often sacrificed their lives producing it, the nation would not have become the industrial workshop of the world in the nineteenth century, nor remained a major international power in the twentieth.

---

[*] The saying was already common at beginning of the seventeenth century.

Fine particles of sea coal on Saltburn Sands in 2007. By the time this image was taken the larger pieces of coal which had been washed ashore had been collected to be burned in open fires.

The initial phase: coal collecting

Archaeologists have found coal on local Roman sites, including Hadrian's Wall.[3] Despite this evidence that coal was in use in Northumberland around two thousand years ago, there is no evidence of a trade in coal until the thirteenth century.[4] Initially, coal in the North East was not mined or even dug. Charters were granted to monks to collect it. Quite literally, they picked 'sea coal' up from beaches.*

> The dawn of the coal trade would seem to have begun … where fragments of the mineral, quarried from their native bed by the surge of the North Sea, lay strewn among the shingle on the open Northumberland coast. The strange black stones, which could be burned like charcoal, and were seemingly brought there by the waves themselves … [were] christened 'sea coal'.[5]

---

* Later, the term was used more generally for coal mined in the area. Later in the seventeenth century, the use of the term *sea coal* began to decline and was replaced by the more general term *coal*.

The evolution of the coal trade

Until the eve of the First World War (when it was matched by South Wales), the most productive English coalfield was the Great Northern coalfield of Northumberland and Durham.[6] A complex mining industry emerged in and around Tyneside at an early stage, at a time when inland coal fields were still extracting coal from outcrops or rudimentary open-cast workings.[7] Ready access to the sea gave Tyneside coalfields a marked advantage over inland fields which could only transport their coal by land, river or canal. The trade in coal from Newcastle to London began at least as early as the thirteenth century. References to a Sacoles (Sea Coals) Lane in London have been found in records dating back to the thirteenth century, along with several mentions of the arrival of sea coal in the capital. The trade increased significantly during the second half of the century when a fleet of ships took coal from Newcastle to London.[8] The growing use of coal by smiths, lime-burners, brewers, dyers and other trades was often unpopular. The smoke produced by coal was considered at best annoying and at worst harmful to health. The concern became so widespread that in 1306 a royal proclamation prohibited workers from using sea coal in their furnaces. The ban seems to have been widely ignored but for another three centuries 'coal continued to be regarded by the upper classes in London as a most inferior and objectionable fuel'.[9] Yet by 1369 the trade in coal had become so significant that the City of London appointed four officials to supervise the unloading of coal, collect the duties imposed by the City and Crown as well as protect buyers from being given short measure. Coal that left the Tyne was not only landed in London. It was unloaded in numerous locations between the North East and the south coast and coal was also exported to the Continent, particularly to France.[10]

In 1377 about 70,000 tons of coal were shipped from Newcastle to London and it was during the reigns of Edward III (1327–77) and Richard II (1377–99) that recognisable coal capitalists and shipping magnates emerged. By the fifteenth century, coal was employed in a wide range of industries. Moreover, as wood became scarce, coal was used increasingly in homes and houses constructed with chimneys to take away the offending smoke. There was also an expanding export trade for coal – to such an extent that in 1549 there was a proposal to prohibit the export of coal to the French. It was said that French craftsmen could no more survive without Tyneside coal than fish could survive without water. Their need for the coal was reflected in the price they were prepared to pay for it. At a time when coal could be purchased for about 11*d.* a chaldron at Newcastle, it was sold in France for over £4.[11]

In the fourteenth century, an increasing number of landowners in Northumberland and Durham leased their land to those prepared to mine the coal that lay beneath the surface. From the pits, the coal was taken to staithes on the river bank. Because the river was shallow and difficult to navigate small, shallow-draught keel boats were used to take coal to the larger sea-going craft moored below Newcastle Bridge.* Keelmen enjoyed the protection of the monopolistic system that governed life on the Tyne but that does not mean they had a comfortable existence. Their work was seasonal because it was often too dangerous to sail colliers in the winter. Even during the rest of the year, because of interruptions in coal deliveries from the mines, work could be intermittent. The keelmen's work was always arduous. Their first task was to load coal into the keel from wooden chutes on the riverside called *spouts*. Their second was to navigate the keel to the waiting collier. Leaving on the ebb tide from the up-river pits, keels were propelled by a combination of the outgoing tide and a pair of oars, steered from the stern by a 25-foot *swape*. Iron shod poles called *puys*, on either side of the keel, assisted it over the shallows. A single square sail was used when the wind was favourable.† Once moored alongside an anchored collier, the coal had to be 'cast up' using a shovel. As the difference in height between an unloaded collier's deck and a loaded keel's gunnel could be as much as eight feet (2.4 m), the work was extremely demanding.‡ A separate keel worked on each side of the ship and, if necessary, loading continued until after nightfall.[12] Once having finished discharging his own coal, a keelman was expected to help the crew of other keels belonging to the same owner.

Customs dues were paid on the coal shipped, so some standardisation was necessary for those who derived an income from the mining and shipping of coal. The chaldron was the original standard measure. In the fourteenth century, keels carried about 20 chaldrons, about as much as could be conveyed by a cart with one horse. However, when keels themselves became the *de facto* measure, some enterprising traders evaded the duty by using keels that carried more than 20 chaldrons. In 1421, in an attempt to curb this loss in revenue, all keels had their carrying capacity measured and marked with a load-line by the king's commissioners.[13] Over time, traders went back to using the chaldron itself as the *de facto* measure but then devised another ingenious way to evade duty. The size of the chaldron was gradually increased so that 250 years later it was $2\frac{1}{2}$ times its original size.

In 1368, Edward III agreed that the burgesses of Newcastle could raise a levy on coal sold from the Tyne. By the end of the reign of Elizabeth I, this raised about £10,000 per annum for the corporation, the equivalent of

---

* Newcastle's ancient stone bridge prevented navigation further upstream.

† In later years a sprit sail and stay sail were carried, together with a rudder, which improved the keel's performance, but the tide still provided the main source of motion.

‡ During a keelmen's strike in 1819, they demanded an extra shilling per keel for every foot of the side of the ship above five feet. By then vessels had become bigger and higher, making loading progressively more difficult. Later, a removable section of the bulwarks, opposite the mainhatch, made the work easier. Many colliers built expressly for the trade during the eighteenth century were built with rails not solid bulwarks.

about £20 million in 2014. In 1599 the burgesses agreed to share the revenue from this lucrative trade with Elizabeth I. She received 1 shilling (5p) for every chaldron sold to 'the free people of England' – the 2014 equivalent of about £100 on each chaldron.[14] The levy applied only to coal sold from the Tyne. An additional 5s. per chaldron tax, the 2014 equivalent of about £500, was levied by the Crown on coal sold to foreigners from all ports. So the principle of taxing fuel, which in the case of petrol has become such a lucrative earner for the Treasury in recent years, is nothing new.

From what Galloway calls 'time immemorial', the sale of coal on the Tyne had been handled by a guild of middle-men known as 'hostmen'. They alone handled transactions between the owners of coal mines and the merchants who bought coal from the Tyne. They also provided the keels that took the coal to the anchored ships. The increased demand for coal greatly strengthened their power and influence. Elizabeth I regularised it by incorporating the Society of Hostmen, and confirming their exclusive right to load coal on the Tyne (between the Sparhawk and Hedwin streams). Their privileged position did not come without conditions. As well as the 1s. a chaldron tax referred to above, the hostmen agreed to limit the price of coal.[15] At the time of their incorporation, there were 48 hostmen (although in 1602 only 28 were active).* Together, they handled nearly 200,000 tons of coal, using 85 keels. About 200 hoys (a type of flat-bottomed ship) took coal from the Tyne to London alone – often with an armed convoy, such was the importance of the trade to the capital. A further 200 ships supplied other ports.[16]

In the sixteenth century, an increasing number of collieries came under the control of the merchants of Newcastle. They exploited their near-monopoly in a predictable way. The price of coal rose sharply and no less a person than the Mayor of London registered a formal complaint about the 'monopoly and extortion of the owners of the Newcastle coals'.[17] From the second half of the sixteenth century the quantity of coal shipped from the Tyne increased markedly. Hatcher concludes that between the 1560s and 1590s it grew almost four-fold and as much as 97 per cent of the coal sent to coastal ports or overseas had come from Newcastle.[18] Finch maintains that 'the Hostmen's Company of Newcastle, with the coal trade secure and the government of the port and river in their capacious pockets were rightly dubbed the Lords of Coal'. [19]

By the close of the century, the hostmen of Newcastle were handling about 474,000 tons annually.[20] Not all of the increase was for domestic heating. In the early seventeenth century, glass manufacturers began to

---

* The term probably derives from a 1404 statute which specified that foreign merchants should stay with appointed 'hoostes' in the towns they visited. Curiously, visiting merchants were also known as hosts or oastes. That explains why the seal of the company of hostmen represents a hostman grasping the hand of a newly arrived stranger saying 'Welcome, mine oaste'.

perfect coal-fired furnaces. In return for the promise of £1,000 per annum (the equivalent of about £2 million in 2014), the king granted Robert Mansell a monopoly of this new development and banned both the manufacture of glass with wood and the import of glass from abroad. It was on Tyneside that Mansell's efforts proved most profitable. By 1624 he employed 4,000 people. From being a valuable item left to one's descendants, glass became a relatively commonplace commodity and windows became as normal a feature of domestic architecture as doors and chimneys.[21] The only significant time the position of Newcastle was undermined came during the Civil War. When Newcastle sided with the king, Parliament blocked the Tyne. Sunderland, on the River Wear, however, came out in favour of the parliamentarians and helped make up the loss. When peace returned, it had become a serious competitor to Newcastle and by 1660 had increased its coal production 50-fold. Despite that, its coal output was still significantly less than that shipped from the Tyne.[22]

Newcastle was not so predominant in collier ownership. Finch cites figures from Brand's *History of Newcastle* which included a list of ships 'useing the Coale Trade at Newcastle' in the years 1702–04'. Top of the list was Yarmouth with 211 followed by London with 168. Newcastle and

East-coast collier barque c.1750. Barques were three- or four-mast ships with a distinctive sailing rig. They were smaller and easier to handle than fully rigged ships and have been described as the work-horses of the golden age of sail.

| Shiels to Shields

The Low Light, 1828. This painting is by Robert Salmon (1775–1845). Born in Whitehaven, he went on to become known as father of Luminism, landscape painting characterised by the effects of light. To the left of the base of the Low Light a wagon can be seen being pushed towards the opening that will deliver the coal into the waiting collier. To the right, a section of Clifford's Fort can be seen.

Whitby shared third place with 98 colliers. Many other ports had 40–50 colliers calling into Newcastle. The ownership of colliers was complicated. Some of the Tyne's coal-owners were shareholders in ships, including those registered at other ports. The masters of colliers might also own shares in their ships, although seldom a majority holding. Ship chandlers, sailmakers and the owners of rope works often established their right to supply vessels by taking part ownership in colliers as did some other merchants so that they could exercise influence over return cargoes. Shipbuilders sometimes retained a share in the vessels they had built on a speculative basis.[23] During the seventeenth century, colliers made up about one-sixth of all Britain's sea-going merchant vessels. Even so, more of the coal that left the Tyne was carried by foreign ships. In 1616, for example, seven times more foreign colliers left the Tyne, despite the very high customs charges imposed on exported coal.[24]

By the nineteenth century, industrial manufacturing had developed at an unprecedented rate and coal and the steam engine played a major role in facilitating the development of the powered factories that made Britain the workshop of the world. The combined impact of coal and the steam engine also revolutionised transportation as locomotives opened up the country for freight and passengers. Coal was also used to produce coal gas, which lit streets and homes throughout Britain until well into the twentieth century.[*] It was then used in the twentieth century to generate electricity. In addition, the distillation of coal provided the basis of a huge range of products, for a variety of industrial, domestic and medical purposes.

The cumulative significance of these developments led to the nineteenth century being described as 'the great age of coal'.[25] Ironically, the very developments that coal made possible weakened Newcastle's grip on the coal trade. Coal-powered steam locomotives were a safe, all-year mode of transport. Coastal sailing, particularly in the winter months, was always hazardous. Despite colliers from the Tyne sailing for only 8–10 months of the year, many ships and lives were lost. No comparable problems existed for those moving coal from inland fields by railway. Because the duty imposed on Tyneside coal since 1599 applied only to sea-borne coal, coal mined from inland mines could be priced more competitively. The cost of the duty which had once been easy to accommodate when Newcastle was so dominant in the coal trade, now appeared unreasonably discriminatory. Despite the fact that it was not in tune with the free market philosophy of the times, the case for a reduction in the duty on sea-borne coal was conceded only gradually. It was first relaxed on so-called small coal in 1816 and 1823; then on coal carried to London in 1824. It was reduced on exported coal in 1831 and 1834 and abolished altogether in 1845 on coal carried in British ships. Only in 1850 were all duties on sea-borne coal removed.

These and other developments destroyed the way of life of the keelmen. At the peak of their activity in the late eighteenth century, there were about 400 keels on the Tyne.[26] Thereafter, the number declined as the increasing mining of coal from pits lower down the Tyne coupled with the relaxation of the Newcastle monopoly meant that coal could be loaded directly into colliers. For a time, keelmen still had a role to play. Coal staithes were in relatively shallow water and, to prevent ships grounding, the final stages of loading were still completed from keels in the traditional manner.[27]

---

[*]   When my grandmother Lawrence died in North Shields in 1953 her home still had a coal gas lamp. In 1949, about half the 3,082 street lamps in North Shields still used gas, even though the town had built its first electricity power station in 1901.

However, the dredging of the river after 1851 made it easier for colliers to be loaded with full cargoes at the staithes. In addition, the introduction of 'drops', which lowered a whole wagon onto a waiting collier, had the advantage of reducing the distance the coal had to fall once the hinged base of the wagon was released. That had the advantage of reducing the breaking up of coal into smaller pieces.[28] Such developments finally brought the days of the keel and the keelmen to an end.*

The supreme irony for North Shields is that when the Newcastle hostmen eventually lost their monopoly of the local coal trade, Tyneside as a whole was facing intense competition from inland coalfields. So when free at last to compete with Newcastle, North Shields had also to contend with other major competitors, something its rival Newcastle had not had to do on the same scale in earlier centuries. Nevertheless, the demand for coal was so great that this period in coal mining still proved crucially important to North Shields and to the area immediately around it. The fortunes of individual mines and mine owners, which had fluctuated over the centuries but always been restricted by the monopoly enjoyed by the Newcastle hostmen, improved towards the end of the eighteenth century. Indeed, by then, the primary focus of mining operations on Tyneside had already begun to move away from Newcastle toward the coast. That was in part because mines farther from the river were becoming less productive. More significantly, it was because the use of steam engines allowed access to the renowned Main seams of coal in the Tyne basin that were readily acknowledged as the best available for household purposes. The nineteenth century saw a surge of mining in the areas immediately around North Shields, in Wallsend, Percy Main, Howdon, High Flatworth, Shire Moor and Backworth, as well as Preston Colliery and Chirton Colliery in North Shields itself. It was such mining developments in the closing decades of the nineteenth century which brought my Lawrence ancestors to the north-east of England. They moved in 1871 from Cornwall to County Durham and subsequently to a township called Allotment in Northumberland, three miles north-west of North Shields near to the Shiremoor and Backworth collieries.

Britain is still heavily dependent on fossil fuels. At the time of writing, a third of our electricity is generated from coal. However, a political policy to close most of Britain's mines in the late twentieth century means that Britain now has to import large quantities of coal. When boasting of its recent achievements, the Port of Tyne noted that the *importation* of coal into the Tyne had increased from zero in 2003 to almost 5 million tonnes

---

* The keelmen's hospital in City Road, Newcastle, remains as a lasting testament to this historically important group of workers.

Alam Penting,
bringing 75,000
tons of coal *into*
the Tyne.

in 2013. Instead of dredging the river to aid the export of coal, the river was deepened in 2011 to receive the *Alam Penting* which brought a record 75,000 tonnes of coal into the Tyne from New Orleans. The following year, the *Alam Pesona* arrived with over 76,000 tonnes.

The once familiar ironic expression *It's Like Taking Coal to Newcastle* is now devoid of meaning.

4

Free at last: economic change since the eighteenth century

'Beginning in the eighteenth century, demographic, economic and political forces arose in Europe that were truly revolutionary.'
(Peter Stearns).[1]

Tynemouth Borough coat of arms: *'Messis Ab Altis'* – 'Our Harvest is from the Deep'.

T HE precise impact of these forces depended on local circumstances. In the case of North Shields, the demographic, economic and political changes coincided with the decline in the monopolistic position which Newcastle had enjoyed on the Tyne in previous centuries. The combination of these general and particular developments provided commercial opportunities for local entrepreneurs beyond the dreams of those who had lived in earlier periods. Many became rich and influential in the process.

At the beginning of the eighteenth century North Shields was still physically limited to the narrow strip of land that ran alongside the river, close to the entrance to the Tyne. Almost all its inhabitants, permanent and transient, earned their livings directly or indirectly from the river and the sea. By the end of the twentieth century, the river and the sea had become minor factors in the life of North Shields: a decline characteristic of many British ports.

Such a profound shift would have seemed inconceivable to those who, in the eighteenth century, were about to transform the fortunes of North Shields. Nor was such a decline imaginable when the Borough of Tynemouth was established in 1849. Its coat of arms reflected its past, present and future. The past was symbolised by a shield of three crowns, representing the three kings buried at Tynemouth Priory. The present and future were symbolised by a sailing ship above the shield, with a coal miner to the left and a sailor to the right. The motto, *Messis ab Altis* (Our Harvest is from the Deep) was a reference both to the coal below the surface of the land and to the sea, to which the population of North Shields had ready access for food and trade. The symbols and motto were well chosen. The development of North Shields in the eighteenth and nineteenth centuries was based, directly and indirectly, on industries relating to coal mining and to the sea. Salt making, so important to North Shields in the seventeenth century, was not included because it had gone into a marked decline early in the eighteenth century.*

Fortuitously, as North Shields entered the eighteenth century, new sources of employment emerged alongside more traditional occupations. It was transformed from a tiny struggling riverside community into a thriving nineteenth-century town. Industrial development was accompanied by a flourishing commercial sector, a growth in public utilities and opportunities for professional employment. Serving the rapidly growing population was a growing leisure sector and an explosion of church building. The buildings constructed during this period were not the ramshackle affairs that had grown up on the riverside in earlier centuries but imposing structures built not just to serve a function but to impress: a far cry from the quick to erect, unimpressive structures that occupy some of the same plots today.

The scale of economic activity in North Shields in the nineteenth century is readily illustrated by the trade and commercial directories published during this period. Pigot's *National Commercial Directory* for 1828–29 is a good example.

> North Shields, a sea-port and market-town … is most advantageously situated for the purposes of commerce on the northern shore of the Tyne, at its junction with the German Ocean, opposite to South Shields; and, like that town, has risen, in modern times, from the rank of a humble village, consisting of a few fishermen's sheds, or shiels (a provincial name for mean huts) to that of a populous and well-built thriving town. … The staple trade of this place is coal,

---

* In 1707, there were 27 saltpans in operation. By the end of the century most had gone. Writing in 1907, Craster noted that 'only a single salt manufactory existed till recently' (p. 310). Since one of my own relatives was described as a salt worker at the time of the 1881 census, it is probable that he was working at this establishment at the Low Lights. The decline in salt making in North Shields does not indicate a general decline in the demand for salt, only that the use of sea-salt was gradually superseded by rock salt.

but other branches of great consequence and magnitude have, within the last half-century, insinuated and established themselves here; amongst which are roperies, tanneries, potteries, chain cables, and various other productions from iron; and ship building. At one time the principal trade of Shields arose from the salt pans, and to this time the salt works continue of importance.[2]

The Directory listed (in addition to 83 members of the gentry and clergy) over a thousand firms operating in over 100 broad categories of employment plus over 20 more listed as miscellaneous. Given that some of these categories, such as boat and shipbuilding, encompassed many separate trades and skills, the range of occupational categories in which people were employed in North Shields at the time was very extensive. Twenty years later, Gibson wrote:

> The manufactures carried on at North Shields cannot be adequately described in our present limits. But it may be mentioned that there are five iron-foundries, that there are extensive works where chain-cables, anchors, and windlasses are made; shipbuilding yards and dry docks; an extensive tannery yard; sail-cloth, block, and rope-manufactories; two salt-works; manufactories of earthenware; steam-mills for grinding corn; manufactories of hats, tobacco and lesser matters; and there are staithes from which coal and lime are conveniently shipped in large quantities. There are several breweries in North Shields and no end of public houses for the consumption of the beverage which those breweries produce.[3]

Many of the commercial undertakings listed in the Pigot Directory had equivalents in other towns. North Shields pottery is an obvious example. Established at the Low Lights early in the nineteenth century, under a number of owners but principally the Carr family, it continued pottery production until 1893 and then concentrated on glazed bricks until 1913. Usually employing about 140 people, the company's products were sold worldwide and are still collectable. Other obvious examples of products made in other large towns were beers, biscuits and non-alcoholic beverages. But many local industries were unlikely to be found anywhere else but in a coal-mining area or riverside port like North Shields. There is space here to discuss only a few of them: specifically those that relate to the coal trade, shipping, shipbuilding and fishing along with a sample of the commercial activities which grew up to support them.

Examples of Carr's pottery manufactured in North Shields. Carr's pottery was exported around the world. These particular examples have been selected because of their local significance. The plate reads 'Northumberland 74'. The mug in the centre reads 'Success to the Coal Trade'. The Jug to the right reads 'Tynemouth Haven'.

The rise and fall of coal

North Shields and its adjacent townships sit on numerous layers of coal, no fewer than eight of which are thick enough to have been mined economically. As the diagram shows, coal is nearest to the surface towards the sea, in the immediate vicinity of North Shields. But, even when near the surface, mining was never straightforward. Many seams had been disrupted by volcanic activity in the distant past, and the original layers broken up by faults, which resulted in the same seams being found at different levels. Miners dubbed these deviations 'troubles' because a good seam could end suddenly with no easy way to determine where it continued. If it had been thrust to the surface, weathering might have destroyed it altogether. In some instances, molten lava had flowed into the faults and formed igneous dykes. The Tynemouth Dyke, for example, about 12 feet (3.7 m) wide, runs under the Priory and Castle just a short distance from the pier.[4]

The alignment of coal strata in and around North Shields, adapted from a diagram in *Tynemouth, 1849–1949*, p. 124.

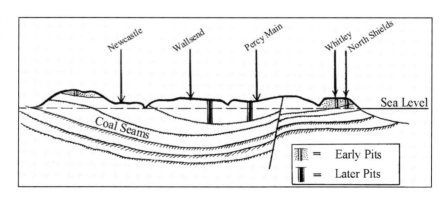

| Shiels to Shields

Tynemouth Priory was deriving an income from coal as early as the thirteenth century. Although details of early mining ventures are sparse, there is evidence that coal was being mined in Preston in 1584 and in Tynemouth in 1590. In that period, mines were typically no more than 30 feet (9 m) deep. However, from the seventeenth century the pace of local mining activity accelerated and mines were sunk farther from the coast where seams were deeper. They were established in Billy Mill, Murton and Shire Moor; Flatworth, Preston, East and Middle Chirton and Monkseaton. The developments in Shire Moor, Billy Moor, Flatworth and Chirton were particularly significant because they provided access to the better quality High Main coal. Technical problems and failures to renew leases meant that some of these early mines had closed by the start of the eighteenth century but others were developed to take their place.

With the relaxation of the Newcastle monopoly of the Tyne, North Shields benefited from its proximity to mines producing both high-quality coal for household consumption and low-quality coal for industrial use. It also benefited from the increased demand for coal which came with the reduction and then abolition of the duties on coal for export. Its position at the entrance to the Tyne made it an obvious port of call when colliers were no longer obliged to meet the loading stipulations imposed in the past by Newcastle. North Shields was, of course, not the only Tyneside port ready to exploit this new freedom. South Shields, immediately across the river, was in a similar position. Nearby, Cullercoats and Seaton Sluice also developed during the same period.

The increase in trade provided an incentive to improve the way coal was taken from the mines to waiting colliers. Hartley (Salt) Pans was renamed Seaton Sluice in the sixteenth century after sluice gates were constructed to flush the harbour at the turn of the tide to make it easier to ship coal and other products. At Cullercoats a pier and quay were built to ship the coal from Whitley and Monkseaton mines. The means for transporting coal to North Shields and other places on the Tyne was also improved. Conveying coal on rudimentary roads was hopelessly inefficient and from the beginning of the seventeenth century wooden waggonways were used around the coalfield. By road, a horse could pull around 18 cwt. (914 kg) of coal but on wooden rails and, after 1768 iron-capped or entirely iron rails, it could cope with 42 cwt. (2,134 kg). By mid-century a series of waggonways was in use, including the Whitley waggonway which took coal to the staithes at the Low Light (as well as magnesian limestone from the Whitley Quarry to the North Shields Lime Works by the Pow Burn) and a waggonway from the mines around Backworth to the Northumberland Dock.* Fixed steam engines later replaced horses and pulled wagons along the rails by rope.

---

* Several of these nineteenth-century waggonways have now been transformed into walking and cycling routes by North Tyneside Council.

Coal Mines in and around North Shields, adapted from a diagram in *Tynemouth, 1849–1949*, p. 123.

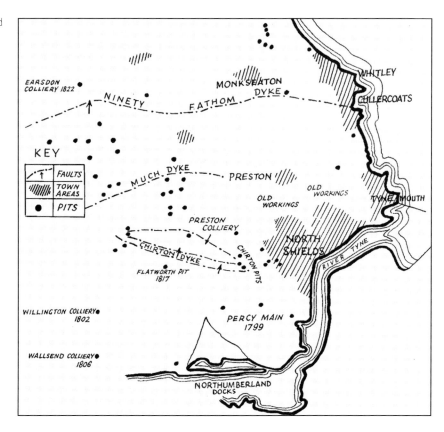

Their presence is still recorded in such place-names as Middle Engine Lane, the location of North Tyneside's Stephenson Railway Museum. But, thanks largely to the work of this local engineer George Stephenson; they were in turn replaced by steam locomotives. An uneducated man, who began his working life operating a brake to prevent horse drawn waggons running away on declines, Stephenson's crucial early developments were made in Killingworth, just a short distance from North Shields. He went on, with his son Robert, to build the world's first public railways.

Mines were often subject to flooding but, with the introduction of the steam pump, deeper and more productive seams could be reached. In 1767 coal was being mined at Shiremoor at a depth of 120 feet (37 m). By 1817 it was mined at 510 feet (157 m) at Howdon and at 803 feet (247 m) at Percy Main.[5] Unfortunately, there was a downside to such advances.

The venture into greater depths in pursuit of greater coal output was pushing contemporary technology to its limits, and the toll of death and injury expanded with the number and depth of pits. Apart from a stream of small-scale accidents involving death or injury to an individual or a small group the larger, deeper collieries with their larger work force, were the scene of a long list of tragic large-scale disasters.[6]

Coal-driven steam engines not only transformed the extraction of coal: they also greatly increased the demand for it. 'Small' coal, which in the past had been used to heat salt pans, mend roads or even dumped because it was unsuitable for household use, could now be used to drive stationary and mobile steam engines.[7] Although 75 per cent of sea-borne coal was still carried by sailing ships as late as the 1860s, coal-owners increasingly gave priority to screw-driven steam colliers at coal drops.[8] They could make 30 to 36 voyages a year, so even a short delay could make a difference to their profitability. In contrast, collier sailing brigs only managed 10 to 12 voyages, and a few days' wait was not considered significant.

The advantages of steam-driven colliers were more than economic. They were safer: a significant consideration in an industry where loss of life was commonplace. Unfortunately, the traditional collier fleet began to cut corners in order to compete.

> In 1862, 100 colliers were posted at Lloyd's as wrecks as the result of a large fleet of sailing colliers taking the risk of putting to sea in doubtful weather, and 1865 also saw heavy losses of lives and ships for similar reasons. The once-proud fleet of sailing colliers was now associated with 'bad gear, rotting timbers and inadequate crews'.[9]

The other downside of the advent of the steam collier was that the work became even more routinised and unrelenting.

> The grind of a continual and unremitting round; loading of the staithes, clearing for sea, the journey to the Thames, discharging and then, with the hull pounding and the screw thrashing, without a pause, the passage back to the Tyne, produced a tread wheel of existence. A screwcollier arriving at Tyne Dock at one or two o'clock on Saturday afternoon was expected to, and did, 'save the weekend' and load and sail the same night. Overtime was unknown and working hours were whatever the master thought necessary.[10]

By this time, the main focus of local mining had shifted to an area to the north-east of North Shields (beyond the Earsdon colliery shown on the diagram opposite).

The first Backworth colliery pit was sunk in 1813 and produced its first High Main coal at a depth of 517 feet (159 m) in 1818. It continued working until 1980. Three additional pits (B, C and D) were sunk which continued working until the 1890s. What became known as the Maude Pit opened in 1872 and produced coal until 1960. The Prosperous Pit opened in 1906 and produced coal until 1960. The Backworth pits were soon followed by mines at Earsdon, Holywell, Burradon, Seghill, Shiremoor and Allotment.[11] The Shire Moor Coal Co. was formed in 1874 and its Blue Bell pit continued in operation until 1915. It was followed by the Algernon Pit near Prospect Hill in Allotment which opened in 1853 and continued working until 1966.*

By the end of the nineteenth century, the Tynemouthshire collieries, as Craster called them, were producing about two million tons of coal a year. That not only meant work for miners and wealth for coal owners but the opportunity to service the activities associated directly and indirectly with mining. The miners needed to be housed, clothed and fed. The mines needed engineers and book-keepers. The ships that took the coal from the Tyne needed provisions and repairs. The sailors who came in the colliers needed to be fed and entertained while their ships were being loaded.

As the twentieth century developed, seam after seam in the area became exhausted. Preston Colliery, the last mine operating in North Shields, closed in 1926 although the desperate shortage of coal after the Second World War led to some open-cast mining for a few years about two miles north of the town, near to the Fox Hunters Inn. The use of the term 'open' needs some clarification given that the coal was at a depth of about 55 feet, deeper than the mines of the sixteenth century. Most of the coal extracted was better suited for industrial than domestic use. The remainder was of such an inferior quality that it could be sold without the rationing controls imposed after the war.[12]

Shipping

The Tyne was not an easy river to enter, navigate or leave and licensed pilots were appointed from the sixteenth century to try to minimise the risks. Before the advent of steam vessels, they would sail their cobles sometimes considerable distances beyond the harbour entrance 'seeking', that is touting for business. Over the years, many of them lost their own lives in the process. The Tyne presented several dangers to seamen and it is a testament to what Tyneside had to offer that it was used so much despite them.

The easiest way to illustrate the problem which an unfavourable wind could present to a ship entering the river is to describe the experience of Robert Lowery in the early nineteenth century.† After a difficult voyage up the east coast, the crew had given up hope of reaching the Tyne for Christmas but were confident they could make it by New Year.

---

* It was on Prospect Hill that my father was born in 1904. His father and two uncles, all three born in Cornwall, had made their way to the area via coalfields in Durham before finally settling in this part of the Borough of Tynemouth.

† Robert Lowery was born in North Shields in 1809 and went to sea in his early teens on a brig in the North America timber trade. In his later life, he became a prominent Chartist and later a temperance advocate.

On the eve of New Year's Day, a little before dark, we saw Tynemouth Castle. … About six p.m. we were abreast of the bar, knowing it would not be high water for us to enter until near eight. The harbour lights were bright and clear, as if beckoning us in, and we had hoisted our signal for a pilot, and expected one quickly, and all was expectation and delight. Suddenly the sky darkened, and a violent blast blew from the westward, and it came so suddenly and with such force, that our chief sails shattered to pieces, and we were blown far off the land, almost over to Norway, and we did not get into Shields harbour until a fortnight after, and by that time … our candles and oil were consumed, and we had to burn strips of pine in the binnacle to enable us to see the compass; or steer by the stars during dark.[13]

Before ships were powered by steam, the wind also determined how easy it was to leave the river. With a prolonged strong easterly wind, vessels could not escape the river at all. For example, in the winter of 1847–48, 1,700 vessels were wind-bound in the Tyne for several weeks. But even escaping the river was no guarantee that a vessel had done so unscathed. Keels could be damaged by the shifting bank of sand, shingle and rock, spread across the river mouth from North Shields to South Shields known as the Shields Bar. Hitting it could create leaks that would sink a vessel several days later.[14]

The *Oregis* on the Black Middens in 1974. This is just one of numerous ships that have been wrecked or damaged in the entrance to the Tyne, often with the loss of many lives. This relatively recent example illustrates that, even after the building of the piers and with all the benefits of modern technology, the mouth of the Tyne can still be dangerous.

The Bar was 800 feet (244 m) long and 600 feet (183 m) wide. At low water mark there might be no more than 4 feet (1.2 m) of water above it. Indeed, during a low spring tide in 1824, three Tyne pilots walked right across the river in no more than 2 feet of water. At high tide on the same day, the Bar was almost 25 feet (7.6 m) beneath the surface.

Once inside the Tyne, seamen had to confront the infamous Black Middens, an area of rocks close to the shore in the area now dominated by Collingwood's Monument. They were a particular danger to ships which had jettisoned their ballast early to reduce the risk of fouling the Bar. That made them less stable, so any deterioration in the weather increased the risk they would be driven onto the Black Middens or other danger spots at the river entrance. Although the risks were reduced with the advent of powered vessels and the building of the piers at the entrance to the river, they did not disappear as the image of the stranded Oregis amply illustrates.

To help sailors navigate, three lighthouses had been in use since the sixteenth century. One stood on Benebalcrag.[15] It was, initially, a coal fire in a brazier on a castle turret. When the stairs to the turret collapsed, it was replaced in 1664 with a new tower on the north-east corner of the promontory. That was rebuilt in 1775 and from 1802 an oil lamp with revolving reflectors was used. The Castle lighthouse was eventually made redundant and demolished in 1898 after new lighthouses were built at Souter Point (near South Shields) in 1871 and St Mary's Island (near Whitley Bay) in 1898. The second and third lighthouses were located in North Shields from as early as 1536. The Low Light stood on the east side of the Pow Burn. The High Light was built at the top of the bank on the other side of the Pow Burn. Because the sand banks in the river moved over time, the towers needed to be realigned at intervals, often quite quickly. In October 1667, for example, sailors were informed that the High Light had been moved northward. In April 1668 they were informed that it had been moved again. The Low and High Lights erected in 1727 were subsequently superseded between 1806 and 1808. All four buildings survive to this day.*

Standing by, helplessly, when ships were wrecked on the river's sand banks and rocks, encouraged local people to take a lead in the development of lifeboats. After the loss of the *Adventure* with all hands during a storm in 1787, a committee was formed which invited the submission of boat designs to help save lives in such circumstances. Only two of those submitted appeared practical. One was designed by William Wouldhave of North Shields: the other by Henry Greathead of South Shields. The *Original*, built at Greathead's South Shields boat yard, incorporated ideas from both

---

* Originally, only a single tallow candle was used. Later, two were lit and then, in 1727, three. Copper reflectors were added in 1736. Oil lamps eventually replaced the candles in 1773.

designs. It was launched in 1790 and subsequently used to save hundreds of lives.* These early lifeboats were essentially beamy rowing boats, steered with a single oar, with a substantial belt of cork to give added flotation. Their range was limited by the strength and stamina of the crew in often extreme conditions. Despite this limitation, each coastal community along the north-east coast followed the example set by North and South Shields.

North Shields men left their mark on shipping in other ways. James Whitehead, the North Shields master-owner of the brig *John and Mary*, was determined there should be an agreed way to anticipate the course of screw-colliers at night and fought to have his idea of red and green lights adopted to make navigation safer. His attempts to solicit support proved unsuccessful until taken up by W.S. Lindsay, the MP for Tynemouth (1854–59). With a merchant navy background before setting up his own shipping company, he saw the merits of Whitehead's proposal and brought it before Parliament. Whitehead's perseverance was eventually rewarded when his idea was incorporated into the Rules for the Prevention of Collision at Sea.[16]

Despite the hazards associated with entering, navigating and leaving the Tyne, shipping flourished in the eighteenth and nineteenth centuries. Today, when it is possible to stand on the Bank Top and see only an occasional ship entering or leaving the river, it is difficult to appreciate the scale of activity that existed in earlier centuries. When looking at old paintings it is tempting to think that the artists may have exercised a deal of licence when portraying the traffic on the river. The truth is that the river *was* crowded with ships. For example, in 1836 alone, 11,226 colliers *left* the Tyne.[17] To get some idea of the volume of traffic on the river one must take into account the fact that these same ships had earlier *entered* the river. In addition to the colliers, merchant ships carried other cargoes into and out of the river. As well as coastal shipping in British waters, trade was carried on with the East Indies, North America and the Baltic ports. Early in the nineteenth century, according to Craster, 200 vessels sailed annually from North Shields to America.[18] Add to these merchant ships, the vessels of the Royal Navy; the fishing boats; the local river traffic of keel boats, tugs, ferries and dredgers; the ships coming into the river for repair and those leaving it after having being built or repaired, and one then begins to realise that those artists of yesteryear may have actually exercised licence in the opposite direction.

This is how Thomas Dibdin described the activity on the river during a brief visit in the 1830s.

---

* The design also drew on Lionel Lukin's ideas for watertight compartments and cork gunwhales. Lukin and Greathead profited from their ideas. Wouldhave, whose ideas were also integral to the design of the *Original* did not. He died penniless and unrecognised in 1821.

The High and Low Lights. The yellow lines show the alignment between the related High and Low Lights. The 1727 buildings are to the right. The 1808 buildings are to the left. Note how the wall of the earlier Low Light which faces the sea was painted black to avoid confusion with the later building.

One day was given to sight-seeing; and what sights should those be but North and South Shields. … How am I even to attempt the description of these parallel towns, intersected by a river, upon the breast of which, all day long, colliers, and steamers, and wherries, and cock-boats, are in a constant state of movement and excitement! Never had such a scene before presented itself to my view. … We now crossed the river, a good width, and all in a ferment with navigation of every possible description, and in every possible direction. Echoing shouts of men, splashing of oars, roaring surf round the steamers' prows, swelling sails, and fluttering flags, caught the ear and eye wherever they wandered.[19]

North Shields in the nineteenth century was at last able to derive direct advantage from its position at the mouth of the Tyne. In 1833, the Lords of the Treasury empowered custom house officers at North Shields to clear vessels loading below Hebburn Point without any reference to Newcastle. In 1848 further progress was made when North and South Shields were together constituted as an independent port known as Shields, with the customs house located at North Shields. The 1851 Ranger Report noted that the harbour of Shields was able to accommodate about 1,000 vessels; that 75 per cent of the over 20,000 vessels that arrived in the Tyne each year remained within the boundary of the Borough of Tynemouth; that of the 3 million tons of coal shipped from the Tyne each year over 66 per cent was shipped from North and South Shields and that 'the maritime population of the Tyne was estimated at about 14,000 persons, nine-tenths of whom resided in and around the Boroughs of Tynemouth and South Shields'.[20]

Subsequently, in 1865, North and South Shields became ports in their own right with their own marine board.[21] As part of the same body of reforms, in a major effort to improve the Tyne for shipping after centuries of neglect, the 1850 River Tyne Improvement Act took the conservancy of the river away from Newcastle Corporation and placed it in the hands of independent commissioners: precisely what Ralph Gardner had sought to achieve at the time of the Civil War.* Within a few years, conditions at the entrance to the river had been transformed. Major dredging operations started in 1861. They not only deepened the naturally shallow river to allow larger ocean-going ships to use the Tyne but also removed the treacherous Shields Bar across the entrance to the river. Similar dredging work removed the sands at Dotwick and Whitehill Point. Between 1861 and 1914 about 133 million tons of material dredged from the river was dumped at sea.[22] Northumberland Dock near Flatworth was opened in 1857. At the time, this 50-acre site was the first enclosed dock to be opened on the Tyne and was used to export coal from local collieries as well as for other imports and exports.† That was followed by a proposal to construct another dock a little further up-river in Coble Dene. That proposal revived the centuries-old opposition of Newcastle to developments at the entrance to the river. When the proposal was debated by Newcastle Council one speaker felt obliged to remind his fellow councillors that when Newcastle had been responsible for the river it had done nothing to improve it despite the huge revenues it had received.[23] The Coble Dene project went ahead and the Albert Edward Dock was opened officially in 1884.‡

The Tyne Commissioners also decided to build two huge piers and lighthouses at the entrance to the river. Work began on the north pier at Tynemouth in 1854. It was scheduled to take seven years but took over half a century. The project was plagued by disasters and the architects greatly underestimated the power of the sea at the entrance to the river, a power against which seamen in small wooden vessels had risked their lives for centuries. In 1867, with 1,920 feet (590 m) of the projected 2,959 feet (910 m) pier completed, gales and heavy seas destroyed almost 480 feet (148 m) of the stone structure. By 1893 the pier was almost complete when movement was detected during severe winter storms. The damaged section was repaired but further movement was detected in 1895. Victory

---

* The Port of Tyne Authority replaced the Tyne Improvement Commission in 1968.
† In 1953 it was closed and filled in.
‡ It is now an attractive marina surrounded by housing.

Albert Edward Dock, photographed by Gladstone Adams of the Royal Flying
Corps in 1917.

against the elements finally appeared to be in sight in 1897 when the pier
and lighthouse had been completed. Then freak gales and unusually heavy
seas lasting for two days again breached the pier. Initially, 110 feet (34 m)
of the stonework collapsed but eventually the damage extended to nearly
300 feet (92 m), leaving the lighthouse marooned. It then became a case of
'back to the drawing boards'. In 1898 a decision was made to rebuild the
pier to a different design. The plan for a curved pier was abandoned and
replaced with a design in which the pier followed a straight line. Rebuilding
began using old sections of the pier as shelter. This time, the work went
more or less according to plan. The lighthouse was commissioned in 1908,
and the pier completed in 1910 – 56 years after work had first begun! But,
even after the building of the piers, it is still possible for ships to founder
in bad weather. For example, in 1963, the 3,725-ton freighter *Adelfotis II*
went aground on the Herd Sands in a winter storm. In 1974, after a major

The completed Tynemouth pier and lighthouse to the right and South Shields pier to the left. This aerial image shows the difference in the shape of the two piers following the many problems encountered during the attempt to construct the north pier to match that to the south.

refit, the 9,000-ton *Oregis* ran aground during an easterly gale on the Black Middens where it remained for four weeks despite several attempts to re-float it.

The relaxation of Newcastle's grip on the river encouraged more local people to move into the expanding world of shipping. For convenience, I shall concentrate on two examples. Both illustrate that it was possible for people of modest origins to build significant shipping empires but also that even successful entrepreneurs could not escape the upheavals that ruined the lives of so many people during the First World War.

The Knott Prince Line

James Knott, the son of a Howdon grocer, was born in 1855.[24] The family moved to North Shields where his father, after a spell as a customs officer, took over the Old Inn in Nile Street in 1864 and later turned it into a wine and spirit merchants. James was educated at the school attached to the Scotch Church in Howard Street and then went to work at a firm of merchants and shipbrokers in Newcastle. By the time he married in 1878, James had become a ship broker (an agent for ship owners) and ship-owner in his own right – albeit on a small scale. His early ventures were not encouraging. His first ship was a 45-year-old collier brig, *The Pearl*. His next ship, the 32-year-old brig *Rival*, was bought in November 1879 but wrecked in December. His third ship was 35 years old and lasted no more than six months. But Knott did not give in easily and by 1881 had done well enough to order a new cargo steamship from Swan and Hunter's at Wallsend. The *Saxon Prince* was the first of the subsequently world-famous Prince Line. In 1866 Knott sold his sailing ships and by the end of the decade owned 29 steamships trading all over the world. Three years later his fleet was 47 strong. Despite his burgeoning business, Knott did not devote himself exclusively to his shipping empire and at the age of 30 was admitted to Gray's Inn and called to the Bar in 1889. It seems that Knott expected a similar degree of hard work and commitment from his ships' officers. He insisted that: 'All accidents are the result of carelessness.' If a Prince Line ship was involved in a collision or stranded, all its officers were compelled to resign.

James Knott played a role in the development of the Parsons' steam turbine which revolutionised the way ships were powered. Having experimented with a steam turbine in his yacht *Turbinia*, Charles Parsons, who was a neighbour of Knott, wanted to develop it further and bought the *Eastern Prince* from Knott in 1887. That association may have been a factor in the ship-owner Knott being made president of the Institute of Marine Engineers in 1908.

By the early part of the twentieth century, Knott's business was enormously successful. With success came a change of address. The family moved from North Shields although they retained their link with the area by acquiring what is still known as Monks Haven in Cullercoats. Knott's second son James and youngest son Henry became partners in the company in due course and the future of Knott's family and international company seemed guaranteed. At the age of 55, in 1906, Knott stood for the short-lived constituency of Tyneside. He was unsuccessful but in January 1910 was elected as a Conservative MP for Sunderland. His political career was brief. Ill health prevented him from contesting the subsequent election in December 1910. That disappointment was soon followed by tragedy, with the outbreak of war in 1914.

James had three sons. Henry Basil, the youngest, was the first to die. Within ten months after the declaration of war he had volunteered for the Northumberland Fusiliers, been promoted to the rank of captain and died of the wounds he received at the Battle of Ypres. Knott's son Thomas James was reported missing presumed dead during the Dardanelles

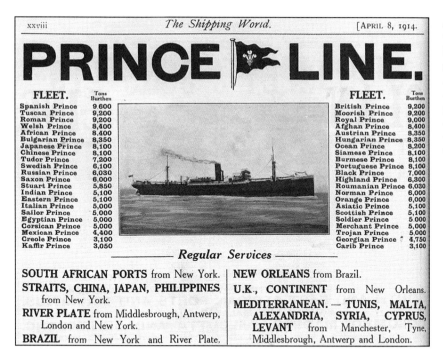
Advertisement for the Prince Line, which appeared in *Shipping World* in 1914. Twenty-one Prince Line ships were lost during the First World War.

campaign in November 1915.* James Leadbitter, like my grandfather Thomas Smith, was in the West Yorkshire regiment. Both took part in the 1916 Battle of the Somme. As a corporal, my grandfather probably had little understanding of the strategic thinking behind the offensive. As second in command of his battalion, the 34-year-old Major James Knott DSO, who was killed advancing on German lines after a huge but largely ineffective artillery bombardment, probably knew that the enemy positions had been reinforced. His last letter home leaves no doubt that he was aware that his death could be imminent. Unlike my grandfather, who recovered from his shrapnel wounds, Major Knott was killed. His letter, marked 'Only to be sent in the event of my death' read:

> I hope and desire above all things that you will not unduly grieve. …
> My medals are yours, but I would like them destroyed when you both
> join me – My clothes, furniture and motor-car must be immediately
> disposed of, everything which reminds you of my death must be
> removed – this is my urgent desire and wish.†

---

* After three years of commemorating his death, the family learned he had survived and been imprisoned in Germany.

† James left over £104,000 in his will: the equivalent of £48 million today relative to the total output of the economy at both dates.

When the death of James was announced in July 1916, it was widely reported that all three of Knott's sons had been killed. His ordeal was not yet over. Although he may have been cheered by being made a baronet in 1917, he lost his brother Stanley who, after serving three years in France, died unexpectedly at a camp in the UK early in 1918. Knott was so devastated by this succession of tragedies that he sold his company with its fleet of modern steamships for £3 million (equivalent to about £800 million in 2014) and devoted much of the rest of his life to philanthropic work. He established and endowed the Knott Memorial Fund, initially to help the widows of men who had been killed in battle. But such was his business acumen that when he died in 1934, his estate was valued at £34 million (the equivalent of about £5 billion in 2014). Fortuitously, or by virtue of careful planning, he was living in the Channel Islands and his estate was not subject to death duties.[*]

Robinson Stag Line

James Robinson, the founder of the Stag Line, was born in Whitby in 1768.[25] He moved to North Shields when still a first mate in 1796. He subsequently became a ship's captain but not a ship owner until 1817 when, aged 49, he took advantage of the drop in the value of vessels at the end of the Napoleonic Wars and bought the 12-year-old 221-ton brig *Blessing*. It did not make James his fortune. On the contrary, the continuing depression in trade obliged him to raise a loan against the ship which was still outstanding when he died in 1833. The vessel was inherited by his widow Grace and commanded by her two sons, Captains John and Joseph Robinson. In 1843, Joseph assumed responsibility for the loan and following the death of his mother became the sole owner.

When the *Blessing* was lost in 1846, Joseph used the insurance money to order a new vessel from a South Shields shipbuilder. He named it *Stag*. It was an opportune time to do so because the demand for shipping was then increasingly rapidly. Robinson bought several other ships over the next few years and by 1850 Joseph Robinson & Company owned a fleet of eight barques and one brig.[†] The company bought its first steam vessel in 1871, following the opening of the Suez Canal in 1869, and by the end of the decade had switched entirely from sail to steam. By then, the company owned 11 vessels, totalling 16,113 tons. At the time of his death in 1889, Robinson had built up a fleet of 16 steam vessels. In 1895 all the ships were

---

[*] Knott's name and tangible examples of his good works survive in North Shields and the Sir James Knott Trust is still active. The Prince Line in various guises continued until it celebrated its centenary in 1984 but by then had been reduced to just two container ships. The line now exists in name only.

[†] At the time, the ownership of ships was usually divided into 64 shares. While Joseph owned a large part of the shares in each ship, others were owned by relatives, local traders and professional men.

transferred to a limited liability company, the Stag Line, with 72 per cent of the shares held by the Robinson family. The remainder were owned by friends and local traders. As the century closed, the company replaced its vessels with larger, more modern ships and, although at the outbreak of the First World War the company owned fewer ships than when Captain Joseph died in 1889, the total tonnage of the 12 vessels (as against the 16 owned in the earlier period) was 65,460 tons (as against 28,302 tons).

The company paid a heavy price during the Great War. It lost seven ships, including the two most recent additions to the fleet built in 1917 and 1918. At the end of the war, government restrictions and a recession necessitated a reconstitution of the company. Stag Line Ltd was registered in 1918 with just two ships. By 1928 business had recovered sufficiently for the fleet to have grown to six ships of 35,173 tons in total (about half the tonnage owned at the outbreak of war) but then the depression of the 1930s brought the company to its knees. Vessels were laid up for lengthy periods and no company dividends were paid for eight years. At the outbreak of the Second World War the company owned seven ships. Of these, four were destroyed by enemy action within 12 months. At the end of the war, a new intake of family members took the company forward and by 1958 the Stag Line had a fleet of six modern, dry cargo bulk carriers. Indicative of the company's enterprise, it was two Stag Line ships that were the first to be chartered to load in the Great Lakes after the opening of the St Lawrence Seaway in 1959.

The Stag Line Building. Completed in 1807 as a subscription library for the Tynemouth Literary and Philosophical Society, it was used between 1895 and 1980 as the headquarters of the Robinson Stag Line. It is now used by the Superintendent Registrar for civil wedding ceremonies.

AUTHOR PHOTOGRAPH

The company continued to prosper during the 1960s and fared reasonably in the 1970s but ceased trading in the early 1980s when hit by a deepening world recession. By the end of 1982, 7 per cent of the world's dry cargo fleet had been laid up and ship owners faced what was arguably a worse situation than during the 1930s. The Stag Line building at 1 Howard Street, which the company had occupied for 90 years, was sold. This imposing building, which had originally been the home of the Literary and Philosophical Society, is now occupied by the Superintendent Registrar of North Tyneside. With its fine views over the river it makes an impressive setting for civil marriages.

Shipbuilding

North Shields was never as important a shipbuilding town as its neighbour Wallsend but it did build ships on a significant scale.

For example, during the war against the American colonies as many as 30 ships a year, including frigates and gun-brigs, were built by the several yards in the town. A similar impetus was given to shipbuilding by the boom in the fishing industry in the second half of the nineteenth century. 'It was not unknown for a steam trawler to be built from keel to maiden voyage in less than 40 days.'[26] The type of boat built most often by smaller shipbuilders was the 20–35 foot Northumbrian coble. The larger yards built mainly wooden sailing collier brigs but later steam driven vessels.

North Shields' shipbuilders are known to have built at least 1,221 vessels between 1772 and 1910. Table 5.1 (*opposite*) is based on research by David Waller, which is on-going, and in time both the number of shipbuilders and figures in the right hand column will almost certainly be greater.

President Barack Obama at the Resolute Desk. This famous desk built from the wood of the North Shields-built *HMS Resolute* also featured prominently in the film *The Da Vinci Code*.

Table 5.1 Known North Shields shipbuilders

Shipbuilder	Dates	Known ships	Shipbuilder	Dates	Known ships
Thomas Anderson	1829–51	8	Edward Moseley	1795	1
R. Banks	1846	1	Mr. Oliver	1859	1
Andrew Bell	1836–46	11	J. Pletts	1814–19	2
J. Bell	1852	2	J. P. Rennoldson	1866–70	14
Daniel Bider	1854	1	Edward Robson	1833–34	2
John Brodie	1868–78	5	T. Shelton	1828	1
Brodie & Maxwell	1866–74	19	Smith's Dock	1899–1910	280
James Dunn Burdis	1860–70	20	G. K. Smith	1882	3
Stephenson Chisholm	1856–59	2	Thomas & William Smith	1839–90	135
Coble Dene	1857–66	4	Softley Bros.	1876	4
J. Cooper	1845–65	4	J Softley & Sons	1877	3
W. Cooper	1843–54	22	David J. Stewart	1867–72	13
W. Cooper & J. Gardner	1840–43	8	Richard & Robb Stobbs	1852–81	36
J. Couley	1876	1	William Stokelle	1847–53	2
John Ralph Curry	1848–49	5	Joseph & John Straker & Isaac Pearson	1839	1
James Davy Jnr	1854	1			
Edward Dawn & Robert Davison	1828	1	R. Swan	1856	1
			Thorburn & Grant	1848–54	15
Charles William Dodgin*	1869–76	37	Thorburn & Alman	1856	1
James Dowey	1828–58	38	W. Thoburn	1856–64	5
Edwards Bros.	1893–99	133	J. Turnbull	1862	1
Thomas Ellis	1840–42	4	Unknown builders	1823–56	199
Gardiner	1859	1	Garthum Wall	1859	1
J. Grant	1851	1	Thomas Murray Wall	1825–26	3
Hall & Bell & Co.	1850	1	James Walmsley	1795	1
Thomas Hearn	1787–94	3	Thomas Walmsley	1798–1801	3
D. & G. Heckels	1869–74	7	A. Woodhouse	1858	2
Hepple & Co.	1881–1903	72	Richard Wouldhave & William Johnson	1875–85	26
Hepple & Landells	1851–61	28			
Hughes & Driver	1881	1	William Wright	1828–30	2
Francis & Thomas Hurry	1805–06	2	Richard Wouldhave	1873–79	3
Francis Hurry & Co.	1802–03	2	Emmanuel Young	1868	1
Laing Bros.	1855–59	2	Thomas Young & Son	1819–54	6
Richard Landells	1862	4	William Young	1841	1
Mark Melvill	1840	1	*Total known vessels built*	1772–1910	1,221

Source: D. Waller, 6 April 2014, *personal communication*.
See also *Tyne Built Ships: A History of Tyne Shipbuilders*, http://www.tynebuiltships.
co.uk/NorthShields.html
* North Shields Fish Quay was built in part on the site of Dodgin's shipyard.

In time, the North Shields yards amalgamated and larger companies such as the Tyne Dock and Engineering Company and the Smiths Dock Company emerged. The roots of the latter go back to 1756 when, to provide a living for his son William, Thomas Smith of Heaton Hall bought Rowe's shipyard near Newcastle. In 1849, the company moved to a more convenient location in North Shields. One of the earliest ships built there, in 1850, was the barque *Ptarmigan*.* It had an interesting career. It was bought by the Royal Navy and renamed HMS *Resolute*; fitted out for Arctic service and despatched to Canada to look for Sir John Franklin's ill-fated expedition which had been searching for the North-West Passage. When it became ice-bound the ship was abandoned. It was later found adrift, 1,200 miles away, by an American whaler. As a goodwill gesture, HMS *Resolute* was re-fitted, sailed back to Britain in 1856 and presented to Queen Victoria. In due course, when the ship was retired, the queen ordered two richly carved desks to be made from the ship's timbers. One was presented to the President of the United States in 1880 and the Resolute Desk has been used in the Oval Office of the White House in recent years by presidents John F. Kennedy, Jimmy Carter, Ronald Reagan, Bill Clinton, George Bush and Barack Obama. The other desk is kept in Windsor Castle. Smith's shipyard went on to make iron ships for both the coal trade and fishing. For a short time, Smith's even took up fishing. Following the take-over of the established businesses of H.S. Edwards & Sons and Edwards Brothers in 1899, Smith's became the owner of four steel-hulled herring drifters. At the time it was widely believed that the salt used in preserving herring would corrode the steel hulls. Eustace Smith, who then controlled the company, knew better. Smith's had experience of steel vessels that carried salt as their main cargo, so he had the vessels registered in his own name.[27] Smith's Docks eventually moved out of shipbuilding and after 1909 concentrated exclusively of ship-repairing.†

When boats were still built of wood, and the expanding coal mines needed props to shore up excavated tunnels, a ready supply of timber was needed and huge wood yards were established in North Shields, stimulating trade with Baltic ports.

Other associated industries developed alongside the shipyards. These included iron foundries and manufacturers of anchors, chains and cables. Pow and Fawcus became one of Britain's biggest manufacturers of anchors, chains and other marine ironwork, but left North Shields in 1875.[28] Making

---

* Barques were three- or four-mast ships with a distinctive sail rig. They were smaller and easier to handle than fully rigged ships and have been described as the work-horses of the golden age of sail.

† There was a widespread belief in my day that Smith's Dock in North Shields was the biggest ship repair yard in the world. That claim is still being repeated in recently published local histories. Smith's Dock only ever claimed to be the biggest specifically ship-repairing *company* in the world. Smith's had other docks on Teesside.

ropes and block and tackles, to enable weights to be lifted more easily using pulleys, were also big business in North Shields. By 1825, there were five rope factories in the town.[29] Four ran north to south and one east to west. Pearson's (later Linskill's) Ropery, on the west side of Church Street, extended from Albion Road to Tyne Street. Together with Stephenson's (later Mitcalf's) Ropery, located between Stephenson Street and Norfolk Street, which also ran north to south, the long sheds of these two factories influenced the development of the town. Because they ran down to the river bank, they separated Charlotte Street from Saville Street, the main roads

Smith's Dock, once the home to the biggest ship repair company in the world. Smith's merged with Swan Hunter and Wigham Richardson in 1966 and closed in 1987 although its docks continued to be used by other companies. The site has now been cleared in anticipation of another residential development on the banks of the Tyne.
BY COURTESY OF TYNE AND WEAR ARCHIVES & MUSEUMS

which paralleled the river. These two thoroughfares remained unconnected until 1884. Farther to the west of the town, Popplewell's Ropery (also known as Chirton Ropery), ran from Albion Road down to Hylton Street. Although affected by the construction of a deep cutting for the main railway line to Newcastle in 1854, it continued in operation until about 1885. Also running north to south but above Albion Road was Knott's Ropery which from 1826 to 1856 ran from the east side of Spring Terrace from Albion Road to a point near to Etal Villa (owned by the Pow family). Unlike the other rope factories, Matthew Waters' ran along the Bank Top, parallel to the river, from Coach Lane to Little Bedford Street in the period before the 'Cut' (Borough Road) was constructed in 1854.

Fishing

By the nineteenth century, North Shields was able to take advantage of major development in the fishing industry. A market was built in 1820 and the Union Quay in 1823. Much of the subsequent growth in the industry followed the creation of the Borough of Tynemouth. The construction of North Shields Fish Quay as it exists today began in 1870. Between then and the close of the century it was developed in stages as fishing grew in scale and importance to the local economy.

Until the 1860s, the North Shields fishing fleet consisted mainly of sailing smacks and luggers. Steam vessels driven by paddles were in use but mainly as tugs to pull vessels in and out of port when the wind was against them. However, in 1877, a local man, William Purdy, stumbled on a way of fishing that transformed the industry. A fishing smack (the *Zenith*) became becalmed off the Tyne. The tug *Messenger*, captained by Purdy, towed it back into harbour. The smack's trawl net, used to catch bottom-feeding fish such as cod, haddock and sole, had been left down during the return to port. When the catch was unloaded, it was larger than usual. That gave Purdy the idea of towing a trawl net behind his own steam tug. He bought some second-hand nets and left the fish quay on 2 November 1877 to the jeers of onlookers. After a couple of such trips, from which he returned with more than respectable catches, other tug owners followed his example and within a year there were 50 steam trawlers in service.[30] In time, purpose-designed steam trawlers were built and paddles gave way to screw propellers. A little later, steam was used to power drifters which used 16 yard deep (15 m) vertical nets to catch fish, such as herring and mackerel, which swim closer to the surface. According to Craster, between 40 and 70, 50–55 yard-long nets (46–51 m) were kept in place by floats attached to a rope that ran along the top of them.[31] Joining the local fishing boats during this period were vessels not only from the rest of the east coast of England but also Scotland and even as far away as Cornwall.

The impact of this changed pattern of fishing was staggering. Before it,

North Shields
Fish Quay, c.1930.
This busy scene
is not very
different from
the way in which
I remember the
Fish Quay when I
was a boy in the
1940s.
BY COURTESY OF
DISCOVER NORTH
TYNESIDE

about 370 tons of fish were landed at North Shields annually. By 1880 the figure had risen to 2,430 tons and, by 1885, 4,328 tons. The introduction of the otter trawl, patented in 1895 by another local man, Robert Scott, sent the catch soaring still further. It grew from 8,832 tons in 1895 to 10,430 tons in 1900 and 12,485 tons in 1905.[32] By then, there were 143 first-class fishing vessels registered in North Shields, in addition to many other second- and third-class vessels, and sheds enclosing 11,000 square yards had been erected at the Fish Quay. *

The fact that more capital was needed to buy steam vessels and finance the long-distance trips that became increasingly necessary as local fish stocks were depleted by the new techniques, resulted in fishing becoming increasingly the preserve of big businesses rather than one man businesses. Some of the entrepreneurs who shared in this boom came from beyond North Shields. Others were born in the town. The most successful was Richard Irvin. He was born in North Shields in 1858. At 16 he owned a marine store. At 19 he was the part owner of a trawler. Since it was called the *Zenith*, it is reasonable to assume that is was the same *Zenith* that

---

* First-class vessels were over 15 tons; second-class less than 15 tons and third-class with a keel less than 15 feet in length.

Purdy's steam tug towed into the harbour in 1877. Irvin soon owned a steam trawler himself, the *Enterprise*. From then, he never looked back.

By the close of the nineteenth century, fish were being caught in quantities far in excess of local requirements and were being sold much farther afield. Even as early as the 1850s, Mayhew recorded that the smell of fish pervaded the rooms of London's poorest families. The salted herrings they ate would probably have come from fishing ports such as North Shields.[33] To preserve the fish, it was salted or smoked. Gutted and cured herrings were also exported in barrels. Then, after the Northern Counties Ice Making and Cold Storage Company facility had been built on the Fish Quay in 1898, Irvin, Purdy and other local business men, established their own Shields Ice and Cold Storage Company in 1901, to enable fish to be kept fresh for sale in more distant markets.[*] Yet, even with ice available, fish catches still exceeded demand and substantial quantities were sold to a local factory to make fertilizer.[†] Irvin then decided to add what became known locally as the tin factory to his growing methods for getting fish to other markets. His tinned fish were sold under the trademark Tyne Brand. He first tried haddock, which did not prove popular. When he tried the same technique with herrings, it was a runaway success. Tyne Brand went on to become a nationally known brand which sold a wide range of other tinned products.

By 1913, Irvin's company owned 50 steam trawlers, had a controlling interest in a further 70 vessels, and owned the Shields Engineering and Dry Dock. He was also head of an extensive international business empire. As well as branch offices in many other British ports he had fishing-related businesses in South Africa (in Cape Town, Durban, Johannesburg, Port Elizabeth, Bloemfontein and the Marion and Prince Edward Islands) and Portuguese West Africa. In addition, he was chairman of the Southern Whaling and Sealing Company with stations in South Georgia, the Falklands and Port Alexander (in Alaska).[34] Despite all these international interests, Irvin remained firmly rooted in his home town of North Shields.[‡]

Wartime advertisement for Tyne Brand Products, from the *Sunday Post* newspaper, 28 September 1941.

BY COURTESY OF THE BRITISH NEWSPAPER LIBRARY

---

   *   W.H. Storey, a local owner of a fishing fleet, held shares in both.

   †   It was still in operation during my childhood and given an ill-wind the smell from the factory was awful.

   ‡   Irvin's former offices on the Fish Quay were converted into apartments and a restaurant in 2009. At the time of writing in 2014, the nearby derelict remains of the Tyne Brand factory remain a local eyesore.

It is noteworthy that complaints of over-fishing were already being voiced in the closing decades of the nineteenth century. Following the introduction of steam trawlers, a scarcity of fish in shallow waters was reported by fishermen in villages like Cullercoats all the way up the Northumbrian coast. The complaints were taken sufficiently seriously for the Northumberland Sea Fisheries Committee to be formed under the provisions of the 1888 Sea Fisheries Regulation Act.[35] Subsequent falls in fish stocks indicate that this legislation was ineffective. The combined effect of dwindling catches, coupled with the protectionist measures of Iceland and the fishing policies of the European Union, have had a devastating effect on North Shields. According to a recent analysis by Brookfield *et al.*, the local fleet now catches only 10 per cent of the total catch landed and the fish market is only viable in winter because of the visiting Scottish fishing fleet. In 2000, only 2,361 tonnes of fish were landed at North Shields Fish Quay, less than 20 per cent of the catch a century earlier. However, the Quay remains economically significant for the landing of shellfish, which exceeded 1,100 tons in 2000, and because of the growing number of visitors it attracts both because of its iconic status and the wide range of restaurants that are housed in buildings that just a few decades ago were used to prepare and sell fresh fish.

The expansion of commercial services and utilities

The boom in economic activity created a need for a variety of commercial services and utilities. Initially, North Shields' banks were branches of Newcastle and Northumberland companies but, in 1818, Robert Spence (a Quaker draper) and William Chapman (a rope-maker), in conjunction with Edward Chapman who had family links with Whitby bankers, set up the North and South Shields Bank. Spence (who owned 25 per cent of the shares) had day-to-day responsibility for it. The bank issued its own notes, was well funded, and within four years had branches in South Shields, Newcastle and Morpeth.* After the death of Chapman in 1836, it became part of the Newcastle, Shields and Sunderland Joint Stock Company.[36] Unfortunately that failed in 1847. It was not the first such banking failure in the area and led Gibson to jest that a new local charity was needed: an *Asylum for Betrayed Shareholders in Joint Stock Banks* – to furnish a warning against 'placing confidence in hollow systems and unworthy persons'.[37] Twenty-first century readers might consider such a charity is still needed. Four banks were listed as having offices in North Shields in an 1854 Trades Directory: The National Provincial Bank, The Northumberland and Durham District

---

* Cash was conveyed more securely than on the stage coaches featured in so many Hollywood western films. It was packed in a strong oak box reinforced with iron and placed in the boot of the coach after it had been padlocked to the heavy iron chain which was securely attached to the coach boot.

North and South Shields bank note. This bank note sold at auction for £365 in 2004. Appropriately, it was bought by the owner of a business on North Shields Fish Quay.

Bank, The Union Bank and the Savings Bank (which had been established in 1836 as a provident institution to afford 'a safe and profitable investment for the savings of the industrious classes'.

Mutual marine insurance clubs emerged in the late eighteenth century, consisting of groups of ship owners, usually from the same port, who insured one another's vessels by paying an annual premium calculated on their potential losses. The first such club was the Union Ship Insurance Company established in North Shields in 1778.[38] By 1848 there were 29 such clubs in North and South Shields.[39] Other insurance associations and benefit societies soon followed.[40] By 1897, Ward's Trades Directory listed 37 of them.

Prompted by their own need for a supply of water, six brewers were incorporated by a 1786 Act of Parliament as the North Shields Waterworks. It is ironic that it was the brewers of the town who provided teetotal residents with their water.[41] The first coal gas works were established in the town near to the Low Light in 1820 by the North Shields Gas Company.[42] The Tynemouth Corporation Electricity Works followed, 80 years later, when it opened on the site of the former Richardson's tannery in 1901.

By the close of the nineteenth century, North Shields was close to the peak of its economic success and the huge increase in the range of its economic activities and associated developments had brought about enormous changes in the built environment. Land previously devoted to agricultural or horticultural purposes was now occupied by a wide range of businesses and a great variety of public, private and commercial buildings. It is to this transformation of the North Shields' built environment that we now turn.

5

Transformation of the built environment

T HE POPULATION of England and Wales increased greatly during the nineteenth century. In 1801 the census enumerated 8.9 million people. By 1901 it had reached 32.5 million: an increase of 366 per cent.[1] The proportion of the population living in urban areas had also increased markedly, although the often repeated assertion that by 1851 a majority of the English population lived in towns is an over-interpretation of the statistic that 50.1 per cent were living in places with over 2,000 inhabitants. It is more realistic to suggest that it was 1881 before *urban society* became the normal milieu for more than half the population.[2]

During the nineteenth century there was also a substantial increase in the population of what local residents today think of as North Shields. However, care is needed in interpreting the census statistics. The primary unit for census data was the Tynemouth Registration District, used for the recording of births, marriages and deaths. The Registration District is shown on the map below by the area enclosed by both the yellow and pink shading. It extended far beyond the boundaries of the parish, township and village of Tynemouth. Tynemouth Parish is indicated by the yellow shading. The constituent townships of Tynemouth Parish are identified on the map below by the red boundaries and red upper case names within the area of yellow shading. Tynemouth village was much smaller and included only the small settlement at the north entrance to the river. The fact that these and other administrative units with different boundaries were all labelled *Tynemouth* is a reminder of how the adoption of 'real' place names for bureaucratically contrived administrative units can be confusing. As the nineteenth century progressed, *Tynemouth* was adopted as the name for yet more administrative units. Tynemouth Parliamentary Borough, created in 1832, included only the five townships of North Shields, Tynemouth, Chirton, Preston and Cullercoats (and not the other three townships within the parish of Tynemouth). In contrast, the Tynemouth Poor Law Union created in 1836, included, initially, all eight townships in the parish of Tynemouth; the chapelry of Earsdon and eight others. Subsequently, five other neighbouring townships were added. Later, when Tynemouth was constituted as a borough in 1849, its boundaries coincided with that of

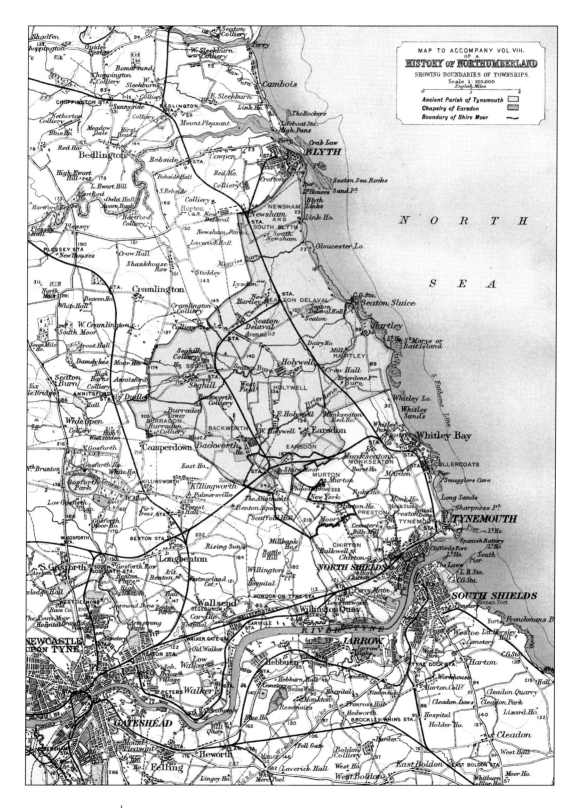

opposite Map 6.1 Tynemouth parish and the chapelry of Earsdon. The yellow area shows the boundaries of the ancient parish of Tynemouth. The pink area shows the boundaries of the chapelry of Earsdon. The original township names are in red capital letters.

SOURCE: CRASTER, 1907 P.XV. COURTESY OF H.E. CRASTER'S FAMILY

the Parliamentary constituency, that is incorporating just five of the eight townships of Tynemouth Parish.

When early census statistics were published, registration districts were divided into sub-districts, parishes and townships.[3] In terms of area, North Shields was the smallest of the eight townships that comprised the parish of Tynemouth. It was limited to a narrow strip of land along the northern bank of the Tyne. The only place for it to expand was on the Bank Top, on land officially within the township of Tynemouth. Subsequent developments spread into the neighbouring townships of Preston and Chirton. So the residential and commercial developments from 1763 on, although in reality extensions of North Shields, were in terms of local boundaries in the three predominantly rural townships adjacent to North Shields.

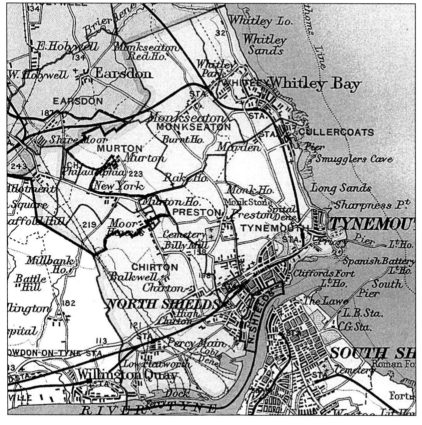

Map 6:2 Tynemouth parish and its constituent townships. Note how the original North Shields (the area in red labelled N. SHIELDS) was limited to the very small area alongside the river.

SOURCE: CRASTER, 1907 P.XV. BY COURTESY OF H.E. CRASTER'S FAMILY

The history and topography of Tynemouth Parish and its constituent townships means that it is not possible to give precise figures for the population growth of what we now think of as the town of North Shields. We know that the combined population of North Shields and its three adjacent townships increased from 12,719 in 1801 to 49,623 in 1901: an increase of 390 per cent, a little greater than the national figure. We also know that the bulk of the population growth was on land immediately adjacent to North Shields, which belonged to other townships. What we lack are precise figures on how the population of this extended North Shields increased as it spread outwards into the townships of Tynemouth, Chirton and Preston. The raw figures in Table 6.1 might suggest, to those unfamiliar with the area, that it was the township of Tynemouth that grew most: from 3,856 in 1801 to 24,881 in 1901: an increase of 645 per cent. In contrast, over the same period, the recorded population of the township of North Shields fell from 7,280 to 5,737: a decrease of 21 per cent. However, as Map 6.2 shows, the major part of the urban development within the township of Tynemouth

Table 6.1 Population figures, 1801–1901

Date	Shields	Tynemouth	Chirton	Preston	Total
1801	7,280	3,856	1,152	431	12,719
1811	7,690	5,834	3,116	445	17,085
1821	8,205	9,454	4,351	627	22,637
1831	6,744	10,182	4,973	765	22,664
1841	7,509	11,854	4,360	919	24,642
1851	8,882	14,493	3,960	983	28,318
1861	9,595	16,560	5,544	1,456	33,155
1871	8,619	19,326	8,005	1,593	37,543
1881	7,250	22,548	11,448	1,707	42,953
1891	6,046	23,678	13,066	2,178	44,968
1901	5,737	24,881	15,668	3,337	49,623

Source: N. Price, 'Housing Access and the Marginal Poor: Housing in North Shields, 1850–1940' (unpublished MA thesis, Newcastle Polytechnic, 1988), p. 6.

Note: It is not possible to determine how these statistics were affected by North Shields being a port. In 1841 seamen on shore on census night were counted in the same way as the rest of the population, but no provision was made for recording local seamen at sea. In 1851 seamen on board ships in port or docked on rivers were recorded separately. In 1861 seamen on board all ships in port or docked in rivers were recorded along with, for the first time, those 'on the high seas', but there is no record of the home port to which they belonged. For the 1881 census there is a separate index of all named merchant seamen, along with an index of vessels. Those sailing on Royal Navy ships were also enumerated but that information is provided in a different set of records. So, even if all this material were readily available it would still be beyond the scope of this project to determine the ways in which being a port affected the population counts of North Shields over time.

was immediately adjacent to and in reality an expansion of North Shields. The decline in the population of the township of North Shields reflects a fall in the population density of the riverside area, as alternative dwellings became available on the Bank Top. In the same way, the increase in the population of the neighbouring township of Chirton (from 1,152 in 1801 to 15,668 in 1901) is testament to the outward expansion of North Shields to the west and north-west. The same applies to the recorded growth in the population of the township of Preston. It grew from 431 in 1801 to 3,337 in 1901 but, again, most of that growth can be accounted for by the expansion of North Shields into land formally designated part of Preston.

Map 6.3 provides a graphical representation of the physical growth of North Shields in five phases up to 1949 when the Borough celebrated its centenary. In the first it was restricted to the narrow strip of land alongside the river. In the second, between 1773 and 1849, it expanded into a relatively

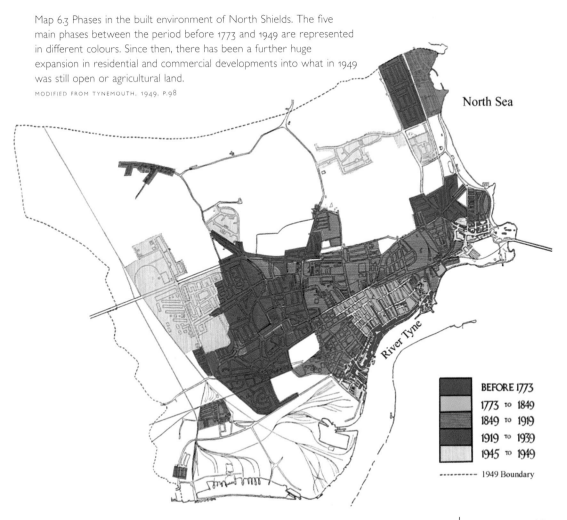

Map 6.3 Phases in the built environment of North Shields. The five main phases between the period before 1773 and 1949 are represented in different colours. Since then, there has been a further huge expansion in residential and commercial developments into what in 1949 was still open or agricultural land.

MODIFIED FROM TYNEMOUTH, 1949, P.98

North Sea

River Tyne

BEFORE 1773
1773 TO 1849
1849 TO 1919
1919 TO 1939
1945 TO 1949
-------- 1949 Boundary

Transformation of the built environment | 83

small area immediately north of and above the small riverside town. In the third, between 1849 and 1919, growth was mainly to the north and west of the second phase developments. In the subsequent fourth and fifth phases the town expanded primarily (but not only) to the west.

The long narrow street

Early schematic maps of North Shields, for example those of Gardner (1655) and Fryer (1727) show North (and South) Shields with a double row of buildings straddling a road running along part of the riverside. In the nineteenth century that route was extended. In 1803, the Duke of Northumberland constructed the 'New Quay', at the foot of what is now Borough Road (also known as Borough Bank) to provide not only a deep-water mooring but a large area suitable for markets and the impressive stone-built Northumberland Arms. Then, in 1823 a new quay was built to the east, connecting the original area of building with the bridge over the Pow Burn. The Low Street, as it was commonly called (despite different sections bearing different names), then ran from the Pow Burn in the east, to the New Quay and past it to the Bull Ring in the west. For most of its length, its crowded dwellings were packed into short courts, on quays resting on piles driven into the riverbed or on the steep (about 45°) bank rising from the river. There was virtually no public space for recreation, a point deplored by the 1851 Ranger Report on the sanitary condition of the town. The inhabitants did not even have a direct public route to the sea; something the Report remarked was scarcely credible for a population which lived so close to it.[4]

The permanent residents of North Shields did not find it easy to move beyond the confines of their small town when England was still without a decent road system. Even trips across the river to South Shields, or up the river to Newcastle, could be difficult or even impossible when the weather was bad. However, despite these difficulties, they were not cut off from the rest of Britain or the wider world. Living in a port at the mouth of the River Tyne, they witnessed a continual flow of visitors from further afield.

Shut out from all but the most limited communication with other parts of England by the almost impassable roads, intense local jealousies and uncertain vagrancy laws of the time, the population, wholly seafaring, or drawing its means of subsistence from the sea, knew less of England and its people than of countries across the main … But if access to inner England was barred for the Shieldsman, he had his compensation in the extraordinary and ever-changing variety of sea-borne folk bearing up for the shelter, or trade, or protection … of his almost natural harbour.[5]

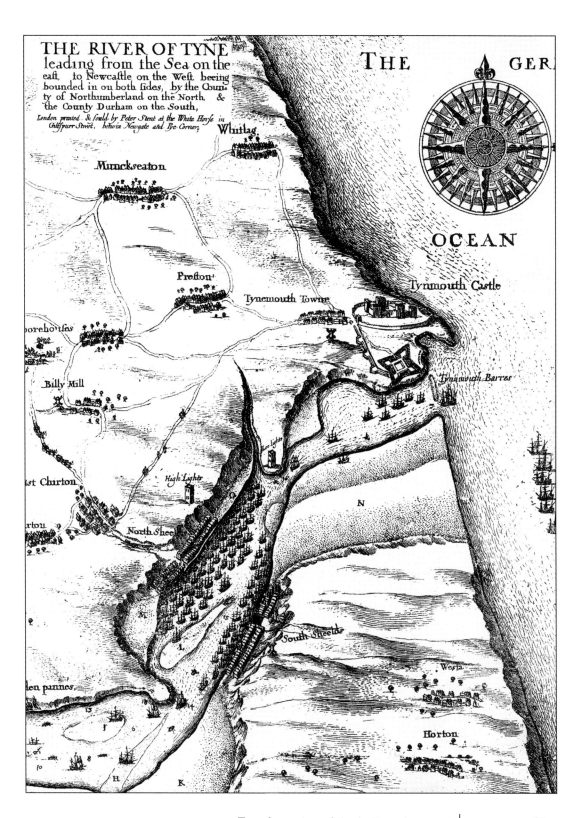

THE RIVER OF TYNE leading from the Sea on the east, to Newcastle on the West. beeing bounded in on both sides, by the County of Northumberland on the North, & the County Durham on the South,

London printed & sould by Peter Stent at the White Horse in Giltspurr Street, betwixt Newgate and Pye Corner;

THE GER...

OCEAN

Whitlag

Murckseaton

Preston

Tynemouth Towne

Tynmouth Castle

...orehouses

Billy Mill

...st Chirton

...rtou

High Lights

North Sheel...

Tynmouth Barres

N

M

L

South Sheelds

West...

...en pannes

Horton

H

K

The Bank Top

In 1539 the possessions of Tynemouth Priory were surrendered to the Crown. In 1637, after a series of transfers, its land became the property of the tenth Earl of Northumberland. Traditionally, the plateau immediately next to North Shields, 70 feet (25 m) above the river, was common land, virtually free of dwellings.[6] However, in 1649 the earl's tenants agreed to it being enclosed (that is, formally divided into distinct areas). What was in effect a form of privatisation, led to the creation of nine freeholds and thirteen leaseholds.* Two of Tynemouth's three fields continued to be farmed but the third, the 188-acre south field of Tynemouth, was sold and subsequently developed as the first phase of the North Shields that is recognisable to this day.

The twenty acres of Tynemouth's south field allocated to John Carruth were sold in 1667 to Edward Toll. When Toll's grand-daughter Elizabeth married Josias Dockwray, the land eventually passed to their son Thomas Dockwray, the vicar of Stamfordham (a parish about 20 miles west of North Shields).† Dockwray, who has been described as the founder of the modern

---

*   Those interested in the details of the original strip-holdings, enclosure allocations and subsequent land transfers should consult Craster, *Northumberland County History*, pp. 247–80.

†   Some local writers describe him as the vicar of Tynemouth. He was not, although there have been two vicars of Christ Church called Thomas Dockwray. The first served between 1668 and 1673. He was succeeded by his son Stephen. On his death in 1681 he was succeeded by his brother Thomas. He died in 1724. During the period when Thomas Dockwray began developing his land in North Shields, the vicar of Christ Church was Emmanuel Potter (from 1749 to 1789).

Map 6.5 Fryer's 1773 Map of North Shields. Based on information derived from Fryer's 1773 map and the inset in Rook's 1827 Post Office map of North Shields. Note the building on Dockwray's land and the roperies on the land owned by Stephenson, Pearson and Waters.

AUTHOR MAP

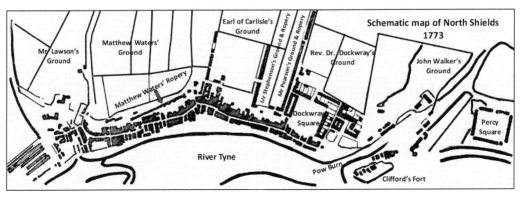

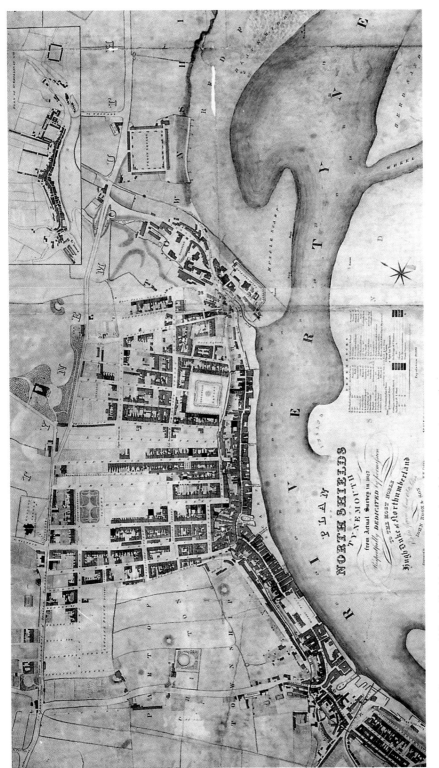

Map 6.6 Rook's 1827 map of North Shields. Note the scale of development over the
54 year period since 1773, as shown on Map 6.5.

town of North Shields, began building on his land in 1763. Dockwray Square came first.

> This was a great event in the history of North Shields, being the commencement of the high town. The plan of a square was drawn and each intending resident then bought a piece of the ground, and built upon it his own house, or two houses, of whatever size and height seemed best to him. The result was a square with one side open to the river, the three remaining sides consisting of houses considered to be very elegant.[7]

Toll Square followed and, after his death, Dockwray's representatives built on the whole of his Toll inheritance.

Dockwray's example was followed by the other freeholders. The result was that the south field of Tynemouth became effectively part of North Shields. The new developments were a mix of dwelling houses, public buildings and places of employment. The scale of development over the next 50 years is readily evident in Rook's 1827 map of North Shields. By 1856, as the Ordnance Survey Map shows, the development had continued at a rapid pace.

The 29 acres of land to the east of Dockwray's, originally allocated to the Quaker Robert Dove, eventually passed to another Quaker, John Walker. Then a resident of Dockwray Square (but originally from Whitby and friend of Captain Cook) it was the Walkers who developed Walker Place to the east of Dockwray Square, along with its surrounding streets. Land owned by the Walkers was also put to important industrial use. Late in the eighteenth century, a glass works, an iron foundry and a tannery were established on the southern section by the Low Light. The part of Walker's land which he leased to his fellow Quaker John Richardson was originally inhospitable marshland. Once drained, it became the site of a successful tannery and substantial house with attractive gardens.[8] The tannery continued in business until 1889 and the steep descent from Tynemouth Road to the riverside is still called Tanner's Bank. The site was later used for a steam saw mill until 1897 when it was purchased by the Borough council for an electricity generating plant.*

Across the Tynemouth to North Shields road, the land was owned by the Duke of Northumberland. In 1878, at the instigation of the then mayor, he offered Tynemouth Corporation ten acres of it, in Spital Dene, for a public park.† Surprisingly, some of the corporation's members actively opposed

---

* For a more detailed account of the developments in and around the Pow Burn see Coates, *The Pow Burn*.

† The name Spital Dene is thought to be a derivative of (Ho)spital Dene. During the excavations for the park, the foundations of St Leonard's Hospital and burial ground were uncovered. Dating back to the late thirteenth century, the hospital was probably

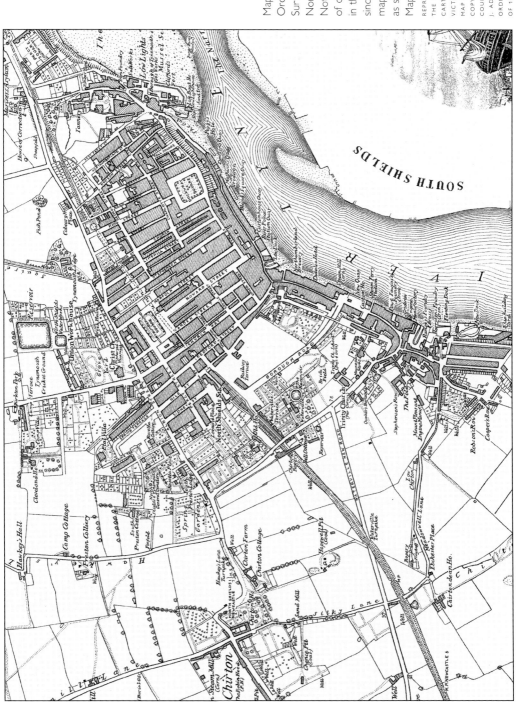

Map 6.7 1856 Ordnance Survey map of North Shields. Note the scale of development in the 29 years since Rook's map of 1827, as shown on Map 6.6.

the idea and the offer was declined. Subsequently, during a depression in shipbuilding in the 1880s, Ald. J.F. Spence persuaded the Duke to renew his offer so that it could provide work for the unemployed. Northumberland Park was officially opened by the Duke in the summer of 1885.[9]

Adjacent to Dove's freehold, were 33 acres which eventually passed to Anthony Pearson, a North Shields rope maker. He subsequently transferred them in 1768 to his son-in-law, William Linskill. Part of the eight acres of land originally held by William Collinson also passed in time to Linskill.* The boundaries of his estate are still evident in the triangular residential area between Tynemouth Road, Washington Terrace and Linskill Terrace. The remainder of the Collinson inheritance eventually finished up in the hand of the Stephenson family.

The 50 acres allocated to Lord Howard in 1649 remained in his family until 1796 when they passed to John Wright, a Newcastle attorney. His land extended from the Bank Top to the road between Tynemouth and North Shields. Its eastern boundary was the present-day Norfolk Street and its western boundary Bedford Street. It is Wright who is credited with transforming most of this land into the thriving commercial and retail district at the heart of Georgian North Shields. He named Norfolk, Howard and Camden streets which ran down to the Bank Top; and Bedford Street which ran right down to the riverside.

Wright had wanted to extend Saville Street (named after his home in Newcastle) to the east to make it a southern thoroughfare for the town but was unable to do so because of the rope works which ran down to the edge of the Bank Top. Instead he built himself a mansion on Norfolk Street facing west along Saville Street. After his death, in 1806 it became the Albion Hotel. The Albion Assembly Rooms were opened immediately adjacent to it on Lower Norfolk in 1853. Its fine architecture was not untypical of much that was being built in North Shields at the time. It was constructed of polished ashlar masonry. Above three shops with ornate decorations at ground level was an 85 foot × 36 foot (26 m × 11 m) hall, almost 30 feet (9 m) high with a cantilevered, decorated cornice. It was finished in a bold ornamental style with wood panelled walls behind which there was a regulated current of air to provide ventilation. The circular windows had pilasters with carved caps running between them, each with a truss running up to meet the moulded beams which divided the ceiling

---

administered by Tynemouth Priory (in conjunction with the Benedictine Nunnery of St Bartholomew in Newcastle). As well as an isolation hospital (perhaps for lepers) it was a place where food and medicines were dispensed to the poor. The last recorded burial was in the early eighteenth century. The remains of the hospital are now a Grade II English Heritage listed building and a programme of archaeological excavation was begun at the site in 2011.

   * William Linskill, a descendant of the original William Linskill, became the first mayor of the newly constituted Borough of Tynemouth in 1849.

OLD NORTH SHIELDS. 88.

into compartments. In each of them was a ventilator decorated with an ornamental centre flower. When there was insufficient daylight, the hall was lit with four specially designed circular chandeliers, each with 60 gas jets. Above the spacious staircase was a gallery capable of accommodating over a hundred people.

Only in 1884, after the council acquired the land, was the hotel demolished to allow Saville Street and Charlotte Street to become a single thoroughfare.* By this time, North Shields was not only a successful port with numerous manufacturing businesses but also a flourishing retail centre. In Britain as a whole, it was during the second half of the nineteenth century that retailing underwent a transformation. But that process, in which small local shops were joined by specialist retailers and department stores, was already well underway in North Shields.[10] Hill Carters, for example, had its origins in 1825; the Howard Stores 1856 and Walkers (The House of Quality) 1880.

Wright's two sons built Howard Street, much of it unchanged to this day.† They also laid out the still fine Northumberland Square.‡ The north

Wright's Mansion and the Town Hall. The mansion was still blocking access between Charlotte Street and Saville Street in the early 1880s when this image was taken.

---

* The Albion Assembly Rooms remained in use.

† At the bottom of Howard Street, by the Bank Top, there had been active coal mining until earlier in the century.

‡ The town's replacement public library was built in the south-west of Northumberland Square in 1975 in an architectural style not in keeping with the rest of the square.

Advertisements for three of North Shields' department stores. From left to right: Hill Carters on Union Street, Howard Stores at the junction of Howard Street and Saville Street and Walkers on Borough Road. There were other department stores in the town, including Bell Bros on Bedford Street.

side was constructed on the site of a substantial mansion built by George Wakefield, another Quaker businessman, during the boom in trade which accompanied the Napoleonic Wars. He built it despite the advice and misgivings of his fellow Quakers and responded to their criticism by leaving the Society of Friends. Within six months he was dead and his family was forced to sell the contents of the house. His widow could not find a buyer for the property and eventually his creditors pulled it down and used the stone to face the houses still standing on the north side of the Square.[11]

In the late eighteenth century, another housing development took place at the west end of the town. Land that had been owned by the Milbournes of Chirton House was developed in the 1780s, following close on the developments in the east end of the town. The largest houses were built on the edge of the bank top above the Limekiln Shore and enjoyed commanding views. However, these were eventually ruined by the huge Ballast Hill which grew from the predominantly flint and chalk offloaded from ships. The houses were also close to the site of the 'one o'clock gun' which, from 1863 to 1905, was fired each day at precisely 1 p.m. to allow ship's captains to set their chronometers.*

---

* As the character of the area changed, better-off families began to move away. By the time my maternal grandparents lived there in the early decades of the twentieth century it was an area largely for the poor.

Some of the remaining fine buildings on Howard Street. North Shields has lost numerous fine buildings since the 1950s. Many had to be demolished after they were neglected or subjected to arson attacks.

AUTHOR PHOTOGRAPH

From these initial housing developments, North Shields expanded at a staggering rate. Numerous flights of steep steps built into the bank side now connected the Low Street to the Bank Top.[12] Several of them are still in use.* Just a glance at the 1856 Ordnance Survey map is sufficient to give an indication of the scale of the development in the less than 100 years after Dockwray's property development in 1763. Most of the land south of the Tynemouth to North Shields Road had been built on, as far as Bedford Street to the west. To the north-west of the railway station, which had been built near Bedford Street in 1839, there was a residential development as far as Cecil Street. To the south-west of the station there was still no significant development. That was initiated at a later stage by George Rippon (one of the brewers who founded the North Shields Water Company in 1786) and Alexander Scott. Both lived for a time in Waterville (sometimes called Water Villa); a John Dobson designed residence built for the Waters rope-making family. It originally stood in its own extensive gardens but became 42 Stanley Street West, off Coach Lane, after Rippon

---

*   The stairs probably inspired the 1932 Oscar-winning comedy film *The Music Box* in which Laurel and Hardy struggle to deliver a piano to a house at the top of a long flight of similar steps. Stan Laurel lived in North Shields as a boy between 1895 and 1905 (see Lawrence, *The Making of Stan Laurel*).

and Scott bought the land between Borough Road and Coach Lane in 1856 and developed the area.*

The opening of the Northumberland and Albert Edward docks encouraged the town's westward growth, and a further stretch was added to the road paralleling the river. Saville Street connected with Prudhoe Street, at its junction with Borough Road. That then connected with Howdon Road at its junction with Coach Lane. The route eventually continued alongside the riverside past Percy Main, Howdon, Willington Quay and Wallsend to Newcastle. A railway line followed a similar route. Both provided access to the shipyards and engineering companies that lined the riverside route from North Shields to Newcastle.

There were no further major residential developments in North Shields until after the First World War. The widespread concern that the 1917 Russian Revolution might encourage Bolshevism in Britain was used by Lloyd George as a rationale to persuade his Cabinet colleagues to pledge that they would make the country 'a land fit for heroes to live in'. As a consequence, the inter-war period ushered in an unprecedented involvement of central and local government in the provision of housing. The further development to the north-west and west of the town centre are described in Chapter 11 (II).

During the Second World War, North Shields was subjected to intensive bombing raids. The warning sirens of impending raids were heard over 250 times and, although the bombers often flew past because they were targeting other locations, a surviving Luftwaffe map shows that many of the selected targets were in North Shields itself. Official records estimate that at least 310 high explosive bombs were dropped on the town, along with 18,000 incendiary bombs and 19 parachute mines. They resulted in 447 properties being demolished or damaged beyond repair. A further 9,928 were damaged but judged reparable. Despite the provision of air raid shelters, 225 people died, 150 suffered serious injuries and a further 325 were slightly injured.[13]

The 1947 Town and Country Planning Act was passed following the war to encourage local authorities to plan for the future rather than leave developments to the vagaries of the market. The planners in the Borough of Tynemouth came up with a bold redevelopment scheme in time for the Borough's 1949 centenary. They recognised that traditional industries could no longer provide sufficient work for the population and had acquired West Chirton Farm as a site for the West Chirton Trading Estate. Residential estates had already been built at West Chirton, Lynn Road and Cullercoats and the 333-acre site of Marden Estate, designed to house 9,000 people, was under construction. But the proposed new civic buildings did not materialise. The same was true of the 'much more handsome version of Saville Street cutting through the centre of the town'; the envisaged new entertainments centre, general post office, hotel and airport.[14] Instead, the

----

* Waterville was destroyed by enemy action on 30 September 1941.

Shiels to Shields

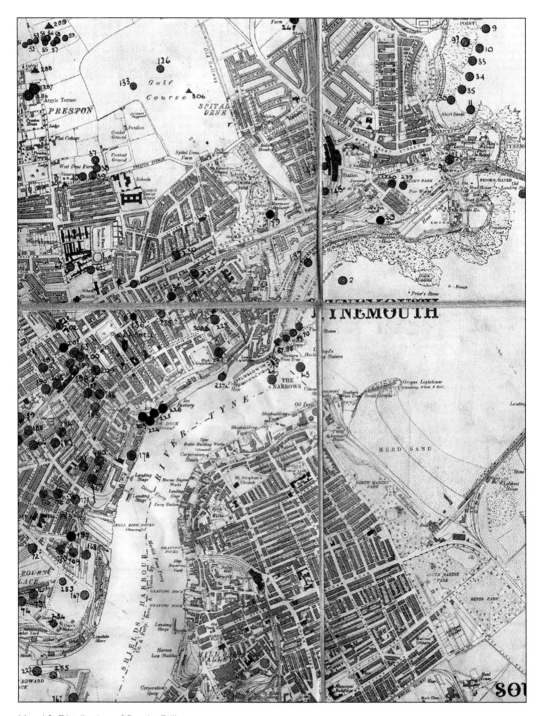

Map 6.8 Distribution of Bombs Falling on
North Shields, 1940–43
BY COURTESY OF THE TYNE AND WEAR ARCHIVES

Transformation of the built environment | 95

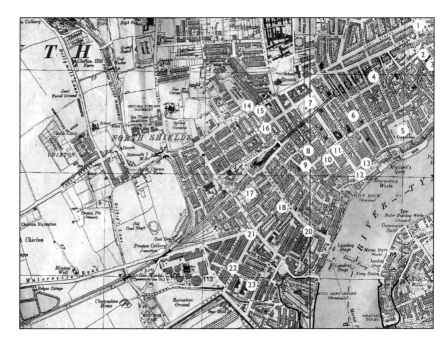

Map 6.9 Public bomb shelters in North Shields.

1. Washington Terrace [trenches]; 2. 11 East Percy Street [basement]; 3. 12 East Percy Street [basement]; 4. Wilkinson's Lemonade Factory [basement]; 5. Dockwray Square [trenches]; 6. Police Dwellings, Stephenson Street; 7. Northumberland Square [trenches]; 8. Church Way [surface shelters]; 9. Fifty Shilling Tailors, Saville Street [basement]; 10. Public Conveniences, Church Way; 11. Public Library, Howard Street [basement]; 12. Library Steps, Howard Street; 13. 77 Tyne Street [basement]; 14. Rosella Field, Albion Road [trenches]; 15. 2 Bedford Terrace [basement]; 16. McCombies, West Percy Street [basement]; 17. Alexander Scott Park [trenches]; 18. 50 Prudhoe Street [basement]; 19. Preston Park (beyond map) [trenches]; 20. Bonded Stores, bottom of Borough Bank [basement]; 21. 2 Howdon Road [basement]; 22. 27 Penman Street [basement]; 23. Junction Penman Street and Lawson Street [basement].

BY COURTESY OF PETER BOLGER AND WWW.NORTHSHIELDS173.ORG. THE MAP IS BASED ON FIGURES RELEASED BY INSPECTOR WHITE, DEPUTY ARP CONTROLLER IN OCTOBER 1944.

town of North Shields slowly went into a decline as a retail and commercial centre as a result of competition from Newcastle, 'out-of-town' retail parks, and major developments such as the Cobalt Business Park which is home not only to many businesses but also North Tyneside Council. Private house-building also continued on a major scale in the second half of the twentieth century and into the twenty-first but at the expense of large tracts of farmland and open public green space. Sites once occupied by schools, playing fields, retail premises, a swimming pool, hospital and theatre have been 'in-filled' with housing. People have also taken up residence by the riverside to live in houses and apartment blocks built on the sites which once gave the local economy its distinctive character.

6

Beyond Shields

A T THE START of the eighteenth century, large stretches of land still separated North Shields from its neighbouring townships. The routes between them were difficult in bad weather and, by today's standards, primitive. This had implications not only for the movement of people but also the delivery of letters and parcels. When the *Newcastle Courant* announced the appointment of a new deputy postmaster in North Shields in 1760, it added that letters would be forwarded from an office in the Fish Market at 6 p.m. but only on three days a week.[1] Each letter was logged and the charge determined by the distance it had to travel and the number of sheets of paper it contained. Sometimes letters were paid for by the recipient rather than the sender. As a result, coded information was sometimes written on the cover of a letter, allowing the recipient to decipher it but then decline to pay for its delivery!

Access by river

Ferries carrying passengers between North and South Shields were running as early as 1377 and from at least 1588 a 'horse boat' was carrying livestock and other goods across the river. For centuries, the dean and chapter of Durham Cathedral enjoyed exclusive customary rights over these ferries, although they were leased to others to operate. In the eighteenth century, the lease was awarded to Newcastle Corporation, giving it an effective monopoly of a river crossing several miles away. The monopoly was eventually successfully challenged by Robert Wallis, a South Shields shipbuilder, who ran partially covered sculler-boats (rowing boats known locally as 'comfortables') between North and South Shields.[2]

The sometimes perilous crossing of the river in such small craft prompted proposals for radical alternatives. In 1797, Ralph Dodd proposed a 400 yard (366 m) tunnel from Clifford's Fort in North Shields, with a diameter of 4.7 yards (4.3 m) to make it wide enough for loaded wagons. He maintained that a tunnel made more sense than a bridge because it would not be subject to extreme weather conditions. No action was taken – which may have been fortunate. The construction of a tunnel Dodd had designed under the Thames, between Gravesend and Tilbury, was started in 1798 but abandoned in 1802 because of engineering problems. It took over 150 years for Dodd's dream of a Tyne Tunnel to be even partially realised when a pedestrian tunnel was completed in 1951. A road tunnel was not available until 1967. Despites Dodd's reservations, others did propose a bridge between North and South Shields. In 1801, an improvised bridge was made using keel boats. In a second successful experiment, a boat capable of carrying 300 soldiers and equipment was pulled across the river from Clifford's Fort using a system of ropes. In 1824 Samuel Brown proposed a suspension bridge based on his patented wrought-iron chain links, which he had already used successfully in eight bridges, including the Union Chain Bridge across the River Tweed, the largest iron suspension bridge in the world when it opened in 1820. A prospectus for what would have been a toll bridge was issued at a public meeting in North Shields in 1825. The renowned road and bridge-builder Thomas Telford declared it to be a practical proposition; tenders were sought and half the required shares sold. Then progress faltered, primarily to do with the state of the money markets at the time; the project was postponed and eventually abandoned.

Fortunately, given the failure of the proposals for a tunnel and bridge, passage across and up the river was made safer and more efficient with the advent of steam vessels, although not everyone welcomed this development.

> At the Low Light House and New Quay, small boats can be obtained for an easy row seaward, or among the mass of shipping on either side of the river. It will be an act of charity to engage one of these small boats for an hour or two, for the scullermen who ply them are worthy old fellows whose occupation has been nearly destroyed by the steamers.[3]

A steam boat service ran between North Shields, South Shields and Newcastle as early as 1814, but the first boats were uncomfortable and, although the fare was lower than for the 15 horse-drawn gigs, five horse-drawn omnibuses and three coaches which travelled between Newcastle and North Shields daily, they usually made the same journey in half the time. As steam vessels improved in comfort and speed they became more popular and by the 1830s a service ran several times a day between Newcastle and the two river-mouth towns; more than 30 were available for hire between Newcastle and the mouth of the river. Following the success of the original company, the Port of Tyne Steam Navigation Service was introduced, leading to a marked improvement in both the frequency of the service and conditions on the steamers (for example, stoves were provided in cold weather).

The North and South Shields Ferry Company started a steam service across the river in 1830. Its vessels ran from the New Quay to Dean Street near the South Shields Market Place. The 1d. price charged for foot passengers at the time may seem cheap. However, converted into a comparable figure for 2014, it works out at about £3.50 for a journey of

300 yards (275 m). Horses and carriages, cattle and goods were charged by weight. The charges reflected not just the running costs of the ferry but the obligation to pay about seven per cent of the annual profits to the dean and chapter of Durham Cathedral in lieu of their ancient rights to provide ferries across the river.

In 1848, a rival Tyne Direct Ferry Company provided a slightly shorter and quicker crossing. For decades thereafter its ferries were nicknamed The Ha'penny Dodgers because of their lower fare and tendency to weave in and out of the heavy river traffic. The companies later merged. In 1856 another company introduced a ferry service between Whitehill Point in North Shields and the Penny Pie Stairs in South Shields but, under the provisions of the Tyne Improvement Act of 1861, which empowered the commissioners to purchase rights in any ferry company on the river, both companies were then taken over by the Tyne Commissioners. They established the North and South Shields Ferry Company in 1863 and went on to purchase new vessels and to improve the ferry landings. In 1865 they were also given the power to purchase the ancients rights of the dean and chapter of Durham to the ferries and bring an end to this centuries-old anachronism.

Other companies provided services which criss-crossed the river. For example, in 1859, The Red Star Line operated six steam vessels which called at several points on both sides of the river en route between Newcastle and Prior's Haven in Tynemouth. It was subsequently absorbed into the Tyne General Ferry Company which secured the right to carry passengers,

Tyne General Ferry Company paddle steamer alongside Tynemouth Priory. This postcard was issued by the company to help publicise its regular half-hourly journeys between Newcastle Quayside and the river mouth at Tynemouth.
CONTEMPORARY POSTCARD

"Doon the river to Tinmuth," on a Tyne Ferry Steamer.

HALF HOUR SAILINGS FROM QUAYSIDE.
FARES { 6D. SINGLE. 9D. RETURN.

Printed and Published by ANDREW REID & CO. Ltd. 50 Grey Street Newcastle-on-Tyne

animals and goods within the area of jurisdiction of the Tyne Improvement
Commission. By the 1860s it was operating 17 boats (nicknamed the ladies
of the river because they all carried female names) which called at 26
landing places at half-hourly intervals. They became increasingly popular
because their fares were lower and could sometimes out-perform the Tyne
Commissioners' vessels. In 1872 they carried about 4 million passengers,
rising to a peak of almost 7 million by the turn of the century, despite the
introduction of 'workmen's trains' with cheap fares on the riverside line
from 1880.

Growing competition from road, rail and trams brought about the
company's downfall. It ceased trading in 1909 after the Tyne Improvement
Commission declined to intervene to save what many at the time still saw
as a vital service for workers and employers. However, a direct ferry from
North Shields to South Shields continues to this day.

Access by road

The roads leading from the North Shields Low Street at the start of the
eighteenth century were steep and had poor surfaces. The road to the ferry
landing was described as 'so bad a horse going to the boat is in danger of
having its legs broke'. The road down Coach Lane to the Bull Ring was
described in 1747 as being 'so deep and ruinous that travellers cannot pass
without danger'.[4] Roads in general in England at this time were of poor
quality: a particular problem for businessmen who needed to convey goods
beyond the area in which they had been mined or manufactured. Two main

responses emerged. The first was a system of canals. They became a key means of transporting goods elsewhere in Britain but were not developed in the north-east of England. An elaborate canal network was proposed in 1795, which would have started from North Shields, but no canals were ever constructed.[5] The second response was to encourage private companies to improve the road system. In return for the construction and maintenance of a given stretch of road they were allowed to erect turnpike gates at intervals to exact tolls from the travellers who used them: the same principle embodied in the M6 toll road which opened in 2003. The scheme gave an impetus to both the quantity and quality of England's roads. Since the days of the Roman occupation, the engineering skills needed to build good roads had been neglected but the work of engineers such as Metcalfe, Telford and Macadam transformed road building in the eighteenth century. By 1830, there were about 22,000 miles of turnpike roads in England. About half were well constructed. The 100,000 or so remaining miles of roads that remained under the control of parish authorities continued to give cause for concern.

The first Turnpike Act to involve North Shields was passed in 1749. The Tynemouth to Newcastle road was improved and toll gates erected near to what are now the Master Mariners Homes on Tynemouth Road and at South Preston, Chirton and Percy Main. By the time of Pigot's 1829 Directory, there were several passenger coaches a day to Newcastle. Another coach left Cullercoats each morning for Tynemouth to allow people to catch the coach to Newcastle. In addition, on Tuesday afternoons, a coach took passengers to Morpeth. Pigot lists ten destinations for carriers. Most ran once or twice a week but those serving Newcastle and Seaton Sluice carried goods most days. By 1832, a horse omnibus left North Shields for Newcastle every hour. A century later, after the advent of the internal combustion engine, and UK car production approaching 200,000 per annum, there was a major new development when the first section of the dual carriageway between Newcastle and North Shields (the Coast Road) was opened in 1927.

The general improvement in roads and growing expectation of shorter journey times led to new proposals for a bridge between North and South Shields. The case for one was strong. Ferries did not run at night or when the river was foggy and even in good conditions the vehicular ferry ran at only half hour intervals and could not carry many vehicles. The 10-minute passenger ferry struggled to cope with the numbers wanting to cross the river on special occasions. Ferries cutting across the river were an obstacle and potential danger to the then huge number of vessels moving up and down the river. The route they took represented something comparable to an unregulated crossroads on a motorway. Those who lived at the entrance to the Tyne felt, not unreasonably, that they were badly served compared to their Newcastle neighbours. Newcastle and Gateshead had five bridges while the residents of North and South Shields were forced to rely on ferries to cross the Tyne. Newcastle might have lost the monopoly of trade it had

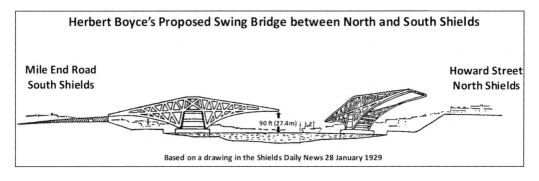

Herbert Boyce's Proposed Swing Bridge between North and South Shields

Mile End Road
South Shields

Howard Street
North Shields

90 ft (27.4m)

Based on a drawing in the Shields Daily News 28 January 1929

Boyce's proposed swing bridge between North and South Shields. This 1929 proposal was just one of several bridges which never materialised.

enjoyed in earlier centuries but it still enjoyed significant advantages over the two competing settlements at the entrance to the river.

A joint committee of Tynemouth and South Shields Councils made no progress when it convened in 1887 to discuss a proposal for a bridge. A second proposal made by a South Shields councillor in 1893 was rejected by the Tyne Improvement Commissioners because they considered it might obstruct river traffic. More promising was a proposal to build a transporter bridge (comparable to the Middlesbrough Bridge). The Shields Bridge Company was incorporated to pursue the project. It was to be of a proven design and have the added advantage of joining up the tramway systems of the two towns. The proposal passed the scrutiny of a House of Lords committee in 1901 but was rejected by a committee of the House of Commons after the Tyne Improvement Commissioners lobbied against it. Subsequent proposals for an opening cantilever bridge; a bridge to be accessed by spiral ramps at either end (to gain the necessary height to overcome the shipping clearance problems voiced by the Tyne Improvement Commission); and for a novel cantilever swing bridge all came to nothing. They foundered in part because they were proposed at a time when the country had entered into the years of the inter-war depression when the economy of the north-east of England was particularly hard hit.

Access by rail

The Newcastle and North Shields Railway Company ran one of the world's first suburban passenger-carrying railways as early as 1839. The economic case for it, as explained by Tomlinson in his encyclopaedic *The North Eastern Railway*, was the estimated number already making that journey by road and river: a minimum of 478,000 per annum and possibly as many as 896,000. Even so, at £36,000 per mile (the equivalent of £100 million relative to national economic output then and now) it was much the most expensive of the lines built north of the Humber during this period. Contributing to the high cost was the viaduct across Willington Dene, between Wallsend and Howdon, and that across the Ouseburn valley, between Byker and

Newcastle. That private investors were prepared to invest so much in the project is an indication of the growing commercial importance of North Shields. Their confidence was justified. It was reported in 1843 that they were receiving a return of 6 per cent per annum.

The line encountered predictable opposition from those already offering transport between the two towns. There was also concern in Newcastle that it would reduce the number of ships loading and unloading there and increase the likelihood that it would lose its custom house to North Shields. In North Shields, tradesmen were concerned that it would encourage local people to shop in Newcastle. The first two locomotives, which pulled ten and eight carriages respectively to North Shields, were the Wellington and Hotspur, both manufactured by Robert Stephenson's Newcastle Company. A ferocious thunderstorm on the opening day seems not to have deterred the 700 guests from celebrating the occasion in an open-air event at Tynemouth.[6] In due course, twenty trains a day ran from Newcastle to Nile Street in North Shields and the railway soon carried around 800,000 passengers annually. The journey could be made in 20 minutes. In recording

North Shields Railway Station and European Hotel. The large covered area beyond the clock was not part of the original station. Note the European Hotel on the right. Today the nearest hotels to the station are in The Royal Quays, Tynemouth and the Cobalt Centre.
BY COURTESY OF DISCOVER NORTH TYNESIDE

Beyond Shields |

this fact, Gibson added that the journey 'before the opening of the railway was made in purgatorial vehicles which plied occasionally and consumed more than two hours in creeping eight miles.[7] Subsequently, a very steep New Cut was excavated through the Ropery Banks in 1844 to provide access to the station from the New Quay. To restore the right of way along the Bank Top, a timber bridge was constructed across the cutting, which was replaced by an iron structure in 1937. The extension of the railway line from North Shields to Tynemouth was a massive undertaking because it required the excavation of deep cuttings through North Shields town centre and beyond, so that much of the track could be below road level. The Tynemouth extension ended with a station at Oxford Street (not the current station site) in 1847.[*]

Other rail lines followed, such as the Blyth & Tyne Railway in the 1860s from Newcastle to Tynemouth via Gosforth, Benton and Monkseaton. Eventually, both lines were integrated under the control of the North Eastern Railway (NER). The section of the Blyth and Tyne line between Monkseaton and Tynemouth, which had originally followed the route of the former Whitley waggonway through what is now the Marden Estate, was rebuilt closer to the coast with new stations at Whitley Bay, Cullercoats and Tynemouth. The Newcastle and North Shields line was then re-routed to join up with the new Tynemouth station.[†] 'Workmen's trains' were introduced on a riverside branch in 1880 to service the shipyard and engineering works along the riverside. Subsequently, when electric trains came into use after 1900, the NER electrified the line using a third rail system. It went into operation in 1904, beating the electrification of the Mersey rail system by a few weeks.

The development of the railway system prompted further proposals for a rail bridge over the Tyne. Projects were advanced in 1853 and 1864 but eventually dropped even though, in the latter case, land had already been purchased in Camden Street for the northern pier.[8] The advent of the railway age also revived the idea of a tunnel under the river between North and South Shields. A proposal for a fast shuttle service of electric trains between Bedford Street in North Shields and Mile End Road in South Shields was put forward in 1902. It received parliamentary approval but was subsequently abandoned. A similar proposal with a slightly different route was also abandoned at the outbreak of the First World War. In 1923, there was a further proposal, from E.W.C. Kearney, an Australian engineer, to build an innovative monorail tube system between North and South Shields.[9] A prototype carriage designed to run at up to 60 mph using a combination of electric motors and 1 in 7 gradients (to reduce the amount

---

[*]   The original stone-built station is now incorporated into a residential development.
[†]   The restoration of Tynemouth Station was completed in July 2012 at a cost of £3.6 million.

of electricity needed and heat produced) was built by the Brush Company of Loughborough.[10] A Bill went through both Houses of Parliament in 1928 but failed at the committee stage because, though supported by South Shields Council, it was not supported by Tynemouth Borough Council.* Kearney made three further proposals to improve communications between North and South Shields in 1934, 1939 and, finally, 1955, but all three failed to elicit sufficient support to be taken further.†

The first North Shields tram service was horse-drawn.[11] The Tynemouth and District Tramways Company built a track between Camden Street in North Shields to the Grand Parade in Tynemouth, which opened to passengers in 1880. Although the company went bankrupt in 1881, it was soon replaced by the North Shields and District Tramways Company which introduced steam trams and extended the line to Prudhoe Street in 1884. Within a few years it too went bankrupt and between 1886 and 1890 the company's six tramcars were mothballed. Then another new company, the North Shields and Tynemouth District Tramways Ltd. re-opened the line in 1890 and ran it until it was taken over by the British Electric Traction Company in 1899. It changed the name of the company to The Tynemouth and District Electric Traction Co. Ltd and built a new electric tramway from the New Quay in North Shields to Whitley Bay which opened in 1901, after Tynemouth Corporation had enhanced its electricity supply. The line was further extended to the Whitley Bay Links in 1904.‡

Accidents to pedestrians were not uncommon and the steep descent to the ferry landing on the New Quay remained difficult even after electric trams came into use. Initially, when the Tynemouth and District Electric Traction Company opened the line, the Board of Trade insisted that it run only single deck trams down the 1-in-10 gradient of Borough Road. Nevertheless, a tram ran out of control, jumped the rails and fell on its side in 1903. The single-decker rule was later relaxed, with the proviso that two people were on hand to apply the brakes. Despite an incident when another tram ran out of control and was de-railed, this safeguard was relaxed in 1906. More accidents followed. In 1914, 17 people were injured. In 1919, a building was destroyed. In 1921 five people died and 32 were injured, nine seriously. The 1919 and 1921 incidents were both caused by the brakes failing to hold after rain. There was also evidence that drivers frequently

---

* The Brush prototype carriage remained in their sheds, unused, until at least the 1960s.

† The failure of Kearney's ambitious plans did not prevent work on a much less ambitious project. A pedestrian and parallel cyclists' tunnel which was started in 1939, but brought to a halt by the Second World War, was recommenced in 1947 and completed in 1951.

‡ The original tram car shed, running down the back of Norfolk Street from Suez Street, was not large enough for the expanded fleet of 22 tram cars and additional premises were opened in John Street, Cullercoats, in 1902.

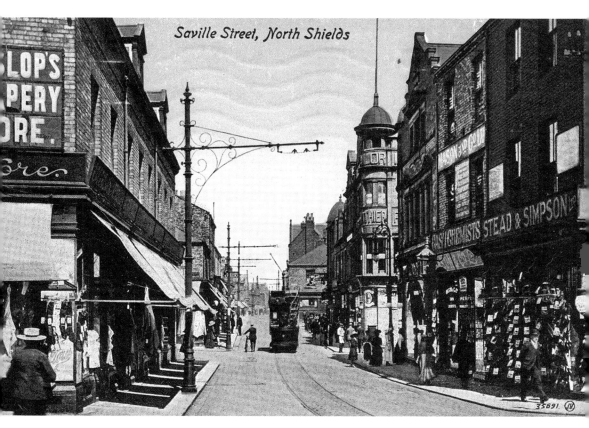

A tram running along Saville Street. Note that at this point on Saville Street
there appears to be only a single tram track.

ignored the low speed limit set for Borough Road and the inquiry report
recommended that in future it should be no more than 4 mph. The Dianunti
family, which ran a café on the New Quay, suffered particularly badly in
these incidents. The tram which ran out of control in 1919 smashed into
their New Quay café, tore it from its foundations and pushed the building
to within a few feet of the river. Miraculously, Contasto Dianunti sustained
only minor injuries. The same café was destroyed in the 1921 accident but,
fortunately for the Dianuntis, it was closed at the time. Although colliding
with the café probably prevented the tram from ploughing into the river,
the deflection caused the double-deck tram to topple on to its side. That
threw the upper deck passengers onto the Quayside and contributed to the
high death and injury toll.[12]

An additional tram line from North Shields to Wallsend was opened in
1902, by the Tyneside Tramways and Tramroads Company. An extension to
Gosforth followed in 1904 along with a link with the Newcastle tram system

at the Wallsend boundary. At this point, it was possible to travel by tram all the way from North Shields to Gosforth or the west end of Newcastle. It was also possible for the residents of all the places along the route to travel via North Shields to enjoy the pleasures of the coast. As well as the natural attractions of the bays and beaches, there were now commercial ventures in operation such as the huge Tynemouth Aquarium and Winter Garden (later called the Tynemouth Palace and subsequently the Plaza), overlooking Tynemouth Long Sands, which opened in 1878. Trimmer notes, however, that it was not possible to make this journey in an entirely straightforward way because of the different track gauges used by the Tynemouth and Tyneside operations. 'Where they met in Prudhoe Street, North Shields, was the only mixed gauge tram track in England.'[13]

In 1922, the Tynemouth and District Electric Traction Company was authorised to run the North Shields to Whitley Bay line for a further 21 years provided it improved the line and carriages. It complied but ran the trams for only a further nine years. The last one ran on 5 August 1931 although by then buses had actually been running along the same route for over a year. Interestingly, Trimmer recalls people referring to the route of the number 8 *bus* as the *tram route* well into the 1950s and, although the company changed its name in 1934 to the Tynemouth and District Transport Co., Trimmer's bus pass was still stamped Tynemouth and District Electric Traction into the 1960s. Sections of track are still being uncovered during repairs to the services below the current road surface.

As the original settlement of North Shields expanded into its neighbouring townships, and the scale of its economic and commercial developments increased, the inadequacy of its system of local government became increasingly obvious. The changes that followed are described in the next chapter.

7

Civic pride and independence

U NTIL 1828, local public affairs were managed by the parish vestry. Commonly called the Four and Twenty because it was made up of 24 prominent, unelected local individuals, this form of local government, which dated back to the early seventeenth century, was rendered inadequate by the transformation that took place in North Shields during the eighteenth and nineteenth centuries. The town's 1828 Improvement Act acknowledged that and, as well as establishing new administrative boundaries which corresponded with the urban development on the Bank Top, transferred responsibility for 'paving, lighting, watching, cleansing, regulating and improving the town of North Shields' to a newly constituted 92-strong board of commissioners.

The national standing of North Shields was given a further boost when it became the major part of one of several new parliamentary boroughs created under the 1832 Reform Act. The commissioners who made the recommendation reported in the following terms in 1831:

> The condition of the town of North Shields is certainly prosperous; it is progressively increasing in importance, and the port was described as the second in this kingdom for tonnage registered as belonging to this port. ... Much building is in progress, and many improvements have been both commenced and agreed upon; new roads are to be made through the parish towards the west and north-east, a railroad is to connect this town and Newcastle, which will pass through the township of Chirton. The town is chiefly extending itself in the west and north-west into Chirton and Preston townships, and in the direction of the town of Tynemouth. There is little doubt that in a few years the village of Chirton will be nearly united to the town of North Shields in a continuous street, and that a great portion of the township of Preston will be occupied by that town. Already several buildings of a superior class have been erected in that township in its immediate neighbourhood, and the whole of a small part of that of Tynemouth, which juts out in the form of a peninsula on the south-west adjoining both Preston and Chirton, is either covered with new building or marked out as their future site.[1]

Following the 1834 Poor Law Amendment Act, workhouses were built to serve groups (unions) of parishes. In the south-east corner of what was then Northumberland, the Union Workhouse was located in North Shields, in 1836, on Preston Lane (now Preston Road), close to Christ Church. In addition to North Shields, it served the other townships in the parish of Tynemouth, as well as the townships of Earsdon plus Cowpen, Bebside, East Hartford, West Hartford, Cramlington, Horton, Long Benton and Wallsend; and later Walker, Willington, Willington Quay, Weetslade and Camperdown.

In the aftermath of the 1832 Reform Act, which extended the number of people with the vote, a Royal Commission made recommendations on the future of local government. Under the subsequent Municipal Corporations Act, 178 municipal boroughs were created. Although North Shields was not amongst them, after two unsuccessful bids, 'the Queen in Council granted a Charter of Incorporation to the Borough of Tynemouth' on 6 August 1849. It was seen as a great local achievement and 'four days later the shops in the town were closed and business entirely suspended in celebration of the event'.[2]

The boundaries established for Tynemouth Borough were the same as those adopted for the parliamentary borough of Tynemouth: the townships of Tynemouth, North Shields, Preston, Chirton and Cullercoats. The new Borough Council was made up of a mayor, six alderman and 18 councillors representing three wards. The first election was held on 1 November 1849. Only those who had lived in the borough for at least three years and were sufficiently well off to contribute to the poor rate had the right to vote. The newly elected councillors took over the building on Saville Street, between Howard and Norfolk Streets, which had been designed by the architect John Dobson for the Improvement Commissioners in 1845.

In 1904, Tynemouth became a county borough, responsible for an extended range of services. The number of elected councillors was increased from 18 to 27 and the number of appointed aldermen from six to nine.[3] Amid the further celebration at that time, no one could have foreseen that the Borough of Tynemouth would be legislated out of existence just 70 years later when, in 1974, it was incorporated along with other local government areas, into the newly constituted Metropolitan Borough of North Tyneside.

Component parts of Tynemouth Borough

At the start of the eighteenth century North Shields was still limited to its one long narrow street by the riverside. The 1828 Improvement Act, however, in taking note of the transformation that had taken place in the interim, officially refined the boundaries to correspond more closely with the new reality.

To the east, a line drawn in a south-east direction from the correction house to the River Tyne; to the north, the turnpike road from the said correction house to the south-west corner of the churchyard; from thence the west wall of the said churchyard to the north-west corner thereof; and from thence a line drawn in a north-north-west direction to the lane or road called Hawkey's Lane, leading from the Newcastle turnpike to the village of Preston; to the west, a line drawn from the termination of the said northern boundary in Hawkey's Lane to the end of the road leading from the Newcastle turnpike to the town of North Shields; and from thence the said lane or road leading therefrom to the town of North Shields as far and unto the south end of the Quakers' burial ground on the west side of the said lane; and from thence a line drawn straight therefrom to the north-west corner of the Milburn Place; and from thence following the boundary between the townships of North Shields and Chirton to the river.[4]

North Shields, within its original boundaries, was dwarfed by the neighbouring townships that became part of Tynemouth Borough. Chirton had 2,576 acres; Tynemouth 1,347 and Preston 646 acres. Only Cullercoats with 15 acres was smaller than North Shields' 103 acres. Its other neighbouring townships, which remained separate in terms of local government, were also much bigger. Monkseaton was made up of 1,344 acres, Murton 680 and Whitley (Bay) 658.[5] Nevertheless, it was North Shields and not any of its neighbouring townships that experienced the enormous dynamic growth that justified the establishment of Tynemouth Borough in 1849.

Although the names and general locations of these neighbouring townships are still used by local people, the boundaries between them have become obscured by the urban sprawl that is now, in local government terms, North Tyneside. At the beginning of the eighteenth century, however, these townships were still distinct entities.

Tynemouth and Cullercoats

To the east, residents of North Shields were able to cross the Pow Burn by a bridge and from there make their way to Tynemouth. Unlike North Shields, the township of Tynemouth escaped the industrial revolution virtually intact. It increased in popularity when the fashion for sea-bathing developed around 1760.[6] By 1846, by which time the village had spread a little to the west, 91 lodging houses were advertising accommodation in addition to 15 inns. Even in the closing decades of the nineteenth century Tynemouth was still described in Lamberts' Handbook in the most flattering terms.

The little watering place of Tynemouth is year by year assuming more and more the character and proportions of a fashionable town. From a single street, flanked by a couple of narrow lanes, it has risen to boast of handsome terraces, picturesque villas, and wide, open thoroughfares. Every summer hundreds of strangers from all parts of the kingdom come here to seek health, or change, or pleasure; and from May to October, beauty and fashion, in the streets, on the cliffs, and along the sands – for we meet them everywhere – indicate the increasing popularity of the village.[7]

Among the visitors to Tynemouth were many celebrated Victorians. Perhaps the best known was Charles Dickens. He was, literally, bowled over by the place as he wrote in a letter to Georgina Hogarth on 6 March 1867.

The atmosphere is so very heavy [in Newcastle] that yesterday we escaped for a two hours sea-walk. There was a high north wind blowing, and a magnificent sea running. Large vessels were being towed in and out over the stormy bar, with prodigious waves breaking on it; and, spanning the restless uproar of the waters, was a quiet rainbow of transcendent beauty. The scene was quite wonderful. We were in the full enjoyment of it when a heavy sea caught us, knocked us over, and in a moment drenched us and filled even our pockets. We had nothing for it but to shake ourselves together and dry ourselves as well as we could by hard walking in the rain and sunshine. But we were wet through for all that, when we came back here to dinner after half an hour's railway ride.[8]

The incident loomed so large in Dickens' mind that he described it in several other letters, and Pearson suggests that it is one of the factors which contributed to Dickens' declining health.[9] Harriet Martineau, the writer and social reformer, lived in Front Street between 1839 and 1845.* William Wordsworth visited in 1838. Herbert Spencer, the evolutionary sociologist who after reading Darwin's work on 'natural selection' coined the phrase 'survival of the fittest', called in to Tynemouth for a brief stay after a visit to Scotland and described it as 'this picturesque old place'.[10] Other famous visitors included the future Prime Minister Gladstone in 1862 when Chancellor of the Exchequer in Palmerston's government.

Cullercoats, a short distance from Tynemouth, became a separate township in 1690, in an acknowledgement of its growing population. At the beginning of the eighteenth century it was altogether more industrial than it is today. Coal was being mined and used, among other things, to fire

---

* Martineau came for the sake of her fragile health and because of several close family connections by marriage between the Martineau, Greenhow and Rankin families, something not explored in Postlethwaite's otherwise valuable account of Martineau's stay in Tynemouth.

Front Street, Tynemouth.

17 salt pans producing over 2,000 tons of salt a year. The decline of mining at Cullercoats, and closure of a mine in Whitley, contributed to the decline of the salt industry and it was only then that Cullercoats emerged as 'the chief fishing village along that part of the coast'.[11] Even then, coal had not completely disappeared from the local economy. In 1770 it was still being mined close to the harbour, 'a considerable way below the flow of the tide, without the least difficulty'.[12] Fortunately, the nature of the fishing from small cobles did not detract from the natural attractions of Cullercoats Bay. On the contrary, it helped Cullercoats become an inspiration for artists, including the celebrated American Winslow Homer.*

Although Whitley (Bay) and Monkseaton were not incorporated into Tynemouth Borough, they are such close neighbours that they warrant a brief mention. Whitley is named after the de Whitby family who were tenants of Tynemouth Priory for about 300 years. Coal was mined in Whitley from the seventeenth to the nineteenth century and magnesian limestone was quarried for many years off what is now the Broadway. The Quarry Inn still stands as a reminder of the now residential area's industrial past. To service the mines and quarry, a wagonway was constructed connecting

---

* The area, and its residents, inspired the celebrated American artist Winslow Homer so much that he stayed longer than he originally intended. His Cullercoats' paintings are among some of his most admired works and many critics suggest that it was his Cullercoats period which transformed him from a good into a great artist. Cullercoats also attracted many other artists in the same period.

| Shiels to Shields

the Cullercoats Main Colliery and Whitley limestone quarries with staithes on the Tyne. By the time I was born, mining had long ceased at Whitley. It had become a combination of a residential area and seaside resort with an amusement park, arcades and ballroom. Today most of those seaside attractions have gone, but the natural appeal of its beaches and links remain.

Monkseaton, like Whitley, has a long past. It was granted to the monks of Tynemouth during the reign of Henry I (1100–35) when it was known as Seton. The prefix Monk was added two centuries later, possibly to distinguish it from North Seton which also belonged to Tynemouth Priory. Tomlinson, writing in 1893, remarked that 'its rural character and proximity to the sea make it a popular place of residence and health resort'. The coal mines in Monkseaton seem to have become exhausted by the early eighteenth century, and by the nineteenth century the most conspicuous buildings were two breweries and a handful of inns and churches. During the twentieth century, it became a popular residential area.

Preston and Chirton

Half way along the North Shields Low Street the swampy area known as the Dogger Letch was crossed by a wooden bridge. From the bridge, a causeway led to the Bank Top. A road continued north on what became known as Church Way. It led to Christ Church and, beyond, to the village of Preston. As late as the nineteenth century, Lamberts' Handbook described the route from North Shields to Preston as a quiet country walk (despite the

Preston Village, c.1950, as I remember it as a boy.

fact it passed the parish workhouse) and Preston village as 'standing in an airy and pleasant situation'. By then, 26 acres of Preston had been allocated for the Borough of Tynemouth's new cemetery, with separate chapels for Anglicans and Dissenters and different plots within it for Roman Catholics and the Society of Friends. The still rural Preston was also the home of many large and impressive houses built or lived in by those making their fortunes in North Shields. The houses and their owners are described in detail in Smurthwaite's *Our Heritage. Preston Township and Preston Village.*

Farther west, a route from the Bull Ring near the present ferry landing went up Coach Lane where it met the Tynemouth to Newcastle road.

East Chirton lay a short distance to the west of the junction. Lamberts' Handbook describes Chirton, even in the late nineteenth century, as a rustic village. At various times it had been the home of the North Shields hero Ralph Gardner, the infamous Duke of Argyll, and the family of Lord Collingwood.[13]

Originally, Chirton comprised three elements: East Chirton; Middle Chirton or Balkwell; and West Chirton and Flatworth. It enjoyed a natural landing place on the river just beyond North Shields, formed by the confluence of the Red Burn, which flowed from the north-west through Coble Dene, and a second stream which flowed north to south through Chirton Dene. On the west, Chirton's boundary was with the Howdon Burn. The township stretched north as far as Shire Moor, with an irregular boundary drawn from Moor Houses to Murton Row.[14]

| Shiels to Shields

Silkey's Lane continued north to the once famous local landmark of Billy Mill. Despite a history that can be traced back to 1320, and the efforts of a scout troop to give it a new lease of life in the 1950s, it was eventually pulled down in the 1960s. Beyond Billy Mill, the route went to Moor Houses where it joined a medieval road from Tynemouth to Morpeth known as North Street. From Moor Houses, it passed through Murton and Earsdon before crossing the Seaton Burn at Holywell.

Records show that farming in Middle Chirton or Balkwell generated income for Tynemouth Priory at least as early as 1292.[15] By the beginning of the nineteenth century, when the 544-acre Balkwell Estate was sold in four lots, it comprised land in East as well as Middle Chirton in addition to Shire Moor.[16] In 1655 West Chirton contained 466 acres of pasture and 404 acres of meadow and arable land.[17] The character of the area underwent significant change when a colliery was opened in Percy Main in 1799. In the wake of the industrial development that followed, the name West Chirton was almost forgotten. Along the riverside frontage, the Northumberland Dock was opened in 1857, enclosing an area of 55 acres. The Albert Edward Dock, enclosing 24 acres, was opened by Prince Albert in 1884.[18] Despite these changes, and although the hamlet of West Chirton had disappeared without trace, Craster still described it as a predominantly rural area in 1907 and noted that Flatworth Mill still remained on the right bank of the Red Burn at the mouth of Coble Dene.

Although Howdon and Willington Quay were not incorporated into Tynemouth Borough, as near neighbours of North Shields they, like Whitley and Monkseaton, warrant a brief mention. Willington existed at least as early as 1072 and there are records of a mill in that area in 1299. Subsequent references mention a salt pan and up to eight farms. By 1839, there were six farms in the area and Willington itself was a two-row village with a green located around a cul-de-sac, known later as Engine Inn Road. The later history of Willington and its neighbour Howdon, like that of Percy Main, was dominated by industry. Coal mines were linked to staithes on the river by wagonways and railways and, in addition, there were rope factories, a brick and tile works, aluminium, lead and other smelting works, shipbuilding, and a glassworks which had been established as early as the seventeenth century.

Public utilities and services

The changes in local government introduced in the nineteenth century brought about consequential changes in public services. The measures introduced by elected councillors began to supplement and/or replace previously uncoordinated commercial, private and voluntary initiatives. However modest they may have been, they were important because the public provision of services was seen by many to be at odds with the prevailing ideology of *laissez-faire* principles of market economics.

Police and emergency services

Britain entered the nineteenth century without a nationally organised police service. Criminal acts were tackled by local arrangements. North Shields parish employed four constables, but a victim of crime was expected to foot the bill for apprehending the criminal and bringing him or her before the courts. For that reason, groups of people came together to share the cost. Thousands of such bodies were set up around the country including the *North Shields and Tynemouth Association for the Prosecution of Felons*, established in 1791.[19]

In 1792 a House of Correction was built on Tynemouth Road, opposite Tanner's Bank, with 14 cells for the temporary confinement of prisoners. Cases were heard by visiting magistrates at an adjoining courthouse. Those given custodial sentences would normally serve them at the county gaol in Morpeth. In 1828, under the town's Improvement Act, watchmen were appointed with power 'to arrest all suspicious persons, prostitutes, nightwalkers and persons misbehaving themselves within the town of North Shields'.[20] Each watchman was provided with a board to fix above his door which read, 'A CONSTABLE HERE'. Initially 16 watchmen were appointed although, within a year, the number was reduced to 12. Four years after the Improvement Act, the parish stocks which stood on land opposite Christ Church were used for the last time. Those subjected to this final public indignity were two youths who had been betting at 'pitch halfpenny' on a Sunday. It was hoped that making an example of them in this way would discourage others from doing the same on the Sabbath Day.[21] When Tynemouth became a fully fledged borough in 1849, there was, initially, little change with respect to the role of police officers but a new court house and police station were later incorporated into the Town Hall buildings on Saville Street.

A second private body, the *Victorian Association for the Prosecution of Felons*, was founded in 1841.

> The object to this Society shall be to protect the persons and property of its members and their families, from the commission of violence or crime of every description; and for that purpose to pay out of its funds all expenses incurred under the direction of its committee in the management of the association, or in discovering, prosecuting and bringing to justice person guilty or suspected of any crime or misdemeanour upon such persons or property.[22]

As Peel emphasises, this Association, like its earlier counterpart, was designed specifically for the protection of subscribing members rather than the common good. Indeed because the list of its members was published in the local newspaper, would-be thieves were effectively encouraged to target those who were not members of the Association; in much the same way that CCTV cameras and visible burglar alarms encourage today's burglars to switch their activities to properties that are unprotected.

These two private bodies co-existed with the newly constituted North Shields' police service until late in the nineteenth century. When the first professional police service was established in London in 1829 by Sir Robert Peel, to allay concerns that the police might be used by the authorities as spies, they were required to wear their uniforms both on and off duty. Moreover, because there was concern that the police might become tantamount to a para-military force; their uniform consisted of blue tail-coats and top hats. Helmets were not introduced in North Shields until 1872. The nearest thing to a weapon carried by the police was a truncheon (concealed in a coat tail pocket). Policemen also carried a pair of handcuffs and, initially, a wooden rattle (replaced by a whistle in the 1880s) to help solicit help should they need it. The North Shields regulations maintained that 'no qualification was more indispensable [to a policeman] than a perfect command of temper'. A policeman should never 'be moved to the slightest degree by any language or threats', and it was maintained that 'if he do his duty in a quiet and determined manner, such conduct will probably induce well-disposed bystanders to assist him should he require it'.[23]

Newly recruited police officers did not receive any kind of systematic training. Nor were they particularly well paid. Their £1 a week wage was about the same as that of miners. For that, early Victorian police worked seven days a week, with only five days unpaid holiday a year. They had no security of employment and their lives were strictly controlled. They were not allowed to vote; they required permission to marry, and even had to seek permission before sharing a meal with a member of the public. Constables were instructed to live on the beat to which they had been assigned and, initially, the police superintendent and sergeant were expected to live in accommodation in the police station.

Robert Mitchell, the first superintendent of police, was pessimistic about the prospect for curbing crime when he presented his first report in 1850. He claimed that scores of lodging-houses were hideouts for thieves, built with trapdoors so that criminals had a better chance of evading capture, and that his task was made worse by the fact that some local marine stores were ready to accept stolen property.

> In one house, the notorious *Sally Joyce* on the Steam Mill Bank, I found one night eleven persons who had been living for a considerable period of time on no other visible means than that of pilfering. The most of them had been convicted thieves and were the associates of thieves. They had been regaling themselves with a piece of beef, eggs, tea and some hot whisky toddy.[24]

Door head from the original Tynemouth Police Station. The station was opened in 1878, closed in 1926 and the building demolished in 1970. The door head was preserved for posterity by Father Pickering.

THIS DOORHEAD IN THE FORM OF THE BOROUGH ARMS, IS FROM TYNEMOUTH POLICE STATION, WHICH STOOD IN OXFORD STR. OPLNED, 1878.IT CLOSED AS A POLICE STATION IN APRIL 1926 AND FINALY DEMOLISHED IN 1970. THE DOORHEAD WAS PRESERVED BY FATHER PICKERING M.A. JE JACKSON 1996

The comparable annual report for 1878 stated that over the year the police had dealt with 158 thieves, 157 vagrants, 301 prostitutes and 628 habitual drunkards. Such figures explain why prostitution was thought of as *the* great social evil in the Victorian era and why there was a comparable concern with what today would be termed alcohol abuse.

A second police station was opened in Tynemouth with accommodation for two sergeants, their families and five constables. A third followed in the Bull Ring area of North Shields in 1883. Anyone arrested in that part of the town was kept in the station until 2 a.m. and then shackled by the legs and taken to the main station in Saville Street. When the site was needed for an extension to Smith's Dock, a replacement station was set up in 1905 which contained six cells and accommodation for a sergeant and three constables. Both divisional stations were closed in 1925 and replaced by 23 (*Dr Who* Tardis-style) wooden police boxes. These contained telephones and allowed policemen walking their beats to contact the central station. A blue flashing light was used to summon constables to a Police Box when necessary. In a period when very few houses were equipped with telephones, each box was also provided with a telephone for emergency use by the public to summon help from the police, fire or ambulance services.

England was also slow to organise public fire services. The need for a more organised approach was obvious after the Great Fire of London in 1666. In its aftermath, a number of laws were passed in the capital to try to reduce the potential damage from future fires. Each quarter

The New Quay
Police Box. This
box was one of
many used both
by the police
and the public
who needed
to summon
the emergency
services in the
days when few
houses had
telephones.
BY COURTESY OF
DISCOVER NORTH
TYNESIDE

of the city was provided with 800 leather buckets, 50 ladders and other fire-fighting equipment. Each house had to have buckets, and occupants were required to participate in hand-to-hand bucket brigades. Another law allowed insurance companies to be set up to indemnify property-owners against fire damage. This was a significant development, but still a terribly inefficient arrangement. Each of the many companies put up its own distinctive sign over the door of a policy holder's property. In the event of a fire, someone was expected to inform the responsible insurance company. They maintained their own equipment but, for many years, this consisted of little more than hand-pumps and barrows with lengths of leather hose.

By 1849 things had moved on and in North Shields the local water company was supplying water to about 65 hydrants. That provided a modest degree of support for fire-fighters – but only if the fire broke out during the day. That was because the private water company chose to cut off the supply at night rather than run the risk of water being drawn by people who had not paid for it. So the chances of successfully tackling a fire during the hours of darkness were greatly reduced. On the night of 1 December 1851, the North Shields theatre at the junction of Union and Howard Streets caught fire and was totally destroyed. At the time, there was only one small fire engine in North Shields. By the time a horse-drawn military fire engine arrived from Tynemouth Castle, and two from South Shields, there was nothing left for them to save.[25] Even 50 years later, when the Norfolk Street fire station opened in 1907 (in a former school rather than a purpose-built

Tynemouth County Borough's Fire Brigade in action. This 1985 fire destroyed the Albion Assembly Rooms at the junction of Saville, Charlotte and Norfolk streets.

building), the situation was still inadequate. The station was equipped with a horse-drawn steam fire-engine, but the horses had to be borrowed as required from neighbouring stables. Given this kind of inefficiency, it is hardly surprising that music hall sketches involving incompetent fire brigades were popular elements in the repertoires of the great music hall comedians Dan Leno, Rob Wilton and Will Hay.

North Shields' first fire engine with its own motor was ordered in 1917. By 1940, equipment had improved significantly and included a fire engine with a 100 feet (30 m) turntable ladder which, as a boy, I found hugely impressive. Communications had also greatly improved by the mid-twentieth century, thanks to the development of radio. However, since most houses were without telephones there could still be a considerable delay while the person trying to report a fire made his or her way to the nearest public telephone. Despite improvements, the fire service was still overwhelmed at times, and especially so when North Shields was a target for the incendiary as well as explosive bombs of the Luftwaffe during the Second World War. During a single night (12 April 1941) the fire brigades of North Shields and the immediately surrounding areas were called to 265 fires. A few months later, the fire service was nationalised.

A Police Ambulance Corps was established in North Shields in 1888. After four months training, 33 policemen were awarded certificates and received arm-bands to signify that they were qualified. Despite the fact that we now have a professional paramedic ambulance service, the tradition of training the police in first aid has continued to this day and all policemen are expected to hold a St John's Ambulance Certificate.

Water and public health

North Shields' first piped water supply was provided by six brewers under a 1786 Private Act of Parliament. This represented an obvious conflict of interest. At a time when beer was drunk as a safe alternative to impure water, a widely available supply of cheap, safe drinking water would have made inroads into the brewers' profits. For that reason, it is not surprising that the company provided water primarily for the needs of industry rather than residents and laid no pipes at all outside North Shields. Most people in the Borough beyond North Shields depended on private wells. There were several in Tynemouth, in addition to a single public well. Cullercoats had three private wells, but I have found no evidence of a public well. The water that had been available from the Marden Burn disappeared after a new colliery shaft was sunk in the vicinity. By the middle of the nineteenth century, the pressure to improve the supply of water was growing. The Public Health Act of 1848 gave local authorities the power to make changes to the way water was supplied, provided that an inquiry confirmed that change was needed. That case was more than easily made in the Borough of Tynemouth. A team of investigators reported in 1851 that the conditions in the Borough were appalling and that the case for improved sanitation in the town could not possibly be stronger. With respect to the hopelessly inadequate water supply to domestic dwellings, it concluded that 'nothing less than the introduction of water into every habitation will successfully combat the evil'.[26]

The inadequacy of the town's water supply, which rendered its population more vulnerable to infectious diseases, was studied at first hand by Dr Edward Headlam Greenhow. Born in 1814 into a North Shields medical family he practised medicine in the town alongside his father for 18 years.[*] His appreciation of the need for public health reform was heightened by the

---

[*] He was the grandson of E.M. Greenhow, MD, of North Shields and the nephew of T.M. Greenhow, MD, FRCS, who was an innovative surgeon at Newcastle Infirmary and a notable advocate of sanitary reform. The Greenhows were not the only notable medical men from North Shields. Sir Byrom Bramwell (1847–1931) was born in North Shields where his doctor father had a medical practice. He worked with him for a time but made his mark in Edinburgh where he wrote several important textbooks which were translated into numerous languages. George Grey Turner (1877–1951) was born in Cambden Street, North Shields (in what is now the Magnesia Bank pub). His pioneering surgical skills were widely recognised and, in 1946, he was appointed President of the International Society of Surgeons. A particular type of bruising is still known as Grey Turner's sign.

cholera outbreaks of 1831, 1849 and 1853. In 1851 he assumed the role of chairman of Tynemouth's first Local Board of Health but in 1853 accepted an invitation to move to London. Losing Greenhow's expertise and energy probably made a significant difference to the Borough's response to the 1851 Ranger Report. Although a plan was drawn up in 1854 by R. Rawlinson for the Tynemouth Local Board of Health, to provide drains and sewers for North Shields and the rest of the Borough, even according to the Borough's own assessment little was done to improve matters until the Public Health Act of 1875.[27] The cost was not the only reason for the delay. There was also disagreement about the appropriateness of sewers as a solution to the problem. Even among those who favoured their introduction, engineers disagreed about the most effective way to provide them.[28] In the case of the Borough of Tynemouth, Rawlinson emphasised that it was 'not an easy place to sewer and drain', and his report is impressive both in terms of the range of considerations he took into account and the level of detail in the proposals offered.[29]

Greenhow's move to London may have been a loss to North Shields but it was very much to the nation's gain. John Simon, who had been impressed by Greenhow when a member of the 1854 Royal Commission into the cholera outbreak in and around Newcastle, advised the Board of Health to appoint Greenhow as a medical officer to one of the London districts most prone to cholera. He also helped secure Greenhow the appointment of Britain's first lecturer in public health, at St Thomas's Hospital. It was while there that some of Greenhow's most influential epidemiological work was conducted and it proved crucial to the decisions that were made about the future of public health provision in the late 1850s.

In the absence of significant public health reforms, the population of North Shields was in an unenviable position. The water company piped water to only 406 of the town's 3,225 houses. Those who lived in the other 87.5 per cent of dwellings (probably in excess of 90 per cent of the population), had to obtain water from one of the 18 pumps from which it could be purchased during the day (but not at night). Private wells were frequently contaminated by midden-heaps of dung and other refuse.[30]

In 1869 the water company had the opportunity to merge with the Newcastle and Gateshead Water Company. Choosing not to do so was a costly mistake. The company struggled to meet the growing demand for water and shortly afterwards was obliged to start buying bulk supplies from the Newcastle and Gateshead company – at the going market rate. As the company's financial situation deteriorated, so too did the quality of the water it provided. Much of it was pumped from a disused colliery shaft in Shiremoor and was polluted before it reached the surface. From there it drained through fields 'heavily manured with town refuse'. The water then made its way to the Red Burn, where it was further polluted by the red precipitate which gave the stream its name. From there, it was sold to the consumer without any filtering and the precipitates in the water were sometimes so substantial that they blocked water pipes. Other, more particular problems arose from time to time. In 1889, for example, there were complaints that the supply of water to some houses was unusually variable: some families enjoyed full pressure while others had virtually none. Seven eels were found in the pipes; three feet (91 cm) long and six inches (15 cm) in diameter.[31] Because the water company declined to provide a separate supply of water for cleaning the streets, when the corporation did flush them it used pumped sea water which left a residue of dry salt on the surface which reportedly blew around the town in white clouds on windy days.

The Public Health Act of 1872 placed an obligation on local authorities to provide a water supply and yet, twenty years later, less than half had taken direct responsibility for it.[32] The Borough of Tynemouth was among them. However, growing dissatisfaction with both the quantity and quality of water provided by the water company led to an 1892 meeting of ratepayers who wanted to set up a municipal water company. Involving ideological as well as practical considerations, the proposal failed to secure a majority in the subsequent poll of local opinion. All that was achieved that year was a specific court injunction to stop the water company using the water from the Shiremoor mine shaft. The company continued to resist the demand that it also stop using water from the Red Burn. That no doubt fuelled the continuing demand for change, and five years later the case for public intervention was accepted by sufficient local ratepayers. The 1897 Tynemouth Corporation Water Act gave the council the power to acquire the undertakings of the North Shields waterworks. The following year, arrangements were made to greatly increase the capacity of the existing reservoirs at Brock Farm (between Drummond Terrace and the rear of the workhouse on Preston Road); in Meadow Well; in the former limestone quarries at Whitley Bay and at Billy Mill.

A new reservoir was also constructed about 25 miles north-north-west of North Shields, fed by the River Font. When it was completed in 1908 it held 722 million gallons of treated water. In the meantime, a 1901 public inquiry had revealed that the profit motive had driven the directors of the private water company covertly to flout the 1892 court injunction to stop using water from the Shiremoor mine shaft. When later compelled to stop drawing water from the Red Burn, the company directors had ordered their employees to use 'an ingenious and secret contrivance', locked and enclosed with brickwork, to intercept once again the water from the mine shaft to sell to its customers.[33] Despite the marked improvement in the water supply which followed the opening of the Fontburn reservoir, the increasing demand for water meant that additional supplies had to be obtained from elsewhere in subsequent years. Even the four million gallons a day available by 1934 was deemed insufficient and it was necessary to keep on increasing

provision. By the time I was born in 1940, most North Shields' households (including my own) still lacked the three basic amenities of an indoor toilet, plumbed bath and hot water supply, but we did enjoy clean cold water on tap, which to most people in North Shields in the eighteenth and nineteenth centuries would have seemed an unattainable luxury.

The supply of water once again became the responsibility of private companies during the flurry of privatisations that took place in the 1980s and 1990s. Those who advocated it claimed that it was an appropriate service to be returned to the free play of market forces, unaware that this had not been the predominant view a century earlier. As Wohl notes, even ardent advocates of *laissez-faire* economics accepted the argument for the municipal ownership of water.

> Water is as essential to the health and comfort of mankind as the air we breathe, and when mankind congregate in masses counted only by tens of thousands, it is essential to the public health that it should be most abundant, not doled out to yield 30 per cent interest, but supplied from the public rates and at net cost.[34]

It is hardly surprising that those familiar with such inglorious histories as that of the North Shields' Water Company should have been sceptical about the alleged advantages of returning the supply of water to private enterprise in 1989 and dubious about the ability of public watchdogs to supervise the new private water companies properly. What one assumes the government did not anticipate is that most of the privatised water companies would soon be owned by foreign companies.[35]

Public baths

In recognition of the need for easier access to water for bathing and laundry, the Borough Council opened public baths at the junction of Saville Street and Church Way in 1854. The front of the building housed six baths for women but ten for men, in an acknowledgement that much of the work they did was 'dirty'. In addition, there were two showers and some salt water baths. At the rear of the building, were 20 separate recesses for washing clothes. Each contained three wooden troughs provided with hot and cold water. This wash house area was also provided with mangles to squeeze excess water from the laundry before it was taken to a double range of drying closets. The baths and laundry cubicles were closed in 1939, despite the fact that the majority of the town's population still did not have access to piped hot water let alone a bathroom in their own homes. The facilities were

North Shields Public Baths and Wash House The baths closed in 1939 and were never re-opened despite the fact that thousands of local houses did not have baths or a plumbed hot water supply then or for decades subsequently.

BY COURTESY OF DISCOVER NORTH TYNESIDE

still in demand at the time but increasingly unpopular because the bath's furnaces produced so much smoke. For the duration of the Second World War the building was used as a mortuary, and the baths did not reopen after the cessation of hostilities.

Gas and electricity
The first coal gas company was founded in London in 1812. From then, the industry spread rapidly. Private companies usually operated by making an arrangement with local authorities to light streets. This was tantamount to a 'loss leader' but gave the companies the right to lay gas pipes to private and business consumers (who provided the companies with their main source of revenue). At this stage, coal gas was used almost entirely for lighting. The provision of coal gas to heat homes and for cooking only developed significantly in the latter part of the nineteenth century. The North Shields Gas Company was formed in 1820 and streets were lit by coal gas for the first time in 1822.[36] Prior to that, only a few oil lamps alleviated the gloom and even they had met with some local resistance.

> It was a great shock to all preconceived notions when some daring innovators proposed to dispel a little of the darkness of the streets during the long winter evenings by a few oil lamps. The project was thought most revolutionary, and a crowded meeting was held to oppose it. Eloquence might be lacking amongst the opponents of change, but strength of lungs was present in full force and the stragglers for light were howled down. One worthy stood upon a form, waving his arm and shouting 'Nee leets! Nee leets!' … The victory won at the meeting was not a lasting one. The oil lamps were soon hung in the streets, and gas lights followed in their turn.[37]

As a result of a dispute about street lighting between the North Shields Gas Company and the North Shields Improvement Commissioners, the Borough of Tynemouth set up its own gas company. Within five years the two companies had amalgamated to form the Tynemouth Gas Company. By 1850 it provided 194 street lights in North Shields but they were only illuminated between September and April of each year. A new gasworks opened at the other end of the town, in Minton Lane, in 1872. It produced coal gas until 1930, when it ceased full-time production and the contract to supply gas to the town was awarded to a company outside the Borough. Gas production was ramped up again during the Second World War, until the gas industry was nationalised in 1948. A 90-foot gas holder, built in 1906, which could hold 1.4 million cubic feet of gas, continued to dominate the local area until it was demolished in 2012.

When it came to the supply of electricity, Tynemouth Borough decided not to repeat the problem that had arisen with the supply of water and acted to forestall the entry of private companies into the local energy market. The town council made use of the provisions of the Electricity Lighting Acts of 1881 and 1888 and applied for permission to construct its own generating facilities. Agreement was reached in 1891 and a power station later completed on Tanner's Bank, on the site of what had been Richardson's tannery. The first business premises to be lit by electricity were those of the 35,117 square feet department store, D. Hill and Company (later D. Hill and Carter's) on the junction of Howard Street and Union Street on Saturday, 17 April 1897. The over 600 lights were switched on at 7.15 precisely, at an event to which the public were invited 'to see the First Business Premises in the Borough to be lit up by Electricity'. As the demand for electricity exceeded the local supply, the council decided to buy additional supplies from Newcastle rather than extend its own plant and, in 1910, Tynemouth Borough gave up generating its own electricity altogether. Although electricity eventually ousted gas in terms of street lighting, as late as the 1950s about half the street lights in North Shields were still illuminated by gas.

Public libraries

The Public Libraries Act was passed in 1855 but it was not until July 1869 that a meeting called for its adoption in North Shields. The fact that a public library could be opened by January 1870 was due to the generosity of two voluntary bodies. The first was the Tradesmen's and Mechanics' Institute which donated its fine, ten-year-old building at the south-east corner of the junction of Saville Street and Howard Street, along with its book collection. The second was the Tynemouth Literary and Philosophical Society (established in 1835) which also donated its collection of books to the new public library. The first Borough librarian, George Dixon, was a member of the Tradesmen's and Mechanics' Institute as was the secretary to the library committee J.S. Edington. He too showed a marked generosity by donating his collection of engravings by British artists, which was believed to be the second largest of its kind in the country, exceeded only by that held in the British Museum.[38] The institute's science and arts classes continued in the library until 1880.

The Borough began to establish branch libraries elsewhere as early as 1883, but the main library on Saville Street was still in use when I was a boy and I found the building and range of books awe-inspiring when I graduated to it from the junior library.* Ironically, the building was pressed back into service in 2011 when the 1975 replacement library built in Northumberland Square was in need of extensive refurbishment.

---

* What I had not appreciated until I was conducting research for this book is that the junior library, adjacent to the main library in Howard Street, was not opened until 1945 and that I was among its earliest customers. Living so close to it and being so in love with books I must also have been one of its most frequent customers.

North Shields' first public library. Originally The Tradesmen's and Mechanics' Institute, it was initially stocked with books from the institute's library and that of the Tynemouth and Literary and Philosophical Society. Note the prominent four-faced clock on the corner of the building.

Given the scale of the social problems generated by Britain's predominantly *laissez-faire* political and economic system, these public utilities and services may have had only a modest positive impact on the lives of the people of North Shields. Nevertheless, the very creation of *public* services at a time when there was a widespread view that *private* enterprise was the key to the future is not inconsequential. What became known as 'gas and water socialism' might have been dismissed by Marxists (because it diverted attention away from fundamental questions about political economy) and criticised by capitalists (because it interfered with the free play of market forces) but, whatever its limitations, it undoubtedly improved the lives of many ordinary people. The local investment in these services is one of the reasons why there was so much resentment when the national governments of the 1980s embarked on a systematic programme of privatisation. Many people felt that local public facilities belonged to the locality that had created them, and that central government had no right to acquire them by some legal device only to sell them back to the private sector from whom they had been rescued in the first place.

The industrial and commercial developments described in earlier chapters, and the introduction of public utilities and services identified in this chapter, brought about significant changes in the economic, social and political structure of North Shields. The lot of ordinary people still left a great deal to be desired, as later chapters will show, but compared to earlier centuries there was a growing sense of optimism. That was not limited only to material and secular matters. The nineteenth century also saw another remarkable transformation, as church after church was built to cater for the growing number of people who wanted to give public expression to their optimistic personal faiths.

8

Religious institutions

L IVING in a society where many people are indifferent to religion, it is difficult to appreciate that 'religious thinking, religious practices and religious institutions were once at the very centre of the life of western society'.[1] By the eighteenth and nineteenth centuries, religion may not have been as pivotal a factor in the country's affairs as previously, but it still retained considerable significance. Throughout the nineteenth century religious differences impacted on social relationships and influenced the way in which people behaved in public and private. Religion also influenced the way in which people conceived of the world and their place within it. That is why Charles Darwin's *On The Origin of Species by Means of Natural Selection* had a rough ride when it was published in 1859. Darwin's ideas challenged the universal Christian belief that men and women were created by God in his own image, and were in fact products of the same evolutionary process as animals.

In North Shields, the sacred and the secular expanded side by side. The perceived need for so many new churches was in part a function of factionalism among non-conformists but, given that splits were usually based on issues of principle, even that confirms how passionate people were about their religious beliefs. The new churches were built to impress, with capacity to spare: a testament to the optimism of those who paid for them.[*]

This chapter begins by outlining the growth of organised religion from the sixteenth century through to the nineteenth and ends with its decline in the twentieth century. The main issues in the sixteenth to eighteenth centuries were about who should have power and authority over religious matters. It was also the issue of 'who governs' which was central to the dissenting movements which rejected the authority of the bishops within

---

[*] There are gaps in my coverage. Spiritualism was the subject of a lecture in Cambden Street in 1884 and there was a Spiritualist Church on Saville Street at the turn of the century. It moved later to Waterville, a substantial building on Stanley Street West. After Waterville was destroyed by enemy action in 1941, it was replaced by the building still in use today. I understand that it has a small but active membership. Unfortunately, I have had no response to my requests for further information. I have also had no response from the Jehovah's Witnesses who meet in Norfolk Street, nor from the Church of Latter Day Saints who meet in Preston Grange. It has also not been possible for me to describe the history of independent churches in the town.

the Church of England. However, in the nineteenth century, the key issue was the importance of a personal faith.

Organised religion from the sixteenth to the mid-nineteenth century

Roman Catholicism

Until the sixteenth century, to be a Christian in England meant being a Catholic. Those who worshipped in Tynemouth Priory took part in religious services that would be recognised throughout the international orbit of the Roman Catholic Church. But when Henry VIII's behaviour led to his excommunication and the establishment of the Church of England, those who remained within the Roman Catholic tradition became a vulnerable minority. Henry was sympathetic to traditional Catholic doctrines but his Archbishop of Canterbury, Thomas Cranmer, was not. He was free to act on those sentiments after Henry's death in 1547. Many churches were stripped of their religious artefacts; the rituals surrounding the Mass, the most sacred act of Catholic worship, were changed; the sacraments of penance and the last rites of the dead were abolished; purgatory was deemed not to exist; prayers for the dead were declared pointless and priests no longer obliged to be celibate. Those who wanted to remain Catholics were faced with a terrible dilemma. To keep their faith meant putting their lives at risk. Such a huge transformation in religious expression must have been bewildering to the ordinary people of places like North Shields.

For the next two centuries, the pendulum between Catholicism and the Church of England swung back and forth but the fundamental movement away from Catholicism proved inexorable. The population of England was effectively bullied into deserting its long-established and familiar form of Christianity to follow the state-sanctioned alternative. There were attempts to reverse the process. Following the death of Edward VI, Mary, a confirmed Catholic, came to the throne and tried to restore England's link with Rome. During her short reign, she was responsible for about 300 executions, including that of Cranmer. Another of her victims was John Dudley, who had been assigned the lands and temporal rights of Tynemouth Priory. When captured by Mary's forces he claimed to be a Catholic, in the vain hope that it might save his life. On the day before his planned execution he took part in a Catholic communion and maintained that 'the plagues that is upon the realm and upon us now is that we have erred from the faith these sixteen years'. Despite his confession, Dudley was beheaded the following day. When Elizabeth I succeeded Mary in 1558, the religious changes introduced by her sister were reversed. To follow Catholicism became a crime against the state. Elizabeth's successor, James I, despite being the son of the Catholic Mary Queen of Scots, chose to continue Elizabeth's policies. In retaliation, a handful of Catholic extremists tried to blow up Parliament. It was difficult to argue for religious tolerance in the face of the evidence that at least some influential Catholics were prepared to resort to gross acts of violence. During the succeeding reign of Charles I, religious tensions were inflamed further when the King chose to marry a French Catholic; raised an Irish Catholic army to fight the Protestant Scots and, eventually, embroiled the country in a prolonged and bloody civil war. His actions proved a particular disaster for England's Roman Catholics. They were not only on the losing side but, following seven years of bitter conflict, had to contend with a fiercely puritan government backed by a trained army.

The subsequent restoration of the monarchy in 1660 provided no relief for Roman Catholics. Although Charles II was a Catholic at heart, he bowed to anti-Catholic feeling rather than risk losing the crown. Several pieces of legislation were passed to ensure that there would be no turning back.* Yet fears of a 'Popish Plot' continued and ultimately led to the so-called 'Glorious Revolution' of 1688 in which King William III and Queen Mary II of Holland were invited to invade England and take the throne as a way of protecting England from the perceived threat of Catholicism. With the final defeat of James's heirs in the 1745 rebellion, and a parliamentary inquiry in 1767 which estimated there were by then no more than 70,000 practising Catholics in the country, some felt it was safe to reduce the discrimination against them. The first Catholic Relief Act of 1778 allowed Catholics to own property and join the army provided they took an oath of allegiance. However, this relaxation of religious discrimination underestimated the strength of popular feeling against Catholicism. When the MP Lord George Gordon initiated a campaign against the legislation, about 60,000 people marched on Parliament in 1780 to present a petition against it. Riots followed for more than a week. By the time the violence was suppressed, 285 people had been killed in the worst episode of rioting ever experienced in Britain. Despite such popular resistance, there were further relaxations of the restrictions against Catholics in 1791 and 1829. By then, the only significant stipulation left in place was that a Catholic could not succeed to the throne. But it is plain that in the over 200-year period between Elizabeth I coming to the throne in 1558 and this gradual relaxation of discrimination against Catholics, being a practising Roman Catholic demanded considerable courage as well as deep religious conviction. Not surprisingly:

---

* The Licensing Act prohibited any publication which did not conform to Anglican teaching. The Corporation Act made taking communion in the Church of England a precondition for holding public office. The Test Act obliged anyone holding a civil or military office to take an Oath of Supremacy and Allegiance and subscribe to a declaration against the Catholic belief in transubstantiation. Subsequent legislation extended such stipulations to include peers and members of the House of Commons.

No trace of Catholic worship can be found in the district of Tynemouth and North Shields for nearly two centuries and a half after the surrender of the Abbey in 1539. ... Those of the people who remained faithful to the old religion either practised it in secret or fled across the sea that they might follow the dictates of their conscience in peace.[2]

Catholicism only returned to being a more public form of religious expression in North Shields towards the end of the eighteenth century. A Roman Catholic mission to the town was established in 1784, six years after the first Catholic Relief Act. A priest made a 20-mile journey from County Durham, once a month, to say mass in a hired room in Milburn Place.[3] As an anonymous writer remarked in 1849, these services were in marked contrast to how the Catholic Mass was celebrated in Tynemouth Priory 250 years earlier.

> What a change is here! – a room in Milburn Place, where the priest enters by a miserable lane, to meet some twenty or thirty devout souls, who form his congregation, who kneel before his portable alter, where everything like pomp and ceremony is out of the question ... Where now is that long procession which accompanied the previous celebration of the Mass in Tynemouth Abbey; the train of mitred abbots, prelates, bishops and archbishops, covered with gorgeous vestments studded with pearls and precious stones, that moved along the spacious nave, accompanied with all the ceremony and splendour which adorned the service of the Church in the days of Faith?[4]

The next significant development in the revival of Catholicism in North Shields came as a result of the revolution taking place in France. In 1792, the new, anti-clerical regime passed a resolution ordering all clergy who declined to take the civil oath to leave the country. As a result, about 8,000 Roman Catholic priests sought refuge in England – along with many nuns and lay people. On 5 October 1793, 295 of these French refugees arrived in North Shields. Most moved on but a few remained in the town and held services in the little chapel in Milburn Place.[5] Three died but two others continued for several years to hold services in a hired a room in Norfolk Street.[6]

Soon after his appointment to a Newcastle church, the Rev. James Worswick began to visit Tynemouth and North Shields. Initially, he had very small congregations. For example, on one Easter there were only 14 communicants.[7] The congregation increased significantly during the Napoleonic Wars when a Catholic regiment (probably the Second Royal Lancashire Militia) was stationed at Tynemouth Castle. Worswick then made use of a building in Union Street as a Catholic chapel with the soldiers making up the bulk of his congregation. However, it seems that many Protestants also went to hear Worswick out of a sense of curiosity 'and it is said that nurses sometimes took those under their charge to the chapel, in order to show the children a real, live, genuine, popish priest'.[8] When the regiment left Tynemouth, the use of the Union Street chapel was discontinued but Worswick continued to ride the eight miles from Newcastle to Tynemouth on horseback to celebrate mass once a month. A contemporary recorded that, 'Many times in winter he arrived in Shields covered with snow but nothing ever prevented him coming on the appointed days in exact time'.[9]

Worswick is a pivotal figure in the history of Catholicism in North Shields. The son of a wealthy English banker, he had studied in France for ten years before the National Assembly passed its anti-clerical resolution and he was obliged to return to England. He was the major figure in the Shields Mission and used his influence and personal fortune to help re-establish Catholicism in the town. He made a point of introducing himself to ordinary people during his visits and was always pleased to report that despite being a Catholic he was invariably treated with respect. Over the years, he became a popular figure in both Newcastle and North Shields, not least because he seems to have been prepared to go where some other clergymen of the period chose not to. The following account may be biased because it comes from Worswick's obituary in the Catholic magazine *Tablet* but is consistent with other evidence about his character and down-to-earth manner.

> Regardless of his own personal safety he not only visited continually the wretched abodes of disease in all parts of the town, but the workhouse, the prison, and, above all, the fever wards in the infirmary were the daily scenes of his heroic ministry. This fearless indifference to danger … where no other clergyman of the town ever dared to enter, drew from the leading medical attendants strong expressions of admiration. … His manifold charities were only bounded by his means, and they were distributed to all in want, without regard to their religious opinions.[10]

It was primarily as a result of Worswick's efforts that the large and impressive St Cuthbert's Catholic church was opened in 1821, at the top of Bedford Street, no more than 100 yards from the Anglican Christ Church. It was built on a scale which seemed unnecessary given the still small Roman Catholic population of the town. Despite that, the new church could not hold the thousands of people who wanted to attend the consecration service. Once opened, the church was 'crowded every week' and within a short time the congregation was the largest among Catholic churches in Northumberland with the exception of Newcastle. That was in part because

St Cuthbert's Roman Catholic church. Robert Giles, *South West View of the Roman Catholic Chapel, North Shields*. Opened in 1821, the church was situated on the corner of Albion Road and Bedford Street.

Bell Anti-Catholic Emancipation Mug. Bell, one of the unsuccessful candidates in the local 1826 election, remained vehemently opposed to equal treatment for Roman Catholics.

there were no Roman Catholic churches between North Shields and Morpeth to the north; North Shields and Newcastle to the west and North Shields and Sunderland to the south. I should add, for those unfamiliar with the area, that other than Tynemouth there is nothing but the North Sea to the east. So, in addition to local people and visitors, the congregation was drawn from South Shields, Jarrow, Percy Main, Howdon, Willington, Wallsend, Backworth, Earsdon, Cowpen, Seaton Sluice, Whitley, Cullercoats and Tynemouth.[11] St Cuthbert's congregations were also increased by the growth of the Catholic population of North Shields and Britain more generally. Between 1800 and 1850, the proportion of Catholics in the population increased from 1.2 per cent to 4.1 per cent. Given that the overall population was growing rapidly during this period, the increase in absolute numbers was even more marked.[12] Not all of it can be attributed to immigration from Ireland or a natural increase in the indigenous Catholic population. There were also a significant number of conversions from Protestantism. The Rev. Gillow, who was the priest at St Cuthbert's from its opening in 1821 to his death in 1857, claimed that he had received 'nearly 1,000 converts into the bosom of the Catholic Church'.[13]

Worswick and Gillow appear to have been respected and popular and, according to Stark; St Cuthbert's 'became the most fashionable place of worship in the town for upper class Protestants'. Even though some may have left after the sermon and before the celebration of the mass, the fact that prominent local Protestants should attend a Catholic church at all is remarkable given the bitter conflicts which had driven Catholicism underground for so long.[14] This does not mean that all anti-Catholic feeling had disappeared. In 1830, some local Protestants were so concerned about the popularity of the newly opened St Cuthbert's church that they invited a lecturer to preach against 'popery' in the Scotch Church on week-day evenings. Catholics who attended to try to contradict what they regarded as false assertions were 'forcibly turned out' and had to resort to publishing and distributing a pamphlet to try to mitigate the ill-will the lectures were generating.[15]

The Established Church

During the Civil Wars (1642–51), the local population lost access to the parish church and their vicar. They lost access to their church because it was within the walls of Tynemouth Castle. They lost James Hume, their vicar, because he refused to endorse the abolition of the Episcopacy (government by bishops) that was agreed by Parliament in 1646. He was punished for his stand by being ejected from his 'living'. As a result, the next four ministers were appointed by the Commonwealth Commissioners. By this stage, Cromwell's Commissioners had reported that the church within Tynemouth Castle was 'quite ruined'.[16] For a period, services appear to have been held in the open air but, in 1650, a malting house belonging to Ralph Gardner was used until 1659. At that point, there is evidence that some services returned to the church in Tynemouth Castle even though it was still in a state of disrepair.[17] Any hope of a replacement depended on the permission of the Commonwealth Commissioners for Propagating the Gospel. Fortunately, in 1652, they concluded that 'The town of North Shields being a populous place of itself, it is fit that a parish church be built there'. Two years later, Tynemouth parishioners sent this request to the Earl of Northumberland for a plot of land on which to build a new parish church.

> The petitioners to their great grifes have found theis 12 or 13 yeares past bin deprived of hearing God's holy word in their usuall church, it being within the castle, which is garrisoned soe that manie tymes they have been forced to heare the same in the open fields. That your petitioners, not having anie hopes of the use their church againe and well knowing your honor's piety and zeale to soe good a work, are emboldened to becaome most most humble suitors, beseeching your honor to be pleased to graunt unto them a proportion of ground to build them a church on, also for a buriing place, and they humbly conceive if it be with your honor's pleasure that a corner of a close there called Brocks close by the highway wilbe most convenient for that purpose.[18]

The Earl asscnted and made a piece of land available where the road from North Shields to Preston met the road from Tynemouth to Newcastle. It is a testament to the growing significance of North Shields that it was deemed more appropriate to build the church there than in Tynemouth where the original had been. Fund raising began in 1657 when the Four and Twenty directed that the church rates (taxes levied locally on houses and working buildings such as farms, mills and salt pans) were to be 'given for and towards the erecting of the new church at Brocks Cloase'.[19] However, there was little prospect of raising sufficient funds locally so a case for raising the money county-wide was put by Tynemouth parishioners to the quarter sessions held in Morpeth in 1658. The bid was successful and building began in 1659. If there had been any need for further proof that a new church was necessary it was provided later in the year when the roof of the old church in the Castle collapsed and killed several soldiers. Work on the new church proceeded slowly, affected among other things by an outbreak of plague in 1666 and the need for additional funding; nevertheless, the building was completed and Christ Church was consecrated in 1668. Although work on it was not very advanced when the monarchy was restored in 1660, its architectural form left no doubt that it had been designed in the days of the Puritans. One of only two parish churches built in Northumberland during the Interregnum, the original structure conformed to the simple style preferred by the Puritans.

According to one published source the original building was made of brick but Scott's meticulous research suggests that then as now it was built of stone. Most subsequent modifications to the building were to increase its capacity, but in 1788 a steeple with six bells was added.[20] Despite the alterations made over nearly 300 years, Adamson concluded that Christ Church 'remains to this day as it was from the beginning – a plain utilitarian structure'.[21] As a building, it has had few admirers but many critics. In 1849 Gibson described it as 'a nondescript structure … the style of which has been as far as possible removed from the ecclesiastical, and in the shape of which there is not one of the distinctive features of a church'.[22] During a discussion about church insurance in 1859, the then vicar interrupted a churchwarden with the remark, 'Upon my word, a good fire would be the greatest blessing to the church. I can assure you that I would not bring one can of water to put it out.'[23] Writing toward the end of the nineteenth century, Haswell was equally dismissive. He described it as 'perhaps the ugliest church in England', but then, in an attempt to be fair, added, 'an opinion deprecated by the folks of the town only to the extent of a pleading expostulation that it is not so bad as St Hilda over-the-water – an uncomely enough sister one had to admit'.[24]

Thomas Dockwray served as the first vicar from 1668 to 1672. He combined his role as a clergyman with that of a naval chaplain. In return for the latter role, Charles II required the University of Cambridge to 'admit Thomas Dockwray … to the degree of Doctor of Divinity, without the customary exercises, in reward of his faithful services as a chaplain in the fleet'.[25] Thomas did not enjoy his honorary title for long. He was killed at the Battle of Southwold Bay against the Dutch in 1672. The vacant living went to his son Stephen who remained vicar until his death in 1681.

By the time Christ Church opened, the upheavals nationally had weakened the authority and influence of the established church. The situation deteriorated further during the period that a second Thomas Dockwray (the son of Stephen) was vicar between 1682 and 1722. The 1689 Act of Toleration improved the situation of non-conformists to only a limited extent but any relaxation of the rules relating to non-conformity weakened the position of the established church and encouraged the emergence of a market for religion. In future years, vicars of Tynemouth had to contend with what was, in effect, a marketing onslaught from the local Methodists who went into the highways and byways to 'sell' their religious product to a market that had long been neglected by the previous, complacent, close to monopolistic supplier. This is why Gilbert described the period up to 1830 as an 'era of disaster' for the Anglican Church.[26] Even in the face of this increased competition, there seems to have been an unusual degree of complacency in the parish of Tynemouth. The Rev. Christopher Reed, vicar from 1830 to 1868, was absent from the parish for the last twelve years of his life and his brother John officiated at services – the same John Reed who had told the churchwarden that a good fire would be the greatest blessing to Christ Church!

In the parish of Tynemouth, this post-1830 period was accompanied by some not-so-little local difficulties. Originally, church rates had been raised to cover the cost of maintaining law and order, repairing the roads, and supporting the poor. In time, responsibility for such matters was transferred to the town council and poor law guardians, but church rates were still needed for the upkeep of the church. They were supposed to be levied on all parishioners, whether or not they regarded themselves as Anglicans, although in many parishes this obligation was 'honoured more in the breach than the observance'. That was not the case in Tynemouth. In 1852 Christ Church churchwardens acted like bailiffs and removed goods from the Quaker Meeting House to the value of the rates owed by the society's members. This heavy-handed action proved counter-productive. In retaliation, every item in the Christ Church accounts was scrutinised for irregularities. They were not difficult to detect and, as a result, payment of the church rates also became voluntary in the parish of Tynemouth.[27]

Old Dissent

At the time of Henry VIII's break with Rome, there was a wider challenge to Catholicism from the protest movement now known as the Protestant Reformation. Critics complained that Catholic worship was empty ritual, that many priests were lax or corrupt and that Popes, and that their bishops tended to act more like secular kings and princes than Christ's disciples. Christians were increasingly faced with a stark choice: continue to be Catholic, or embrace one of the emerging strands of protest against it. Such decisions were not solely private matters. They were intimately associated with the struggle for power between and within nation states and for many people became a matter of life or death.

Old Dissent is a label for those English denominations outside the Roman Catholic Church and the Church of England which have their roots in the Protestant Reformation.* Although the members of these groups welcomed the break with Rome, they did not welcome the replacement of one religious hierarchy with another. What they had in common was a conviction that local congregations should not submit to the authority of bishops – whether Roman Catholic or Anglican. Presbyterians were prepared to submit to the rulings of a regional or national synod of elders. Congregationalists and Baptists insisted that local congregations should be completely autonomous. George Fox's followers, popularly known as the Quakers, went still further and emphasised the principle of personal autonomy.

It was the conviction that the Church of England would never provide a form of church government in which everyone had even a nominally equal say that helped prompt the 1620 voyage of the Pilgrim Fathers in the *Mayflower* to found a colony on the other side of the Atlantic. It must have seemed that their dangerous venture had been unnecessary when puritan Protestants gained political ascendancy in England and set about imposing their religious will on the rest of the country. However, this period was short-lived and with Cromwell's death and the restoration of the monarchy, the religious pendulum swung back in the opposite direction. In 1662, at the midpoint of the period between the conception and consecration of Christ Church, Parliament passed an Act of Uniformity that imposed the use of the Book of Common Prayer on all churches and insisted that clergy subscribe to official Anglican doctrine. A deadline of 24 August 1662 was set when all ministers were required to conform – or face the consequences of their non-conformity. Over 1,700 ministers refused to comply and were ejected from their homes as well as their churches. More restrictions followed. The Conventicle Act made it illegal for the ejected ministers to meet for worship and the Five Mile Act required that they live more than five miles from their old congregations. Some ministers ended up in prison for failing to observe the rules.†

Although the old dissenting groups that emerged proved influential, Gilbert estimates that, even at their peak around 1700, no more than 5 per cent of the population belonged to them and that by 1740 support had fallen to about half that figure.[28] So, although an investigation by Daniel Neal, in 1715–16, estimated that there were about 1,150 congregations of dissenting Protestants in England and Wales, most must have been small.

---

* The label distinguishes them from New Dissent churches founded later in the eighteenth and nineteenth centuries.

† The most famous was John Bunyan, author of the allegorical *Pilgrim's Progress*, who spent several years of his life in jail for his non-conformity.

Neal labelled 673 of the congregations Quaker, 638 Presbyterian, 333 Baptist and 203 Independent (Congregationalist).* By the nineteenth century, Presbyterian numbers had declined although Baptist and Congregational numbers increased. Quaker numbers were also in decline but exercised much greater social influence than would be expected from the size of their membership.†

Presbyterians and Congregationalists
The roots of Presbyterianism in North Shields can be traced back to 1662.[29] Among the local Anglican ministers ejected from their parishes because they refused to conform were Alexander Gordon, vicar of Tynemouth; William Henderson, vicar of Earsdon; and John Lomax, vicar of Wooler.[30] Lomax chose to settle with his family in North Shields where he made a living as a surgeon and set up the town's first apothecary's shop.[31] He also continued to preach.[32] At first his congregation met in secret some distance from the town but, in 1672, he obtained a licence to be an 'independent' teacher. Although never imprisoned, in 1682 he was fined £5 (the equivalent of about £8,000 in 2014) for preaching and illegally keeping a conventicle – an unauthorised building for religious meetings.[33] The first known regular Presbyterian meeting-house used by Lomax and his followers was a small stone building on what later became known as the Magnesia Bank.‡ A larger chapel was erected off Bell Street, a section of the Low Street, in the early eighteenth century. Lomax remained in North Shields until his death in 1694, six years after the accession of William and Mary and the relaxation of the laws against Protestant non-conformists.

A theological dispute divided the congregation in the mid-eighteenth century when the then minister became sympathetic to Unitarian beliefs, such as that the notion of the Trinity was without biblical foundation and that Jesus was an exceptional man rather than the God-made-man Christ of Christian orthodoxy. Those who preferred traditional Presbyterian doctrines established their own church in 1759 and became affiliated to the Church of Scotland. When their numbers grew, they moved to a new building (called the High Meeting to distinguish it from the Unitarian Low Meeting) on the

---

* The term Independent came into use in the seventeenth century and was in use in England until the end of the eighteenth century. It relates to those churches we now know as Congregational.

† As early as 1758, they protested against the slave trade and subsequently dissociated themselves from any members who were involved in it or who owned slaves. Although the trade in slaves was banned in 1807, the institution of slavery was not abolished within the British Empire until 1834. Quakers were also actively involved in the demand for penal reform.

‡ The Magnesia Bank was a bank in the geographical sense though, to confuse matters, the public house now called the Magnesia Bank occupies a building that was once a financial bank, that of Lambton & Co. The original Presbyterian meeting house became a bakery.

'Scotch' church (now the Salvation Army Citadel), Howard Street. Built in 1810 this John Dobson designed 'High Meeting' Presbyterian church, which was affiliated to the Church of Scotland, is now the Salvation Army Citadel.

AUTHOR PHOTOGRAPH

Ropery Banks above the New Quay. In 1810 they moved again; this time to a still surviving, imposing John Dobson building in Howard Street, with accommodation for 700. Affiliation to the Church of Scotland came with the stipulation that the minister must be a licentiate of that church and it was that which gave it its popular name of the Scotch Church.

In 1818 theological differences led to a further split, and St Andrew's chapel opened in adjacent Camden Street with seating for 650. In 1822 it joined the recently formed Durham and Northumberland Congregational Union. Although Congregationalism was part of the Old Dissent movement, its main growth period came in the eighteenth and nineteenth centuries, a period more closely associated with New Dissent. The Congregational Union went from having 229 churches in England and Wales in 1718 to 3,244 by 1851.

A subsequent difference of opinion in the Church of Scotland, about how much independence churches should enjoy, prompted a shift in the affiliation of the original Howard Street congregation. In the 'Disruption' of 1843, 451 of 1,203 ministers left, together with a third of the lay members, and set up the Free Church of Scotland. The congregation in North Shields shared the minority view and disassociated themselves from the Church of Scotland but chose to switch their allegiance to the newly formed Presbyterian Church in England.

Despite its nickname, most of the members of the Howard Street 'Scotch' church were English. However, another church in North Shields did cater for a primarily Scottish congregation. In 1781 several Scottish families living in North and South Shields, who otherwise had to travel to Newcastle to find a pattern of worship that suited them, established a branch in North Shields. From 1783 they met in a disused North Shields theatre but moved to a small chapel at the foot of Church Way in 1788. At this stage, the membership was large enough for a separate congregation to emerge in South Shields. The North Shields church moved to a location between Church Street and Queen Street until 1812, when it transferred to premises on the Ropery Banks. Their next base, in 1821, was a substantial building on Lower Norfolk Street, before finally moving into their John Dobson designed church in Northumberland Square, with seating for 600. It became popularly known as the *Square Pres*.

Baptists

Baptists, like Congregationalists, insisted that local congregations should be autonomous. They differed by emphasising the importance of the baptism of believers rather than infants too young to make a decision for themselves. The first reference to a Baptist congregation in North Shields is in 1798, by which time the new dissenting movement of Methodism was already underway. With the support of a Newcastle congregation, a church was established and met in a house in Walker Place. The following year, the congregation moved to a rented hall in Stephenson Street. It prospered sufficiently for their rented premises to be purchased and improved in 1804. By 1845, with a membership of 215 and a 150 strong Sunday School, supported by 30 teachers, it was sufficiently well endowed to buy an additional plot of land in nearby Howard Street. It commissioned John Dobson to design a church, with provision for the total immersion of adults. It opened in 1847 with the Stephenson Street premises retained for a time for both the Sunday School and the day school then in operation during the week.*

The Society of Friends (Quakers)

The origins of the Society of Friends lie in a group known as the Seekers who remained outside established denominations because 'they could discover no form of church government which could claim divine origin'.[34] It was George Fox, an itinerant preacher, who, despite insisting the only ecclesiastical authority was Christ, and that his authority should be felt at the level of the individual, succeeded in creating an acceptable organisational framework. Fox had already established contact with sympathizers in and around North Shields five years before establishing his missionary

---

* The church moved its Sunday School to the Howard Street premises in 1902. In 1923 it sold its old premises in Stephenson Street and acquired additional accommodation adjacent to the Howard Street church.

Shiels to Shields

base at Swarthmoor Hall in 1652.* In 1647 he was entertained by John, William and Mary Dove and when in the area again in 1658 wrote: 'A very good meeting we had at Lieutenant Dove's, where many were turned to the Lord and His teaching.'[35] In 1661, after Parliament had passed legislation in an attempt to suppress the Quakers who were deemed 'dangerous to the public peace and safety', the Doves and other local Quakers were arrested and imprisoned for a month in Tynemouth Castle. Undeterred, John Dove made public his association with the Quakers by setting aside a piece of land in Cullercoats to be used for the burial of members of the Society of Friends. The first recorded burial there was in 1661; the last was in 1818. When Tynemouth Corporation wanted to extend John Street to join with Whitley Lane, it could only be achieved at the expense of the burial plots. The 'key-keeper' (who had relatives buried in the little cemetery) objected but the Borough's employees ignored his protestations and the headstones and human remains were transferred to Preston Cemetery.

Persecution of the Quakers continued but despite, or perhaps because of it, they consolidated their position. A growing sense of solidarity among the originally scattered local groups encouraged the formation of a loose federation. The building of meeting houses which had begun in the 1650s continued and when Fox, who had been imprisoned between 1664 and 1666 was released, he spent much of his time organising monthly meetings and, in 1678, a national representative body. Sporadic persecutions continued for some time. For example, in 1681, Richard Pinder of North Shields was brought before the quarter sessions charged with hosting a Quaker meeting. But, within a decade, the worst of the persecution was over, and the restriction on Quaker meetings lifted when William and Mary came to the throne. In 1694 a newly built brick building was opened near the Bull Ring. To complement it, a plot of land for Quaker burials was bought in Coach Lane in 1729. It remained in use after meetings were transferred to a building in Stephenson Street in 1801, with room for 300. An additional burial ground, was opened opposite it in 1811.† The Stephenson Street meeting house was later enlarged in 1849.[36]

During the nineteenth century, there were several notable Quaker families in North Shields. They included John Walker, a ship-owner who came from Whitby (and to whose company James (later Captain)

---

*   Quakers today have a reputation for their quiet, inoffensive manner and personal piety but in their early years were prepared to shout their message from the proverbial rooftops.

†   Each Meeting was asked to provide a separate burial ground as 'a testimony against the superstitious idolizing of those places called holy ground'. Both the Stephenson Street and the older burial ground near the Bull Ring were subsequently closed under the provisions of the 1854 Burial Act and from then on Quakers were buried in a designated section of the public cemetery. The ownership of the Coach Lane burial ground remained in Quaker hands until 2013 when it was sold to a developer and eight town houses erected on the site. The 244 interred bodies were moved to Preston Cemetery.

Cook was apprenticed). The Walker family occupied the largest house in Dockwray Square. The same John Walker helped his fellow Quaker John Richardson set up his tannery. There are other comparable examples of business success among North Shields' Quakers which led at times to uncomfortable debates about whether or not the way in which their success had been achieved was at odds with Quaker principles. For example, many Quaker shipowners were ostracised when their ships were involved in military action. Boyce records that when members of some previously well-known Quaker families were asked in later years why they were no longer Friends, they explained that their fathers had been 'disowned for carrying guns on board their ships'. Such breaches of Quaker principles led to a number of probably apocryphal stories. One of the most popular was that of a Friend who took to his cabin to show that he was not in any way associated with the battle about to ensue. Watching from the cabin window, he saw that his shipmates were about to make a big mistake and at that point his seamanship prevailed over his Quakerism. He shouted to the man at the helm, 'I have nothing to do with it, but if thou dost mean to hit her, then starboard, John!'[37]

New Dissent

Whereas Old Dissent developed in the seventeenth century, New Dissent developed in the eighteenth and nineteenth centuries. It was primarily a reaction against the Church of England.

Methodism

New Dissent is most closely associated with Methodism and the brothers John and Charles Wesley, the sons of an Anglican minister. John returned to Oxford University as a Fellow following his ordination. He and similar minded Christians met regularly for Bible study and prayer, and their devout, methodical behaviour was so unusual that they were dubbed the Holy Club or Methodists. Their behaviour was also unusual because they attempted to provide spiritual comfort to those on the margins of society, such as paupers and prisoners.

In 1735 the Wesley brothers went as ministers to the American colonies. The posting was of pivotal importance because during the voyage they encountered members of the religious group known as Moravians who had broken with Rome more than a century earlier than Luther. The Wesley brothers renewed their contact with the Moravians on their return to England and, within days, each had undergone a profound religious experience. The following year, Wesley organised the first Methodist Society and started to preach in the open air. During the following half-century he became an extraordinary traveller, covering huge distances to preach his evangelical message of personal salvation, often several times a day and sometimes to thousands of people. It was a propitious time for his evangelical message. The

Church of England seemed remote to most ordinary people.* In contrast, Wesley reached out to them and asserted that they could use their free will to secure salvation if they had faith in God and followed the teachings of Christ in their daily lives. As a committed Anglican, he famously insisted, 'I live and die a member of the Church of England', and initially expected his followers to attend their local parish church. He saw Methodist societies as complementary to conventional church membership. But, in parishes where the Anglican Church was weak, there was a tendency for Methodists to regard their society as their primary home. Despite Wesley's initial hopes, Methodism drifted inexorably towards becoming a separate denomination. As early as 1740, when his followers were denied communion by Anglican clergy, he administered it himself in his own meeting houses. Then, in 1784, he took another significant step when he ordained two ministers who had been rejected by the Bishop of London. Such acts of defiance, and the strength of the revivalist movement he had helped create, made a split from the Anglican Church inevitable.

Wesley visited North Shields in 1759, 1761, 1764, 1766, 1780 and 1788.[38] The first recorded Methodist chapel was opened in Milburn Place in 1786 but within three years there were the first signs of the factionalism that was to plague the development of Methodism. The members of the Milburn Place chapel declared themselves independent of the Newcastle circuit, following a dispute over their right to refuse the preachers sent to them: this was a foretaste of things to come at the national level after Wesley's death in 1791.

Wesley had exercised tight personal control over the emerging Methodist movement.[39] Indeed Currie described Wesley as 'Methodism's executive, legislature and judiciary'.[40] Aware of the problems that would arise after his death, he appointed 100 preachers as a Methodist Conference to be the heirs to his authority. However, with the need to respond to such contentious issues as the growing demand for political reform, conflict within Methodism was inevitable.[41] Wesley's own political instincts had been deeply conservative, but many of his followers favoured political reform and this fundamental division of opinion found expression in arguments about how Methodism itself should be governed.[42] The disputes became increasingly focused on Alexander Kilham who, as well as urging further separation from Anglicanism, and a closer affiliation with the Old Dissenting tradition, demanded more lay control within Methodism. Kilham was eventually expelled in 1796. Other preachers left with him and together formed The Methodist New Connexion (MNC), in which administrative responsibilities

---

* At the beginning of the nineteenth century, 7,000 parishes had no Anglican priest and 50 per cent were administered by curates on behalf of 'non-resident' incumbents. In others, Anglican priests did little more than go through the motions of ministering to their flock, and it was not uncommon for communion to be held only a few times each year.

were shared jointly by clergy and lay people. The Methodists of Milburn Place were among those who joined the MNC but in the country as a whole it grew slowly in the face of continued opposition from the original Wesleyan Methodists who sometimes used litigation to prevent the MNC taking over the chapels built before the split. That did not happen in the case of the Milburn Place chapel and in 1808 the Wesleyan Methodists built their own 1,200 seat church in Howard Street (which later became the Howard Hall theatre then cinema). A second MNC congregation was established on the bankside in Bell Street in 1801, which, in 1838, moved to the newly built Salem Church in Linskill Street.[43]

The next significant splits represented further reactions to the religious and political conservatism of the Methodist Conference. From 1820 until 1851, it was presided over by Jarez Bunting, who opposed religious revivalism and political radicalism and sought to expel Methodists who refused to comply with his position. He insisted that 'Methodism was as much opposed to democracy as to sin'.[44] He favoured recruiting members from the more respectable sections of society; denounced female preachers and even had reservations about the teaching of reading and writing in Sunday Schools.[45] During his period of office there were further splits. Tent Methodists went their own way as did Bible Christians. The latter were concentrated in the South West but the migration of Cornish miners to the North East brought their special brand of Methodism with them.[46] The next departure was the most significant. In 1807 Hugh Bourne and William Clowes held American-style, day-long, open-air revivalist meetings and incurred the wrath of the Methodist establishment who refused to admit their converts into membership of the church. When Bourne and Clowes refused to stop holding 'camp' meetings they too were expelled. They retaliated in 1811 by setting up the Primitive Methodist Church. The name was chosen with care to suggest continuity between their way of preaching and the open-air meetings prominent in Wesley's day.

William Clowes first visited North Shields in 1821 at the invitation of disaffected Wesleyan Methodists.[47] A return visit in 1822 at the instigation of Joseph Peart, a Wesleyan Methodist local preacher, gives us a revealing insight into the differences within Methodism at the time.

> I had a very strong debate with a professor of the dead languages, who, as well as myself, belonged to the society of Old Methodists. While contending with him in vindication of the rationality and great utility of such a work as had been effected in North Shields (about five years previous to that time) by an extraordinary outpouring of the Holy Ghost, he (by way of derision) said: 'You should have been a Ranter.' It powerfully wrought on my mind, as I sat in the room, that it was my indispensable duty to send for the 'Ranters' (so called). The circumstance was very singular, for I had never heard, nor

never seen, any of them. I was not disobedient to the heavenly call but wrote for William Clowes, who shortly arrived at our house, and stopped till the cause got established.[48]

A class was formed after Clowes' first meeting. Clowes preached again on the following two Sundays, with the result that another nine members joined. Another class was formed shortly afterward 'at the upper end of the town'. From then on, the Primitive Methodists met in the Union Street premises that had previously been used by the Catholic regiment based at Tynemouth Castle. The Primitive Methodist style of preaching earned it the nickname, the Ranters' Chapel. From there, missions were sent to other parts of Northumberland, including the rapidly expanding coal-mining communities in the area. The message and style of Primitive Methodism was well received by the miners and their families, and societies sprang up in almost all the many pit villages in the area. The Primitive Methodists' behaviour as well as their religious message helped to consolidate their position. For example, during the cholera outbreak of 1832-33, 'in North Shields the preachers prayed, ate, drank and slept among the dying and the dead'.[49]

Another group of expulsions and resignations led to the formation of the Protestant Methodists in 1827, a body which joined forces with other breakaway groups who wanted increased independence for local circuits in 1834. A suggestion that the new alliance unite with the MNC was rejected and instead a new body formed, the Wesleyan Methodist Association (WMA). About a thousand members of existing Wesleyan Methodist chapels joined the WMA and by 1837 it was 21,000 strong.[50] Other critics of Bunting's regime continued the fight within the original body. It culminated in what has been described as 'the declaration of the last and greatest war in Methodism'.[51] The reformers demanded the right to do what they wanted in their own chapels, but behind this formulation lay more profound issues relating to the rights of ordinary people in relation to their social betters. The struggle came to a head in 1850 when the new Conference President Thomas Jackson demanded that, 'Everywhere persons taking part in agitative meetings must be expelled'. The outcome was that over 100,000 members were excluded or forced to resign.[52]

This purge produced a quick reaction in North Shields. The Wesleyan Association, the Protestant Methodists and another small group known as the Arminian Methodists came together. Initially, they met in the Norfolk Street Temperance Hall until they built a new chapel in Howard Street in 1856 opposite the Scotch church, coinciding with the formal establishment of the United Methodist Free (UMF) Churches, which incorporated these and other reform groups. The North Shields Circuit report to the UMFC's magazine in 1859 was decidedly up-beat. For example, it described the fortnight of revival services held in North Shields in these terms.

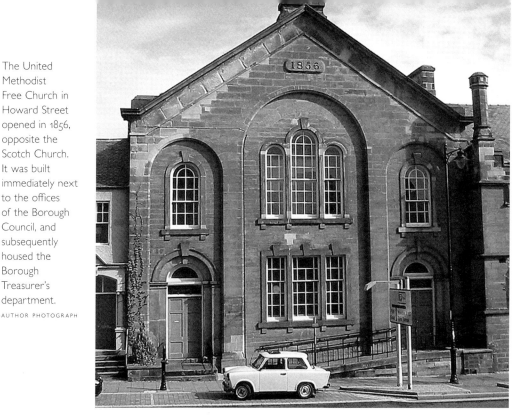

The meetings were well attended, well sustained by praying men, and the Divine Presence was powerfully felt. There was little or no noise in the meetings, but the moral tone of the services was deep and subduing. The singing was hearty, the prayers were fervent and earnest, and the good is now manifesting itself. Nearly every class in the Society has received some additions.[53]

Religious institutions in the mid-nineteenth century

A plan to include a question about personal religious affiliation in the 1851 census was abandoned after opposition from Anglican bishops. Instead, a census of religious worship was conducted to provide information on attendance at services. The subsequent 1854 report showed that there had been a total of almost 12 million church *attendances* at morning, afternoon and evening services. Allowing for some people attending more than once, it was estimated that 7.6 million people had been to church on 30 March 1851. On the assumption that only about 58 per cent of the population would have been free to attend church (because about 42 per cent were too young, too infirm or obliged to work on the day of the count), that suggested that over 50 per cent of the eligible population had been to church: a huge figure by today's standards. Applying the same assumptions to the Borough of Tynemouth's returns, suggests that of the eligible population of 37,263, 46 per cent had attended church. My attempt to extract the corresponding figures for North Shields in particular proved unsuccessful. The available microfilms of the returns are indecipherable and I was denied access to the originals by the National Archives. Nevertheless, the overall findings are still of interest.

Table 8.1   Church provision and attendance in
the Borough of Tynemouth, 30 March 1851

Churches or denominations	No.	Total seats	Morning service	Afternoon service	Evening service
Roman Catholic	2	700	220	95	0
Church of England	12	6,965	3,706	1,535	1,719
Presbyterian Ch. in England	3	1,500	1,150	0	465
United Presbyterian Church	4	1,273	872	474	392
Independents	4	1,815	860	84	777
Baptists	1	690	220	0	260
Society of Friends	1	400	78	0	85
Wesleyan Methodists	25	6,512	2,055	1,035	2,884
Methodist New Connexion	7	2,066	840	145	1,057
Primitive Methodists	13	2,686	526	1,003	1,617
Wesleyan Reformers	11	2,132	931	414	1,433
Undefined	2	200	0	15	45
Latter Day Saints	1	/	20	30	50
Jews	1	30	20	17	17
Total	87	26,969	11,498	4,847	10,801

Table 8.1 shows the absolute numbers attending churches in the Borough on 30 March 1851. Table 8.2 shows, in percentage terms, the relationship between seating capacity and actual attendance. Unfortunately, a failure to submit an attendance figure for a large Catholic church (presumably St Cuthbert's) means that Roman Catholics numbers cannot be compared with the rest. Of the three main Protestant traditions, it is striking how closely seating capacities paralleled attendances. Anglican churches had 25.8 per cent of capacity compared to 23.8 per cent of attendances. Old dissenting churches had 21.1 per cent of the capacity and 19.1 per cent of the attendances. The breakdown within the old dissenting traditions were 10.3 and 11.2 per cent for Presbyterians; 6.7 and 5.8 per for Congregationalists (Independents); 2.6 and 1.6 per cent for Baptists and 1.5 and 0.5 per cent for the Society of Friends. The combined capacity in Methodist churches was 49.7 compared to 46.9 per cent of the attendances. The breakdown here was

24.1 and 20.0 per cent for Wesleyan Methodists; 10.0 and 10.5 per cent for Primitive Methodists; 7.9 and 9.3 per cent for Wesleyan Reformers and 7.7 and 6.8 per cent for the Methodist New Connexion. With the exception of the Baptists and Society of Friends, the total attendance during the day of the census was very close to or exceeded the total number of seats available for each denomination.

Table 8.2   Church attendance in the Borough of
Tynemouth as a percentage of seats, 30 March 1851

Churches or denominations	Total seats	% seats	Total attendance	% attendance	Attendance as % of seats
Roman Catholic	700	2.6	315	1.1	45.0
Church of England	6,965	25.8	6,960	23.8	99.9
Presbyterian Church in England	1,500	5.6	1,615	5.4	107.7
United Presbyterian Church	1,273	4.7	1,738	5.8	136.5
Independents	1,815	6.7	1,721	5.8	94.8
Baptists	690	2.6	480	1.6	69.6
Society of Friends	400	1.5	163	0.5	40.8
Wesleyan Methodists	6,512	24.1	5,974	20.0	91.8
Methodist New Connexion	2,066	7.7	2,042	6.8	98.9
Primitive Methodists	2,686	10.0	3,146	10.5	117.1
Wesleyan Reformers	2,132	7.9	2,778	9.3	130.3
Undefined	200	0.8	60	0.2	30.0
Latter Day Saints	?	?	100	0.3	?
Jews	30	0.1	54	0.2	180.0
Total	26,969	100	29,924	100	111.0

Religion and social class

From the standpoint of the twenty-first century, the 1851 church attendance figures seem very high. Yet Horace Mann, who analysed the data, considered them low: 'The most important fact which this investigation ... brings before us is, unquestionably, the number of non-attenders. ... A sadly formidable portion of the English people are habitual neglecters of the public ordinances of religion.'[54]

Mann went on to claim that most of these 'neglecters' were in the labouring classes. If true, church attendance among the smaller middle class must have been correspondingly higher, lending support to Thompson's assertion that 'regular church or chapel going was universal among the middle classes ... not to attend was scandalous or bohemian'.[55] What Mann did not appear to consider were variations in attendance between sections of the 'labouring' classes: an important consideration because more recent analyses suggest that, at least in non-conformist churches, skilled workers were more often church members than had previously been assumed.[56]

Disquiet about the under-representation of working-class people in church congregations represented more than a concern for the fate of their immortal souls. It was widely assumed that ungodliness was associated with social unrest – a view consistent with Marx's assertion that religion was the 'opium of the masses'. This was a source of particular unease in the first half of the nineteenth century when there was widespread fear that revolution might spread from the continent to Britain. Mann himself, it should be emphasised, was not censorious. For the period, he was unusually empathetic. Long before the term secularisation became common currency among sociologists, Mann used it to suggest that its growth was encouraged by the way in which ordinary people had to struggle to make ends meet. The exigencies of their daily lives predisposed them to think only in terms of their immediate problems and ignore issues relating to the possibility of a life hereafter.[57]

Mann outlined four hypotheses to explain why working-class people were reluctant to attend church. The first was that working-class people felt at best ill-at-ease and at worst humiliated when they did attend. McLeod put the same point more recently: 'The poor who did attend such churches were likely to feel themselves marginal members of the congregation. … Hierarchical seating arrangements emphasised their inferiority.'[58]

In the case of Christ Church, hierarchical seating was introduced when the church was built. Individuals were encouraged to contribute to the cost by paying for one or more pews and then acted as if they owned them, in some cases recouping their contribution by selling or even auctioning them off. People moving away from the district often retained their pews but rented them out. By the middle of the century some parishioners had accumulated several pews and those not used by their family and servants were sub-let for the best rent available. Writing of the period when he lived in North Shields and attended Christ Church, Haswell described the contrast between 'owned' pews, and those available for those who could not afford them, in the following way.

> On the ground-floor were pens – they could not be called pews – for the poor; down the centre of the main aisle, conspicuously exposed to all present and securely isolated, ranged short benches in which the school-boys, the paupers, the lame, the halt, the blind and, separately, the workhouse children – in short, all objects of charity. For the rest, as rigorously preserved as game coverts, were the square wells over the high sides of which occupants glared at the hapless visitor who in nervous bewilderment sought a place in the House of God.[59]

An 1840 attempt to end the practice of 'owning' pews led to stormy public meetings. Change came only in 1869 when the old box pews were removed.[60] Interestingly, when work on St Augustin's church began in 1881, the loan secured from the Incorporated Church Building Society included the condition that 'all the sittings are for the free use of the parishioners'.[61]

Charging rents was not limited to the established Anglican Church. In the Borough of Tynemouth as a whole, 55 per cent of seats were (to use Mann's term) 'appropriated'. To sit in any of the 45 per cent of 'free' seats was an indication of inferiority in the very place where all men and women were allegedly equal in the sight of God. As Table 8.3 shows, the highest proportion of appropriated seats was in the old dissenting churches, ranging from 71.9 per cent to 93.3 per cent. The proportion in both the Catholic and Anglican churches was 61.3 per cent. It was only among the Methodists that the proportion fell below 50 per cent. The range there went from 14.4 per cent for the Wesleyan Reformers to as high as 71.3 per cent for the Methodist New Connexion. That latter figure helps to explain why William Booth, the founder of the Salvation Army, was criticised for welcoming 'riff-raff' to his services when he was a Methodist New Connexion minister. It was suggested that such people should enter and leave by the rear door of the chapel and once inside remain behind the pulpit rather than sit with

Table 8.3 Appropriated seats in churches in the
Borough of Tynemouth, 30 March 1851

Churches or denominations	Free seats	Appropriated seats	Total seats	% appropriated seats
Roman Catholic	271	429	700	61.3
Church of England	2,480	4,265	6,965	61.3
Presbyterian Ch. in England	100	1,400	1,500	93.3
United Presbyterian Church	157	1,116	1,273	87.7
Independents	510	1,305	1,815	71.9
Baptists	100	590	690	85.5
Society of Friends	400	0	400	0.0
Wesleyan Methodists	3,508	3,004	6,512	46.1
Methodist New Connexion	592	1,474	2,066	71.3
Primitive Methodists	1,733	953	2,686	35.5
Wesleyan Reformers	1,826	306	2,132	14.4
Undefined	200	0	200	0.0
Latter Day Saints	?	?	?	
Jews	6	24	30	80.0
Total	11,883	14,866	26,969	55.1

the rest of the congregation. Even the most apparently proletarian of the Methodist factions, the Primitive Methodists, had 36 per cent of its seats appropriated, not markedly out of line with the figure of 46 per cent for the more conservative Wesleyan Methodists.

Mann insisted that whatever the disadvantages of appropriated seats, getting rid of them would not make a significant difference. Just being in the same place as middle-class people was enough to make working-class people feel uncomfortable because 'their tastes and habits are so wholly uncongenial with the views and customs of the higher orders'. He then offered a solution reminiscent of the arguments used to justify separate provision for black people in the USA during the days of segregation.

> The same disposition ... will forever operate to hinder their attendance at religious services, unless such services can be devised as shall become exclusively *their own*. ... It has consequently been proposed to meet so far the prejudices of the working population; and to strive to get them gradually to establish places of worship for themselves. Experiments have been already put in operation with the persons lowest in the social scale; and Ragged Churches are in several places making a successful start. In several places, too, among Dissenters, special services in halls and lecture rooms are being held, intended wholly for the working class; and the success of these proceedings seems to prove that multitudes will readily frequent such places, where of course there is a total absence of all class distinctions, who would never enter the exclusive looking chapel.[62]

The extraordinary notion that separate religious provision for the working class could be equated with 'a total absence of all class distinctions' is reminiscent not only of the arguments used to justify segregation in the USA but also that of apartheid in South Africa.

Mann's second hypothesis was that the poor were alienated because religious institutions seemed indifferent to the social conditions of the poor. The third hypothesis was that the less well-off people in British society doubted the motives of clergymen and other ministers when they tried to encourage members of the working class to attend church. At worst, it was believed that ministers wanted to increase their flock for primarily pecuniary reasons. A more generous interpretation was that they did so only because it was part of their professional duty – not because they really cared. Mann's fourth and final hypothesis was that the conditions in which working-class people lived were actually inimical to religious sentiments.

> The vice and filth which riot in their crowded dwellings, and from which they cannot fly to any less degraded homes; what awfully effective teaching, it is said, do these supply in opposition to the few

infrequent lessons which the Christian minister or missionary, after much exertion, may impart.[63]

Based on his four hypotheses, Mann recommended that 'the people who refuse to hear the gospel in the church must have it brought to them in their own haunts'.[64] There is considerable evidence of such missionary activity in North Shields in the second half of the nineteenth century. The following examples are not comprehensive but give an indication of the scale of missionary work and the range of churches engaged in it. In 1852, the Town and River Mission was set up in a small room on the Low Street. That was followed by the Mission to Seamen in 1857. In 1860 the Wesleyan Methodists set up a mission in an old tenement room in the Bull Ring and then moved to larger premises three years later. In 1861 the Mount Pleasant Mission was established in Milburn Place. In 1864 Christ Church set up St Faith's mission, originally in the premises of the Seamen's Loyal Standard Association and eventually, after several moves over the next 30 years, to a chapel in Hudson Street where it remained until it closed in 1955. In 1866 the United Presbyterian Mission, on the Union Stairs in North Shields, began a penny saving bank to try to encourage thrift among the people in the area. The following year, a Scandinavian Lutheran church was built on Borough Road for Norwegian seamen visiting the Tyne. It was hoped it would enable them to resist the 'temptations to which seamen are subjected in British ports'.[65] It was probably not a coincidence that in the same year 'Bible women' from the Town Mission went out and invited 'street girls [i.e. prostitutes]' in for supper. The Low Lights Mission obtained new premises in Northumberland Street in 1880 (and, remarkably, had a single secretary, Miss Edith Moffat, for at least 65 years). The Baptist Church opened a mission in Milburn Place in 1882. The Seamen's Mission was opened in Mill Dam in 1885 and, five years later, The Evangelistic Mission was founded on the Wooden Bridge Bank with an associated Bible Class and Sunday School in Camden Lane. Then, in 1903, the Town Mission built new premises at the southern-most point of Lower Rudyerd Street, close to the edge of the Bank Top.

Churches offered more than Sunday services. They provided a wide range of diverting activities for weekdays, many of which had no overt religious content. Although provided primarily for members, non-members were welcomed in the hope that their involvement would encourage them to become regular church members. McLeod notes, for example, that 'many poor families came to depend on the free breakfasts and other benefits and treats provided by churches and chapels'.[66] Although some people may have focused their social lives on one particular church, others took advantage of what was available, irrespective of denomination, especially when, in the second half of the nineteenth century, concerts, excursions and evening classes were on offer and, from around the 1880s, churches were actively promoting 'healthy' sports such as football, cricket and boxing. Large numbers of working-class children were happy to attend Sunday School because of the benefits to be derived from this single hour per week investment. An elderly professor of sociology once told me how he and his friends joined several Sunday schools after first researching how many attendances were necessary to qualify for their annual Christmas parties and summer outings!

One possible reason for the subsequent decline in church attendance is that in later periods churches had relatively less to offer in terms of diverting activities.

> The many extrinsic factors that had increased church membership at attendance for much of the nineteenth century had largely disappeared, and the churches were forced to rely on the intrinsic attractions of their message and of the fellowship they offered. … Smaller families meant that fewer women were perpetually tied to the kitchen. But where the mother of six in 1880 had gratefully seized the opportunity of escaping from home to an occasional Mothers' Meeting, the mother of one in 1930 found a much wider range of commercial operators competing for her increased leisure time.[67]

Consolidation and decline

In the closing decades of the nineteenth century and in the twentieth century there was an absolute and proportionate fall in church attendance. Initially there was continued growth in the Protestant dissenting traditions, but over the longer term they have lost ground and the pendulum has swung back a little in favour of the Catholic and Anglican traditions. These general trends have been evident in North Shields too but particular church openings and closures have also reflected shifts in population: initially from the old town by the river on to the Bank Top and then, in the twentieth century, to the suburbs.

Roman Catholicism

The gradual removal of discrimination against Catholics culminated in the 1829 Catholic Relief Act. Although Clark's claim, that removing the supremacy of Anglicanism fundamentally undermined the cultural hegemony of the old elite, is generally considered to be overstated, there can be little doubt about the symbolic significance of the legislation. However, as with legislation against racial discrimination in the twentieth century, passing an Act in Parliament did not change the views of people on the street or their behaviour in private. Many continued to see 'popery' as a threat. In the case of North Shields, such anti-Catholic sentiment was reinforced by a more general prejudice against the Irish immigrants who arrived in the town in significant numbers following the potato famine in Ireland – where they had been faced by the stark choice of emigrate or starve. The underlying prejudice was brought to the surface in the late 1860s when William Murphy, who was touring the country giving anti-Catholic lectures, came to North Shields in 1869. His visit so stirred up religious and communal tensions that it precipitated rioting. Several hundred predominantly Irish residents attacked the hall where he was due to speak and some shots were fired into the building before the crowd was beaten back by the police. In the face of such opposition, the town authorities refused to allow Murphy to continue with his lectures. What they could not stop was a dramatic debate in the House of Commons which focused on an Englishman's right to free speech, in which the events in North Shields received a specific mention. The Liberal MP for Devonport was concerned that:

> At North Shields there was an attempt, not by a sudden, but by a concerted riot, to prevent him from delivering them. People came from a distance, across a ferry, with that deliberate object. Well, were they within the law? Of course they were breaking it. As each one joined the others for the purpose of taking a journey to create a tumult, every word they uttered and every step they took in furtherance of their object was a breach of the law. They were guilty of conspiracy to make a riot, and all the force of the law might be fairly invoked by any English citizen against whom they thus put themselves in array.[68]

In response, the Liberal MP for North Shields emphasised that:

> Murphy came to Tynemouth and delivered lectures which were exceedingly insulting to a large number of the inhabitants. The result was a riot. Murphy left the town, but returned again, and the Mayor thought it his duty to apply to the Home Secretary and, under the authority of an Act which was not obsolete, the right hon. Gentleman put a stop to Murphy's lectures in Tynemouth. That act of the Home Secretary had the approbation of the whole of the orderly and well-disposed inhabitants, whatever religious denomination they belonged to. Had Mr. Murphy confined himself to vindicating the doctrines of Protestantism his lectures would have been popular in Tynemouth; but he had insulted the Roman Catholics in a gross and aggravating manner.[69]

There was continued immigration into North Shields from Ireland in the latter half of the nineteenth century and an associated increase in the number of Roman Catholics in the town. This, and the higher rates of fertility in the then predominantly young immigrant Irish community, increased Catholic congregations significantly and encouraged the building of more Catholic churches. In Tynemouth, in 1871, the Catholic Church of Our Blessed Lady and St Oswin, was opened and mass celebrated in Tynemouth for the first time since the Reformation. During the twentieth century, four more Roman Catholic churches were built in and around North Shields. St Edward (the Confessor) in Whitley Bay came first in 1911; followed by St Joseph's in Balkwell in 1935, The Immaculate Heart of Mary in West Monkseaton in 1960 and St Mary's in Cullercoats in 1970. The original St Cuthbert's church in North Shields was replaced by a new St Cuthbert's church not far away on Albion Road in 1975. There is now a residential home for the elderly on the site of the original church.

The Established Church
An increase in the number of Anglican churches, clergymen and communicants after 1830 reflected an overall increase in the population not a proportionate growth in Anglicanism.[70] In North Shields, as the population increased and the town expanded in all directions, a single parish church was no longer adequate. Holy Trinity church was built on Coach Lane in 1836 to cater for the population to the west of the town where further major housing developments were to take place. In 1860 St Peter's was built at the bottom of Borough Road close to those who lived on or near the Low Street. In 1877, a proposal was made to build St Augustin's in Washington Terrace for the growing population on the former Linskill estate. Raising sufficient money proved difficult and when the church opened in June 1884 it was still without the planned chancel, tower, vestry or organ chamber. New parish churches were also built in the vicinity of North Shields. To the east, Holy Saviour's church was consecrated in Tynemouth in 1841. A temporary church was established in Percy Main in 1862 and land acquired the following year for the permanent St John the Evangelist church which is still in use. St Paul's was built in what is now Whitley Bay in 1864 and St George's, on the sea front at Cullercoats, followed in 1880.

This expansion in and around North Shields does not mean that all was well within local Anglicanism. Conflict arose with the emergence of the Oxford Movement which perceived the Church of England as a branch of the Roman Catholic Church, along with the Greek and Russian Orthodox churches. In many Anglican churches Catholic practices were re-introduced and holy communion became more central to church services. In 1853, a Christ Church curate preached a sermon in which he appeared to advocate a return to the Catholic belief in transubstantiation. That led to a petition being sent to the bishop by a group of parishioners, urging him not to ordain the curate because of his Roman Catholic sympathies. However, within a few years, when the Rev. Thomas Brutton became Vicar of Christ Church (1868–99), Christ Church became a high (as distinct from low evangelical)

St Peter's Church, built at the bottom of Borough Road in 1866 to serve the population in and around the Low Street. It closed in 1936 after a major slum-clearance programme had moved many people away from the area.

Anglican church. When there was similar shift in patterns of worship at Holy Trinity church, congregations increased, suggesting that the trend towards high Anglicanism was not without popular support.[71]

Changes within Anglicanism in North Shields in the twentieth century are in part associated with movements in population. The closure of St Peter's in 1936 coincided with a programme of slum clearance which robbed it of its congregation. By then, St Luke's Mission had been established in Balkwell. It was subsequently renamed St Peter's and a new church built on the site in 1938 as the population of the area increased. St Aidan's was built in Billy Mill in 1955 to cater for another new housing development. Similarly, the first Anglican service in the newly built Marden estate took place on Christmas morning 1954 but it was 1966 before St Hilda's church opened, at the interface between the Marden and Preston Grange estates. Further afield in Percy Main, the merger of St John's with the Methodist church in 1974, coincided with the displacement of population when a large section of the village was redeveloped. In contrast, the closure of Trinity Church in 1982, when it was still in a densely populated area, is more easily explained by a decline in religious observance. There had also been no significant change in the local population when, as an alternative to the closure of St Augustin's, it was merged with Christ Church in 1987, and a new parish of North Shields formed with a team ministry.

Old Dissent

By 1877, both the Northumberland Square and Howard Street Presbyterian churches had become members of The Presbyterian Church of England, making them, effectively, two churches of the same denomination scarcely 100 metres apart. Initially, the Howard Street congregation was larger but within ten years it had been overtaken by the Northumberland Square church. Both then went into a decline and eventually merged in 1949. At that point, the Northumberland Square church adopted the current name of St Columba's. It went on to build a new church on Verne Road in the Balkwell area in 1954. But All Saints survived only until 1986. The church has since been demolished and the site is now occupied by a block of flats.

Stephenson Street Congregational church in North Shields had its origins in the temperance campaign of the Wesleyan preacher John Broadbent. His enthusiastic followers initially met in a room over the George Tavern in Charlotte Street. When Broadbent moved, his congregation reformed itself as the Evangelistic Temperance church. It opened new premises in Stephenson Street in 1875 and became a Congregational church three years later, although just a short distance across Northumberland Square from the St Andrew's Congregational church at the top of Cambden Street. When St Andrews closed in 1947, the members joined the Stephenson Street church. Their building became a furniture salesroom. The origins of the Northumberland Street Congregational church lie in a mission in the 1870s to what was regarded as a deprived area near the Low Light. New building

St Andrews, Camden Street, as it looked after it closed in 1947 and was converted to a furniture mart.

work was undertaken in 1886 and 1902, giving it a 250 seat capacity. In 1929 it became a Congregational church in its own right but closed its doors for the last time in 1964. Its members too merged with the congregation of the Stephenson Street church. The Northumberland Street building became a timber merchant's. At that point, the Stephenson Street church adopted the name St Andrew's. It survived only until 1973 when the site was bought by the local council; the church was demolished and an office block erected on the site. Tynemouth Congregational church, founded in 1866 with seating for 500, was dissolved in 1973. The grade II listed buildings was then sold and converted into The Land of Green Ginger shopping complex.

St Columba's, with about 150 members at the start of the twenty-first century, is all that now remains of several once flourishing Presbyterian and Congregational churches. It belongs to the United Reformed Church, a title adopted to reflect its Reformation origins. It is astonishing to reflect that this is all that is now left in North Shields of a movement that once split England apart and brought about the beheading of its king.

The only other remaining old-dissenting church in North Shields is the Baptist church in Howard Street. Its numbers have also declined but the congregation is sufficiently active to have been able to undertake a significant refurbishment of the church in the late twentieth century. Initially, the North Shields' Baptists regarded themselves as Particular Baptists – as distinct from General Baptists – and subscribed to the view

St Columba's, Northumberland Square. Now a United Reformed church, this is the only remaining Presbyterian or Congregational church in North Shields. The section of the building on the right is now used as residential premises.

Baptist Church, Howard Street. This formerly Strict and Particular Baptist Church hosted a Moody and Sankey revivalist meeting in 1874.

AUTHOR PHOTOGRAPH

that Christ died only to save particular individuals who were pre-destined by God to be saved. General Baptists subscribed to the view that Christ's death made possible the salvation of all men who chose of their own free will to believe in him. It is not clear what the Particular Baptist viewpoint meant in practice. But the announcement in 1872 that it was no longer a 'Strict and Particular Baptist Church' and that communion was now open to members of all recognised Christian denominations was obviously a very significant change. Two years later, the church hosted a revivalist meeting by the world-famous American evangelists Moody and Sankey, who preached that Christ had died on the cross for all, not just an elect few.

The Society of Friends continued to meet in Stephenson Street until 1928 when the meeting was discontinued.

New Dissent

Methodism grew fastest in the period 1740–1840 and in 1841 registered members represented 4.5 per cent of the adult English population. According to Gilbert, the initial growth came mainly from the working class but in later periods Methodism became increasingly dominated by the middle class. After the mergers described above, there were still five distinct groups of Methodists, numbering about 540,000. The original Wesleyans remained the largest group and their membership grew steadily from 320,000 in 1861 to 455,000 by 1901. The Primitive Methodists at 128,000 in 1861 and 189,000 in 1901 also grew steadily. The remaining three groups did less well. In 1901 The Bible Christians numbered 28,000, the NMC 32,000 and the 1857 UMFC amalgam 73,000.[72] However, although Methodism continued to grow in absolute numbers, relative to the growth in population it had actually been in decline since 1841. As a percentage of the British population aged over 15, only the Primitive Methodists had shown any significant growth and even they peaked as early as 1871 when their members made up about 1 per cent of the over-15 population. This proportionate (and later absolute) decline accelerated in the twentieth century.[73] Overall, Methodist membership had fallen from 3.9 per cent of the British population in 1841 to 2.5 per cent by 1931.[74]

This continuing decline prompted further mergers. In 1907, the so-called Liberal Methodists (i.e. The Bible Christians, New Connexion and United Methodist Free Churches) came together to form the United Methodist Church. After years of protracted negotiations, the Wesleyans and Primitives then merged with the United Methodist Church and came together in a single body in 1932. The union, which many members of the three separate branches entered unwillingly, did not produce the revitalised Methodism its advocates had predicted. As Currie concludes:

> Since 1900, half-a-dozen denominations have surrendered both convictions and existence to make the present Methodist Church possible. Since 1932, thousands of private members have been evicted from their chapels. Minority traditions have been overwhelmed by the majority, but the 'great forward movement' which might justify these sacrifices has never come.[75]

These trends in consolidation and then decline are clearly evident in North Shields. In 1860 the Wesleyan Methodists established a mission in the Bull Ring and built a new church in Chirton. In 1870 they built a larger chapel in Tynemouth, with seating for over 700. In 1883 they built a new church in John Street, Percy Main, followed closely by another in 1889 in Coach Lane, North Shields (for a congregation which until then had been meeting in Collingwood Street). Then, in 1891, the Wesleyan congregation meeting in the Howard Street premises the church had occupied since 1808, moved into a new church built on the then arable land on the north side of Albion Road at the junction with Stephenson Street. This impressive building was funded by the ship-owner Joseph Robinson and opened in 1891.* The Methodist

---

* It was named the Wesleyan Memorial Methodist Church in memory of his daughter Elizabeth Amy and extended twice during the 1890s to provide accommodation for its Sunday School.

groups identified by Currie as least strong nationally seem to have been in the same relative position in North Shields. The UMFC moved from their Howard Street premises to a new chapel in Dene Street in 1871 with room for a congregation of 350, in addition to a school room for 200 pupils. In 1878, a congregation which since 1868 had been meeting in Simpson Street, Cullercoats, moved to a new church on the boundary of Cullercoats and Whitley Bay.* A Sunday school building was added to it in 1891. That was closely followed in 1902 by a new UMF church in New York. When the UMF church on the Whitley Bay boundary was destroyed by fire in 1903, it was quickly rebuilt and reopened in 1905. The MNC seem to have been less active over this period but even they built a new Sunday school to replace their original 1813 building and extended their Salem Church premises in Linskill Street.

In North Shields, as nationally, it was the Primitive Methodists who consolidated their position most strongly before the period of decline. In the circuit of which North Shields was part, membership increased by 600 in the two-year period 1868–69 alone. In 1861 the Primitive Methodist church in Union Street, which had been in use for 40 years, was replaced by a large and impressive new church in a central position in Saville Street. Patterson records that it was built at a time when Primitive Methodism in North Shields had never been on a more 'elevated plane' and, for the benefit of those who believe the term has a more recent origin, described the period as 'the swinging sixties'.[76]

The Percy Main Primitive Methodists 1829 chapel was enlarged in 1864 and again in 1884 before it was replaced in 1902, alongside the recently opened school house in Burdon Row. The original church was subsequently used by the Churches of Christ. Primitive Methodism began in Cullercoats in 1833. Originally, services were held in an old chapel shared with Presbyterians and Congregationalists but in time it became the exclusive preserve of the Primitive Methodists and they rebuilt it in 1868. Known as the 'fishermen's chapel' it attracted large numbers of summer visitors to its services. A new chapel was built alongside it in 1900. It proved not to be the auspicious start to the new century the congregation had anticipated. Until then, the members of the chapel's well-known Fisher Choir wore the characteristic local fisherman's jersey or fishwife's shawl, garments which figured prominently in the 1880s paintings of Winslow Homer. When John Lisle, the choirmaster of 35 years, was replaced in 1899, the new choirmaster deemed local dress inappropriate. His decision had far-reaching consequences. In a tightly knit fishing community, where loss of life was common, and the Lisle family itself had lost several of its members in an 1848 tragedy, the local garb had deep symbolic significance

---

* The church was renamed St Margaret's Church Methodist Church in 1932. My wife attended the church, and she and I were married there in 1966.

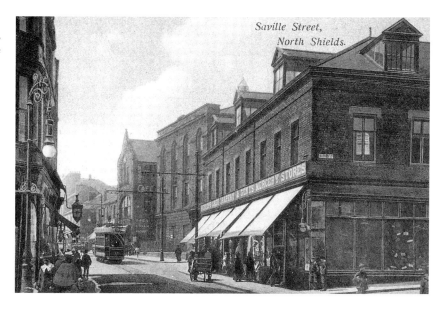

Saville Street, North Shields.

Primitive Methodist church, Saville Street. The stone building in the centre of the image, between the two redbrick buildings, was built during the 'swinging sixties' in 1861; it was sold to Woolworth's in 1931. At a later date the top storey was removed. The congregation moved to the newly built Primitive Methodist church in Hawkeye's Lane.

and many members chose to leave both the choir and the chapel following the change. In 1905, the original choirmaster John Lisle then established an independent Fishermen's Mission, initially in rooms above a shop but later in a modest hall. This new choir went from strength to strength and performed throughout the region. The mission's present home on the boundary between Cullercoats and Whitley Bay was opened in 1931 on the site of what had been Nater's House. Primitive Methodism came to the adjacent village of Whitley in 1823 at a time when it was a colliery village and most of the members were miners. In the closing years of the century, as Whitley Bay was transformed into a residential area and seaside resort, the Primitive Methodists held services in the Assembly Rooms until a site was secured in Oxford Street in 1899 and a new church opened in 1904. A Primitive Methodist church was established in Willington Quay in 1881 and a chapel in Earsdon in 1886. Three chapels were built in Backworth (formerly known as East Holywell) in 1854, 1868 and 1901. A brewery which closed in 1866 was turned into a chapel in the Allotment in 1868 and another chapel built not far away in Shiremoor in 1902. The impressive Primitive Methodist church on Saville Street, North Shields, was sold to Woolworths in 1930 but replaced by a new church outside the town centre in Hawkey's Lane in 1932.

Currie's observation that the re-unification of the Methodist church in the 1930s failed to deliver the new dynamism its advocates had hoped is an under-statement in the case of North Shields. Broadway Methodist church in Cullercoats, and Trinity Church in Preston Grange (which absorbed the congregations of the two Methodist churches in the nearby village of New York), may have opened in the mid-1950s but the predominant pattern has

C H I R T O N !

been the closure of one church after another. The United Methodist church in Howard Street was bought by a compulsory purchase order in 1936 and became the office of the Borough Treasurer. What had been the Primitive Methodist chapel in Cullercoats was destroyed by a bomb in 1942. Although the congregation continued to meet elsewhere for some time, their church was never rebuilt. In 1954, Tynemouth's Methodists and Congregationalists came together and the Methodist church sold and transformed into the Carlton cinema. In 1956 the congregation of the John Street Methodist church in Percy Main united with the church in Burdon Row and their church became a warehouse. Salem Methodist church closed and became the subject of a compulsory purchase order in 1965. The Ridges Mission followed in 1969. By 1974 the combined attendances at the Methodist church in Percy Main had fallen so low that the congregation amalgamated with the Percy Main St John's Anglican church. The Memorial Methodist church on Albion Road was the next to close in 1980. The impressive premises with seating for 1,000 became the home to Frank Wappat's non-denominational Byker Mission. This charismatic figure (and radio broadcaster), who had been brought up a Primitive Methodist, drew large congregations for some time to his unorthodox services, in a way reminiscent of nineteenth-century revivalist preachers. But in time the numbers fell there too. The building is now home to a children's play centre. Trinity Methodist church in Coach Lane (which despite the 1932 reorganisation was still known

Trinity Methodist Church, Chirton Grange estate. The final Methodist church built in North Shields. Opened in 1956, it closed in 1994. The building is now used by a veterinary practice. The symbol of the cross can still be discerned on the front of the building.
AUTHOR PHOTOGRAPH

locally as Wesley Coach Lane) also closed in 1980. It had been destroyed by a fire bomb in 1941, rebuilt in 1957 with funds from the War Damage Commission but was obliged to close, like so many others, because of a dwindling congregation. St Margaret's, on the border between Cullercoats and Whitley Bay, closed in 1989 when the trustees were unable to meet the cost of repairs demanded by the Health and Safety Executive and then demolished. In 1994 it was the turn of the short-lived Trinity Methodist church in Chirton Grange to close. West Allotment chapel closed in 1999, followed by Chirton Chapel in 2002.

The formerly Primitive Methodist church on Hawkey's Lane, is now *the* North Shields Methodist church: the sole remaining Methodist church in North Shields.

The Salvation Army

William Booth, the founder of the Salvation Army, was originally a Methodist New Connexion minister. However, his determination to reach the down-and-outs of Victorian society was not easy to reconcile with the respectable niceties of mainstream mid-nineteenth-century Methodism. The more successful he became, the more doubts were raised about his approach and in 1857 he was told he must give up his role as an itinerant preacher and return to work within a single Methodist circuit. In 1858 (after a brief spell in industrial Yorkshire) he was appointed pastor of the

Bethesda Methodist New Connexion chapel in Gateshead, about ten miles from North Shields.

Within a short time Booth was drawing crowds of as many as 2,000 to his services. His wife Catherine was also active: ministering to down-and-outs and preaching. Booth would probably have stayed on Tyneside had the lay officials of the church agreed to him combining his work as a pastor with that of a travelling evangelist, but they refused and so the Booths moved to London. In time they emerged as the leaders of the East London Christian Mission. As the mission's work spread throughout the country, the name Salvation Army was adopted in 1878. Military-style uniforms and terminology were adopted as was the brass band music that became the Army's hallmark. The early Salvationists made a point of taking their gospel message onto the streets and the music was said to calm the rowdy and sometimes hostile crowds. However, when Booth visited North Shields in 1897 and 1900 it was to address meetings of 'salvationists', the already converted, at the Howard Hall.

Booth, like Wesley, was an autocrat. It suited him to be the undisputed head of his own army. He valued the work of lay people but not to the point of sharing authority with them. He was also initially reluctant to allow women equal access to the pulpit but his wife persuaded him otherwise and women went on to play a key role in the Army. Murdoch even argues that had it not been for the central role of women, the Salvation Army might not have stood out from the hundreds of other inner-city missions that existed at the time. Booth seems to have acknowledged that with his wry remark that, 'Some of my best men are women'.[77]

In 1879 Booth sent six young women, dubbed Hallelujah Lasses, to Tyneside. They began to hold evangelistic meeting on both sides of the river and targeted the poorest sections of society. Their meetings were packed and paved the way for William and Catherine Booth's return to the area a few months later. Booth was a pioneer in exploiting publicity and appears to have believed that any publicity was good publicity. He would appear to have been correct. Although his revivalist meetings met with a mixed reception in the press, within nine months 18 Salvation Army corps had been set up in the North East. The North Shields corps was established in 1878, the 39th to be founded in Britain. It appears to have been highly regarded because its captain, Emma Westbrook, was reassigned to be one of the seven Hallelujah Lasses who helped establish the Salvation Army in New York in 1880. Unlike so many other churches in North Shields, the Salvation Army has soldiered on throughout the twentieth century and into the twenty-first century. It moved into the vacant premises of the Howard Street Presbyterian Church in 1950 where, despite a much reduced membership, activities still take place each day of the week.

Other religious groups

Among most other religious groups in North Shields, the pattern has also been one of decline. The original Town Mission Hall on the Low Street was demolished in 1939. The Norwegian Seamen's church closed its doors for the last time in 1966: a reflection, among other things, of the declining trade with Scandinavia. The Rudyerd Street Town Mission closed in 1972 although the remaining congregation continued to meet for a time in the local YMCA. The earliest available records indicate that a gathering of the North Shields (Plymouth) Brethren first met in the lower part of Collingwood Street near the Bull Ring in 1897. Around 1912, when about 30 strong, the assembly moved to a hall in Waterville Road which had originally been built for Spiritists (a movement similar to spiritualism). They held open-air meetings on Saturdays in Rudyerd Street about half a mile away, carrying a harmonium with them from their Waterville Road premises. They also held services in the workhouse each Sunday afternoon. By 1981, with numbers peaking at about 80 (which included some former members of the Evangelistic Mission), they moved to the vacated premises of the former Wesleyan Trinity Methodist church on Coach Lane. Since then, membership has fallen. At the time of writing only about 30 gather each Sunday in the Coach Lane Gospel Hall.* The Waterville Road Gospel Hall was sold to the Pentecostal Assemblies of God in 1987, who subsequently adopted the name Lighthouse Christian Centre. The premises were refurbished in 1990 but abandoned in 1994 after a series of burglaries. For a short time the centre was based in the vacant premises of the former Trinity Methodist church in the Chirton Grange estate, but that building now houses a veterinary practice.

The Jewish community
According to Rabbi Salis Daiches, North Shields had 'the oldest [Jewish] congregation in the north'.[78] Jews arrived at least as early the beginning of the nineteenth century and there are references to a Jewish burial ground in 1806 and to a synagogue in 1827.[79] An 1827 Directory states that 'The Jewish Synagogue stands on the declivity of the bank in which Tyne Street is built', and added that the Jewish cemetery was situated at the north end of Preston village. That suggests that there may have been more than one Jewish cemetery because Craster describes it as 'a small burial ground at Billy Mill' which corresponds with its location on the west side of Billy Mill Lane on an 1856 Ordnance Survey map. It certainly was small: apparently just 20 square feet! When the plot was excavated during the construction of a housing estate in 1924, 17 skeletons were found beneath two headstones.[80] The only clear date on them indicated that one of the

---

* I am grateful to Dr S.M. Menzies for providing me with the local information.

burials was in 1806. The remains were moved to Preston Cemetery where, by a coincidence, the first internment, in 1856, had been that of a Jewish lady, Sarah Isaacs.

Whatever the size of the Jewish population in the early decades of the nineteenth century, Pollins' examination of the names on census returns suggests that in the second half of the century it peaked in the decade 1861–71. From a high of 84 in 1861, when it received a visit from the Chief Rabbi, it fell to 78 in 1871 and was as low as 37 in 1881. In 1864, there was an appeal in the *Jewish Chronicle* for funds to build a synagogue for the use of residents of both North and South Shields. It noted that, 'The Brethren, although not at present numerous in these two towns, are … for the most part, in poor circumstances …'[81] At the time there were about 40 Jewish adults in North *and* South Shields plus about 30 children, just enough to support a shared synagogue in a small terraced house in Linskill Street.[82] The synagogue that had been open in the 1840s at 57 Church Road appears to have been no longer in use because a report in the *Jewish Chronicle* in 1874 notes that the Jews in North and South Shields 'have been for some time without adequate provision for public worship and for the religious instruction of their children'.[83] Those Jews who travelled from South Shields, like the South Shields Roman Catholics who worshipped at St Cuthbert's, had to cross the Tyne to do so, often in unpleasant and sometimes dangerous conditions. Olsover is confident that they must have been orthodox Ashkenazi Jews because they paid the ferry dues in advance on a weekly basis, so as not to desecrate the Sabbath.[84] The estimated numbers are consistent with the accommodation in the building occupied in 1876, where two small rooms had been knocked into one to provide seating for 70 people, with an additional school room for about 12.[85] By 1880 the community may have been smaller but appears to have been better established. They bought what had been their previously rented accommodation and enlarged it to form a permanent synagogue. The main hall for worship was on the first floor. It contained an ark, a reader's desk and rows of polished benches.

Craster, writing in 1908, noted that the Jews in North Shields were 'formerly more numerous than they are at present'.[86] That observation accords with Pollins' more recent remark that, although there was a time when the Jewish communities of north-east England were 'numerous and vibrant, most of them have declined or disappeared'.[87] Even as early as 1911, Daiches remarked that there was 'scarcely a minyan left in North Shields', i.e. the minimum ten Jewish adults needed for a service. Olsover concludes that the Jewish community of North Shields remained small because immigrants saw advantages in moving to the bigger industrial centres of Newcastle and Sunderland where there were 'better social facilities for their children amidst Jewish surroundings' and they could 'look forward to better opportunities for meeting Jewish partners in marriage as they grew up'.[88]

The interior of the small synagogue at 29 Linskill Street, shown here in about 1955. The synagogue closed in 1965.

The Ashkenazi Orthodox membership of North Shields seems to have remained around 40 in the first half of the twentieth century. By 1953 the synagogue was no longer in use.[89]

A huge gulf now exists between the scale of religious conviction and observance in North Shields in earlier centuries and the situation at the time of writing. In the eighteenth and nineteenth centuries, the secular and the sacred developed side by side and in various, often complex ways, affected one another. Today, because religion belongs to the realm of minorities rather than the mainstream, and has little discernible impact on how most people live their daily lives, it is tempting to disregard its social, political and economic significance. But, to understand how our own society evolved and, in this particular instance, how North Shields developed, it is vital to remember that for many centuries religion was vitally important to large numbers of influential as well as ordinary people. It is for that reason, that it has been necessary to devote so much space to the role of religion in North Shields. Not to have done so, would have meant being guilty of what Banton calls 'presentism', that is making the mistake of interpreting past events and beliefs in terms of the taken for granted assumptions of the present – rather than the taken for granted assumptions of the period under investigation.[90]

9

Leisure time

Constraints and influences

How people used their free time could never be a purely personal matter. It inevitably reflected considerations of class and status. Class position set limits to how much time was available for leisure and what pursuits could be afforded. Status determined what pursuits were deemed suitable and what, if any, social distance was maintained between those taking part. Religion too, directly and indirectly, played a role in how people spent their leisure time, although it affected the middle class more than the upper or working class. In the early nineteenth century, the application of the moral code derived from evangelical Christianity effectively defined middle-class respectability. It was based on the notion that the world was inherently evil and that god-fearing people had to be constantly on their guard against corrupting influences.

> An unguarded look, a word, a gesture, a picture, or a novel, might plant a seed of corruption in the most innocent heart, and the same word or gesture might betray a lingering affinity with the class below.[1]

The reference to 'the class below' relates to the widespread middle-class view that members of the lower orders were morally suspect, so staying appropriately aloof from them was a necessary part of appearing respectable. Another way to demonstrate one's respectability in public was not to be frivolous in the use of leisure time.

> To be serious, to redeem the time, to abstain from gambling, to remember the Sabbath day to keep it holy, to limit the gratification of the senses to the pleasures of a table lawfully earned and the embraces of a wife lawfully wedded, are virtues for which the reward is not laid up in heaven only.[2]

The reference to 'the embraces of a wife lawfully wedded' reflects the discrepancy between outward displays of respectability and the real world lives of many middle-class men. Middle-class women were expected to be chaste before and faithful after marriage but it was widely accepted that many middle-class men would indulge their sexual appetites before marriage and be unfaithful afterwards. In the main, it was to working-class women that middle-class men turned when they paid for the services of a prostitute, enjoyed a casual liaison, or took up with a regular mistress. That is not to suggest that prostitutes did not have working-class clients. Sailors were predominant among those of prostitutes in North Shields, and in such a thriving port the demand for their services was considerable. In 1878 the still small police force of North Shields was aware of over 300 *active* prostitutes.[3] Moreover, as Mayhew's work revealed, the actual number of women who had been prostitutes at some stage in their lives was probably ten times greater. The fact that such large numbers of working-class women resorted to selling their bodies is testament to their vulnerable position in a society in which people were expected to fend for themselves.

Another way in which religious thinking manifested itself was in opposition to traditional sports and pastimes which involved brutality towards human beings and animals. Macaulay's belief in progress encouraged him to exaggerate the differences between the Britain of the late seventeenth century and that of the mid-nineteenth century, but cultural change was undoubtedly underway which, at the time, was regarded as evidence of moral progress.

> Fights compared with which a boxing match is a refined and humane spectacle were among the favourite diversions of a large part of the town. Multitudes gathered to see gladiators hack each other to pieces with deadly weapons, and shouted with delight when one of the combatants lost a finger or an eye.[4]

Haswell, who was brought up in North Shields, drew a similarly graphic picture of some popular traditional sports at the beginning of the nineteenth century.

> The sports and pastimes of the poor were in the main cruel and mean and cowardly. ... Each squalid town had its Bull Ring where, in the eyes of even children, a poor infuriated animal secured by a rope was torn by dogs amid the shouts and cheers of the crowd.* ... The same children might see – nay, could not fail to see – their fathers busied in cock-fighting, dog-fighting, ratting, ferreting, and the meaner cowardice of coursing; might see disgusting eating competitions, man and dog fights, furious prize-ring encounters, with the gentry in full force hounding on the brute-like champions.[5]

---

* The iconic British bulldog was bred specifically for the purpose of bull-baiting.

Hogarth's portrayal of cock-fighting. Cock-fighting was a popular 'sport' in the North East, and continued for a time in a clandestine way after it was made illegal.

CONTEMPORARY PRINT

Blood sports were not the exclusive preserve of the poor. They were supported by the better-off who often gambled large sums of money on the outcome. The *Newcastle Courant* reported in 1768 that 'the *gentlemen* of the town had *graciously* [my emphasis] provided a bull for the amusement of the poor' and that, in 1774, Newcastle's magistrates had enjoyed a bull-baiting to the accompaniment of 'ringing of bells and firing of guns'.[6] The most popular spectator sport on Tyneside in the early 1800s was cock-fighting.[7] There were numerous cockpits in the area, including one which can still be seen in a cellar in Front Street, Tynemouth.[8] Prior to being made illegal in 1835, cock-fighting was well organised, with pre-arranged fixtures, and enjoyed the active support of such notables as Earl Grey, the Northumberland-born prime minister. Concern about the abuse of animals was channelled through the Society for the Prevention of Cruelty to Animals (later the RSPCA), founded after the Cruel Treatment of Cattle Act of 1822 had not included bull-baiting in its provisions. Pressure to remedy that, and other omissions, led to the Cruelty of Animals Act of 1835 which extended protection to bulls, dogs and bears and expressly prohibited bear-baiting and cock-fighting. However, although dog- and cock-fighting were no longer advertised in the newspapers, and devotees had 'to guard against the visits of the men in blue', they continued in a clandestine form at least until the end of the century.

Those at the top of Britain's hierarchical society were less constrained in their leisure pursuits than the members of the middle or working classes. Their wealth left them free to do more or less what they wanted and their social position was so unassailable that they did not need to concern themselves with the niceties that mattered to status-conscious members of the middle class. At times, this led to outrageous behaviour that shocked those from other social classes.

One local example is Archibald Campbell, the first Duke of Argyll, who separated from his wife in 1696 and set up home in Chirton Hall with a mistress. He moored his yacht at North Shields to make travel easy; was a keen follower of the turf, and a racehorse owner. He appears to have devoted his life to the pleasure principle and died in 1703 from stab wounds received in a brawl in a brothel after having lived what a contemporary described as a lewd and profligate life.[9]

A second local example is Francis Blake Delaval, whose family had been associated with the area since 1095. In 1728 the family moved into the newly built Sir John Vanbrugh-designed Seaton Delaval Hall about six miles from North Shields. Francis, the eldest son, delighted in playing outrageous practical jokes on visitors. The walls of one bed chamber could be raised to expose guests when they were undressing. In another, the four poster bed could be lowered into a tank of cold water. Most bizarre was a room in which the furniture was stuck upside down on the ceiling with a chandelier attached to the floor. Drunken guests were put to bed in the dark and woke to think that they were lying on the ceiling. Not content with life on the family estate, Francis sold his inheritance to his younger brother John and moved to London. As a result of a combination of influential contacts and good luck he became an MP, received a knighthood, temporarily solved his financial problems by marrying an elderly widow, and went on to spend her fortune indulging his whims. Passionate about acting, he hired the Drury Lane Theatre at a cost of £1,500 (the equivalent of over £1 million in 2014) to put on a performance of *Othello* with himself in the title role and family members in the leading parts. The House of Commons adjourned early that day so that fellow MPs could attend the performance. Sir Francis plainly saw himself as a member of what Veblen would later term the leisure class. It was not enough to be wealthy: it was necessary to flaunt wealth – although Sir Francis flaunted his so much that he died in considerable debt.

Other privileged local people used their free time for industrious rather than self-indulgent purposes. John Delaval, to whom Francis had turned over the estate, with the help of his brother Tom, established the Royal Northumberland Glassworks in 1763. By 1777 it was producing close to 2 million bottles a year. To facilitate the loading of the glass, as well as the coal and salt produced on the estate, John commissioned a major engineering project which necessitated cutting a 900 feet (274 m) channel through sheer rock to give easier access to the harbour entrance. The sluice gates at either

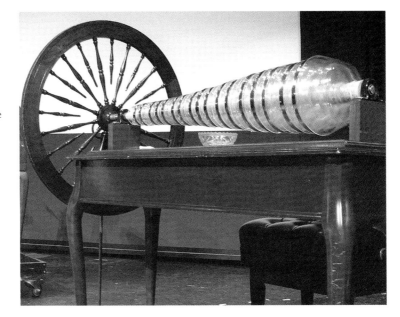

Benjamin Franklin's glass armonica. This early nineteenth-century example is now in the Museum of Fine Arts in Boston, USA.

end created a deep water dock to aid the loading and unloading of ships. John's brother Edward used his free time for scholarly purposes. He was a fellow of Cambridge's Pembroke College; a member of the Royal Society in recognition for his research in chemistry and shared the Copely Medal for his work on metals and glass. His indulgence was playing music on wine glasses and it has been conjectured that it was his public performances which inspired Benjamin Franklin to develop his famous glass armonica.[*]

At the other end of the social scale, there was relatively little time for leisure. Workers at the beginning of the nineteenth century toiled for long, relentless hours and pitifully small wages. Government inquiries reported that manual workers typically worked twelve to fifteen hours a day, six days a week – and, in addition, might have to make lengthy journeys to and from their workplace on foot. Coal hewers, in compensation for the appalling working conditions, worked fewer hours but the hours worked and conditions endured by seamen and fishermen were long and comparably dangerous. And yet for many workers in North Shields, wages were so low and periods of unemployment so frequent, that they would have readily exchanged even more hours at work for their minimal free time.

Domestic servants often had very little free time. The 1851 census recorded about 1 million *female* domestic servants out of a total female

---

[*]   An iron rod passed through a hole in the top of 37 glass hemisphere from the largest to the smallest and was linked to a wheel with a foot treadle. The instrument was played by moistened fingers held against the glass rims as they turned, producing a sound similar to that of musical glasses. Mozart composed two pieces for the instrument and Beethoven wrote a short melodrama in which a narrator was accompanied by the armonica.

population of 5.5 million aged between 15 and 65.[10] Most were not employed in grand houses but in middle-class homes with little or no time to themselves. Towards the end of the century they might get an afternoon a week off but most had to spend all their time at the beck and call of their employer. Work could start as early as 5 a.m. and continue until the end of the evening.[11] For the majority of women servants, this life of relative servitude lasted until they married. Their new life was often just as arduous but, when circumstances allowed, they were at least free to attend church, go for a walk and enjoy the company of friends when it suited them.

Employing one or more servants, did not free middle-class women from all domestic chores. In upper-middle-class Victorian families it might have been possible to leave all the housework to domestic servants. For lower-middle-class families the reality was different. They may have employed a 'daily' but domestic *help* was no more than that. The labour-intensive nature of housework was very time-consuming. Rooms were kept warm with coal fires which demanded much more work than the twiddle of a central heating thermostat. The previous day's ashes had to be removed and the grate cleaned before a new fire could be lit. The coal on the fire had to be replenished throughout the day to ensure it did not go out. Shopping, cooking, cleaning, washing and a great many other domestic tasks in the nineteenth century bore scant resemblance to the way in which their functional equivalents are conducted today. Before the advent of fridges, freezers and microwave ovens, most meals were prepared from fresh ingredients. Cleaning the house had to be done without the aid of electrical appliances and washing clothes and bedding was a particularly labour-intensive operation.

To illustrate the point, I am fortunate to be able to draw on the memoirs of Alice who, although born in 1907, spent much of her childhood in the company of her grandparents and recorded how their households were organised, in addition to her own. Despite the services of a daily domestic 'help', she and her nine siblings were expected to share in the housework and the older children were expected to help to take care of the younger. As with most middle-class families, washing clothes, towels and sheets was an arduous task undertaken at home. Most houses did not have a plumbed-in supply of hot water so cold water had to be carried to a copper boiler and heated by a coal fire before the process of washing could begin. Clothes more than slightly soiled were scrubbed on a bench or wash board or pounded in a wooden or metal barrel filled with hot water, known locally as a *poss* (or *dolly*) tub, with a wooden or metal *poss* stick. This was demanding work and because one of Alice's grandmothers was regarded as 'weakly', her husband had built her a primitive labour-saving device. Their *poss* stick was tied to a heavy spring attached to the scullery ceiling. Although his wife had to push down on the *poss* stick, the spring returned it into its initial position for the next downward push. Excess water was squeezed from clothes by a mangle (also known as a wringer). This involved feeding them through wooden or rubber rollers with one hand whilst rotating a heavy handle with the other. The clothes were then hung outside to dry on a line of rope, secured by wooden pegs. All that hard work did not guarantee the clothes would be clean when they were brought back inside, because the use of coal in domestic fires and industrial processes meant that the outside air was invariably dirty. The final part of the process, removing creases, involved using an iron heated over a naked flame.

The dirt in the air meant that furniture needed to be dusted frequently. Alice recalled that one of her jobs was to wash and polish the wooden blades of the venetian blinds at their sitting and dining room windows. She vowed that if she ever had her own house it would never have venetian blinds! Furniture was polished regularly and the well-used piano keys given a daily rub with a wash-leather. Even keeping house plants required significant effort. Every week, four aspidistra plants were submerged in a tub of water for two hours. Their leaves were then washed with a cloth dipped in diluted milk before being polished with a piece of chamois leather.

Victorian leisure in the home

In *The Rise of Respectable Society*, Thompson devotes a lengthy chapter to what he calls 'Play'. It is an unfortunate choice of title because, to most people, that term suggests activities undertaken purely for pleasure. Yet Thompson emphasises that much spare time in the Victorian period was used for self-improvement or the *re*-creation of the person in ways which were edifying, useful or, ideally, both.[12] Reading, especially of literature with moral messages was encouraged, as were useful home-crafts such as needlework and embroidery. Children's toys were often not designed primarily to entertain but to instruct, and also to reinforce the then marked gender differences in social roles. Alice's father (born in 1877) made violins for a hobby. Her grandfather (born in 1844), made model ships in his spare time and entered and won prizes in numerous competitions. Her uncle's main hobby was landscape painting. The family were all taught to play the piano and, in keeping with the romanticised view of the Victorian family, did stand around it singing popular and religious songs in four-part harmony.

There was much less scope for such activities in the households of the working classes in North Shields. Their cramped almost invariably overcrowded and uncomfortable dwellings did not provide them with the same opportunities for the pursuit of hobbies and pastimes. However, as rates of literacy rose, their homes were places where newspapers, pamphlets and books could be read. Residents no longer had to rely on word of mouth communications, or the announcements of Tynemouth Borough's town crier (the last of whom, John Scarth, retired after 40 years in the post in 1905). At least 18 newspapers were published for the North Shields area between

1819 and the end of the century. Many were short-lived. For example, the *Shields Monthly Mirror* was issued only from 1819 to 1820; the *Tynemouth Gazette* from 1870 to 1872; and *Shields and Tynemouth Argos* from 1881 to 1882. Others were long-lived. What was originally the *North and South Shields Gazette* began publication in 1849. Although it has undergone name changes and now serves only South Shields, it is the country's oldest regional newspaper. Augustine Yorke, the original publisher of the *Gazette*, severed his links with it in 1864 and set up the *Shields Daily News* which served the whole of the Borough of Tynemouth. Both the *Gazette* and *Daily News* (like the *Newcastle Chronicle* and *Newcastle Courant*) adopted a Liberal perspective. Its first editorial even declared, 'No daily newspaper could be established in this country in 1864 whose conductors should for a moment think of opposing the onward march of the people.'[13] Its fashionable format at the time consisted of several columns of closely set type, with no headlines and few illustrations. It covered national as well as local issues and the 'latest intelligence' from abroad via 'the electric telegraph'.

By 1909, the days of small, family-owned provincial newspapers were virtually over and the *Shields Daily News* was bought by the Northern Press Association. In time there was a change in format. News rather than advertisements dominated the front page and content was made easier to read, with larger typefaces, headlines and more white space. The column inches devoted to national and international news declined; new features such as crosswords and children's sections were introduced and photographs appeared for the first time during the First World War. Ironically, as the proportion of the population who were literate increased, the level of literacy needed to read the newspaper decreased. The supreme irony is that literacy rates were at their highest when the newspaper closed in 1984. By then, radio and television had become the main source of news.

Working-class children, like middle-class children, may have played cards, board games and with toys at home, but the overcrowded conditions in which they lived made it more obvious for them to make the streets their playground and they devised numerous free ways of entertaining themselves.[14] Working-class women often had very little time for anything resembling the leisure pursuits of their middle-class counterparts. For working-class men, much of their play and the scope for self-improvement focused not on their overcrowded homes but on the world outside it, including North Shields' numerous public houses.

Victorian leisure outside the home

Churches, clubs and societies
Even Victorians with a relaxed view of religion could not ignore the prevailing, ultimately religious, moral sentiments of the period without running the

risk of undermining their local social status. This affected women more than men. Although not usually expected to work, it was assumed that they would be gainfully employed in some other way. Typically, what free time they had would revolve around church or charitable work of some kind.

> There were so many Victorian charities and so much philanthropic activity that ... it could easily have taken up all the spare time that middle class women had left after running their homes. ... The closest the Victorians came to having an apparatus of social services was ... the largely unsystematized efforts of vast numbers of individuals and voluntary organizations, mainly inspired by religious motives, and sustained by the work of armies of middle class women.[15]

A wide variety of social activities took place in the churches and chapels of North Shields, ranging from prayer meetings, bible study classes and choir rehearsals, to social activities such as magic lantern shows, teas, bazaars, fetes, picnics and 'days out'. The roots of the Thomas Cook travel agency can be traced back to such outings. When an active Baptist, Cook arranged for a train to take people from Leicester to a temperance rally. It was from that modest beginning that his international travel agency was born. Towards the end of the century, churches also provided respectable alternative environments for the kind of events which had commercial equivalents, such as dances, socials and whist drives. Alice proudly recalled: 'On social evenings, grandmother's rabbit pie suppers were renowned. She would cook the pies at home and then take them in a horse-drawn cab to the church.'

Numerous, many long-forgotten, voluntary societies were formed in North Shields in the eighteenth and nineteenth centuries. Little is known about most of them, but their names are listed in publications of the period. They included the Literary and Philosophical Society, Natural History Society, North Shields Gentlemen's Club, Tyne News Room, Commercial News Room, New Quay Reading Room, Gentlemen of the Friendly Club and Jerusalem Coffee Room. Many of these and similar bodies catered for an exclusively or predominantly middle-class membership.

The working classes also had access to organisations aimed at self-improvement. A Scientific and Mechanical Institution was established in 1825, but collapsed after a few years because it could not recruit sufficient members to make it viable. A second body, the Tynemouth Tradesmen's and Mechanics' Institute followed in 1833. It too struggled and manual workers made less use of it than those who worked in shops and offices. As an attempt to infuse new life into the Institute, Joseph Laing led an initiative to build a library and three-storey museum (called the Athenaeum) on the junction of Saville Street and Norfolk Street in 1846. The Mechanics' Library was transferred shortly afterwards to Tyne

Street, but the museum remained and the rooms used by other local groups (including the Temperance Society) until 1858. At that point, Tynemouth Council took over the Athenaeum and, after alterations, opened it as a Police Court in 1865. By then, a new imposing building was being erected for the Mechanics' Institute at the south-west corner of the junction of Howard Street and Saville Street. The foundation stone ceremony was a grand affair. A procession, which included civic dignitaries from the boroughs of Tynemouth, South Shields and Newcastle, crossed the short distance from the Town Hall to the flag-decorated site, watched by a large crowd. Tea was then served for 600 people in the nearby Albion Assembly Rooms.

The aim of the Institute was to 'spread education amongst the working class'. In 1869 the Institute's building became Tynemouth Borough's first free public library. It still served that purpose in my childhood, a century later. I cannot recall whether the statement 'It is Hard to Enslave a Reading People' was still evident, but the description of the building recorded in the press when it was opened corresponds closely with my own recollections of it in the 1950s. On the ground floor, were two 'conversation' rooms on either side of the main entrance. The passage from the entrance led to a news room, with a wide range of newspapers laid out on wooden lecterns. A spacious stone staircase with an iron balustrade led to the large galleried library, with an adjoining classroom and committee room. The airy library was always well lit thanks to its arched glass roof. When delegates of the 67 branches of the Northern Union of Mechanics' Institutions met in 1894, the North Shields branch (described as the Borough of Tynemouth Public Free Library) came second to Newcastle in terms of its stock of books.

Moreover, the population of North Shields made more use of its collection. Whereas Newcastle's 83,000 books were borrowed on average 2.7 times each year, Tynemouth's 29,000 were borrowed on average 4.5 times. The North Shields' delegates reported that the library was used by about 2,000 people daily and was no longer adequate. But it was another 70 years before it was replaced.[16] When a new library was eventually built in Northumberland Square in the 1970s, the Howard Street library was put to other uses but, in 2012, reverted to its original role while the new building was being refurbished.*

Taking the air

During most of the nineteenth century, those who lived by the river had little access to fresh air, something deplored by William Ranger who conducted the General Board of Health's 1851 enquiry into environmental conditions in North Shields. He described in detail how they spent their lives 'pent up in the close lanes and alleys of the low parts of the town' without even easy access to the sea. By the end of the century, although conditions in the low parts of the town remained overcrowded and squalid,

---

*   I have a soft spot for the original Library. As a babe in arms, along with my mother, sister and many other people, I sheltered there during the bombing raids of the Luftwaffe. Later, after I had graduated from the Junior Library a few doors away, I was drawn to it like a magnet. I loved having access to the newspapers and the privilege of being able to borrow books on a wide range of subjects.

Tynemouth Long Sands as they looked around 1900.
CONTEMPORARY POSTCARD

Ralph Allan, Junr., North Shields.   Long Sands, Tynemouth,   Valentine's Series

access to the wonderful local coastline had been made easier. Prior's Haven nestles south of the promontory on which the Priory was built and King Edward's Bay occupies a comparable position to the north. Beyond that is a glorious almost mile-long stretch of beach known locally as the Long Sands. Tynemouth village was so attractive that it attracted numerous visitors not only from nearby towns but also much farther afield. Still within the confines of the old Tynemouth Borough, visitors could also stroll to Cullercoats Bay whose residents were captured on canvas for posterity by numerous artists. All this meant that local people had a virtual seaside holiday resort on their doorstep, albeit without anything like the scale of commercial development that was taking place elsewhere.

By the end of the nineteenth century, there were also several beautifully maintained parks in the town itself. The designers of Northumberland Park, which was opened in 1885, took advantage of the narrow natural dene around which it was built. The natural contours of the park as well as ponds, trees, shrubbery and floral displays quickly made it a favourite with visitors of all ages and it also provided greens for the first bowling club in the town in 1889.[17] Tynemouth Park followed in 1893 on a site with a view over the sea, alongside the Grand Parade that runs parallel to the Long Sands. It was designed with a large lake for rowing boats and model yachts and also had bowling greens and tennis courts as well as carefully tended gardens and floral displays. The way in which West End Park came into being provides an interesting insight into how local politics worked in those days. Convinced that the west end of the Borough was short of recreational space, a group of men who had to travel across town to Northumberland Park to play bowls, formed a committee to press for a park closer to their homes. Public meetings, a petition, and negotiations with council officials did not produce the desired result. The mainly professional and businessmen on the committee then adopted a different tack. They made a direct approach to the Duke of Northumberland. He supported their proposal and put the local council on the spot by offering them an 11-acre site in the Minton Lane area. The council reluctantly yielded to the Duke's approach and another fine public park was opened in North Shields in 1898. In subsequent years, other parks, playing fields and play areas were provided which, to a degree, compensated for the loss of open and agricultural land as the town continued its relentless residential expansion.

Gardening provided both an open-air pastime and valuable source of food for those lucky enough to have access to a plot of land. However, in densely populated urban areas like North Shields, few had gardens that could be used in this way. To compensate for the loss of common land, the General Enclosure Act of 1845 had specified that some 'field gardens' should be provided for the landless poor but, despite the fact that tending allotments was regarded as a wholesome activity for working-class people, very little land was actually provided for this purpose. It was only after two

further pieces of legislation in 1887 and 1908 that significant progress was made and the allotment movement gathered pace. In North Shields, and elsewhere, it resulted not only in individuals growing food and flowers for their own use but regular competitions in which prize blooms and monster vegetables such as onions and leeks earned prestigious awards for those who had cultivated them.

Sporting activities

During the Victorian period, sports were judged favourably or unfavourably depending on whether or not they conformed to the moral sentiments of the period. When sports were unorganised and unruly they frequently met with criticism. Once rules were codified, and teams organised into competitive leagues, the sports were deemed more respectable. So it is no coincidence that most popular sports had their rules codified and governing bodies established during these years.

Cricket enjoyed the support of and was played by people from all social classes. However, once the game developed a commercial dimension, the class structure of the wider society was reflected in the distinction between amateurs, who could afford to play without payment, and paid professionals. When playing on the same team, amateurs and professionals often had separate changing rooms: a practice which at county cricket level could still be found in post–Second World War Britain. The annual match of Gentleman (amateurs) *v.* Players (professionals) continued at Lord's until 1962.

West End Bowling Greens on Howdon Road, c.1910. My father was a member of a local team and as a boy I spent many happy hours in this delightful park.
CONTEMPORARY POSTCARD

Codified rules and the establishment of the Football Association in 1863 helped render football respectable and suitable for church members and company employees. Many of today's professional teams were originally church teams (including Aston Villa, Manchester City and Tottenham Hotspur) or sponsored by employers (such as Arsenal, Manchester United and West Ham). However, after the game became commercialised it attracted the same criticisms that are commonly heard today. Players were accused of being mercenary and of committing fouls if they judged that they could get away with them. Crowds were criticised for being too rowdy and partisan. Such criticisms helped to alienate the middle classes and football became a predominantly working-class spectator sport.

Those who preferred the game associated with Rugby School, in which handling the ball was allowed, went their own way. Originally there was no limit to the number of players in a game and serious injuries were common, but the need for a single set of agreed rules led to the formation of the Rugby Football Union in 1871. Hundreds more new clubs then formed although considerations of class and regionalism (albeit disguised as amateurism versus professionalism) then brought about the split between Rugby League and Rugby Union in 1895. Other sports codified at about the same time also reflected considerations of class – sometime deliberately and explicitly. When the Amateur Athletic Club was established in 1866 it originally denied membership to anyone who was a 'mechanic, artisan or labourer'.[18]

There is little information available on the scale of informal participation in sports in North Shields but given the known popularity of handball, potshare bowling and quoits in the mining villages of the surrounding area, they were probably popular in North Shields too.[19] One of the attractions of all three traditional sports is that they involved gambling. Handball was sufficiently popular in areas close to North Shields for a number of alleys to have been built: one at the Astley Arms in Seaton Sluice had seating for as many as 600 spectators. Potshare bowling, in which competitors threw a handmade stone ball across a mile long course, with the winner being the person who completed the course in the fewest throws, was even more popular than football in the mining villages until 1914. Quoits was also popular, and could be played anywhere although pubs and working men's clubs were usually the venue for the more organised games which developed towards the end of the nineteenth century. Unusually, the Hawkey's Hall Quoits Club, formed in North Shields in 1860, was an exclusive gentlemen's club with a membership of only twelve. By the time it celebrated its 150th anniversary in 2010, it had only ever had 210 members. The club has used the same site sandwiched between Tynemouth Cricket Club and Tynemouth Golf Club since 1906.[20]

More information is available on formally organised and spectator sports. There is a reference in a local newspaper to the North Shields Cricket Club playing at their ground in Preston as early as 1805 and some of their matches (against South Shields in particular) received a mention in the early records of the MCC. There is evidence that a Tynemouth Cricket Club already existed in 1837 although the Tynemouth Cricket Club which survives to the present day was not established until 1847. Initially, it played on Brock's Farm but, when the water company decided to build a reservoir on the site, it moved in 1854 to an adjacent piece of land on Preston Lane (now Road), opposite Camp Terrace, adjacent to the Tynemouth Union workhouse. By July 1854 Mountford reports that the club was sufficiently established to undertake a small tour to play against teams in Alnwick, Berwick, Kelso and Edinburgh and arrange for those teams to play in North Shields the following season.[21] The Preston Lane ground also became the venue for a variety of other sports and activities. From 1857 it was the scene for weekly brass band concerts and an annual Floral Society show. After a one-off but financially successful Athletics Fete, to coincide with the opening of Northumberland Dock, the Club organised its own annual athletics meeting after 1865.* In the same year Sanger's circus used the ground, and the world-famous French tight-rope walker Blondin gave a demonstration. At other times, the ground was used for croquet, quoits and a velocipede event. From 1874, after a more casual arrangement, the Borough of Tynemouth (Rugby) Football Club was allowed a pitch on the eastern side of the ground next to the reservoir and used it from October to February (when no cricket was being played). The decision to extend Tynemouth workhouse obliged the cricket club to move in 1884 to its present ground off Preston Avenue. The Borough of Tynemouth (Rugby) Football Club moved with it and before the decade was out it was agreed that the Avenue Tennis Club could have three courts on the west side of the ground.

Football became extremely popular in the 1880s with *ad hoc* as well as more established teams playing in a variety of competitions, including the Tynemouth Infirmary Cup which was established in 1904 to help raise funds for the Jubilee Infirmary and attracted teams from the whole of the North East. The current North Shields Football Club can trace its roots back to North Shields Athletics which was formed in 1896 and took over the site of a cycling track on a former Preston colliery site in 1897. Two of its players went on to play for England. The club went into liquidation after suffragettes burned down the uninsured grandstand. It re-formed as Preston Colliery FC before assuming the name of North Shields Association Football Club in 1928, after Preston Colliery closed. Its ground became known as Appleby Park in 1930 after Joseph Appleby, a wholesale fishmonger, donated a new

---

*   In the 1950s the event attracted athletes of the calibre of E. McDonald Bailey, who held the world 100 m record between 1951 and 1956, and Derek Ibbotson who set a new world record for the mile in 1957. I took great pleasure in being in the same competitor area with them when I ran in the boys' event.

1969 FA Amateur Cup Final Programme and return of the North Shields AFC heroes.
In only their fourth year in the competition, North Shields won four regional qualifying
matches, a preliminary national round and five further national rounds to reach the
final. Played at the internationally famous Wembley Stadium, before a crowd of 47,000,
Sutton United went into an early lead but North Shields fought back to win 2–1. Huge
crowds turned out to welcome the team home. The returning heroes are shown here
at the top of Howard Street about to enter Northumberland Square.

CREATIVE COMMONS, BY COURTESY OF ROGER CORNFOOT

club house. A semi-professional team for a time, with three former interna-
tionals on the pay roll in the 1950s, and an aspiration to join the Football
League, it eventually reverted to being an amateur team. Throughout
its long history, the club has won an impressive number of competitions,
including the Infirmary Cup (on nine occasions), culminating in the FA
Amateur Cup at Wembley Stadium in 1969 and the European Amateur
Cup the following season. Sadly, the club ran into financial difficulties and
was obliged to sell its Appleby Park ground for a housing development in
1992 and the team was disbanded. A group of local people then formed
North Shields Football Club (1992) Limited. At the time of writing North
Shields FC are in Division One of the Northern League (the second oldest
football league in the world) and won the FA Vase competition at Wembley
in May 2015.

The Borough of Tynemouth (Rugby) Football Club (BTRFC) which
moved to Preston Avenue with the cricket club in 1884 was soon ousted from
the ground by Percy Park (Rugby) Football Club. That had been formed
in 1872 and initially played at Percy Park in Tynemouth, until its field was
taken over to provide gardens for the residents. It played on temporary sites
until it outbid the BTRFC to use the Preston Avenue ground in 1891. The
BTRFC was wound up soon afterwards. At the time, the price of a ticket

was 3*d.*, but ladies were allowed in free! Unlike the BTFFC, Percy Park were not content with the short season negotiated with the cricket club, and in 1896 rented the land immediately south of the cricket ground, fronting on to Preston Avenue, from the Duke of Northumberland (and subsequently bought it from him in 1949). They have played there ever since, still under the name of Percy Park.

Organised athletics in North Shields can be traced back to the 1870s. The North Shields Bicycle Club was formed in 1876 and concentrated on track racing, first on the Preston Lane cricket field and from 1885 on the Hawkey's Lane bicycle track, laid out on the site of the original Preston Colliery. To make way for the oval track with banked corners, a pit heap was removed, a colliery engine house demolished and two pit shafts filled in. North Shields produced a series of champions. Perhaps the most famous were the brothers Bob and Tom English. Bob was particularly successful. He began as an amateur at 16 and turned professional at 24. His range was phenomenal, winning titles at distances from one to fifty miles. In a report on his tragic, early death at 34, it was noted that in securing trophies 'in all

Map 9.1 Hawkey's Lane Cycling Ground.
1. Preston Colliery. 2. Cycling Ground on the site of an earlier coal mine.
3. Jewish Burial Ground. 4. Jubilee Infirmary. 5. Salt Water Reservoir.

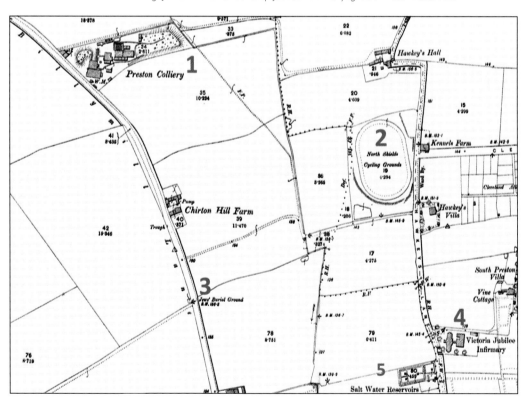

the chief centres of cycling in this country and America, his accumulation of prizes was in itself a history of the sport when the track racing mania was at its height'. Among his more tangible prizes were 'an American 20 guinea gun, a handsome revolver, a diamond pin, 18 clocks, 2 20 guinea gold watches, several silver watches, a sideboard and a £23 Humber cycle'.[22] To help assess the value of these prizes: again using the average earnings index, £20 at the time of his death in 1897 was equivalent to about £7,000 in 2014. Willie Wood was another champion North Shields cyclist. As just one illustration of his popularity and that of cycling as a spectator sport, in 1888 an estimated 2,000 people saw him beat Fred Wood of Leicester over ten miles for a £50 prize (the equivalent of about £22,000 in 2014).

There were also two touring cycle clubs in North Shields for those who preferred to participate rather than spectate. The Priory Cycling Club, founded in 1888, had over 400 members by 1896. The Tyne Cycling Club (an off-shoot of the local Liberal Party which had its HQ on Tyne Street) was formed a little later in 1898.

Pedestrianism was also popular and could attract thousands of spectators. The North Shields Walking Club was formed in 1903 and produced a string of winning athletes. They included Ralph Harrison who was first in the two miles event at the English championships in 1907. He went on to take second place in the Olympic Games ten mile walk in 1908. Tom Payne was also particularly successful over several years. Among his 56 wins were world non-stop records in 1909–10 when he walked over 72 miles in 12 hours and over 127 miles in 24 hours. Cycling and running were added to the club's interests in 1908 when it was re-formed as North Shields Polytechnic.

The proximity of river and sea encouraged rowing, sailing swimming and angling, all of which could be pursued individually and competitively. Rowing was particularly popular on Tyneside in the nineteenth century. Until the closing decades of the century when its popularity began to wane, events attracted huge crowds with large cash prizes and cult status for the winners.[23]

The first Tyne Regatta came off in fine style in the harbour at Shields. The day was remarkably fine, and great numbers of all classes of the inhabitants crowded the banks and shore where the various race boats were expected to pass. … A profusion of flags were flying from vessels in the harbour, and many of the principal shops, were closed during the afternoon. … At about half-past two, when the committee proceeded to Whitley Point, the river was teeming with life. Not a boat on the river was not crowded with spectators, steam-boats loaded with passengers, plying up and down – ships with their flags flying and the river banks crowded with spectators. It was calculated that at that time there would not be less than 10,000 individuals gazing on the scene. The first was a gig race, and was won by the Bee's-Wing, pulled by the Claspers; the Fisher Lass second, pulled by South Shields pilots. The second race was with foy boats, and was won by a North Shields boat, winning by half a length, three other boats starting. The third, a sculler race for 30s, was won by an old scullerman belonging to North Shields, winning by two boat lengths. The fourth, and one of the great attractions of the regatta, was a match for a silk gown, to be rowed for by women, which was won in gallant style by two sisters of the name of Story, belonging to South Shields.[24]

Tyneside produced several rowing heroes during the nineteenth century. Among the most notable was Harry Clasper, a Jarrow pitman turned boatyard carpenter. He designed the Newcastle Oars (to gain an extra inch or two of pulling power) and the fin keel (to improve the accuracy of steering in difficult conditions) and made effective use of the recently introduced sliding seat and swivel rowlock. Along with his four brothers he did very well in the 1845 Thames Regatta (effectively the world championship at the time) and they received a massive civic reception on their return home. When Harry died in 1870, 130,000 people lined the Tyne as his coffin was taken over the championship course as a final tribute. James Renforth (a smith's striker) won the world sculling championship in 1868 and another world championship event at the 'fours' event in Montreal in 1870. He literally rowed his heart out and died between the oars the following year. His funeral was attended by 150,000 people. Robert Chambers, an ironworks labourer, and protégé of Clasper, won numerous titles, including a five length win in the English championships of 1857. Distaste for the extent to which the sport had been commercialised, with prize money and betting, led to the Tyne Amateur Club being set up in 1852 and the Tynemouth Amateur Rowing Company in 1867. Despite its amateur status, this latter body still employed the professional champion Renforth as a coach for a time. The club exists to this day. The most notable early success was at Henley in 1871 when Willie Fawcus, born in Dockwray Square to the Fawcus family (part of the Pow and Fawcus chain and anchor manufacturers) won the Diamond Sculls.

Tynemouth Sailing Club was formed in the late 1880s and is still thriving. Over the years it has produced world champions and staged national and world championships. The Tynemouth Amateur Swimming Club was founded in 1878. People were originally taught to swim in the sea at the Haven until a salt-water reservoir with a uniform depth of 5 feet was made available to the club on Hawkey's Lane in 1907. It had previously been used by the council to hold water for street cleaning and flushing sewers. A bigger filtered sea-water swimming pool replaced it on the site in 1909. By the time I used it as a boy, it used chlorinated fresh water. I can still remember the breath leaving my body as I entered its unheated water. Tynemouth's open air and also unheated swimming pool on the

The opening of Hawkey's Lane Swimming Pool. Generations of young people, myself included, remember how cold the water was in this unheated, open-air pool.

Long Sands did not open until 1925. Unlike the Hawkey's Lane Pool, it still exists but was abandoned after a new heated pool was opened in Preston in 1971. It is now in a ruinous state and a local pressure group has launched a campaign to have it re-opened. Angling was always a popular pastime and one for which it was not necessary to have expensive equipment. Children (including me) who could not afford rods still managed to catch fish, such as mackerel, with nothing more elaborate than a hooked and weighted line.

Other sporting activities attracted smaller numbers of participants but were sufficiently popular to warrant a mention. They include tennis, billiards, snooker and boxing (both before and after the adoption of Queensbury Rules in 1867). A roller skating rink was opened in the North Shields Albion Assembly Rooms in 1873, followed by another in the Aquarium and Winter Gardens in Tynemouth (the Plaza) in 1876. Tynemouth Golf Club was founded in 1913 and its course, designed by the well-known Scottish golfer Willie Park Jnr, opened in 1914.

Outside events

From time to time, North Shields was the scene of organised public displays. In 1862, the world famous tight rope walker Blondin (heralded as the Hero of Niagara) was scheduled to perform at the Preston Road cricket ground on two consecutive evenings in August. Although the first event was cancelled because of bad weather, the following evening about 2,000 people paid for admission to see him – and lengths of canvas were erected to hide his performance from those unable or unwilling to pay the entrance fee. Blondin displayed his talents on a 300 foot rope (91 m) 40 foot

(12 m) above the field. As well as walking along the rope, both forwards and backwards, he 'reclined at full length upon the rope, turned a somersault, stood upon his head, and supported himself on one foot and then one hand'. The newspaper coverage of the event reported that he then undertook even more daring feats. He first walked along the rope blindfolded and enveloped in a sack. He then walked its length while carrying a 12-stone member of his team on his back. He brought his performance to an end by wheeling a barrow to the centre of the rope and 'by his own hands fired a discharge of fireworks, which had a splendid effect'.

This was not the only spectacular outdoor entertainment to be witnessed by the residents of North Shields. In September 1889 a large crowd in and around the Hawkey's Lane cycling ground watched Alma Beaumont ascend about 15,000 feet (4,572 m) in a balloon filled with 12,000 cubic feet (340 cubic metres) of coal gas. She then jumped from it in a way calculated to produce concern among the spectators. Only after a significant free-fall did her parachute open and return her safely to earth. A device on the balloon caused it to turn upside down and also return to the ground. After her first jump, a local councillor expressed moral outrage that the paying customers inside the ground had been outnumbered by the crowd outside who had seen the event for nothing. Obviously the very nature of her performance did not allow the organisers to screen it off, in the way the organisers of the Blondin event had been able to do. A few days later, when a larger 3,000 crowd paid to see Alma perform, collecting boxes were taken round the spectators on the outside. This time, things did not go smoothly for Alma. Her parachute drifted and caught on the top of a 70 feet (21 m) chimney and the first person to attempt to rescue her almost lost his life when the lightning conductor he was climbing up gave way. Two other rescuers then lashed ladders together to reach Alma. She returned to the cycling ground in triumph – though she and the organisers of the event were later successfully sued for damages by the local farmer whose crops had been damaged during the rescue. Outrage of a different kind followed on this occasion. A local vicar complained that such a sensational and dangerous stunt should not have been sanctioned. Alma was unapologetic. She dismissed him as a 'short-sighted sentimental moralist'. However, the vicar had a case. Another professional parachutist was killed when her balloon became tangled in telegraph lines and she fell to her death. Another, only 14 years old, was drowned when her parachute drifted into the Bristol Channel on her very first jump. Such mishaps prompted a cartoon in dubious taste in the magazine *Illustrated Chips*. Two men were sitting in a railway carriage. One confided, 'I've made over £2,000 this year by parachute descents.' The other responded, 'You are a balloonist?' 'No,' the first replied, 'I'm an undertaker!' Alma herself came close to disaster on several occasions during her visit to the North East. For example, in Stockton, her parachute almost collided with an on-coming train. In her final appearance, across the river in Jarrow, she landed in the

Tyne and had to be rescued by a passing boat. [25] Later, in Glasgow, heavy rain made it too dangerous for her to jump and she remained in her balloon in freezing conditions until it came down 60 miles away. The vicar, to his credit, was also not wrong to point to the danger of using coal gas to inflate balloons. In a later descent in Slough, Alma's balloon exploded and several of the spectators received serious burns.

Theatre and music hall

The first North Shields theatre for which there is firm evidence was built on the Bankside in 1765 although, according to an 1896 article in a theatrical newspaper, one had been in operation at an earlier date near the current ferry landing, constructed of slag from North Shields' salt pans. The 1765 theatre opened for three days a week from October to December. The takings from the first performance were donated to a poor widows' and orphans' charity: a not uncommon gesture in the years that followed.[26] The prices charged (the equivalent of about £140 and £70 in 2014) and the plays performed (which included *Hamlet* and *The Tempest*) indicate that the performances were targeted at the well-off and educated. A replacement theatre was opened by the same company in 1783, near to what today is Borough Road. It had boxes as well as a gallery and oil lamps instead of candles, but access to the theatre was still not easy, especially in the winter months. The audience had to climb a steep flight of steps from the Low Street: not the most auspicious start to an expensive evening out. Despite that, the theatre had some influential and enthusiastic patrons, including the Delaval family. It closed in 1798 when a replacement theatre was built as part of a major new development on John Wright's land. Located on the north side of Union Street at the junction with Howard Street, the publicity emphasised that carriages might be driven close to the doors. In the first season, the patrons included numerous local notables such as members of the local Masonic Lodge, Gentlemen of the Friendly Club, the Subscribers to the Jerusalem Coffee Room, William Linskill and Colonel Lawson de Cardonnel and the officers of the Northumberland Provisional Cavalry. Although the theatre could seat several hundred, by 1811 it was said to be 'on too small a scale for a town where the population was advancing so rapidly'.[27]

Some of the plays performed had a patriotic and at times jingoistic flavour. Most tried to combine moral instruction with entertainment. Far from being left implicit, the moralising was often hammered home in the play bills.

(*All that Glitters is not Gold or The Factory Girl*) portrays in strong colours, the inestimable blessings which flow from Education, Industry and Honesty. To the humble and lowly it plainly shows that rectitude of conduct and industrious perseverance will never fail to

Programme for the 1765 opening night of the Theatre Royal on Union Street. The audience was treated not only to a tragedy and a farce but a 'eulogium' on charity and a song.

BY COURTESY OF ROBERT KING FROM *NORTH SHIELDS THEATRES*

Programme for the 1852 opening night of the refurbished Theatre Royal on Union Street, the grand re-opening after the 1851 fire.

BY COURTESY OF ROBERT KING FROM *NORTH SHIELDS THEATRES*

raise them in the estimation of all good men, securing them more real respect and admiration than will fall to the lot of titled indolence. While those who move in the higher circles may learn that Pride and Arrogance, though backed by Riches, may frequently render them objects of ridicule; kindness and condescension will secure them the love of those whom Fortune has placed beneath them.[28]

In 1831 the Roxby-Beverley partnership took over the theatre and ran it until 1861. They undertook an extensive refurbishment for the 1839 season and then completely rebuilt the theatre to a grander design after it was destroyed by fire in 1851. It was at that point it became known as the Theatre Royal. Its artistic focus seems to have been unchanged. For example, of the 44 performances in the 1839 season, 13 were Shakespearean plays. The now five-month season ran from October to February and, for the first time, the theatre opened for six nights a week. In 1862, under new management, the season was extended from October to April. The indications are that performances were still targeted at a well-to-do and educated audience and included occasional operas (including a touring opera company which performed for six nights in 1866) and Shakespearian classics. Edmund Kean, regarded in his day as England's finest Shakespearean actor, performed in North Shields on several occasions when at the peak of his career. As an indication of the respect shown to Shakespeare in North Shields at the time, on the tercentenary of his birth (25 April 1864), in addition to a special musical and dramatic entertainment, there was a gun salute, the bells of Christ Church 'rang a merry peal', and the local population was treated to a half-day holiday. No comparable celebrations attended the quad-centenary of Shakespeare's birth in 1964, despite the advances in literacy and education in the intervening period.

In the 1860s, innovations were introduced in the way in which plays were staged. The buzz word 'scientific' was used to promote the ghost scene in the 1863–64 performances of *Hamlet*. It was described as having 'the assistance of the Great Scientific Wonder of the Day'.

> The attention of the Public is most respectfully directed by the Lessees to the Special Engagement (made at very great expense) of the truly-wondrous Illusion, which has created so vast a sensation throughout the country. Language would fail to convey an adequate impression of this Scientific Marvel, which Walks, Talks, Looks and Thinks like a Human Being, and yet is but a vapour! Possessing apparently the rotundity, solidity and animation of Active Life, most palpable to the eye, and yet is but an insubstantial shade – alike illusory to the sense as it is impervious to the ordeal touch. SEE AND BELIEVE.[29]

Such extravagant language might fall foul of today's Trades Descriptions Act but, like so many of the advertised medical remedies on sale at the time, it may have been readily swallowed by a still gullible public.

There is evidence that the fortunes of the Theatre Royal were declining in the late 1860s because efforts were made to attract a more broadly based audience. Publicity was unashamedly targeted at the working classes.[30] In advertisements, the theatre was described as *The People's Hall* – something unlikely to appeal to its hitherto predominantly middle-class clientele. An 1867 play bill announced 'A Great Treat for the Working Classes – every

Saturday Night at half prices, Pit 6*d*., Gallery 3*d*.' (the equivalent of about £14 and £7 at the time of writing). In an acknowledgement of the growing taste for popular culture, music hall style entertainment was on offer in the summer months (with mesmerists, comics and sentimental singers, tumblers, trained dogs and dancers).

Despite these efforts, the Theatre Royal closed in 1876, probably because it was unable to compete with Samuel Chisholm's Northumberland Music Hall, just a few hundred yards away on Borough Road, which claimed to have room for an audience of 2,500.* Chisholm then applied for a theatrical licence for his Hall. It was refused on safety grounds: a sound judgement because the roof collapsed under the weight of heavy snow in 1878. Chisholm next hired and provided entertainment in the Oddfellows' Hall in Saville Street until his newly built Grand Theatre of Varieties opened with 650 seats, on Prudhoe Street, in 1879.[31] Though a permanent building, like a travelling theatrical booth, it had a platform jutting onto the street for performers to be seen before the show to help drum up business.

Travelling booths, made of wood and canvas, had been visiting North Shields since at least the early part of the nineteenth century. They had a fairground or circus character and sometimes, like the famous Wombwell Menagerie which visited North Shields in 1852, featured animals. They also offered more sensational and sentimental plays than those presented at the Theatre Royal. Many successful actors in the regular theatre began their careers in the booths, while some once-successful theatre actors ended their careers in them. Billy Purvis's Booth was a regular visitor to North Shields, under varying names, as was his rival Thorne's Theatrical Booth. They were erected temporarily on locations such as the New Quay, Bedford Street, Saville Street and Tynemouth Green.

In 1882 Chisholm's Grand Theatre of Varieties, which had already been renamed The Theatre Royal, changed direction. Perhaps in response to competition from the music hall on King Street, and the similar entertainment offered in The Star, a pub situated alongside the Star and Garter Quay on Clive Street, music hall gave way to theatrical performances and, at about the same time, the promenade in front of the building was replaced with a porch. The fare on offer was not as high-brow as at the old Theatre Royal. From time to time there were Shakespearean plays and performances by actors of national standing such as Osmond Tearle but, on the whole, the productions were of a more popular nature, some of which were dismissed by fans of Tearle as 'sensational trash'.[32] Whether or not such harsh criticism was justified, with Chisholm's brother as the scenic artist and his son the manager, the theatre continued to do well.

Ill-health forced Chisholm to retire in 1894 and the following year the

---

* The Theatre Royal was acquired by a local builder and subsequently used for a variety of purposes including a Salvation Army barracks, shops and a billiard saloon.

lease of the Theatre Royal was transferred to Arthur Jefferson. He is now remembered more as the father of Stan Laurel, the creative member of the film comedy team of Laurel and Hardy, but in his day was extremely successful as a theatre lessee, actor, playwright and entrepreneur. The first production under his control was Edmund Tearle's company in a programme of Shakespearean and other costume plays.[33] Visits from Mrs Bandman-Palmer's company offered a similar programme. Theatre Royal audiences were also offered musical comedies and classical plays. However, Jefferson's own play *The Orphan Heiress*, which was well received in December, was more typical. Melodrama of this kind was very popular in England at the time. It often employed elaborate special effects to heighten the dramatic tension, and Arthur had a flair for devising stunts to advertise them.[34] In one, a cage containing a lion and dummy dressed like a man was driven through the streets. A piece of meat inside the dummy ensured the lion would look as if it was devouring a body. As crowds gathered, a canvas was

The Prudhoe Street Theatre Royal, leased by Arthur Jefferson. It is not inconceivable that the boy to the right is Stanley Jefferson, later to become known worldwide as Stan Laurel (the creative member of the Laurel and Hardy comedy team).

dropped to reveal 'Tonight at the Theatre Royal!' In another stunt, a cab was driven around the streets with the cabby apparently unaware that he was sitting next to a man with a dagger in his chest, bleeding heavily from a wound. A third example was the release of a balloon which, on reaching a pre-determined height, emitted smoke and unfurled a big banner to advertise the current production.

In 1897, cinematograph films about 15 minutes long were shown for the first time before the start of the live performance.[35] Jefferson's claim to have been the first to introduce cinema to the North is probably exaggerated, but there is no doubt that he was a pioneer. He went on to make use of Walter Gibbons' Royal Randvoll projector in 1901.

These were not the only innovations introduced by Jefferson. In 1898 customers who bought programmes were covered by insurance for the following week.[*] Others innovations anticipated technical developments to follow in the twentieth century. In 1899 he entered into an arrangement with the National Telephone Company so that subscribers could listen to performances on the telephone.[36] At the time, this was little more than a publicity stunt because there were fewer than 100 subscribers to the National Telephone Company in North Shields, Tynemouth and Whitley Bay, and most were business lines. However, just as the early experiments in cinema gave rise to a huge new entertainments form, so did Jefferson's flirtation with broadcasting. A century later, performances at some of our finest theatres can be seen in real time on cinema screens around the country.

Jefferson could not agree terms when his lease ran out in 1902 and it was taken over by L.M. Snowdon, the lessee of the South Shields Theatre Royal. Jefferson then shifted his attention to the Rudyerd Street Borough Theatre (The Boro') located on a site he had bought in 1897. The wooden building had been run by Henry Alvo Thorpe as a permanent circus but when he died Jefferson was free to convert and re-open it in August 1902 in direct competition with the Theatre Royal. When the Theatre Royal re-opened after renovation the following year, Jefferson was quick to point out that the work had been done by firms from outside North Shields, whereas his Boro' had been built by Boro' (i.e. Borough of Tynemouth) tradesmen, furnished by Boro' tradesmen and was 'liberally patronized by Boro' inhabitants'. He boasted that 160,080 people had paid for admission during his first season. Jefferson regained control of the Theatre Royal in 1904 and re-opened the Boro' as a Theatre of Varieties. However, it struggled, probably because of the competition with the established Central Palace of Varieties on Saville Street. Originally opened as the Central Hall of Varieties in 1899 by William Mould on the site of the Oddfellows Hall, it

---

* In 1900, the proceeds from programme sales helped to pay for meals for the needy of the town. 1,300 such meals were provided by 26 March 1900.

was enlarged and rebuilt to a much higher specification after a fire in 1900. Similar entertainment was provided at the 500-seat Gaiety Theatre on King Street, which became the Gaiety Picture Hall in 1909.

There were also other venues which provided live entertainment, although sometimes on an occasional rather than regular basis. For example, on the night of Shakespeare's tercentenary in 1864, in the Albion Assembly Rooms, Miss Emma Stanley gave a performance of her *Impersonation of the Seven Ages of Women*, a refined musical comedy of the kind offered by Joyce Grenfell in the twentieth century. The former Methodist church in Howard Street became a theatre in 1891. In Tynemouth the Bath Inn provided occasional theatrical performances in the nineteenth century and, in the twentieth, the Tynemouth Palace (the Plaza) incorporated a theatre between 1910 and 1927 and then again in the 1950 and 1960s.[37]

Before Jefferson left North Shields for Glasgow in 1905 he was the lessee of the theatres royal of Blyth, Wallsend and Hebburn as well as North Shields and the Albion Assembly Rooms (which he made available to William Mould for performances in 1900 after the fire at the Central Hall of Varieties). By then the embryonic film industry was beginning to have a marked impact on live theatre. The Howard Hall became a cinema in 1908. The Palace of Varieties, which had been renamed the Comedy Palace of Varieties in 1910, began to show films in 1913 and eventually became a cinema with seating for 800 in 1929. The Boro Theatre was subsequently acquired by George Black, a cinema pioneer, who provided films as well as some live entertainment to his audiences. It was extensively re-built and refurbished after it was gutted by fire in 1910. Interestingly, additional electrically powered ventilation was added to try to minimise the effect of smoking during performances. Another noteworthy feature of Black's presentations at this time were Saturday afternoon programmes, specifically for children, comprised mainly of educational films.* Even when new cinemas were built in North Shields in the twentieth century, they were also equipped with stages for live performances. The 1,000-seat Albion cinema, which opened in 1914, had a stage and four dressing rooms and initially provided an element of live entertainment along with films. The Prince's Theatre on Russell Street (later the Gaumont), was built in 1929 with seating for 1,600 and, as its name implied, was equipped for live performances as well as films. In 1952, Jefferson's by then world famous son Stan Laurel returned to the town, along with his partner Oliver Hardy, and appeared on its stage during a charity concert. Tynemouth Amateur Dramatic Society (TAOS) used the Albion for many years for its annual

---

* By 1912, the Black family controlled a chain of twelve cinemas. George Black Jnr moved to London and, at a later, stage, when director of the General Theatre Corporation, merged it with Moss Empires in 1932. It gave him control of most of Britain's best variety theatres and earned him the nickname *Emperor of Variety*. On five occasions he organised the Royal Variety Command Performance at the London Palladium.

productions before moving in 1951 to the Rex Cinema in the Balkwell area of North Shields when more room was needed. Between 1955 and 1971 the Society used the Gaumont until (like other live productions such as scout Gang Shows) it changed its venue to the Whitley Bay Playhouse.

During the period the cinema began to challenge the theatre as the dominant form of public entertainment, the Theatre Royal resorted to increasingly sensational or sentimental plays e.g. *White Slaves*, *Tainted Goods*, *A Warning to Women*, *No Mother to Guide Her* and *Salome, the Dancing Girl of Galilee*. A spate of war plays were also produced for the period 1914–18. In its final eight years it concentrated on revue and pantomime with only occasional drama. The curtain came down for the last time in 1932. Plans to replace the Theatre Royal with the Cinema Royale with a variety stage came to nothing. It was demolished in 1939. From the 1950s, it was the turn of the town's cinemas to close, one by one, after the advent of affordable television sets. The Boro' closed in 1957; the Comedy in 1958; the Albion in 1976. The Gaumont closed as a cinema in the same year though, like the Rex, it remained open as a Bingo Hall.

Social drinking

Many working-class women had little or no time for leisure either because they had large families to look after – or went out to work – or both. Men were in a slightly better position. After work, numerous, varied, premises were available in North Shields for the purchase and consumption of alcohol. They ranged from respectable inns and taverns to less respectable ale-houses. However, had those who condemned the frequency with which workers paid visits to them understood their several functions they might have been less censorious. Although some pubs were little more than shops, most were much more congenial than the small, usually over-crowded homes from which their working-class customers came. As well as alcohol, they provided light, heat, food, congenial company, games and sometimes entertainment. In short, for many working-class men, the price of a drink was the equivalent of an entry fee to the comforts and amenities of a working men's club.

The consumption of alcohol was high in the nineteenth century but it was not drunk only because it could create a feeling of well-being. Water free from pollutants was often not readily available and beer was a safer alternative. The 1851 investigation of sanitary conditions in North Shields emphasised that there was a 'great deficiency of water' in the town. The situation was still unsatisfactory even at the end of the nineteenth century and only began to become acceptable after the 1897 Tynemouth Corporation Water Act led to a substantial increase in the capacity of the town's reservoirs. The decline in the national consumption of beer after 1900 may, in part, have been a consequence of an improvement in water supplies. Dingle does not consider this possibility in his discussion of alcohol consumption in the period 1870–1914, but it could help to explain why 'perhaps two-thirds to three-quarters of all spending on drink came out of working-class pockets'.[38] What Dingle does note is the nutritional value of beer. Depending on its strength, a pint of beer contained 200–400 calories.[39] There were undoubtedly more cost-efficient ways of obtaining the same calorific value but, along with the function of beer as a substitute for impure water and the fact that many manual workers sweated profusely and needed to drink to avoid dehydration, we must recognise that drinking beer was far from being the unmitigated evil suggested by adherents of the temperance movement.

There is a widespread belief in North Shields that it once had more pubs per head of population than anywhere else in Britain. That claim is unsubstantiated. Nevertheless, there were undoubtedly lots of pubs and whereas pub-building peaked in Newcastle in the 1890s, it continued into the 1900s in North Shields. Pigot's 1829 Directory listed 135 taverns and public houses, plus six inns and hotels. The 1830 Beer Act freed beer from taxation and allowed any ratepayer to sell it provided he or she bought a two-guinea licence from the local excise authority. In freeing licensees from the control of local magistrates it encouraged an increase in the number of places selling alcohol. In response, local magistrates became more relaxed in their provision of licences. Their rationale was that if a drinking place was magistrate-licensed it was at least subject to some local control.[40] In 1853, there were 217 pubs, taverns and ale-houses in the newly constituted Borough of Tynemouth.[41] The greatest concentration was on the Low Street, alongside the river. Map 9.2 identities those on Clive Street, just one small section of the Low Street. Most of the pubs were adjacent to the numerous quays that lined the riverside. For example, the Stone House Inn was immediately adjacent to the Black Cock Quay; the Lombard Arms beside Lishman's Quay and the Tyne Hotel sandwiched between Blackburn's Quay and Bird-in-Hand Quay. By 1903, there were 246 licensed premises in North Shields at a time when the population was 51,366: an average of one to 208 people. In two of the town's districts, with a combined population of 13,727, the average was one to 112 people.

The main clientele of many drinking places, especially those close to the river, were sailors. In *Pages from a Worker's Life*, Foster describes what happened to a fellow seaman who landed in North Shields with the intention of quitting the sea and returning to his native Iowa. He had earned nine sovereigns for the year-long voyage but was only given one sovereign, in advance, for his first night ashore. Foster does not describe how his shipmate spent the night. He does record that when he went ashore on the second day, the still half-drunk sailor handed over more of his precious sovereigns to a man waiting at the bottom of the gang plank with a 'tough-looking' girl.

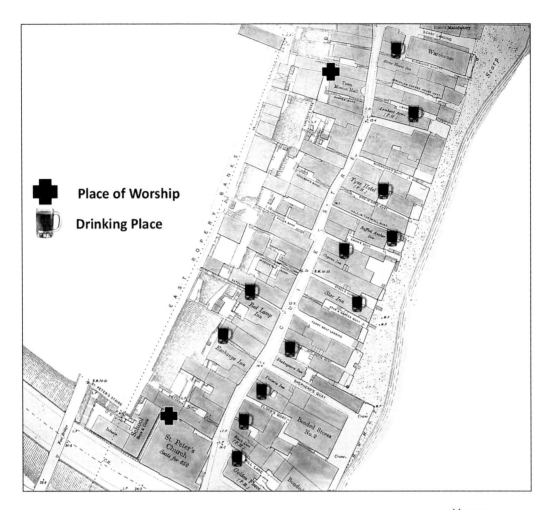

Place of Worship

Drinking Place

Map 9.2
Places for drinking and worship on Clive Street. Clive Street was just one section of the Low Street alongside the river. The map represents the situation in the late nineteenth century.

The rest of Jorgensen's scanty wages went to hell in the next two days in the usual sailor manner. Saloon keepers, prostitutes and other shore sharks soon picked him clean. Jorgensen's hopes and plans for Iowa and a home evaporated with his wages. He was learning again, as he had done so many times before, that it was next to impossible to escape from the sea. In a week, broke and sick, he had signed on another windjammer and was outward-bound, around Cape Horn to Shanghai, China, a ten to twelve months trip each way.[42]

Wright suggests that most of the pubs in the Low Street were 'dens of iniquity'.[43] His examination of the Licensing Victuallers register for a five-year period at the beginning of the twentieth century showed that almost all of the landlords had been charged with one or more offences. The harbouring of prostitutes was a frequent accusation. So too was selling intoxicating liquor to minors (under the age of 14) and to habitual drunkards. In

1878 the police made 914 arrests for drunkenness and disorderly behaviour and that was 50 per cent less than five years earlier. Another common charge against pub landlords was the dilution of spirits. Others were charged with refusing to admit the police to their premises. However, given that in other instances landlords were charged with supplying intoxicating liquor to the police, they may have had good reason to deny them access.

In addition to the consumption of alcohol in congenial surroundings, drinking places were significant meeting places. They were one of the places where oral history was transmitted through the generations. Literate workers read the newspapers provided and the illiterate listened to them read out aloud by people sometimes hired specifically for that purpose. Drinking places, then as now, provided private rooms for formal and informal meetings. For example, the subscribers to the Union Association (for ship insurance), met annually at Thomas Carr's Half Moon Inn.[44] Some justices of the peace met at the George Tavern every Tuesday to hear their cases.[45] The same venue was used for the first meeting of the Poor Law Guardians in 1836. Political groups made use of drinking places for meetings, as did trades unions and those involved in industrial disputes. Pubs and inns were often the place where injured people were taken after an accident, and it was not unusual for them to be used for doctors' consultations, coroners' inquests and the collection of taxes.[46] Drinking places also functioned as the venue where hawkers and tallymen made contact with customers and where members of burial clubs and numerous friendly societies met for their weekly or monthly evening get-togethers. Indeed, the association between friendly societies and pubs was so close that for a period a combined *Friendly Society and Licensed Victuallers Journal* was published in the 1850s. During the moves to change the character of friendly societies in the 1860s, a correspondent to the *Friendly Societies Journal* wrote:

> Mr Editor, I am a temperance man but I must say we owe a debt of gratitude to the Licensed Victuallers Association of England for their kind cooperation and assistance. ... For years they have given us their best rooms to hold our meetings ... too often at a loss to themselves. For years we have sat in comfort doing our business and free of any cost for this accommodation with the exception perhaps of a pint of porter. ... This crusade against public house meetings is mere puritanical cant and humbug, to answer sinister ends; its purpose is jobbery.[47]

Many members of the temperance movement tended to overlook these useful, additional functions served by drinking places. Moreover, their ambition seems not to have been to persuade people to temper, that is to moderate their consumption of alcohol, but rather to abstain from it altogether. The north-east of England had a vigorous temperance/abstinence movement and

The Low Lights Tavern at the bottom of Brewhouse Bank claims to be North Shields' oldest pub. The first documented record of it is in 1834, but it may date back 200 years before that.

in North Shields, like most towns in the area, there were diverse groups of people who had become total abstainers and, with an evangelical fervour, sought to convert others to their way of thinking. For example, those who attended the regular popular concerts at the Howard Hall, organised by the same Mr Hogg who founded the North Shields Amateur Bicycle Club, were obliged to listen to his lectures on the evils of drink in the interval. When a branch of the YMCA (Young Men's Christian Association) was formed in North Shields in 1870, its weekly meetings were held in the Sons of Temperance Hall on Norfolk Street.* A specifically women's temperance organisation was set up following a public meeting in Newcastle in 1876. The British Women's Temperance Association subsequently split in 1893 when some of its members wanted to widen its brief to include women's suffrage. They adopted the name National British Women's Temperance Union and in due course added not only suffrage but welfare, education and health to their concerns. Those who remained focused on the single issue of temperance adopted the name Women's Total Abstinence Union, but were often known as *White Ribboners* because of the white lapel ribbon they wore.† Alice, to whom I referred earlier in the chapter, recalled that her mother was a 'white ribboner' and always wore the small white enamel bow brooch to signify her support for the abstinence movement.

---

* The Sons of Temperance Society still exists but with a dwindling membership of about 8,000.

† The body exists to this day although it now concerns itself with substance abuse of all kinds.

In the latter part of the nineteenth century, working men's social clubs were established in the North Shields area but often provided only the same range of functions already available in many traditional drinking places. As these and other more specialised premises became available, and the homes of ordinary people began to improve, the wider functions traditionally associated with drinking places became less significant. In a port like North Shields, with its distinctive transient population, this change was less marked than elsewhere. Many of the drinking establishments of the late nineteenth and early twentieth century, with their distinctive, often elaborately glazed brick exteriors, survived until my boyhood and were still open at the start of the twenty-first century. Since then, the decline in employment opportunities and retail activity in the immediate vicinity of the pubs, coupled with the ban on smoking in public places, has resulted in many closures. One now has to rely on books like those of Shotton and Steel to understand the dominant and distinctive role public houses once played in the North Shields landscape.[48]

Although even the members of what the Victorians called the labouring classes had access to some leisure activities, it was their position in the economic market place which determined the amount of time they had for leisure as well as, of course, the nature of their every-day lives. It was because they were members of the labouring classes that they did not enjoy access to secure, well-paid employment, and were at a disadvantage in relation to the law and without access to legitimate sources of political power. Before the advent of the welfare state they were also left to cope as best they could with what William Beveridge in the twentieth century described as the five giant evils: squalor, disease, idleness, ignorance and want. It is to an examination of this systematic pattern of disadvantage that we turn in the next three chapters.

10

The labouring classes (I)
Barriers to progress

B Y THE END of the nineteenth century, North Shields was free from intimidation by its Newcastle neighbour and had secured its independent economic position at the mouth of the Tyne. It had outgrown its riverside boundaries, expanded at a phenomenal rate on the Bank Top, and developed a burgeoning local economy. Many people in North Shields benefited greatly from the changes described in earlier chapters and there were undoubtedly significant improvements in the lives of ordinary people during the Victorian period. Even so, at the end of the century, a wide gulf still existed between their lives and the lives of those above them in the social, economic and political pecking order. The harsh truth is that both at the start and end of the nineteenth century, the lot of ordinary people in the town was anything but enviable. Like members of the labouring classes elsewhere, they may have contributed greatly to the success of Britain as the first industrial nation but they were still denied a fair share of the fruits of that economic success. So it is fitting that the lot of ordinary people should be the theme of the concluding chapters of *Shiels to Shields*.

Haswell asserted that the conditions facing them at the beginning of the nineteenth century were so bad that they developed a hatred for their so-called betters. This sweeping assertion came not from a Marxist or any other kind of revolutionary but the son of a local school-teacher who went on to become the managing director of a Midlands engineering company. It was his local knowledge and upbringing which enabled him to empathise with the ordinary people of North Shields and led him to claim that while for reasons of self-interest they may have deferred to their betters in public; their private feelings were very different.[1] While Haswell's assertions cannot be accepted at face value, an examination of the political, legal and economic framework within which ordinary people lived does lend them credibility.

Political oppression

Political oppression is a term ordinarily reserved for regimes without democratic forms of government. In contrast, we commend our political institutions as a model for other countries to follow. Given this prevailing conception of our political system, it is important to emphasise that during most of the period with which we are concerned in this book the ordinary people of North Shields had no access to legitimate forms of political power. After the restoration of the monarchy in 1660, power may have been shared between King, Lords and Commoners but that does not mean that working-class people had any say in the government of their country. They were still without the vote. Even among the few with the right to vote, the electoral process was often corrupt. In small constituencies votes were sometimes auctioned for high prices. In larger constituencies, bribery might only take the form of election feasts and free beer but the overall cost to those nominating candidates could be enormous.* New industrial towns still had no representation in the Commons, yet some rural areas with very few voters retained the right to send one or more members to Parliament. In most of these, the person or persons who owned the estate in which the constituency was located had the right to nominate candidates. This sometimes led to the open sale of parliamentary boroughs for large sums of money.[2]

The blatant disregard of the most elementary principles of democracy in Britain is particularly striking given what had happened in America and in France in the closing decades of the eighteenth century. In 1776, Thomas Jefferson penned the words of the Declaration of Independence, in which thirteen colonies declared themselves to be the United States of America. What is particularly important about the Declaration is that the breach with Britain was justified in the language of democracy.

> When in the Course of human events, it becomes necessary for one people to dissolve the political bands which have connected them with another, and to assume among the powers of the earth, the separate and equal station to which the Laws of Nature and of Nature's God entitle them, a decent respect to the opinions of mankind requires that they should declare the causes which impel them to the separation.
>
> We hold these truths to be self-evident, that all men are created equal, that they are endowed by their Creator with certain unalienable Rights, that among these are Life, Liberty and the pursuit of Happiness. —That to secure these rights, Governments are instituted among Men, deriving their just powers from the consent of

---

* There is an amusing account of electoral shenanigans in Chapter 13 of Charles Dickens' *Pickwick Papers*, published in 1838.

the governed, —That whenever any Form of Government becomes destructive of these ends, it is the Right of the People to alter or to abolish it, and to institute new Government, laying its foundation on such principles and organizing its powers in such form, as to them shall seem most likely to effect their Safety and Happiness. [Original capitalisation and punctuation]

Jefferson may have been a hypocrite in insisting that it was a self-evident truth that all men were created equal. He continued to own slaves and made no provision to free them on his death as other slave-owners had done. Nevertheless, it is still the case that the ordinary people who defeated Britain's trained armed forces were now governed by a profoundly different set of political principles from those that obtained in Britain.

Within a short time, another alarming revolution confronted those who governed Britain. In the summer of 1789, faced with growing violence, French aristocrats surrendered their special privileges and the Declaration of the Rights of Man and the Citizen was formally adopted by the National Assembly.

The representatives of the French people, organized as a National Assembly, believing that the ignorance, neglect, or contempt of the rights of man are the sole cause of public calamities and of the corruption of governments, have determined to set forth in a solemn declaration the natural, unalienable, and sacred rights of man, in order that this declaration, being constantly before all the members of the Social body, shall remind them continually of their rights and duties; in order that the acts of the legislative power, as well as those of the executive power, may be compared at any moment with the objects and purposes of all political institutions and may thus be more respected, and, lastly, in order that the grievances of the citizens, based hereafter upon simple and incontestable principles, shall tend to the maintenance of the constitution and redound to the happiness of all.

This brief statement (albeit long, complex sentence) was translated into every major European language. It became the gospel of the new social order in France and provided a ready-made focus for those seeking political reform elsewhere. Unlike their British counterparts, the people of France, at least officially, enjoyed a written constitution; parliamentary government; equality before the law; and open access to public positions.

Those who held power in Britain were implacably opposed to the revolution. In varying coalitions with other European nations, British people became embroiled in a prolonged conflict with France. What we now know as the Napoleonic Wars lasted from 1793 to 1815. Between 1812 and 1815

Britain was also at war with the United States after continental ports had been blockaded against American vessels.

The American War of Independence and the Napoleonic Wars provided new opportunities for British industry and commerce, and North Shields' entrepreneurs benefited from these military conflicts in a variety of ways. The impact of the wars on the ordinary people of Britain was another matter. In many instances their circumstances deteriorated further. That is why the victory of coalition forces at Waterloo in 1815 did not end the growing demand for political reform in Britain. Even after the restoration of the French monarchy, ordinary people enjoyed more freedom than before the revolution. Encouraged by such developments in France and America, there was a continued demand for fundamental reform of Britain's political institutions. Concerned by this unrest, Parliament passed what became known as the Gagging Acts of 1819. The illiberal thinking behind the legislation was summed up in the preamble which declared that 'every meeting for radical reform is an overt act of treasonable conspiracy against the King and his government'.

The July 1826 election in Northumberland (the constituency of which North Shields was then a part) provides us with a detailed picture of the electoral process in this period. In the whole county there were only about 4,000 voters for two parliamentary seats. For the previous half century, the selection of MPs had been made by agreements between the county's main landowners, saving themselves the expense of a contested election. Unusually, on this occasion, the election was contested: by four candidates, all from major Northumbrian land-owning families. As a consequence, the political differences between them were overlaid with a complex mix of traditional loyalties, family connections, friendships and personal animosities. Without the convenience of a mass media to reproduce the soundbites of the candidates and provide them with photo-opportunities, they had to travel to venues throughout Northumberland and deliver numerous long speeches to expectant audiences. At the time, there were major issues at stake. They included free trade, as distinct from a protectionist economic policy; the Corn Laws which had pushed up the price of bread, the staple diet of the working classes; slavery; and discrimination against Catholics. The main local concerns in North Shields were the downturn in the regional economy following the end of the Napoleonic Wars and the remaining elements of the long-running dispute with Newcastle.

About 10 per cent of those with the vote lived in or near North Shields and during the six-month campaign the town received a succession of visits from the candidates in an attempt to solicit support. Ironically, despite the fact that so few people had the vote, contemporary accounts suggest there was much greater enthusiasm among the disenfranchised majority than there is today when all adults do have the vote. That was, in part, because elections were in effect local theatrical events.

T. Wentworth Beaumont was the first to arrive in North Shields, when he held a meeting at the Commercial Arms on 8 March. Formerly a rebel Tory MP, he emphasised that he was now standing as an independent. The following day, Matthew Bell, a Tory, held a meeting at the Northumberland Arms. On the same day, the Honourable Henry Thomas Liddell, another Tory, invited 'as many of his friends as can make it' to the Commercial Hotel on Howard Street to drink his health on his birthday! Not to be outdone, Matthew Bell then issued a notice on the 10th saying he would 'feel much gratified by the favour of the company of his friends at dinner at the Northumberland Arms' on the New Quay on the 13th. Concerned that votes were already being promised so early in the campaign, Viscount Howick's committee issued a notice which asked freeholders to 'reserve their votes for the present, it being his Lordship's intention shortly to wait upon them to solicit their suffrages'. Howick, a Whig, was the son of Lord Grey, who was to become Prime Minister in the period 1830–34.

Howick had reason to be concerned. Liddell arrived in North Shields in triumphal fashion at the head of a cavalcade on 14 March, accompanied by the ringing of church bells and the firing of guns. Following 'a large body of gentlemen on horseback' came seamen and shipwrights, walking four abreast with banners. They were followed by a band and flags (including one displaying the words *Liddell, the Man of the People*). Bringing up the rear were carriages, more horsemen and yet more banners. On arrival in North Shields, Liddell addressed an enthusiastic crowd of thousands. He talked at length but without touching on a single issue of policy. The following day, he addressed freeholders with the vote, at the George Tavern on King Street. Again, he did little other than issue a string of unctuous platitudes. Although he touched upon the long-running conflict with Newcastle and offered a few words of sympathy he added, 'We must not interfere with vested interests, nor attempt to give more than strict and impartial consideration to the general good, before we meditate a remedy to a particular, but acknowledged inconvenience.' On the issues of free trade and the controversial Corn Laws he said only that he did not claim to understand the issues involved and declined to commit himself to any particular position. 'Upon these points I feel bound to state that I can give no *pledge* whatever of my future conduct, that I must be permitted to decide according to the best of my judgment.' Despite the lack of commitment in what he had to say, he received the promise of 357 votes. By the time Viscount Howick arrived in North Shields a few days later, his cause appeared already to have been lost.

During the long campaign, the candidates were from time to time obliged to confront policy issues. With the exception of the unusually forthright Beaumont, they normally offered reassuring answers that committed them to nothing. Bell, for example, insisted that contrary to a report that was circulating, he was 'a sincere advocate for the *total* abolition of slavery … and nothing would give him higher satisfaction than to see it *instantly* abolished.' But then he added the caveat 'if the measure were practicable'. Liddell, in a later visit to North Shields, tackled the Catholic question in a similarly ambivalent way. He began by insisting that 'no man living is more zealously and devotedly attached to our Protestant church'. He insisted he was 'decidedly opposed to popery' but went on to maintain that because Catholicism was no longer a potent force in Britain it was now safe to relax some of the restrictions on Catholics. Yet, like Bell, he ended with an important caveat. 'I candidly confess it does not appear desirable that Roman Catholics should be eligible to some of our highest offices of state.' Bell was less equivocal when he was joined by 130 'friends' at a dinner at the Northumberland Arms a little later. Despite his claim 'to be a friend to religious toleration', he stated, 'I would have it distinctly understood that I am averse to making further concessions of political power to the Roman Catholics. … I throw myself and my cause into the hands of my Protestant brethren. They will never allow me to be beaten down by the body of Catholics, however formidable.'

Then, as now, the candidates and their followers engaged in negative campaigning. For example, the early front-runner Liddell was obliged to counter an attempt 'to induce some of the less opulent freeholders to break their word' to vote for him because someone had started a rumour that those from North Shields would have to pay their own expenses to travel to Alnwick to cast their votes. As a result, a notice was issued reassuring freeholders that an ample fund had been provided so that no one would be *required* to pay for the 80-mile round trip. It is not clear what mode of transport was used by Liddell's supporters but Viscount Howick took the freeholders pledged to him to and from Alnmouth by steamboat.

Almost all of the speeches made during the campaign contained allegations about the integrity of the other candidates. They in turn not only denied them but made counter-allegations against their opponents. For example, as a result of reports of what Howick's agent had said about him at a campaign meeting in North Shields, Beaumont changed his plans and came to North Shields in person, on 7 June, to deny them. Three carriages left Newcastle. En route, they were joined by large numbers of sailors, carpenters and other workmen as well as a band, and by the time the Commercial Hotel was reached the crowd around it was estimated to be more than 20,000 strong. After his long speech to the crowd from his carriage, he was 'enthusiastically carried over the heads of the people to the door of the Commercial Hotel'. Most of the crowd remained outside while Beaumont and 50 of his 'friends' had dinner and were later treated to 'a brilliant display of fireworks'. Not to be outdone by this show of strength, the favourite Liddell returned to North Shields again in June, once again at the head of a huge cavalcade of supporters.

Unlike the electoral process today, polling took place over a 15-day period. Electors could cast up to two votes, by a spoken declaration, in public, at the 'hustings' in the county town of Alnwick. The cumulative results were announced at the end of each day. Campaigning continued throughout the voting period. After the announcement of the daily count, the leading candidates usually made short speeches thanking their supporters and expressing confidence in the eventual outcome. The candidates facing defeat made longer speeches, often impugning the integrity of their opponents, to try to persuade voters to switch their votes to them. The speeches were accompanied by invariably ill-tempered and often acrimonious exchanges between the candidates, part of the negative campaigning which continued until the very end. The exchanges even led to a duel between Beaumont and Howick's agent Lambton, which fortuitously left them both unhurt.

On the 12th day, when it was obvious that he would come last in the poll, Howick withdrew from the contest. When polling closed at 3 p.m. on the 15th day, Liddell was the clear winner with 1,562 votes. Bell was selected as the second MP with 1,380 votes. Beaumont, with 1,335 votes, was the third and disappointed candidate. The election cost the successful candidates about £30,000 each: a colossal sum equivalent to about £22 million based on average earnings then and now. Beaumont's unsuccessful campaign cost about £40,000. To cover his £17,000 costs, Howick was obliged to sell Ulgham Grange. However, in consolation, later in the year, his political connections awarded him the seat of the 'rotten borough' of Winchelsea.

Mug commemorating the 1826 election victory of Thomas Henry Liddell.
BY COURTESY OF MARTYN EDGELL ANTIQUES

Although there was a widespread demand for electoral reform, most members of the industrial and commercial classes seem to have been prepared to settle for something modest. Their main concern was to share political power with those who already monopolised it. Yet, faced with resistance from the Tories and the House of Lords, and despite strikes, riots and widespread unrest, it took three attempts to get a modest Whig Reform Bill on the statute book. It was eventually passed in 1832. Although little more than a gesture in the direction of democracy, the Act was of major constitutional significance for North Shields. It was one of 43 towns now allowed to elect an MP. Along with Tynemouth, Chirton, Preston and Cullercoats, it was constituted as the parliamentary Borough of Tynemouth and North Shields.

Under the new rules, about ten per cent of local residents now had the vote but 90 per cent remained disenfranchised. For the first twenty years, the constituency returned Whig MPs. The first was the ship-builder George Frederick Young. A vehement supporter of protectionism rather than free trade, Young was unseated by petition in 1838, because 17 of those voting for him in 1837 had contravened the election rules by changing their address between the date of their registration and date of the election. Having had a majority of only 16, Young was obliged to yield the seat to Sir Charles Edward Grey. Originally from Backworth but educated at Eton and Oxford, Grey was a judge and privy counsellor who went on to become governor of Barbados in 1841.* He was succeeded by Henry Mitcalfe (1841–47), of whom I have been able to discover little except he appears to have owned the 447-ton convict ship *William Mitcalfe* launched in Sunderland in 1834. In 1847, the Earsdon-born Ralph William Grey was elected unopposed. In 1852 he appeared to have had the unhappy distinction of being the first Whig to lose the seat to a Conservative. However, the supporters of the winner, Shilbottle-born coal owner Hugh Taylor, were later found to have bribed voters. By then Grey had moved to the Liskeard seat in Cornwall so a by-election was held in 1854 and the winning candidate on this occasion was William Shaw Lindsay, another Liberal.

The 1832 Reform Act may have put Tynemouth and North Shields on the political map, but its labouring classes gained no direct benefit from the legislation and the demand for more fundamental change continued. Tyneside radicalism capitalised on the relative sophistication of the print culture of the area. Newspapers were not only read by the literate members of the working class but also 'hear read' by countless more who were illiterate. In the initial decades after the 1832 Act, protest focused on Chartism. It was a disparate political movement which meant different things to those who supported it, but there were key common elements to which all subscribed. They were that the Charter should secure the vote for all adult males and that there should be annual parliaments, secret voting, equal electoral districts, the abolition of the property qualification for MPs, and the introduction of payments to MPs to make it possible for ordinary people to seek election.

Historians disagree on the character of the support for Chartism in the North East. Maehl asserts that the miners were the backbone of the movement – a claim which Rowe disputes.[3] Nossiter plays down the revolutionary character of North East Chartism but Allen maintains that the call to arms by many local Chartist leaders was no idle threat.[4] What is agreed is that very large numbers of people travelled often long distances to Chartist rallies.[5] It is also clear that the authorities on Tyneside took Chartism seriously. Major precautionary measures were put in place when

---

* Young remains forever associated with the constituency as one of the sample of MPs portrayed in Sir George Hayter's painting of the first session of the new House of Commons, which now hangs in the National Gallery.

the movement was at its height in 1848. In North Shields alone, 900 soldiers and special constables were on standby and a further 1,000 were standing by in South Shields.[6]

The problem facing the Chartists at national and local level was how to persuade – or force – an unsympathetic government to make political concessions. The debate about strategy is usually couched in terms of the use of 'moral force' as distinct from 'physical force' but Kemnitz maintains this is a simplistic dichotomy.[7] Many Chartists who advocated moral force meant much more than an appeal to the heart. They hoped to use economic means to undermine the nation's financial structure, for example by organising a run on savings banks. Others advocated the use of only violent rhetoric (*the language of menace*) to try to frighten the government to yield to Chartist demands. But there were also those who openly advocated the use of force and hoped for a revolutionary situation comparable to that in France. In short, Kemnitz seems to be suggesting that the strategies proposed by the Chartists are better represented as a continuum rather than a dichotomy.

Maehl goes a step further in applying Kemnitz's analysis to Chartism in the North East.[8] He notes that Tyneside Chartists used different strategies in response to changing circumstances. Moreover, the same individuals urged different strategies at different times. Many who had previously rejected the use of violence were prepared to contemplate it when they

Barriers to progress |

feared that they would have to defend themselves against attack from their own government. For example, James Williams, a prominent local Chartist, declared in 1839 in response to the Rural Police Bill, 'I, who have hitherto been and still am a moral force man, will never allow this Police Law to be enforced without arming myself.'[9]

It was at that point in the debate that the Northern Political Union stated that 'it is the sacred and imperative duty of every individual Englishman to be in possession of such defensive arms as are guaranteed by the law'. Chartists who shared this view saw themselves as honest Britons fighting for their birth right and the police as agents of a repressive government, 'trained in order to enable them [the Government] to enforce their cruel, inhuman, un-English, oppressive, and unconstitutional enactments down the throats of the people of this kingdom, at the point of the bayonet.' In a debate not dissimilar from that taking place about civil liberties and the use of the internet in twenty-first-century Britain, other Chartists maintained that the Police Bill was 'intended to take away the last vestige of our liberties'. The 'plan is one of general espionage, by carrying out of which they shall know every circumstance which transpires in the country, whether in the meeting-house, the manufactory, the public street, or the labourer's cottage.'[10]

Robert Lowery, the Chartist leader who had been born in North Shields in 1809, joined with those who suggested that bearing arms was the right of every free Englishman. A contemporary account of a speech he delivered in Newcastle in October 1838 reported that he had argued that:

If the Government granted their just demands they asked no more: but if they did not, it remained to be seen whether a few thousand aristocrats, and twenty or thirty of a standing army were in a condition to put down the mighty and incensed millions of England [Loud cheers]. Resistance to oppression was obedience to the laws of God. Had America trusted to moral force, where had been her republic? The Americans calmly discussed the matter, and when they came to the conclusion that tyranny was to be resisted, they set about it with heart and hand [Loud cheers].[11]

The report on Lowery's speech in Carlisle in the same month indicates that he then used even plainer language.

By law every man was entitled to be in possession of a weapon of defence; and their fathers used to meet on their village greens to practice games of defence. ... He hoped that every man who had the means, and had not already a fire-lock, would with all speed provide himself with one to hang over his chimney-piece. It was the best piece of furniture he could have, for it would protect the other furniture. The villains would scarcely venture to enter his doors for taxes if they saw this [Cheers].[12]

Whether or not Lowery's speeches in 1838 were no more than contributions to *the language of menace*, by February 1839 he seemed close to the physical force extreme of the Chartist continuum. An advertisement appeared in the *Northern Liberator* announcing that muskets were available from Robert Lowery's political bookshop.[13]

The Chartist movement culminated in a miserable failure in 1848. A mass march on the House of Commons was organised to present a petition with over 5 million signatures. Artillery, soldiers and policemen, plus an estimated 170,000 special constables, were deployed at strategic sites to guard against a breakdown in public order, but it did not materialise. The crowd dispersed on the advice of its leaders and from that point on Chartism began to disintegrate as an active political movement.

Allen argues that, despite this, the underlying movement for change continued. New leaders emerged and on Tyneside popular radicalism took on different forms.[14] These included the rise of the Cooperative movement and the emergence of working-class organisations such as Mechanics' Institutes. Though these were established primarily to provide technical education, and were supported by local industrialists such as Robert Stephenson, they also stocked books which increased the social and political awareness of those who read them. As an indication of the depth of political radicalism on Tyneside, Giuseppe Garibaldi, the Italian freedom fighter, was given a warm welcome when he arrived in March 1854, an event which illustrates the international dimension of the struggle for political reform.[15] After previous military failures, Garibaldi had reverted to his original role as a sea captain and when he moored his 1,000-ton ship the *Commonwealth* at North Shields, it was to take a cargo of coal to Genoa. He stayed for a month at what is now Kings School in Tynemouth and used it as a base where he made arrangements for a second Italian war of independence, including recruiting volunteers for a British legion. On the day before his departure, a party of sympathisers visited him on board the *Commonwealth* to express their support and present him with a sword and telescope, paid for by donations from local workers. In his acceptance speech he vowed that the sword would 'never be drawn by me except in the cause of liberty'. His return to Italy from Tyneside in May 1854 marked the end of his five years of exile and in the crucial battle at Volturno in 1860 he drew the sword to

PORTRAITS OF DELEGATES.
No. IX.

ROBERT LOWERY.

Robert Lowery, the North Shields-born Chartist leader. Twelve delegates were drawn for the Charter newspaper at the time of the first Chartist Convention in 1839. Lowery, the Newcastle delegate, was one of them.

lead the charge. Thorburn's, a North Shields shipbuilder, later named one of his tugs *Garibaldi* in honour of the revolutionary leader: one of three River Tyne built vessels named after him.*

Slowly and grudgingly, concessions were made to the disenfranchised in subsequent decades. In 1858 the property qualification for MPs was removed. The Reform Act of 1867 doubled the electorate of England and Wales to almost two million. The Liberal Thomas Eustace Smith, the first MP for Tynemouth to be elected under the new arrangements, was returned in 1868 and remained the MP for the constituency until 1885.† By then secret ballots had been in use since 1872. Further reforms followed in the 1884 Reform Act and the 1885 Redistribution Act – which tripled the electorate, largely by extending the vote to most agricultural labourers. The new MP for North Shields after 1885 was Richard Sims Donkin, a Conservative who held the seat until 1900. Increasingly, voting came to be seen as a right rather than a privilege. Even so, it was not until 1918 when all men over 21 and all women over 30 were given the vote – and not until 1928 that it was given to all women over the age of 21. To put that in perspective, my own grandmother Lawrence did not get the vote until she was 52 years old.

I have included these details on the tortuous routes by which ordinary men and women secured the right to vote for two reasons. The first is to remind readers that during the whole of the eighteenth century and most of the nineteenth, ordinary men and women were denied even a nominal control over their political masters. Some maintain that this is of no great consequence because elections only represent a device to lend legitimacy to the behind-the-scenes exercise of power in society, which lies not with those who control its formal political institutions but those who control its economic resources. That may or may not be the case. What is certainly true is that during the period with which we are concerned, the ordinary people of North Shields and elsewhere lacked any significant influence in either the political or economic spheres. The second reason I have discussed the struggle to extend the franchise is to remind readers, particularly those who no longer choose to vote, that their forebears fought long and hard and in some cases were prepared to die for the right that they now decline to exercise. By the twenty-first century, barely 70 years after women had acquired the same voting rights as men, only a small minority of the electorate voted in local government elections. In 2012 the turnout in what is now North Tyneside was 33 per cent. The turnout in general elections is higher but falling. In the constituency of Tynemouth it was 80+ per cent

---

* His grandson Giuseppe Garibaldi carried the same sword with him when he served with distinction as a volunteer with the British Army during the Boer War.

† His predecessor from 1865–68 was George Otto Trevelyan, who held several senior posts in Gladstone's administration. He was also the author of *The Life and Letters of Lord Macaulay*, the distinguished historian who was his maternal uncle.

from 1900 to 1959. From 1964 to 1992 it fell to 70+ per cent. In the first two elections in the twenty-first century it fell to 60+ per cent.* Ironically, it is members of the working class, whose forebears struggled so hard to get the vote, who are least likely to make use of it.

Economic exploitation

Today, economic exploitation is a term we use for situations in which people are obliged to work in conditions and for wages that would be considered wholly unacceptable in this country. Yet for much of the period with which we are concerned, most ordinary people in England were economically exploited in a similar way. The social and political structures of the period were rigged so that workers could not significantly improve the quality of their lives; no matter how able they were or how hard they worked.

When Parliament consisted mainly of landowners, often unsympathetic towards commercial and industrial capitalists, it sometimes sympathised with industrial workers. In the latter half of the eighteenth century, the situation began to change. More and more landowners were drawn into industry and commerce and redefined their conception of their self-interest. At the same time, the ranks of landowners were diluted by manufacturers who bought land in order to qualify for election to Parliament. Increasingly, social divisions were redrawn so that landowners, manufacturers and MPs saw any worker agitation for improvements in their terms and conditions of employment as a threat to the established order.

Colls maintains that English law was inherently hostile to all combinations of workers: 'a hostility shown in the forty or so eighteenth-century statutes against combination in specific trades, and in the predilection of judges to view all combinations as criminal conspiracies'.[16] In addition, the Riot Act of 1715 (which was not formally removed from the statute book until 1967) allowed the authorities to use force to disperse 'crowds' of twelve or more people if they remained after the relevant clause of the Act had been read out. Those who broke up the gathering were specifically indemnified against any legal consequences in the event of any of the crowd being injured or killed. Amid a growing concern among those in power following the French Revolution, a general ban on trade unions was introduced in 1799. Under its provisions, trade unionists became criminals. Organising to try to increase wages or reduce working hours was expressly forbidden. The penalty for doing so was three months' imprisonment or two months' hard labour in a

---

* I have not included the 1918 election result which followed a month after the armistice which marked the end of the First World War. It used an 8-year-old electoral register and so the turnout figures underestimate the 'real' turnout, that is among those still alive and resident at the time of the poll in the same constituency. I have also not included the 1945 election in which the turnout was also distorted by conditions relating to war (but still 77 per cent).

house of correction. Even attending a meeting to discuss such matters was subject to the same penalties. The decision on whether the law had been breached was taken by a single magistrate – who, given the local nature of most disputes, could even be the accused's employer. But, despite such obviously one-sided legislation, many employers were reluctant to bear the cost of court action, and the reprisals that might follow, which helps to explain why organisations like the coal miners' Brotherhood escaped prosecution in the first quarter of the nineteenth century.[17]

During the nineteenth century, the prevailing ideology was that governments should, as far as possible, refrain from interfering with the way in which employers treated their employees. When governments did intervene, it was to protect women and children from the worst excesses of the market. The prevailing mythology was that able-bodied male workers could look after themselves. The obvious fact that they often could not do so was overlooked. And just to make sure that workers did not succeed in looking after themselves, successive governments breached the principle of non-intervention – in the interests of employers. On occasions, troops actually killed those trying to do no more that secure an improvement in their working conditions. Others were deported to the colonies. Although the Combination Act was repealed in 1824, the strikes which followed created a reaction which led to a number of important restrictions on how trade unions could operate. Workers could combine to negotiate better terms and conditions, but it was unlawful to try to induce workers to breach their contracts or in any way obstruct either employers or employees during a dispute. That made it difficult to organise strikes without running the risk of falling foul of the law especially when local courts were free to interpret terms like obstruction.

The divide that this rigged system created in British society was recognised not just by left wing revolutionaries such as Marx but some Conservatives, for example Benjamin Disraeli. In his novel *Sybil or The Two Nations* he portrays the fundamental divide through a conversation between his character Egremont and a stranger.

'Well, society may be in its infancy,' said Egremont slightly smiling; 'but, say what you like, our Queen reigns over the greatest nation that ever existed.'

'Which nation?' asked the younger stranger, 'for she reigns over two.'

The stranger paused; Egremont was silent, but looked inquiringly.

'Yes,' resumed the younger stranger after a moment's interval. 'Two nations; between whom there is no intercourse and no sympathy; who are as ignorant of each other's habits, thoughts, and feelings, as if they were dwellers in different zones, or inhabitants of different planets; who are formed by a different breeding, are fed by a different food, are ordered by different manners, and are not governed by the same laws.'

'You speak of' – said Egremont, hesitatingly.

'THE RICH AND THE POOR.'[18]

The gross imbalance in power between the two nations is clearly illustrated by the relationship between the mine-owners and the pitmen of the North East. The employers operated a cartel which was of particular value in an industry where supply could easily exceed demand and drive down prices. The cartel operated a policy known as vending, which set limits on coal production to ensure that prices remained high (in the same way that OPEC has until 2015 restricted supplies of oil). By agreeing on levels of production and on the details of the bond (that is, the miners' binding terms and conditions of employment for the coming year), the employers' cartel sought to create a non-competitive situation for themselves. Although a miners' Brotherhood had existed since 1804 (by admitting only to its role as a friendly society), the repeal of the Combination Act allowed trade unions to act openly on behalf of miners. That alone was no guarantee of success. The initial United Association of Colliers on the rivers Tyne and Wear collapsed in 1826. It was replaced by a new body in 1830, headed by Thomas Hepburn, a Wesleyan Methodist preacher. The North Union of Pitmen of Tyne and Wear called a strike to try to reduce the working hours of boys from 16 hours to 12 hours a day, and bring an end to the Tommy Shop principle in which workers were paid partly in vouchers for over-priced goods available at the company store. In order not to fall foul of the 1825 legislation, Hepburn pleaded with his members to keep the strike peaceful although the response of the pit owners made that difficult. They recruited miners from elsewhere in the country and evicted strikers from their homes. Despite lasting from April to September, the strike achieved only minor concessions from employers.

In 1831 there was another strike. This time the demand was for a 12-hour day and a guaranteed amount of work each fortnight. The striking miners also wanted the occupation of houses customarily provided by employers to be separated from the terms of the bond. The owners rejected all but the latter demand and in retaliation sought to move the date of the bond agreement forward from April to February, in the hope that the winter weather would discourage workers from changing employers at the end of the annual period. At this point, no less a person than the mayor of Newcastle suggested that the mine owners had deliberately chosen to adopt this combative stance in the expectation that it would lead to a strike and provide them with grounds for raising the price of coal. On this occasion, the mine-owners' cynical manoeuvre backfired. Within six weeks it was the cartel not the union which had collapsed as mine-owners 'tripped over one another in an effort to reach contract settlements with their workers'.[19]

By the time the next bond came to be agreed, the union was in a weaker position. Its finances had been depleted because of the sickness and death benefits it had paid out to miners and their families during the 1831–32 cholera epidemic. At that point, the union faced a re-forged cartel with a new strategy. While about half of the North East collieries immediately renewed their contracts, the remainder refused to employ union members and by mid-April started to evict unbound union miners from their company-owned homes. They did so with the help of regular troops, London police officers and untrained special constables employed by the coal-owners – but provided with firearms by the army. By the middle of July 1832, General Bouverie, who was supervising the situation, estimated that over 2,000 people had been made homeless. Local banks then provided the coal-owners with funds to recruit 'strangers' to replace the evicted miners. Between June and October, over 3,000 had been recruited, mainly from Cornwall, Wales, Derbyshire and Somerset. In the face of this combined opposition from the employers, the government and local financiers, it was not just the strike but the union which collapsed.[20]

Joseph Skipsey, the Percy Main miner turned poet. When he was four months old his father was killed during an industrial dispute. Aged seven, he started work underground in a local pit for 16 hours a day. He went on to become a nationally known poet.

During the dispute, two men lost their lives. The first was a North Shields miner, Cuthbert Skipsey. He was shot and killed by a police officer while trying to calm the crowd during a disturbance near the still standing Pineapple Inn in Balkwell.* Skipsey left a widow and eight children. The youngest, Joseph Skipsey, only 4 months old at the time of his father's death, went down the pit at the age of seven to work 16 hours a day, but went on to become a celebrated poet.[21]

The constable who shot Cuthbert was found guilty of manslaughter but given only a six-month sentence. A very different fate befell a striking miner, William Jobling. He tried to beg money from Nicholas Fairles, a hard-line local magistrate. When Fairles declined to help, Jobling's seaman companion, Ralph Armstrong, attacked him. Both men then ran off leaving Fairles seriously injured. Armstrong fled the area but Jobling stayed and was arrested. Fairles testified that Jobling had not assaulted him but, despite that, the miner was charged

---

* The Pineapple Inn was the birthplace of the celebrated architect John Dobson in 1787.

with murder after the magistrate died from his injuries. The illiterate Jobling had no legal counsel to argue his case and was found guilty and sentenced to death.*

In passing sentence, the judge conflated the seaman's attack on Fairles with the miners' strike and trades unions in general (which he referred to during the trial as 'these abominations'). He made it clear that he hoped that the sentence that he passed on a man acknowledged to have killed no one would discourage others from taking part in strikes and begging while out of work. Jobling was sentenced not only to a public execution but the humiliation of having his body suspended in chains from a gibbet erected near the scene of the attack.[22] In passing this sentence, Parke acted not just as a partisan local magistrate. Two weeks earlier, the Home Secretary had written to all North East magistrates urging them 'to be vigilant against violent, unjust, seditious, tumultuous, and inflammatory trade union actions'.[23] After his hanging, Joblin's body was covered in pitch and placed in a cage made of flat iron bars. His feet were put in stirrups from which iron bars went up to his head, ending in the ring from which the gibbet was suspended. His caged body was escorted by a large body of soldiers to a point close to Jobling's home, where his wife still lived. The gibbet was attached to a 20-foot high heavy wooden upright, reinforced with steel bars so that it could not easily be sawn through. It was to be the last gibbeting in the United Kingdom. The practice was abolished in 1834.†

It would be wrong to give the impression that, even in these early decades of the nineteenth century, all those in authority were determined to keep workers in their place by whatever means were at their disposal. McCord notes that on occasions the actions of government ministers and officials manifested a genuine sympathy for workers struggling against unfair and sometimes overwhelming odds.[24] Morgan and Ruston also note that government ministers were often irritated by the propensity of North East magistrates to capitalise on the importance of the coal trade to appeal for troops and naval vessels as a first rather than a last resort during industrial disputes.[25]

As the nineteenth century progressed, the legal position of workers in relation to their employers improved significantly. However, there was still a difference between changes to the statute book and changes to people's lives. Some changes could and did take effect more or less immediately. Others, relating to such things as working hours or safety, could only be effective if there was a sufficiently large and vigilant inspectorate to enforce them, which was rarely the case. Indeed even today, laws relating to safety and

---

* The Prisoner's Counsel Act, which introduced legal representation for those charged with serious crimes, was not introduced until 1836.

† According to local legend, after friends took him down from the gibbet, Jobling's body was taken to the Gas Light pub. After nearly two centuries, and despite protests, the historic pub was demolished in 2008 to make way for the second Tyne road tunnel.

the minimum wage are sometimes flouted by unscrupulous employers. But, even in those instances where legislation was fully enacted and a serious effort made to enforce it, the cumulative impact of what had gone before continued for a long time thereafter. The clock could not be turned back for those who had been executed, transported or press-ganged or for the families they had left behind.

Justice and injustice

At the beginning of the nineteenth century, to discourage people from resorting to crime in the face of oppression and exploitation, a harsh penal code was used as an overt instrument of social and political control. It protected the privileged from the under-privileged, the oppressors from the oppressed, and the exploiters from the exploited. It was not just that judges and magistrates were biased. The law's primary function was to maintain the status quo, not only in terms of the distribution of power and wealth but also social relationships, including those between men and women. This is apparent in the range and nature of crimes which carried the death penalty. What mattered was not just *what* was done but to *whom* it was done. The normal penalty for murder was hanging. Someone convicted of high treason was hanged, drawn and quartered in full public view.* High treason did not have to be an act which threatened the country's security. It was defined as essentially *any* act of disloyalty to the Sovereign. The lesser crime of petty treason protected existing patterns of social relationships. In English common law it was defined as an act of betrayal of a superior by a subordinate (a crime which remained in place until 1828). It included a wife killing her husband (but not vice versa) and a servant killing a master or mistress (but not vice versa). Both acts were deemed to threaten the social order and were seen as more subversive than other murders.†

---

* This footnote is unpleasant reading but in a society where we are quick to condemn the punishments meted out in other countries, it is salutary to be reminded of how recently we engaged in what today would be regarded as acts of barbarity. Ordinarily, a man convicted of high treason (women met a different style of death) would be hanged by the short drop method so that their neck would not break. Ideally still alive, he would then be dragged to a quartering table. Water would be used try to revive him if he was unconscious. After his genitalia had been removed, his abdomen would be opened and his intestines pulled out. Only after he was disembowelled and his organs burned before his eyes, would he be beheaded. His body would then be cut into four pieces. The monarch was entitled to decide where the parts would be displayed. The last hanging, drawing and quartering in England was on 1 May 1820, just four years before the birth of my great-grandfather Lawrence.

† Until 1793, husband-murderers were burned at the stake rather than hanged. The crime of petty treason was abolished and husband-killing treated as a common murder from 1825.

At the beginning of the nineteenth century capital punishment was available for 220 crimes, many of which would not be regarded as serious today. Although the death sentence was often commuted, there were still 7,000 executions between 1770 and 1830. Among them was Robert Knowles, a North Shields postman, who was executed in 1777 for stealing a letter which contained two £50 banknotes, each worth the equivalent of about £70,000 in 2014.[26] Today huge crowds converge on Newcastle's Gallowgate to watch Newcastle United play football. In 1777 a huge crowd went to watch Knowles' execution. During the nineteenth century, the number of capital crimes was reduced substantially. The 1860s saw an end to public executions, while the death penalty for murder was eventually abolished in 1969.

An alternative sentence to the death penalty or imprisonment, was transportation to the colonies. It was used for petty and serious crimes. In 1752 a Newcastle schoolteacher was transported to South Carolina for seven years for stealing books.[27] After the American War of Independence, other destinations had to be found. Africa was a disaster. Of the 700 convicts sent to Gambia in 1765, over half died within a year. It was against that background that transportation to Australia began with a fleet of eleven ships carrying 700 convicts in 1787. The youngest was nine years old; the oldest 82. An example of how this serious punishment was used for even petty crime is that of a woman caught stealing a handkerchief during a 1790 trial at the Newcastle Assizes. She was immediately taken before the jury and sentenced to seven years' transportation – in the space of just a few minutes.[28] By the time the practice of transportation came to an end in 1868, about 160,000 men, women and children had been sent to Australia.

Impressment is another example of what today would be seen as grossly unjust. Press gangs were legally allowed to force people to join the Royal Navy against their will. Based on a practice established in 1563, it continued in use until 1815 and remained legal for a further century. It was necessary because the Navy could not recruit sufficient sailors, even after the improved conditions which followed the 1797 Spithead mutiny. Experienced sailors were obviously preferred to landsmen, so North Shields, with its large population of seamen, was a frequent target for press gangs. In 1796, 250 men were pressed into service during an infamous raid in which the town was cordoned off by troops. One of the naval vessels involved in these press gang raids left its name behind. The *Peggy*, which anchored in a deep pool close to Pow Burn, led to it being given the name *Peggy's Hole*. Although press gang raids were governed by explicit rules, they were not always observed – perhaps in some instances because the officers found it difficult to follow the legalistic jargon in their orders. Consider, for example, this notice which was issued in relation to a pressing in North Shields in 1803.

CERTIFICATE OF PROTECTION AGAINST PRESS GANGS

The appended notice to commence a Press at North Shields, &c., may supply Mr W. SABINE with some of the information he seeks.

By the Commissioners for Executing the Office Lord High Admiral of Great Britain and Ireland, etc.

Whereas it is necessary for the more speedy Manning of His Majesty's Ships, to impress all Persons of the denominations exprest in the Press Warrant which you have received from Us, without regard to any Protections, excepting however such Persons as are Protected pursuant to Acts of Parliament, and all others, who by the Printed Instructions which accompanied the said Warrant are forbidden to be imprest and also such as belong to

Transports, Storeships, Victuallers, or other Ships or Vessels in the Service of the Navy, Victualling, Transport, and Ordnance Boards, Ships and Vessels laden by the especial order and under the direction of the Lord Commissioner of his Majesty's Treasury with Provisions and Stores for the use of His Majesty's Armies etc., Vessels and Craft in the Service of the Corporation of Trinity House and Ships and Vessels bound to Foreign Parts which are laden and cleared outwards by the proper Officers of His Majesty's Customs.

And whereas We think fit that a General Press from Protections as above mentioned, shall commence at North Shields and in the Neighbourhood thereof on the Night of Monday next the 7th instant, you are therefore (after taking the proper preparatory measures with all possible Secrecy) hereby required and directed to impress, and to give orders to the Lieutenants under your Command to impress all Persons of the above-mentioned Denominations (except as before excepted) accordingly and to continue to do so until you receive Orders from us to the contrary.

If any of his Majesty's Ships or Vessels, or any hired into His Majesty's Service and Commanded by Commissioned Officers, shall be in the way, you are to communicate these Orders to their Commanders, under a strict injunction of Secrecy, and to settle a Plan with them that a General Press as abovementioned may commence and be carried on at one and the same time, as well Afloat as on Shore, they being hereby required and directed to exert themselves in the execution thereof, and to cooperate with you in whatever may be necessary on the occasion.

Given under Our Hands the 5 day of Novemr, 1803.
To Captain William Charleton at North Shields
By Command of their Lordships
Wm. Marsden.[29]

On occasions, press officers issued notifications that public events could go ahead without fear of a visit from the press gang. Horatio Adamson, a former town clerk of the Borough of Tynemouth, recorded one such advertisement.

On the 3rd December 1781 notice was given that Captain Boyer and Liet. Oakes of the Press Gang had their word of Honour that no Seaman would be interrupted by them between 4 p.m. and 12 p.m. on the play days except such as were found out of the Theatre between 6 p.m. and 10 p.m.[30]

King maintained that some of these advertisements were ruses to press gullible theatre-goers. He cites two examples to justify his cynicism.

The Press Gang have been very fruitful of inventions this Juncture [i.e. in recruiting for the war with the French in North America]; among many others the following Schemes have been carried into Execution with Success: A sturdy Fellow being set on Horseback, and his legs tied under the Belly, with two Men to guard him, have paraded the Streets, whilst others gave out that he was a notorious Highwayman just taken; this drew a number of Fellows from all Quarters, who were directly pressed. Another Scheme they have practised, by going to Shews [Shows] and pressing the Merry Andrew and Servants; but on capitulating with the Masters that they should exhibit their Performance on the Stage to the Populace they should be released: this drew Multitudes of Spectators, out of which they picked a great many able Men.[31]

We have a detailed account of the fate which befell one press-ganged sailor from North Shields. George Haswell's North Shields born seaman grandfather married in 1793. The following day he sailed for Latvia. On the passage home, he and other members of the crew were press-ganged by sailors from HMS *Lizard*, despite the fact that it was illegal to do so while men were at sea. The Liverpool ship-owners protested and, subsequently, the captain of the *Lizard* was court-martialled and dismissed the service. Despite this, the press-ganged sailors were not released and received no redress or compensation.

Haswell served on the *Lizard* for three years. During that time, his grandson claimed that 'an intense, unmitigated hatred of the navy was shared by every tar aboard'.

The one aspiration which animated each soul was to seize the first chance of escape from a dreary round of cruelty and inhumanity. A sense of unappeasable wrath smouldered in the breasts of men who dared not manifest the slightest sign of discontent, for a man might be flogged for even wearing a sullen expression. … With wits sharpened by the extraordinary precautions taken to prevent escape, and by the not infrequent experience, as spectators, of the horrible punishment inflicted upon the miserable beings who made and failed in an attempt, the most unheard-of expedients were in desperation adopted by men attempting to regain freedom. Prize-money, long overdue, was allowed by the authorities to remain due in the hope the prospect of some day receiving it might induce those it was to stick by the ship; yet though the amounts were sometimes very large, they were always joyfully left behind when they might be successfully run away from.[32]

Haswell's grandfather did just that. He escaped whilst HMS *Lizard* was docked at Portsmouth, leaving his prize money and kit behind. He signed on a transport ship but became ill and was discharged at Yarmouth. After recovering, and eventually making his way back to North Shields, he wrote to his wife, who had returned to her birthplace in the Isle of Man, to ask her to come to join him. She must have come close to wondering if she would ever receive such an invitation. Since the day after their marriage, she had not seen her husband for over four years.[33]

Another form of injustice came with the end of the Napoleonic Wars. Haswell maintained that the treatment of those who had served Britain so well in the Napoleonic Wars was indicative of the injustices which characterised British society at the time. Instead of being honoured and rewarded for their service to their country, they were cast aside and forgotten. They may not have been victims of an identifiable legal injustice but suffered from an indifference which was arguably just as pernicious. The ranks of the unemployed in the depression which followed the war were swollen by demobilised soldiers and sailors – many of whom had been mutilated in battle.

The men who did the actual fighting … of these … scores were to be found on the quays, the wharves, the landing-places, and lower streets of old Shields, in every stage of picturesque dismemberment – one arm, one leg, one arm and one leg, one arm and no legs, or a mere trunk, with neither arms nor legs, drawn about on a little trolley, to be propped up against the corner of some quay or entry; the lack of legs, however, curiously exceeding the lack of arms, and grimly suggestive of the peculiar horror of 'tween-deck fighting. … Hardy, patient, long-suffering fellows, … those to whom the fortunes of war had spared the more precious arms and hands, manned the sculler-boats, and waited a turn at the quay landings, or swept a crossing, or lent a hand at any honest job that could be had; no one of them

begging save the poor armless and legless hulk who had no choice.
… Let no man speak of England's glory in the early eighteens until
he has well considered the treatment of those who won her laurels.
It is a chapter of shame.[34]

The legal system changed significantly during the nineteenth century.
Increasingly, the law came to be regarded not as a weapon in the armoury
of those with power and influence but a neutral instrument to be used
to achieve just outcomes. The need for formal equality had been urged,
among many others, by Adam Smith in his influential 1776 book *Wealth
of Nations*. He argued that the 'equal and impartial administration of
justice which renders the rights of the meanest British subject respectable
to the greatest' would, 'by securing to every man the fruits of his own
industry, give the greatest and most effectual encouragement to every sort of
industry'.[35] Equality before the law emerged as voting rights were extended
and people given legitimate avenues to negotiate their terms and conditions
of employment. Marshall maintained this was a key element in the emerging
notion of citizenship. Justice demanded that all people should have the right
to defend and assert their rights on an equal footing, protected by the due
process of the law.[36] Of course, in our adversarial system, the law is never
fully even-handed. Those with the means to do so can employ the most able
legal counsel to argue their case. Nor does equality before the law imply
anything about actual social equality. It may help to level the playing field,
but equal opportunity is not the same as equality of outcome. But, for the
people who lived in North Shields in the eighteenth to twentieth centuries,
neither opportunities nor outcomes were even remotely equal.

11

The labouring classes (II)
Social and economic conditions

T HE framework for this chapter is derived from the 1942 Report of
the Inter-Departmental Committee on Social Insurance and Allied
Services, popularly known as the Beveridge Report, the most important
document in the social policy of modern Britain. Against the background
of the political, economic and social inequality of the nineteenth century
and the economic disasters of the inter-war years, William Beveridge
chaired the committee given the task of planning a system of social
insurance for British people when the Second World War came to an
end. While making the assumption that Britain would continue to be a
capitalist society based predominantly on private enterprise and the free
play of market forces, Beveridge set out a framework within which the
State could intervene to slay what he called the five still-prevalent 'giant
evils' of squalor, disease, idleness, ignorance and want. What I attempt in
this chapter is an outline of how these five giant evils applied to North
Shields in the eighteenth and nineteenth centuries and the early decades
of the twentieth.

Squalor

Eighteenth- and nineteenth-century North Shields was an interesting place
to live. Indeed, some descriptions make it sound positively romantic. As
the harbour became increasingly important, it was filled with the vessels of
many nationalities.

> The Dutch lugger with green painted deck-houses and varnished
> side-swapes (like the elytra of some glorified beetle); the smart
> Norwegian; the poor little French coaster; the stately East Indiaman
> with black hull and painted ports; timber ships from Quebec or the
> Baltic with pine battens or Stockholm tar; collier pinks, barques,
> brigs, schooners, brigantines, sloops, snows, of every shape, size and
> rig; – all lay vast in number, moored in tiers just off the long narrow
> street.[1]

The North Shields riverside in 1891. Painting by
Thomas Marie Madawaska Hemy (1852–1937).

Dibdin, writing in 1838, was struck not just by the extraordinary scale
of activity on the river but also the density and character of the population
on the shore.

Happening to mistake our way, as to the more ready and agreeable
route to the Abbey ruins, we had to thread a few streets – which
can never be forgotten … for their combined narrowness, stench
and dense population. Human beings seem to have been born, and
to have kept together since birth, like onions strung upon a string.
You never see one or two together: they stand still or bustle along, in
fives, *sixes* and *sevens*. It is a rushing stream of countless population.
And what houses! What streets! – what articles for sale! Yet they all
seemed as merry and happy as if they were the *Holmes* and *Lewises*
of Regent Street.[2]

But, however jolly it may have seemed to Dibdin during his fleeting visit; and though this period may have been 'the most picturesque the town has known', with 'Greenlanders, Prussian, Swedes and Spaniards mixing with the burly pilots, the local pitmen, keelmen and scullermen' combining to give the town 'a cosmopolitan air', the day-to-day living conditions of the ordinary people of North Shields were anything but romantic.[3]

The dwellings of those who lived on the riverside were not like the cottages one associates with chocolate-box fishing villages. Those in North Shields were often ramshackle affairs. All lacked the basic amenities we take for granted today.

The long narrow street was … made up of a double row of oddly jumbled red-tiled houses with high-peaked gables – the ones built against the high banks of the river and far over-topped by them, the other sheer on the water's edge and propped up by wooden piles slanting out into the stream like stilts. Here and there at short irregular intervals an 'entry' pierced the line on one side or other and afforded access to a squalid landing-place, where a broken set of wooden steps led precipitately down from a rotting wharf to 'the

shore' … or to narrow break-neck stairs running from the Low
Street to the top of the 'Banks'. … Scarce a house on the river side
of the street but had its ruinous wharf, supported on half-a-dozen
green weed-grown piles, or its tumble-down, gaudy-painted balcony
on which a few fresh herring, split and peppered, were hung out to
dry among the newly-washed 'duds' which bellied out in the wind.
… Public-houses leaning side by side or lurching towards each other
across the street, like half-drunken men seeking a quarrel, were open
at all hours.[4]

It was not just what was on the ground that contributed to the squalor.
The air the people breathed was also unhealthy. It had been like that for
many years. The heavy reliance on the salt trade during the first phase of
North Shields' economic recovery meant that as well as the smoke from the
poor-quality coal that was used to heat the salt pans, dense clouds of steam
'wrapped the place in a white mantle'.[5] So extensive were they that Daniel
Defoe recorded that he could see them as he approached Durham, about 25
miles away to the south. They also appear to have been visible from Cheviot,
over 40 miles away to the north.[6] The local atmosphere led the wife of
Patrick Watt to complain that she had been brought 'frae Norham, frae the
bonny banks o' Tweedy, to Sodom and Gomorrah'.[7] Readers may remember
that Sodom is where, according to the Old Testament, Lot's wife was
turned into a pillar of salt. The reference to Gomorrah, an Old Testament
place made infamous by the licentious and sexually depraved behaviour of
its inhabitants, probably reflected Mrs Watt's verdict on the behaviour of
those who frequented the open-all-hours pubs and other establishments on
the Low Street.

Such personal observations were supported by the General Board of
Health's 1851 *Preliminary Enquiry into the Sewerage, Drainage and Supply
of Water and the Sanitary Conditions of the Inhabitants* of North Shields,
compiled by William Ranger.* Although there were fewer salt pans in the
mid-nineteenth century, air quality was still a major problem. Residents
now had also to contend with 'dense black smoke' from the local factories.

At its eastern extremity it [North Shields] is bounded by the Low
Lights, a locality not inaptly denominated the Valley of Smoke,
where the atmosphere can rarely be seen clearly through, on account
of the almost continual presence of this nuisance. Saltpans, a chain
manufactory, brewhouse, flour-mill, tan-yard, pottery, and gas
manufactory, pour into the atmosphere their share of deleterious

---

* Concerns about public health led to the 1848 Public Health Act. That established
the Board of Health which, in turn, set up inquiries into local sanitary conditions. William
Ranger was appointed to compile the report on the Borough of Tynemouth.

The Low Lights district of North Shields as portrayed in about 1866. Watercolour by James (also known as John) Wilson Carmichael (1800–68). He was born in Newcastle, the son of a carpenter, and spent three years at sea, and completed his apprenticeship as a carpenter, before devoting himself full-time to art and going on to became a celebrated marine artist.

matter, and the smoke arising from the whole collected in a very circumscribed valley, having no outlet but to the sea, darkens the air and renders it very impure.[8]

Each of these industrial units produced its own distinctive smell or, as Wohl put it more eloquently: 'Each trade … had its own distinctive stench which either hung over a district giving it a unique and immediately recognizable odour, or mingled with others into an offensive mélange which pervaded the whole town.'[9] While these smells coupled with the gases and smoke emitted from workshop and factory chimneys were obviously a nuisance, at the time it was less obvious that they were injurious to health. For that reason a Royal Commission on Noxious Vapours was established in 1878. It received medical evidence that offending smells and gases could and did produce nausea, vomiting, bronchial and respiratory complaints, poor digestion, sleeplessness and a general feeling of malaise – and were also injurious to health because their presence meant that people were denied access to genuinely fresh air. In any case, as John Simon maintained, it was not necessary to prove that air pollution caused specific illnesses to determine whether it was injurious to health.

> To be free from bodily discomfort is a condition of health. If a man gets up with a headache, *pro tanto* [to that extent], he is not in good health; if a man gets up unable to eat his breakfast, *pro tanto*, he is not in good health. States of languor, states of nausea, states of oppressed breathing, though not in themselves definite diseases, are *pro tanto* states of unhealth. When a man is living in an atmosphere which keeps him constantly below par, as many of those trade nuisances … particularly do, that is an injury to health.[10]

It was not, of course, only industrial units that produced air pollution. The dependence on coal for domestic heating compounded the problem even in areas some distance away from workshop and factory chimneys. Unfortunately for those affected by the worst of the air pollution, it was accepted with a degree of fatalism. Air pollution was seen not just as a by-product of industry but the inevitable cost of national prosperity; in much the same way that noise pollution close to international airports is perceived today.

Although the worst of the squalor was to be found on the riverside and bank-side, it inevitably affected those who lived in proximity to it on the Bank Top. Indeed, according to Ranger, the area in and around Dockwray Square was already being abandoned in the 1840s by some of those who could afford to live elsewhere, for example in 'the crescents and terraces on the cliffs of Tynemouth where primroses used to grow'.[11]

Ranger recorded that 'the township of North Shields, exclusive of Milburn Place', had just '130 privies for the accommodation of a population of nearly 8,000 persons'. Indeed in the whole of the Borough of Tynemouth, there were only 1,239 privies for a population of 21,710.[12] Moreover, the 'privies' in those days were primitive affairs that were actually part of the problem. Such insanitary conditions were ideal for the spread of the many infectious diseases that plagued urban dwellers in the mid-nineteenth century.

The situation was much the same as it had been in the eighteenth century when 'refuse was allowed to accumulate in the streets and ways were foul'. It seems that most of the scavenging of this refuse was done by genuinely free-range pigs. The freedom that they enjoyed led to additional accumulations of excreta that further encouraged the spread of disease. The Tynemouth court rolls of 15 October 1694 addressed the problem of the 'daily greater numbers' of pigs in staid but graphic terms:

By reason of the narrowness of the streets, and the town of late grown so populous, the keeping of unbowed and unringed swine is very infectious and nautious, especially in the summer time.[13]

Prior to the public health reforms carried out in the latter part of the nineteenth century, refuse and sewage were still just thrown outside. The rain then washed it down to the lowest end of the street where it accumulated, sometimes in such huge heaps that it would completely block the narrow thoroughfares. The following plaintive submission to the Ranger inquiry was made by ten of the inhabitants of Liddell Street and Police Quay.

We, the undersigned, rated inhabitants of the Low-street, beg to represent to you the inconveniences we suffer in consequence of the utter want of drainage, the consequence being that night-soil and other offensive matter is thrown on the shore near our dwellings, and its accumulation, until its removal by the operation of the tide, is the cause of fever and pestilential disease. … We beg the favour of a visit to the locality, where we reside, so that you may be convinced, by ocular demonstration, the truth of our representations.[14]

Ranger did even more. His report included a detailed description of each set of dwellings in the town. He summarised North Shields as made up of hopelessly overcrowded buildings in close and narrow courts, with open ditches by way of drains, and open dung heaps which oozed through the walls of the houses in wet weather. He also noted that animals were slaughtered in open butchers' shops and that blood and fat were left lying on the floor until they putrefied. Not surprisingly the Ranger report concluded that 'few, if any, places stand in more need of the application of sanitary enactments than Tynemouth'.[15]

What is especially noteworthy is that even some of the developments on the Bank Top had not been accompanied by a modern system of drains and sewers. When Wright laid out the land west of Stephenson Street he had done so on a grid system which was intended to include a proper system of drainage. For example, in Howard Street, he had incorporated a sewer '2 feet [0.6 m] in width by 4½ feet [1.4 m] in height, 8 feet [2.4 m] below the surface'. However, a similar provision of drains had not been provided by his sons and successors who had undertaken further developments on his land. As a result, the drainage and sewerage provision for even the then modern part of North Shields would be regarded as completely unacceptable today.

Stephenson Street is nearly one-third of a mile in length, and in two-thirds of its extent densely populated. … It is entirely unprovided with sewerage except for a short distance at the south end. … To the east of it, Linskill-street, Church-street, Queen-street, King-street, Charlotte-street, Reed-street, Hudson-street, and Northumberland-street are all without sewerage. Passing over Bird-street, which has a small sewer leading into the railway drain, Walker-place, Toll-square, and Dockwray-square, have sewerage both scanty and imperfect, and inadequate for the requirements of the population occupying this valuable property. [16]

The Ranger report's several references to butchers' shops warrant an additional note. North Shields was a thriving port. Its butchers catered not just for local inhabitants but the ships leaving the harbour. On average, in the course of a week, 500 sheep, 150 pigs and 80 cows or calves would be slaughtered by 60 butchers, either in small shops or on the streets. Much of the offal, which made up about 30 per cent of the gross weight of the slaughtered animals, was dumped into the river. If a sewer existed in the vicinity, it too would be used to dispose of offal. In other parts of the town, blood and offal were left in the open. There were a few dedicated slaughterhouses, but the entrails from the animals they killed were spread on the fields as manure, which was 'about as damaging to the health of the community as the practice of open-air slaughtering'.[17]

The same casual approach to public health characterised the market on the New Quay, as this extract from an 1850 report sent to the mayor by the superintendent of police makes clear.

The New Quay, as you are aware, forms a sort of market place, though no rules exist for keeping it in order. … In consequence of the stalls being allowed to remain until after 12 o'clock on Saturday night … the whole of the garbage, left after the removal of the meat, fish and vegetable stalls, and of which there is a large quantity, remains over the entire Sunday. The fish market at the end of the New Quay is never cleaned and is therefore always in a most disgusting state.[18]

The comments on Tynemouth Borough (though primarily North Shields) made by the government inquiry into the 1854 cholera epidemic are equally revealing.

The borough of Tynemouth … in a physical and sanitary view presents many points of resemblance both to Newcastle and to Gateshead; … the sewerage, drainage, paving, and privy and ash pit accommodation being probably as deficient there, and the water supply being worse, than in either of those other places: and the whole sanitary condition of the borough, as regards permanent works, being admitted to be but little better than in 1849, when it was very bad, and when the place was most severely visited by cholera.[19]

The particular observation that the water supply was worse in North Shields is a telling one given how often the quality of drinking water supply was linked to the spread of infections. As the Ranger inquiry reported:

> Nothing is more certain than that amongst the inhabitants of North Shields there is a great deficiency of water. In all parts of the town there is a want of it and some of the most needy localities are entirely deprived of any regular supply. One of the worst of these is the township of Shields, where there is more filth of habitation and uncleanliness of person and much more disease and mortality than in any other part of the neighbourhood. Vain indeed, will be any effort, however judiciously made, to improve the persons, lanes, yards and habitations of the people without an abundant supply of water. Nothing less than the introduction of water into every habitation will successfully combat the evil.[20]

As I have already explained in Chapter 7, it was a long time before that ambition was realised.

Ironically, as the worst excesses of surface pollution were tackled by the building of sewers, the pollution of the River Tyne worsened. Once a clean and productive salmon river, it was changed out of all recognition because the 1847 Towns Improvement Clauses Act permitted local authorities to discharge sewage directly into rivers or the sea. So the provision of sewers designed to help keep the streets clean served only to increase the volume of sewage in the river. Not until the latter half of the nineteenth century was it demonstrated that sewage could be treated effectively by filtration on land, and it was only in the second half of the following century that river pollution was taken seriously. While I was living in North Shields, Tynemouth's MP Dame Irene Ward stood up in Parliament in 1958, described the condition of the river as deplorable to the point of being indecent and declared that 'one of my ambitions before I die is to see that the pollution of the River Tyne is dealt with'.*

I have already noted that the dwellings of the labouring classes in North Shields were badly constructed, largely without any system of sewers or drains, and lacking a supply of clean water. They were also very overcrowded. According to Mackinlay, a surgeon who presented evidence to the Ranger inquiry, 'most of the houses occupied by the working classes are let off in single apartments'.

It is frequently found that the number of rooms in a house indicate

---

* Her wish was not fulfilled but in the last twenty years there has been a huge improvement. The Tyne is once again a salmon river and even a seal was seen to poke its head out of the river by the Gateshead Millennium Bridge in 2009.

the number of families resident in it. This is especially the case in the township of North Shields. With very few exceptions there are no wash-houses … the weekly washings are therefore done in the same room in which the family eat and sleep.[21]

There was a growing belief in the importance of fresh air at the time. However, wide-open windows were not something to which the ordinary people of North Shields were attracted. As Ranger noted, 'at present it is hardly to be wondered at if the majority of the poor are either unconscious of the benefits of ventilation or obstinately prejudiced against applying them'.

In too many cases the only result of opening a window in one of the back or narrow streets of the of Low Town is to admit a current of air laden with the stench from an adjoining 'midden', or cesspool, as sickening and unhealthy as the close foetid odour of the over-crowded room itself. Both with regard to ventilation and water supply, it is cruel to charge the poor with being insensible of the benefits of fresh air and water when, as a general rule, their homes have been systematically deprived of both one and the other.[22]

Conditions improved during the second half of the nineteenth century but even the County Borough of Tynemouth's accepted that it was not until well into the twentieth century 'that the Borough redeemed its reputation'.[23] The 1921 census showed that 14 per cent of families in the Borough lived in

Example of Bankside housing before the 1930 Clearance. These were not atypical. The Bankside was full of banks and stairs lined with similar dwellings.

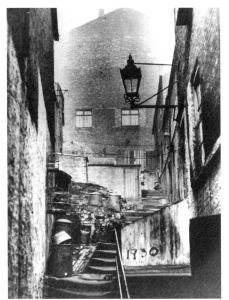

one room and 26 per cent in two rooms (compared to 4 per cent and 11 per cent nationally). Of families with 4–6 members, 29 per cent were living in a single room and 44 per cent in two rooms.[24] The figures for North Shields alone would have been significantly higher.

By the time of the 1919 Housing, Town Planning Act, the Borough of Tynemouth had already purchased land in Balkwell in Chirton in 1912 to build houses for 'better off' working-class families in the hope that this would free up housing for poorer families.[25] By 1930 the Borough had 2,376 additional houses: 39 per cent built by the council and 31 per cent by the private sector with the aid of subsidies. Despite this bout of building, it was insufficient to make a significant impact on the overall housing problem. It did not even match the increased number of families in the Borough, which grew by 2,741 in the period. [26] The problem of overcrowded, slum housing in the oldest part of North Shields, by the riverside, remained essentially untouched. The Union Stairs, for example, housed 48 people living in 17 rooms. They had access to only a single tap. The situation was a little better for the 405 resident of Liddell Street. There were 11 people for every earth privy and 23 people for every tap.

Ridges Housing Estate, now known as the Meadowell Estate.

The 1932 Town and Country Planning Act led to the clearance of the dwellings on the original Low Street and Bankside. Between 1932 and 1936, 33 compulsory purchase orders were served which affected almost 10,000 people.[27] The living conditions of those who were moved from the riverside to the newly built council Ridges estate (later renamed Meadowell) improved beyond recognition. They leap-frogged many of those who remained in the main body of North Shields, who continued to live without the basic necessities of piped hot and cold water, a bath and indoor toilet. Over 2,000 houses with modern amenities were built around three, semi-circular nuclei with private gardens, open spaces, schools and shops. Two groups of houses designed for elderly people were also built at the same time. In addition, three sets of flats were built by philanthropists for families mainly from slum clearance areas. Remarkably, the first two (of 24 and then 48 units) came from an initiative by a group of volunteers from the Northumberland Square Presbyterian church. The third scheme of 135 units was funded by the Sir James Knott Trust. The relatively low cost of land, material and labour in the 1930s also encouraged more speculative private building for owner-occupation in a number of areas within the Borough. Subsequently, in the second half of the twentieth century, there were further large-scale programmes of council house building, several home improvement schemes to improve existing dwellings, and a large number of private developments, primarily for owner-occupation.

Disease

Overall life expectancy in Victorian England was low. It was the youngest who fared worst. Today, mortality rates increase with age. In the middle of the nineteenth century, the opposite was the case. In the Borough of Tynemouth in 1850, 21 per cent of the 2,560 who died had not reached their first birthday. A further 14 per cent had not reached the age of five. In all, 44 per cent of deaths were of people under the age of 20. Robert Spence of North Shields may have been peculiarly unlucky in losing eight of his nine children before losing his wife and then his only surviving child when she was thirteen, but most parents would have experienced the death of one or more of their own children and witnessed the death of nieces and nephews.[28] Those who survived childhood had a chance of becoming elderly. By mid-century, almost 25 per cent of those who died in North Shields were over 60 and 15 per cent were over 70.[29] Sykes could even list 189 people in and around the Newcastle area who had reached the age of 100.[30] The oldest was John Ramsay, who died aged 115. Many were still in 'full possession of all their faculties' until shortly before their death. John Anderson, for example, died while soling his shoes at the age of 108.

During the nineteenth century life expectancy in England increased, but not in a straightforward way. In England as a whole, the average improved from around the mid-30s at the beginning of the century to around the low-50s by 1911.[31] However, there were significant local variations, particularly between rural and urban areas and, within urban areas, between social classes. In a paper *The Waste of Infant Life* (delivered to the National Association for the Promotion of Social Science in 1867) Dr John Curgenven pointed out that whereas the death rate of 0–5-year-olds among the 'educated and well-to-do' was 11 per cent, the equivalent figure for the urban working class ranged from 35 per cent to 55 per cent. Even more startling was his estimate that among children born outside marriage, the rate was 60 per cent to 90 per cent.[32]

Not all infant deaths were due to circumstances beyond the control of their parents. For example, deaths as a result of the over-use of soothing mixtures containing opiates, or alcohol, were sometimes the result of deliberate abuse. They did not loom large in official statistics because infant deaths were so commonplace that murders were easily concealed. 'Victorian social conditions, ignorance and poverty were the legal saving graces against any manslaughter (let along murder) charge.'[33] However, among deaths from recorded homicide it is apparent that infants were most at risk. For example, between 1863 and 1887, 61 per cent of all homicide victims were under the age of one. This phenomenon was not new. The combination of poverty and public shame had always tempted some mothers of illegitimate babies to 'drop' (i.e. abandon) their offspring or practise infanticide. The practice was sufficiently common to warrant a 1624 law which presumed that the mother of a dead bastard was guilty of murder if she had tried to conceal the birth. The onus was put on the mother to prove that her baby had been still-born or had died naturally.

It is not possible to make definitive statements about the causes of infant deaths in the Victorian period because medical terminology was less precise than today. That is one of the reasons why social historians find it difficult to agree on the reasons for the variations and changes in mortality rates. Williams and Galley focus on the 'urban-sanitary-diarrhoea effect' which they maintain helps to explain why infant mortality was higher in towns and why some counties experienced a fall in infant mortality well before 1900, when it began to decline more generally.[34] In a study of several areas, including the Borough of Tynemouth, they suggest that the summer months were a particular risk period for infants because the supply of piped water and provision for sewage removal were inadequate. Smith and Lynch concentrate instead on the kind of conditions children experienced in their early years which, they suggest, is the reason why the cohort born around 1850 experienced a significant improvement in life expectancy compared to those born in earlier decades. In response, Szreter insists that the 1850s saw only an alleviation of the problems that caused premature death and that more significant changes did not come until the 1870s. He also suggests that Smith and Lynch overstate the importance of conditions in early life and play too little attention to other factors such as the adequacy and quality of local water supplies.[35]

What these scholars do agree on is that improvements in mortality rates were not spread uniformly throughout the population. That is readily apparent from a comparison of infant mortality statistics for the Borough of Tynemouth with national rates. In 1851, in the borough, the infant mortality rate (that is, the proportion of children dying before their first birthday), was in the 13.8 to 15.3 per cent band. What is particularly noteworthy about later rates in the Borough is that although the *absolute* figures improved, the borough moved down the *relative* league table. So, while a smaller proportion of infants born in Tynemouth may have died than in the past, the decline was not as marked as in other places. Between 1851 and 1881 Tynemouth was in a middle band for infant mortality. By 1911, it was in the second lowest band. By 1921, Tynemouth was in the bottom band, even though the absolute figure for infant mortality was by then around 9 per cent. The Borough of Tynemouth was still in the bottom band when I was born in 1940 and as late as 1951, when the absolute figure had fallen to 3.6 per cent. It was only in the latter half of the twentieth century that the infant mortality rate moved back into the middle band where it had been a century earlier.[36]

Aggregate figures for life expectancy and the incidence of particular diseases are useful but mask differences between social groups and geographical areas. The reports of the Poor Law Commissioners in 1838 provided evidence of particularly bad health among paupers, and in 1842 Chadwick demonstrated clear occupational differences in mortality rates. The evidence for Tynemouth Borough points in the same direction. The annual mortality rate on the Bank Top was about 2 per cent per annum in 1851. In the old riverside part of the town it was 50 per cent higher. In 1831, when cholera struck the town, a Board of Health door-to-door survey found that 1 in 22 of the population of North Shields had been 'attacked by cholera' compared to 1 in 85 of those who lived in the adjacent village of Tynemouth.[37] In 1849, after a further outbreak of cholera, Dr Fenwick was struck by the fact that it 'was much more fatal in its effects than when it made its appearance in 1831 and 1832'. He concluded that was in part because 'a great part of the more wealthy residents in North Shields have removed to the townships of Tynemouth and Chirton' and that 'the township of North Shields [was] … in an infinitely worse and more filthy condition than in 1831 and 1832'.[38]

Fenwick listed the streets in which cholera had been most evident. These include many of those in which my own forebears were living at the time or lived in subsequent decades. What Fenwick insists is that the key factor in the spread of cholera was not poverty *per se* but that the poor were 'compelled by poverty to inhabit streets and houses whose faulty construction has assisted in the propagation of the complaint'. He also noted that although general statistics showed that men and women were equally susceptible to cholera, in the 1849 North Shields outbreak women were more likely to have caught the disease than men. He attributes this to the fact that 'the employment of the men kept them for the greater part of the day away from the unwholesome air of the district in which they resided, whilst the women were constantly exposed to its bad effects'. While the notion of 'unwholesome air' may no longer have a place in medical terminology, at a time when the mechanisms for the spread of infectious diseases were not well understood, it did represent a step forward in helping to establish a clear causal relationship between environment and disease.

A comparable conclusion about the association between social conditions and disease comes from a study by Gould and Chappel. In 1833, dissenters in the Borough established a separate private cemetery. The registers of the interments there are unusually detailed, and an analysis of 2,610 burials between 1833 and 1853 allowed Gould and Chappel to make some interesting observations on how age at death related to where people lived and their socio-economic status. Age of death was significantly lower for people who had lived in North Shields rather than Tynemouth, particularly so for adult males. The median age of the people of North Shields who were buried in the cemetery was half that of the people from the rest of the parish of Tynemouth 'who would have suffered less crowded conditions, possible free access to water and some may have been able to supplement their diets from vegetable plots'.[39] Despite the inherent dangers in coal mining, from accidents and occupational diseases such as pneumoconiosis, the median age of miners at death was higher than of males in North Shields. Gould and Chappel attribute this to the fact that most coal mining families lived outside the town.

The increasingly crowded urban areas contributed greatly to the spread of serious and often fatal infections. Life-threatening epidemics were common in North Shields before and during the nineteenth century. There were, for example, serious outbreaks of what was then described as 'plague' in North Shields in 1546, 1583, 1604, 1634 and 1666. The 1635 epidemic was particularly severe. According to Howell 'it almost depopulated the town' before spreading up river where it led to the death of 5,037 people in Newcastle and a further 515 in Gateshead.[40] In the nineteenth century, infectious diseases such as cholera led to major loss of life, though it should be noted that the term was used loosely for bowel disorders which did not necessarily have the same cause. However, between 1831 and 1866, Britain suffered four serious epidemics of a specific disease that originated in India and became known as Indian or Asiatic cholera. It spread from the Punjab along trade routes and was eventually brought to the North East on ships from Russia, Poland and the Baltic ports. There were four main epidemics of *cholera morbus*, in 1831–32, 1848–49, 1853–54 and 1865–66.

It appears to have arrived first in Sunderland in 1831. Despite the fact that local doctors were satisfied that the disease was *cholera morbus* and that quarantine was the most appropriate response, probably because of pressure from those whose incomes depended on freedom of trade, they were persuaded to change their minds.* Without quarantine regulations, the disease spread to Newcastle, Gateshead and North Shields where, in all, there were 1,330 cases, 437 of them fatal.† North Shields was also hit by the second epidemic of the disease in 1848–49, but this seems to have been the last major cholera epidemic in the town.[41] There were 722 reported cases and 337 deaths, leaving 106 children without a father, mother, or both.‡

Dr Edward Greenhow, a practising doctor in North Shields at the time, went on to produce a pivotal national report on causes of death in 1858. Influenced by his earlier local experience, he carried out a statistical analysis of previously unanalysed and unpublished national material and found compelling evidence that many diseases and deaths were linked to overcrowding, poor sanitation, inadequate food and particular occupations. More than a century later, the elected mayor of North Tyneside reminded people in his State of the Area address in 2005, that the problem of serious infectious diseases continued into the 1940s. He reminded his audience that just '60 years ago in this Borough we had isolation hospitals for three terrible diseases, tuberculosis, smallpox and diphtheria, which ravaged whole communities and devastated the lives of thousands of people'. Those who lived in the old riverside town were most at risk. In 1933 the overall mortality in the Borough was 12.8 per 1,000. In other words, there were 12.8 deaths for every 1,000 residents. In the riverside area the mortality rate was 20.8. Of every 1,000 children born in the Borough, 83 did not reach their first birthday (compared to 80 per 1,000 in England and Wales as a whole). In the slum clearance area by the riverside the comparable infant mortality rate was 143. The death rate for tuberculosis in the Borough as a whole was 1.4 per 1,000 (compared to 1.15 in England and Wales as a whole). In the designated slum clearance area it was 4.8.[42]

Edward Headlam Greenhow, MD. The son of a North Shields doctor, he followed in his father's footsteps and, after practising in the town, went on to become an important national figure in the field of public health.

---

* Much the same scenario as in the blockbuster twentieth-century film *Jaws* in which, after the sightings of a dangerous shark, local business people refused to close the beaches because it would be 'bad for business'.

† The infection then spread through much of the rest of the country. In London alone, of 9,172 diagnosed cases, 4,218 died.

‡ The 1849 cholera epidemic spread as far as Callington in Cornwall where my great-grandfather was born in 1824. Of the population of 1,630, 700 contracted the disease.

Deaths from communicable diseases were not the only causes of premature deaths. Health hazards of many kinds were associated with particular occupations. Respiratory conditions such as emphysema, chronic bronchitis and pneumoconiosis were widespread among coal miners. Despite being commonplace, it was not until 1831 that 'Black Spots on the Lungs' was recognised as being related to coal mining and not until 1837 that Dr Stratton of North Shields labelled it as a dust disease which he called *anthracosis*, after describing what he encountered during the dissection of the body of a 70-year-old coal miner who had been an inmate of Tynemouth workhouse. Other occupational diseases may not have led to death but greatly affected the quality of life of those who suffered from them, including the eye condition *nystagmus* which was caused by working underground for lengthy periods.[43]

Premature death also resulted from accidents. Large numbers of North Shields' sailors lost their lives during storms or accidents at sea. During the period when wooden colliers were being phased out and no longer maintained properly, the toll was even higher. Deaths from mining accidents were also commonplace. The records maintained by the Durham Mining Museum show that the scale of fatalities increased enormously in the nineteenth century and did not decline significantly until the 1920s. This was in part because inexperienced workers were recruited as the demand for coal grew. Local pitmen, who had been brought up in mining families and gone down the pits as boys had accumulated considerable experience of local conditions before working as hewers. Being 'bred and brought up to it' made them more aware than inexperienced newcomers of the dangers of 'fire damp' and 'choke damp'. But, ironically, the very safety lamps designed by Humphrey Davy and George Stephenson to protect miners' lives indirectly put them more at risk. Safety lamps were seen by many mine-owners as a cheap alternative to improved ventilation. Miners were required to work at greater depths and to 'rob' (i.e. reduce in size) the coal pillars which at an earlier stage had been left behind to support tunnel roofs. In 1852, the first president of the North of England Institute of Mining Engineers confessed in his inaugural address to being appalled by the level of fatalities since Davy's lamp had been introduced.[44] In the North East alone the number of mining deaths ran into thousands.

Until the advent of the National Health Service, the residents of North Shields did not enjoy access to health care that was in any way commensurate

The Stephenson Safety Lamp. Designed in the same year as Davy's lamp, Stephenson's had the advantage that if the amount of firedamp became too high, the flame would be extinguished. A disadvantage was that it could become dangerously hot. Another apparent advantage of his initial design, the use of glass to make the lamp brighter, proved in use to be a disadvantage. It made the lamp less robust and Stephenson subsequently followed Davy's example and used gauze.

with the threats to their health. Public health measures ultimately made the greatest inroads into premature deaths, but many lives could have been saved had access to even rudimentary medical help been readily available. Before 1948, those who could not afford to pay for medical attention had to rely on charitable provision such as the North Shields and Tynemouth Dispensary which was set up in a house in Church Street in 1802 'for the relief of the lame and the sick poor of North Shields and Tynemouth'. It continued to offer such care until the introduction of the National Health Service in 1948. Preston Hospital, which developed as part of the workhouse, and Tynemouth Jubilee Infirmary, the result of a charitable initiative, also played important roles in health care, but the overall inadequacy of provision contributed significantly to the high death rate. In discussing medical facilities in this period, it is important to distinguish between physicians treating disease and surgeons treating injuries. As one physician confided to the antiquarian John Aubrey in the seventeenth century, 'If the world knew the villainy and knavery (besides ignorance) of the physicians and apothecaries, the people would throw stones at them as they walked in the streets.'[45] But, whatever the limitations of pre-scientific medicine in the days before Pasteur and Koch demonstrated the link between bacteria and illness, the value of prompt care by surgeons is demonstrated by the diary kept by a young Newcastle surgeon, Thomas Giodarni Wright, in the 1820s. His services were much in demand and he and others like him were constantly being called out to treat fractures and other, often horrific, injuries caused by accidents in the workshops, furnaces and coal mines in the area.[46]

Thomas Hobbes may have been speculating on what mankind would be like in a state of nature, without the benefits of living in an ordered society, when he described the life of man in *Leviathan* as being 'poor, nasty, brutish, and short'. Yet that is just what life was like for many of those people who lived in North Shields and elsewhere until the twentieth century. The sudden loss of parents and siblings, whether from illness or accident, blighted the lives of countless thousands of North Shields' children, so much so that it was widely believed that it was necessary to harden them at an early age so that they could learn to endure what miseries life held in store for them.

> Horseplay and practical joking of the roughest sort had to be endured. … Young apprentices found they must face for a series of years a course of brutal treatment imposed by, not cruel but, hard-fibred men who … regarded it as a necessary regimen for effecting the 'hardening' of a boy and for developing his manhood.[47]

The fact that death rates eventually fell and more people survived childhood did not necessarily mean that those who grew into adulthood were fit and strong. On the contrary, many adult males at the end of the nineteenth century were so unhealthy that they were judged unfit for military service. In the aftermath of the Boer War there was widespread concern when it was revealed that between 40 and 60 per cent of potential recruits to the British Army had been rejected after a medical examination.[48] Instead of drawing the obvious conclusion that more intervention was needed to protect the health of the population, those who subscribed to simplistic Social Darwinist notions argued that the weak should be allowed to die so that only the fittest survived. Fortunately, accumulating evidence made it undeniable that it was poverty which ultimately lay at the root of much of the ill-health in Victorian Britain.

Idleness

Systematic unemployment statistics did not become available until the introduction of unemployment benefits in the twentieth century but Mitchell and Deane have collated the available information from trade union sources for earlier periods.[49] They leave little doubt that unemployment was a major issue throughout the whole of the nineteenth century. It was a problem for those directly affected because if there was no work there was no pay. It was also a problem for the economy because instead of contributing to it through their labour and purchasing power, the unemployed became a charge on local charities or those who provided poor law relief.

The term unemployment did not come into general use until the 1880s. That may have been in part because until the unemployed began to protest about their plight it was not seen as a particular problem by those in authority. But John Burns (soon to become the president of the Local Government Board in the Liberal government in 1905) clearly overstated his case when he maintained that the unemployed labourer used to be 'a patient, long-suffering animal, accepting his position with a fatalistic taciturnity, looking upon his enforced idleness as inevitable'.[50] Seasonal unemployment was understood. Seamen, for example, expected to be laid off in winter months because of the reduced number of collier brigs leaving the Tyne. Being out of work was also taken for granted during spells of bad weather, most obviously for those who worked in the building trades. Workers were also likely to be fatalistic when personal circumstances plunged them into unemployment because they were sick, disabled or too old to work. Unemployment may even have been tolerated during the 11 depressions in trade between 1815 and 1870.[51] But when unemployment was seen as unfair in terms of traditional expectations, it led to protest and unrest.

Those most likely to be unemployed were unskilled labourers employed on a casual, day-to-day basis. The most significant group of them in North Shields were the dockers who loaded and unloaded the numerous ships which came into the port. Dock work did not have a stable workforce because no one could guarantee when a ship would dock. But, when it did, cargoes needed to be unloaded quickly to minimise dock charges and reduce the risk of perishable goods becoming unfit for sale. So dock companies in the nineteenth and early twentieth centuries typically employed 'permanent men' (my grandfather Smith belonged to this category); 'preference' men who were next in line, although they had no guarantee of employment, and 'casuals' who were only needed at busy times.

Skilled workers were also subject to bouts of unemployment when there were structural changes in the local economy (for example, when innovation in the loading of colliers resulted in keelmen becoming redundant) and, ironically, when the country was at peace. Britain was at war for virtually the whole of the period between 1756 (the outbreak of the Seven Years' War) and 1815 (the end of the Napoleonic Wars). This provided employment in those North Shields companies who supplied goods and services to the military. However, when the conflicts came to an end, many workers lost their jobs. They joined the ranks of demobilised, unemployed soldiers and sailors and those no longer fit for work because of war injuries.

Unemployment eventually became a major public issue in the 1880s. London in the summer of 1887 hosted not only a celebration of Queen Victoria's Golden Jubilee but a parade of the unemployed past St Paul's and Westminster Abbey, with camps in Trafalgar Square and St James's Park. It was the outbreak of violence when mounted police and troops broke up the Trafalgar Square demonstration that led to the coining of the term 'Bloody Sunday'.

> The events of 1886–87 were different in scale and character from anything before. For the first time unemployment became a political issue, perceived as a problem distinct from poverty, caused by factors other than moral failings, deserving of public sympathy and remedial action by the state.[52]

Until the 1870s, the dominant explanation for unemployment was the laissez-faire notion that it was the consequence of a natural balancing of the supply and demand for labour. By the 1880s, when Britain's industrial lead had faltered and the country entered the so-called Great Depression (*circa* 1873–96) such a simple-minded notion was no longer tenable. By 1888, no less an establishment voice than *The Times* declared that unemployment was 'the fundamental problem of modern society, in comparison with which almost every question in politics seems diminutive'.[53]

Others adopted a more fatalistic approach. J.S. Davy, of the Local Government Board which administered the poor law, suggested that the unemployed 'must suffer for the general good of the body politic'.[54] Beveridge offered a middle way. In his book *Unemployment. A Problem of Industry* published in 1909, he argued that, although there was no cure for unemployment, the relationship between the supply and demand for labour could be improved. He recommended setting up a national system of 'labour exchanges'; spreading available work between more workers and providing better assistance for those without work.[55] During the inter-war years, Britain went into a deep depression and the north-east of England was particularly hard-hit. Employment in North Shields' Preston Colliery fell from about 1,400 in 1923 to fewer than 20 in 1929 according to records held by the Durham Mining Museum. The Borough of Tynemouth's own estimate of the number who lost their jobs was 2,000.[56] The Northumberland Shipbuilding Company at nearby Howdon was shut down for the final time in 1930 with the loss of another 1,700 jobs. It had struggled in the years following the First World War, but in 1928–30 had still managed to build 18 tramp steamers as well as other smaller vessels. However, after the *Briarwood* was launched in May 1930 the yard was acquired and dismantled by National Shipbuilders Security which had been set up in 1930 with the express purpose of reducing capacity in the shipbuilding industry. The same fate befell the Tyne Shipbuilding Company of Willington Quay and the much bigger Palmers Company of Jarrow, which prompted the Jarrow March of 1936.

Ministry of Labour statistics for the period 1927–39 show that at the

Situated on Borough Road, the Labour Exchange was known locally as the Dole Office.

BY COURTESY OF DISCOVER NORTH TYNESIDE

start of 1927, 22 per cent of those covered by unemployment insurance in North Shields were unemployed. By October 1928 the figure had grown to almost 28 per cent. After two better quarters, the figure rose more or less steadily to a peak of 46 per cent in October 1932. It fluctuated around the 40 per cent mark until 1936 when it began to fall – but was still at 28 per cent in April 1939 just months before the outbreak of the Second World War. Many unemployed workers who had homes in North Shields were not included in these counts because, like my father, they had gone elsewhere in search of work. Many of those in work were actually under-employed or had been obliged to accept a series of wage cuts, in an ill-judged attempt to ameliorate the country's economic problems. At a time when there was usually only one breadwinner in a family, these high rates of unemployment meant that a much larger number of people were subsisting at or below the poverty level. When the limited unemployment insurance benefit ran out, the unemployed and their families were subjected to the humiliation of the hated 'household means test'. Introduced in November 1931, benefit was paid only after a meticulous investigation of a household's 'means', conducted to ensure that its members had no undisclosed earnings, savings, or other resources to draw on.

Against such a background, the governments that followed the Second World War pursued full employment policies as well as providing insurance benefits for those out of work. But thirty years later, the interventionist and conciliatory middle way of Keynes and Beveridge, which had been adopted by both Labour and Conservative post-war governments, was out of favour again. Mrs Thatcher's governments of the 1980s adopted a hard-line, laissez-faire stance towards 'full' employment, claiming it was responsible for many of Britain's economic ills. Under the new (in fact old) policies, unemployment soared and 1980s Britain was again plunged into episodes of social unrest and public disorder just as it had been in the 1880s.

Ignorance

Most children joined the labour force at an early age in the eighteenth and early nineteenth centuries and received, at best, a very limited education. It is no coincidence that it was only as the use of child labour was regulated, that moves were made to extend educational provision. The underlying principle governing the lives of children seemed to be that if they were not going to work, then they should be educated. Given that kind of thinking, it is not surprising that when education was provided it involved the same kind of rigid discipline which obtained in the workplace.

Child labour
Today, companies in the West are publicly condemned if their products are made abroad in factories which employ child labour. Yet child labour was used extensively in this country in the nineteenth century and deemed to be essential to our competitiveness in the very days when the United Kingdom was regarded as the workshop of the world. Pauper children in the care of the parish were under an obligation to work to help pay for their keep – but a similar obligation held true for children still living with their working-class parents. Many started work aged six or seven or even younger. Eventually, the long hours and horrific conditions in which children worked in mines and factories were documented by public enquiries, and concessions were forced out of unwilling employers. But, initially, they insisted that such reforms would be 'injurious to trade'; they seemed unconcerned that the conditions were injurious to the health and well-being of their young employees. These were not rogue employers. They included, for example, Richard Arkwright and Samuel Courtauld. Both had workforces made up predominantly of children. Arkwright took on children as young as five. Courtauld relied mainly on children from London workhouses, aged ten or more.

Conditions in coal mines were particularly brutal for children. An 1842 Royal Commission reported that in Northumberland some began work underground at the age of four. The youngest were usually employed as 'trappers'. The job involved opening a flap or door when a coal cart passed and closing it immediately afterwards, to maintain the flow of the limited supply of air in the appropriate direction. The task was not physically demanding but critical for safety in Northumberland mines where the danger of flammable gases demanded the best ventilation available. Trappers had to be at work from the opening of mines each day, which could mean leaving home at 1 a.m. or 2 a.m. in time to start a 12-hour shift at 4 a.m. No regular time was provided for meals. Sometimes children were allowed 15 minutes to eat their 'bait', but in many cases the break from work was even shorter. In winter, many young children did not see the daylight for months on end. It was dark when they went down the pit and dark when they returned to the surface. Other than a day away from work on Good Friday and sometimes Easter Monday, the only break child workers were allowed was two weeks over the Christmas period.

Unusually, women were not employed underground in Northumberland, but about a third of underground workers were children. From the age of six they worked to get the hewed coal to the surface. How they did that depended on local conditions. Evidence given to the Royal Commission noted that corves carried a minimum of 5 and a maximum of 10 cwt (half a ton, or 227 kg) and that 'putters' as they were called locally pushed corves an average of about 8 miles daily, often ankle-deep in water. Although the minimum height in which they were expected to work was the minimum height of a corf, that is 3ft 9in (114 cm), witnesses admitted to having seen children pushing shallower corves in even more confined spaces. A Percy Main hewer, who described the appalling conditions in which the children worked, still observed that because of the shallow seams, 'These boys are wanted and must be had. They have great need for boys.' Even after the 1842 Commission, 'putting' was still judged appropriate work for boys aged ten and above.

The following examples from the evidence collected during the 1842 inquiry help convey a sense of what life was like for these young boys working in Percy Main colliery on the outskirts of North Shields.

No. 62 Mark Wood

Aged 9 (the brother of the preceding witness). Keeps the chains in Percy Pit. Puts the tram on the rollers and puts the switch right [for passing places on the underground tracks]. Has been down the pit a year. Kept a door at first. Gets 1s. 3d. a-day now. Leaves home about 3 o'clock and takes his little brother with him. Gets home before 5 o'clock of a night: never later than 5. It is almost always near 5 o'clock when he gets home. The pit makes him sick now and then; has made him sick twice. Threw up his victuals each time. Never sick more than those two times. Head works [aches] sometimes: every two or three days. Feels sore on the top of his head when he is in the pit; never when out of it. Never feels it at home. Never beaten by anybody. Never lamed or hurt. Never worked more than one shift at a time. Cannot read or write. Went to a Sunday School at Shields. Went to a day-school, before he went into the pit for half a year. Does not go to church or chapel regularly. Father is a hewer down this pit. Has another brother a putter, who is 14 years old.

No. 64 Robert Dixon

Aged 9 years. Drives [guides a horse] down Howdon Pit. Has been down Howdon a fortnight. Was at Burdon Main Colliery [in North Shield] six or seven months. Kept a door there. The water in this (Howdon) pit is in some places up to his knees; not in many places; horses splash him. Never feels sick. Feels sleepy sometimes. Works in the night-shift every other fortnight. Is working in the day-shift now. Only the Howdon Pit works a night-shift now. Feels sleepy whiles in the night. Cannot read or write. Goes to no school of any kind. Went to a Sunday-school once. Goes to no place of worship now. Father is a shift-worker. Has two brothers, one 11 and one 14 years of age: one a foal and the other a halfmarrow [both terms for young putters]: both putting down Howdon Pit.

No. 69 John Short

Turned of 10 years. Drives in Percy Pit. Has been down half a year. Was lamed a-fortnight ago by the horses pulling the rolleys [the waggons transporting the tub or corves of coal] off the way [the narrow underground horse route] and jamming him. He was off four days. Likes his work. Goes down at 4 in the morning and rises at 4 at night. His two brothers down the pit; one is driving and is turned 11 years; the other is a foal and is turned 13. Father is a sailor. Cannot read or write. Goes to the Ranters' [Primitive Methodist] Sunday-school but not always, or often to chapel. Went to a day-school when he living at Shields.

No. 76 William Pendley

Turned of 12. Is brother to the preceding witness [aged 8]. Is now going to the Howdon Pit to drive. Has been down pits 3 years. Kept a door for a year and a half. Father is a hewer in Howdon Pit. Drives in the water all day. Stands about in the water many times in the day. This makes his head work and makes him sick, sometimes all night. Was sick most part of last night but did not throw up. Sometimes is sick once, or twice or thrice in a week. Does not throw up his food, never does that. Legs work very often; has pains; pain in his arms sometimes. Was strong before he went down the pit. The pit and the water is making him bad. Has been in it a fortnight. Has felt worse in that pit since she has had water in. Can read. Goes to the Ranters' Sunday-school. Writes his name. Goes to no place of worship. Putter used to beat him sometimes when he kept a door. Used to thrown him down upon the plates and things, and made his head ache. Never laid him off work, nor made the blood come.

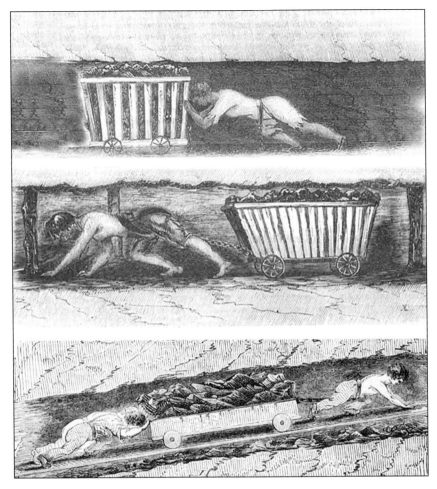

Child putters in coal mines. These are just some examples of the modes used. They varied depending on such factors as the depth and incline of the seam.

FROM THE 1842 COMMISSION ON CHILDREN PP. 78, 79.

Accidents of all kinds were commonplace, but the sub-commissioner for the 1842 inquiry was shocked that in Northumberland no accident records were kept and that the 'colliery medical men 'directly refused to give any evidence'. He added that fatal accidents were not usually made public and it was only by chance that he had become aware of fatal accidents during his visits to the pits. But the health of young children in the mines was damaged in many ways other than accidents. Working in cramped conditions from an early age stunted and deformed their normal physical development. Many became crippled as part of the normal routine of their daily work. In addition, of course, they were exposed to the coal dust which led to serious respiratory problems in later life.[57]

Education

Although education did not become compulsory until late in the nineteenth century, a large number of people were able to at least sign their name in earlier decades. For example, in 1841, only 33 per cent of bridegrooms were obliged to make their mark on their marriage certificate because they could not sign their name. The proportion of those who were totally illiterate fell steadily throughout the century until it reached 3 per cent in 1900.[58] However, although useful as a minimal indicator of literacy, being able to sign a certificate was not the same as being functionally literate. It did not, for example, signify that someone could read a newspaper or write a letter.

Education was available throughout the nineteenth century for those who could afford to pay for it, and there were over 30 small academies listed in the Pigot Directory for North Shields in 1834, Educational provision for the labouring classes was much more limited. As the Inspector of the Privy Council's Committee of Council of Education reported in 1847:

> I have generally found the worst schools in those districts where the best are required, I mean those districts where people are poorest and the most ignorant. This is one of the evils of the entire dependence of education on local resources for its support. It manifests itself particularly in localities on which mining operations are encroaching, in which those persons who draw from them their wealth rarely resided, and from which the gentry have fled.[59]

The very thought that the children of the labouring classes should be educated was seen by many of the better-off as a dangerous notion likely to subvert the social order. As one North Shields ship-owner put it when asked for a subscription to a charity school: 'Eddicashin! eddicashin? Noa! we'll syun hev nee sarvints.'

> The dread conviction [was] that education would emancipate the great suffering class, and enable it ... to compete for the good things so tenderly cherished and conserved by the 'educated'.[60]

The prevailing laissez-faire ideology meant that the state was not directly involved in the provision of education but that does not mean that members of the government did not appreciate its importance. That is evident from the fact that the first members of the Privy Council's Committee of Council of Education were the Lord President of the Council, the Lord Privy Seal, the Chancellor of the Exchequer and the Home Secretary. From 1841, they were joined by the First Lord of the Treasury (the Prime Minister). The committee was set up in this way to avoid the interdenominational rivalry which it was anticipated would beset the educational grant system if it were subject to direct parliamentary control. It allocated grants to voluntary bodies and monitored the education they provided from 1839 until 1899.[*]

---

* At that point it was replaced by the Board of Education.

Most subscription schools receiving the committee's grants were run either by the National Society for Promoting the Education of the Poor in the Principles of the Established Church (usually referred to as National Schools) or the alternative non-denominational British and Foreign School Society favoured by non-conformists (usually referred to as British Schools). It was King George III who provided a rationale for the first subscription school in North Shields. Following his golden jubilee, a group of Quakers called a meeting at which, in anticipation of opposition, they emphasised that to establish a school would be to do no more than meet the King's wishes that 'every poor child in the kingdom shall be able to read his Bible'.

When the school opened in 1811, each of the 188 subscribers was allowed to recommend one scholar. Subsequently, each recommendation required a donation of half a guinea (10s. 6d., equivalent to £340 in 2014). Boys occupied the ground floor of the Royal Jubilee School. A separate School of Industry for girls occupied the upper storey. An equivalent National Society school was not established until 1839. It too had separate provision for boys and girls but within the same building. A Catholic school adjacent to St Cuthbert's church was opened in 1840. Other local schools were funded largely by legacies, such as Kettlewell School which opened in 1826, or by local churches, usually as Sunday schools.

An early attempt by the Committee of Council of Education to establish a supervisory role over schools receiving grants met with such a hostile response from the Anglican Church that the committee was forced to adopt only an advisory role. It was also forced to agree that grants should be awarded only to schools where religious instruction took precedence over secular subjects.[61] A specific condition of enrolment at the British Jubilee School in North Shields was that pupils attend a place of worship on Sundays and that a chapter from the Old or New Testament should be read out at the start and end of each school day.[62] The emphasis on religion was so fundamental that the religious affiliation of teachers was recorded by the Council of Education's Inspector when he visited North Shields' schools in 1840 – something that would be inconceivable today, He noted, for example, that the teacher in the non-denominational British School was actually a member of the Church of England and that the master at Kettlewell School was a Wesleyan Methodist.

The notion that teaching was a profession had not yet been established and the British School was visited daily by one or more of a committee of six governors to ensure the teacher kept to the specific conditions laid down.

He must cause to be entered daily in a book kept for the purpose an account of the lessons performed by each class, and of the absentees from school, or from their respective places of worship on Sundays. To this end he must make out distinct lists of the children who are to attend each particular place of worship, and appoint one boy out of each list as an 'inspecting monitor of worship' who is to report to the master every Monday morning.[63]

The sponsors also insisted on what today would be called a parental contract.

New pupils must be accompanied by a parent or friend, who shall be informed that the children must attend the school regularly at the hours appointed, *viz*, nine in the morning, and two in the afternoon, and be always sent clean and decent, with hair combed, and face and hands washed; and that they will be required on the Lord's day, regularly to attend the place of worship which such parent of friend shall appoint.[64]

The pupils at Jubilee School were drawn from almost all religious backgrounds other than that of the Anglican Church. Among them were 'the Irish Catholic, the Wesleyan, the Primitive Methodist, the Jew, the Scotch Presbyterian, the Baptist, the Independent, the "Salemite", the "New Connexion" boy and the boy from Little Bethel'.[65] It was probably galling to the members of Christ Church that the subscribers chose to build their two-storey British School on a piece of land immediately opposite it but they were probably reassured that the master appointed to teach the boys was a prominent local Anglican.

Admission to the British School was not entirely free. Children paid about 1*d*. a week (equivalent to about £3 in 2014). That did not necessarily mean that the pupils or their parents took attendance as seriously as those who founded the school would have liked. Haswell asserted that 'the boys attended school only when it suited their parents'.[66] His claim is consistent with the findings of the Council of Education Inspector in 1840 that 24 per cent of the boys in the British School were absent as were 26 per cent of the girls. The absentee figures at the National School were 19 per cent for boys and 17 per cent for girls.

Both the British and National schools taught reading, writing and arithmetic, plus a smattering of geography or general knowledge. They made heavy use of the Bible as a textbook. However, once Haswell was well established in the British School for boys he had sufficient confidence to deviate from this narrowly prescribed curriculum. He introduced new subjects and teaching methods – starting with music, followed by astronomy and geometry. More significantly, he taught English in terms of the meaning and derivation of words and also made use of the classics of the day instead of relying exclusively on the Bible for reading material.[67] The inspector reported in 1840 that about a fifth of his boys could read well. Such a low figure would create an outcry today and guarantee that the school be put in 'special measures'. However, it is actually an impressive figure. There was no specified starting or leaving age in subscription schools such as Jubilee.

Jubilee School. Opened in 1811, a small monument at the junction of Albion and Preston Roads now marks the site of the school.

Pupils were admitted from six to fourteen and usually only attended for between one and three years. Consequently, many of those pupils present during the inspection would have been at the school for only a short period and not yet had time to learn to read.[68]

The education of the girls in the School of Industry on the floor above was the responsibility of a different teacher and the curriculum was, intentionally, different. Half the girls' 'education' involved sewing, for which they received payment. Apparently some pupils had earned close to £2 (equivalent to over £1,000 in 2014) by the time they left school. The emphasis on sewing and the fact that the school kept 'a register of behaviour for the use of persons applying for servants' is a strong indication that the girls were being trained for domestic service.

Most schools in this period used the 'monitor' system in which the teacher passed the content of each lesson to selected pupils who then passed on the information to their fellow pupils. Subsequently, the pupils were tested with set questions, to which the class would reply in chorus. An 1842 investigation revealed the risk this method entailed. When the order of the questions was changed, the pupils still gave their answers in the order they had been taught.* When the National School in North Shields was inspected in 1840, there were seven monitors for 220 boys (one per 31 pupils) receiving payment in the form of books to the value of 4d. a month. There were 12 monitors for the 140 girls (one per 12 pupils). They also received payment in kind, in the form of prayer books and bibles. In the more commercially orientated British School of Industry for girls, there were 6 monitors for 100 girls (one per 17 pupils). There is nothing

---

* The monitor system is often ridiculed but actually bears some resemblance to the prevalent system used in universities in which graduate students rather than members of staff provide tutorials and supervision to undergraduates.

in the report to suggest that their 4*d*. a month was received in kind. The fact that the report made no reference at all to the use of monitors for boys in the British School raises the possibility that Haswell taught his pupils without them. Another difference between the four schools is that there are references to modes of punishment in all but the British School for boys.

In the National School, boys were caned: girls were strapped on the hand. In the British School of Industry for girls, pupils were strapped on the hand or given double the usual tasks. The absence of any mention of punishment in the British School for boys raises the possibility that Haswell was able to maintain control without the use of corporal punishment.[69]

A similar school was financed largely by a legacy of £4,000 coupled with a piece of land on George Street from the sail-maker Thomas Kettlewell. The condition of his legacy was that the school should be specifically for poor children. Kettlewell's charitable aim even included a clause that the schoolmaster should be a lame person provided he was suitably qualified.[70] When the school was inspected in 1840 there were about 150 children on the register.*

Kettlewell School. Towards the end of its long life it housed the East End Boys Club. I played football for the club as a teenager.

The education inspector summarised the other schools in the town as follows.

In the Union School for girls under the management of an Independent there were 150 children present; the number on the books was 190. The payments are 1*d*. per week; the dimensions 50 feet by 34 feet. The mistress was trained at the Borough-Road school for about six months some three years back, and she hopes to revisit her old instructors for a short time next year, with a view to further improvement. Her salary is £40 per annum. On the ground floor of the same building there is an infant school, the mistress of which (a Wesleyan) has £30 per annum, house-room and coals. She was trained in the infant school at Newcastle. There were 120 present; the payments 2*d*. per week. There is a small play-ground. The room was well furnished with prints; it is 5 feet longer than the room above. I was told that a school of 300 children attending the Independent place of worship assembled in it on Sunday. In addition to the

---

* One of the first trustees was the artist Miles Birket Foster. After the Second World War, the school became the home of the East End Boys Club. Kettlewell School was demolished in 1964, like so many other interesting buildings in North Shields. The Royal Jubilee School suffered a similar fate. For many years the site remained entirely derelict although it now contains a modest monument recording that it is the site of the school.

above I visited eight schools kept by masters in the town of North Shields; one of these was for those who learnt Latin, the master being a. graduate of Trinity College, Dublin; more than 50 boys were assembled in it; there were, in all, 305 children in attendance at the rest. Some of these were gathered into the most unwholesome rooms I visited during my stay in the North. I heard of a Roman Catholic school but did not visit it; with this exception, I do not think that any school in the town kept by a master escaped me. I visited two dame schools; in the one there were 15, in the other 25 children assembled: 1,530 was given me as an estimate of the number of children in attendance at Sunday-schools.[71]

The Roman Catholic school the inspector failed to visit had only just been established in 1840. Among the others included in the description above was Miss Weir's school, near Dockwray Square which catered for about 30 pupils, the majority of them girls. It is unlikely that the Quaker Elizabeth Richardson's school was included. Founded in 1817 it seems to have closed in 1839, the year before the inspection. It was initially for a small number of girls although it subsequently became co-educational.[72] The school established by the Scotch Church also missed inclusion because it was not established until 1843.

By the mid-1850s it was widely recognised that there was a case for more universal educational provision. However, the royal commission appointed in 1858 to consider 'the extension of sound and cheap elementary instruction to all classes of people' reported that universal and compulsory education was 'neither attainable nor desirable'. The most it recommended was an extension of voluntary provision with more government support.[73] The report also emphasised that schools receiving government grants were not intended to be avenues for social mobility. As Robert Lowe (who was responsible for guiding the legislation through the House of Commons) made plain, the aim of the new arrangements was comparable to that underpinning the Bantu Education Act under the South African apartheid regime a century later.

It must never be forgotten that those for whom this system is designed are the children of persons who are not able to pay for the teaching. We do not profess to give these children an education that will raise them above their station and business in life – that is not our object.[74]

Pugh makes a similar point in her history of London's Foundlings Hospital which for much of the time catered for predominantly illegitimate children. Its inmates were educated to be useful but not on an equal footing with 'deserving' legitimate children. Initially, in the eighteenth century, the governors taught their children to read but not to write because they intended that they should:

> … learn to undergo with Contentment the most Servile and laborious Offices; for notwithstanding the innocence of the Children, yet as they are exposed and abandoned by their Parents, they ought to submit to the lowest stations, and should not be educated in such a manner as may put them upon a level with the Children of Parents who have the Humanity and Virtue to preserve them, and the Industry to Support them.[75]

The government demanded value for money for its investment in education. What was provided was intended to be 'sound but cheap'. The method adopted to achieve that end was payment by results. Government grants were only paid to schools if there was proof that pupils had been successful in a test of the so-called three Rs, that is reading, (w)riting and (a)rithmetic. The House of Commons were reassured in 1862 that though it could not be promised that the new system would be cheap and efficient, 'If it is not cheap, it shall be efficient; if it is not efficient it shall be cheap.'[76] Payment by results proved to be cheap. Within four years the state's financial contribution had fallen by over 20 per cent. Whether the system was efficient is a matter of judgement. The curriculum became even more narrowly focused and teachers and pupils were reported as being demoralised by the new regime.[77]

Educational provision was significantly extended by the Elementary Education Act of 1870, usually known as Forster's Act. By then there was a widespread acknowledgement that Britain needed a better trained workforce to remain competitive in an increasingly industrialised world and that an improved educational system was a necessary preliminary for better technical training. Although a pivotal piece of educational legislation, it still did not introduce a national system of free education. Its primary aim was to bolster existing voluntary provision: 'to fill up gaps, sparing public money where it can be done without.' The narrow focus on the 3 Rs and payment by results remained.

The Act divided the country into school districts. In the case of North Shields, the district coincided with the boundaries of the Borough of Tynemouth. In each district, the aim was to provide adequate accommodation for children aged 5–12, based initially, and ideally, on voluntary places. Only when they were deemed inadequate would a local school board be established and additional places provided in non-denominational schools, funded by local rates and grants from the central government's Education Department.

A School Board was established for the Borough of Tynemouth in 1871. There were already ten schools in operation but far too few places to cater for a 5–12 school career. Over the next few years five board schools were built. The School Board also assumed control of Jubilee School. Poor Haswell, who at the age of 63 had by then provided an education for several thousand young people over a period of 30 years, was subjected to the indignity of demonstrating his competence to the local bureaucrats now responsible for education. He satisfied them and taught on until 1886, dying three years later on his 82nd birthday.

In 1880, further legislation made education compulsory. Parents were required to send their children to school between the ages of 5 and 13. Although the Tynemouth School Board employed staff to enforce attendance, there remained a significant discrepancy between the number of children on a school register and those who actually attended on a regular basis. So, for example, in February 1901, 37 parents were summoned and in some cases fined because their children were not attending school regularly.[78]

Table 11.1   Additional elementary schools
in North Shields after 1841*

School	Established	Denomination
Howard Street	1843	Scotch Church
Trinity	1845	Church of England
St Joseph's	1857	Roman Catholic
Priory	1868	Church of England
Percy (St. John's)	1869	Church of England
St Peter's	1870	Church of England
Christ Church	1872	Church of England
Preston	1872	Church of England
Western	1872	Board School
Chirton	1873	Board School
Eastern	1875	Board School
Percy Main	1894	Board School
Queen Victoria	1897	Board School

Source: Adapted from H.H.E. Craster, *Northumberland County History, Volume VIII: Tynemouth* (Newcastle: A. Reid, 1907), p. 356.

With the subsequent inauguration of Local Education Committees and the abolition of School Boards under the Education Act of 1902, a

---

* Jubilee School closed in 1935. Kettlewell School was extended in 1906 and closed in 1939. The Howard School closed in 1909. Trinity School was transferred to the School Board in 1876 and closed in 1936. Priory School was re-built and re-opened in 1928. St Peter's School was closed in 1935. Christ Church School was extended in 1904. The Infants section closed first, in 1930, followed by the remainder of the school in 1939. Preston School was closed in 1926. Chirton School was destroyed by bombing in 1941. Eastern Board School closed in 1939.

new era in education began. Educational provision continued to improve throughout the whole of the twentieth century. In the opening decades, several new primary schools were built in North Shields. St Joseph's came first in 1907. It was followed by King Edward's in 1909; Cullercoats in 1910; Spring Gardens in temporary accommodation in 1919 and permanent accommodation from 1926; Lovaine Place in 1921; Collingwood in 1929; St Oswin's in 1930; The Ridges (subsequently Meadow Well) in 1937; and Chirton St Joseph's in 1939. In addition, in 1918, an Open Air School was opened temporarily under canvas in the summer months and in permanent buildings from 1925 to provide education for children recuperating after serious illness. The 1902 legislation also allowed local education committees to establish secondary schools. In North Shields, Tynemouth Municipal High School was established in 1904. It was initially housed in an extension to Queen Victoria School until an imposing new building was completed in 1909. Attendance at the high school was based on a qualifying examination but fees had also to be paid which were beyond the means of many ordinary families. Two more secondary schools were established in the inter-war years: Linskill in 1932, and Ralph Gardner in 1935 (which brought about the closure of Jubilee School). However, free secondary education for all had to wait until after the Second World War, when I was among the early beneficiaries of the pivotal 1944 Education Act.

Tynemouth Municipal High School, as it looked in 1916 before houses were built opposite it on Hawkey's Lane. I attended it after passing the '11+ grading exam'. It subsequently became a comprehensive school in 1969. It is now one element of the large and thriving Queen Alexandra Sixth Form College.
CONTEMPORARY POSTCARD

Want

Significant numbers of the British population lived in absolute poverty during the nineteenth century. They were poor, not only relative to other households, but absolutely poor because their household income was insufficient to keep its members healthy no matter how carefully they spent it. There was an improvement in living standards for large sections of the population, including the working classes, in the latter half of the century.[79] But significant numbers still lived at a bare subsistence level and the growing disparity between their position and that of those around them must have made their poverty even more difficult to bear. Still others fell below the poverty line when their circumstances changed, for example when they lost their jobs, became ill, or grew too old to work. There was no system of collective social security to cushion them in those circumstances. The comprehensive provisions of today's welfare state did not come into force until the latter half of the twentieth century.

Four types of factor pushed people into poverty. The first was a rise in the price of essentials. This impacted on the whole population but hit the already poor hardest. The second factor was an inadequate income. Britain did not introduce a national minimum hourly wage rate until 1999. Before that employers were free to set their wage rate as low as the labour market would allow. The third type of factor hit particular occupational groups hardest, for example when the demand for a particular kind of skill declined or even disappeared. The fourth kind of factor impacted specifically on individuals: the early death of a bread winner, for instance. These latter two kinds of factors were often linked. Even when the factor which pushed a family into poverty was an individual event it often had an occupational or community-wide dimension because some occupations were inherently more precarious or dangerous than others. That was the case for many of the occupations followed in North Shields and why the third and fourth factors are considered together below.

Price variations

Factors of the first kind, such as an increase in the cost of bread following a poor harvest, affected the whole population to some extent. However, price rises inevitably had a disproportionate effect on those who had no way to cushion themselves against such eventualities. A modest price rise might have had an insignificant effect on a wealthy family but threatened the very existence of a poor family. Periodic bad harvests hit the poorest particularly hard because from medieval times until the late nineteenth century wheat and other cereals made up the bulk of the diet of ordinary people. As Fraser put it: 'The loaf of bread was probably the principal single component of the working-class diet up to 1914.'[80]

An ability to supplement a grain-based diet with fish may have mitigated the situation for those who lived in North Shields. Nevertheless, the awful circumstances which existed at the start of the nineteenth century had been told to a young George Haswell in such graphic terms that he was still able to recall them many years later.

> In the dark days of January 1800, the grain of the previous autumn lay, yet uncut, rotting in the undrained fields. Such food-stuffs as had haply been garnered were disease-smitten, producing at best a sour, leaden, indigestible mass of dough which, though constituting in many cases the sole, and in most the main article of diet, was so utterly unfit to eat that famished children made a grim plaything of the sorry stuff, and in pulling apart the scanty portion, strove with each other to draw out the glutinous string into which it broke, to the greatest length. When a day old, the loaf became as hard as a block of wood, and stank when cut.[81]

Haswell knew from his experience of life in the town that for some sections of the population comparable hardships continued throughout the nineteenth century. He maintained that even 25 years after the end of the Napoleonic Wars 'an incredible proportion of the people were on the borderland of absolute starvation'. What particularly troubled him was that many of the comfortably-off people in the town appeared unaware or unconcerned by the plight of their fellow citizens.

> No glimmer of a sense of duty towards the people manifested itself … they were habitually spoken of as brutal, cruel, ignorant and vicious … no jot of allowance was made for the hopelessly adverse conditions in which such lives were steeped.[82]

Seen from the perspective of the twenty-first century, it is obvious that the depression, demobilisation and the periodic bad harvests that followed the end of the Napoleonic Wars would increase the numbers in poverty. What is not obvious is that much of the poverty was the result of a rigged market: engineered by the very people who so often complained about the cost of providing relief to the poor. The interruption of grain imports from Europe during the Napoleonic Wars increased the price of flour and bread. That shifted market power towards those landowners and farmers who controlled supply. They took advantage of the situation to push prices far beyond previous levels – despite a nineteenth-century equivalent of the twentieth-century 'digging for victory' campaign when all sorts of land, much of it far from suitable, went under the plough. A resumption of imports from the Continent after the war could have eased the situation. Instead, it was made worse by the government's 1815 Corn Law. Much like today's EU policy on agriculture, it was designed to protect landowners and farmers. Foreign imports of grain were banned unless the price of English corn rose to a specified threshold. Yet even this legislation did not prevent British agriculture from sliding into crisis. As the profits of farmers fell, many tenants were unable to pay their rents. Insolvency became commonplace and the poor harvests of 1828 and 1829 made an already bad situation even worse.

Haswell notes that his school-teacher father encountered the consequences of this situation on a daily basis.

> On all hands lay evidences of that ... insufficiency of food. ... There were sore faces, sore ears, sore eyes, faces tied up for face-ache, carbuncles, boils and abscesses; the children's hands were covered with warts, their feet and hands cracked and bleeding with chilblains; rickety children, deformed children, children disfigured with small-pox, or other unseemly scars and, as the good doctor Owen would sadly tell the Maister [Master] ... it all flowed from a chronic condition of semi-starvation. ... Only a few of the boys knew what it was like to have a good meal, but every boy knew only too well what it was to have more than a full share of suffering.

Ironically, the children in the Union Workhouse were often better fed and cared for than those who remained in their own homes.

> In one respect, indeed, the pauper boys formed a sort of aristocracy – there were no holes or tatters in the shameful garb with which their guardians unnecessarily chose to distinguish them from their fellows. They wore coverings, too, on head and feet, and could count upon regular – if unvarying – food. Not so the rest. Almost without exception poor – extremely poor – ill clad and ill fed. ... The best of the well-to-do lads wore clogs ... but the majority went bare-foot. ... They came from long distances, too, walking bare-footed through mud or snow – and often wet to the skin – from far-off villages, and bearing with them in – oh such tiny parcels, what they called – their dinner.[83]

Of course prices fell as well as rose and, when the cost of living decreased, the purchasing power of incomes increased accordingly. That did improve the situation of the poorest and was tantamount to an increase in wages. Unfortunately, there is no simple way to describe these fluctuations in the cost of living. That is why even today the choice of an inflation indicator to determine pension and benefit rises is so controversial. Nevertheless, broad trends can be discerned. Between 1850 and 1880, aggregate prices rose by about 20 per cent. Thereafter, they fell fairly consistently until almost the end of the century. The importation of grain and meat (made easier by refrigeration from the 1870s) brought about a significant fall in the price of food, although that was offset by a 30 per cent rise in the price of coal between 1896 and 1913. After 1913 the cost of living rose sharply. During and after the First World War there was a marked inflationary trend. Within six years, the cost of living increased by over 100 per cent. That led to industrial unrest in the north-east of England and a government inquiry which acknowledged that 'the high price of staple commodities have undoubtedly laid severe strain upon the majority of the working classes, and in some instances have resulted in hardship and actual privation'.[84] Between then and the outbreak of the Second World War prices fell back but were still 25 per cent higher than they had been at the beginning of the century. In the North East they were accompanied by high levels of unemployment and a widespread dependence on welfare benefits.

Inadequate and irregular incomes

Mitchell and Deane provide convincing figures to show that average wages rose between the middle and the end of the nineteenth century.[85] That does not mean there was a redistribution of income in favour of wage-earners. Industrialisation and the accompanying huge increase in productive capacity in the nineteenth century made it possible for wages to rise without reducing inequality. To this day, there is still a fundamental division of opinion between those who argue for greater equality by narrowing income differentials and redistributing wealth, and those who are content to raise incomes by 'increasing the size of the cake' at the same time as allowing income differentials to widen.

Although *average* wages may have increased during the nineteenth century, by definition all workers did not benefit to the same extent. A significant section of the population remained poor, not because they were feckless but because they still earned poverty-level wages. Others were in poverty because as a result of age, ill health or unemployment, they had no regular income. Moreover, increased wage levels for those in work were of no direct benefit to the retired who had suffered a lifetime of lower wages. Nor could higher wage levels fully compensate for the cumulative effect of years of lower wages for those well into their working lives. That legacy of what had gone before was still reflected in the daily lives of ordinary people in North Shields and elsewhere well into the twentieth century.

The conventional wisdom of the nineteenth century was that poverty was primarily the result of an individual's failure to secure work or spend wages sensibly. It was in part because that view was being challenged that Charles Booth carried out his study of poverty in London. Contrary to his expectations, his first report published in 1889 showed that 35 per cent of London's population were living in what he described as 'abject poverty'. Rowntree carried out a similar kind of investigation in York which demonstrated that Booth's results were not exceptional. His calculated

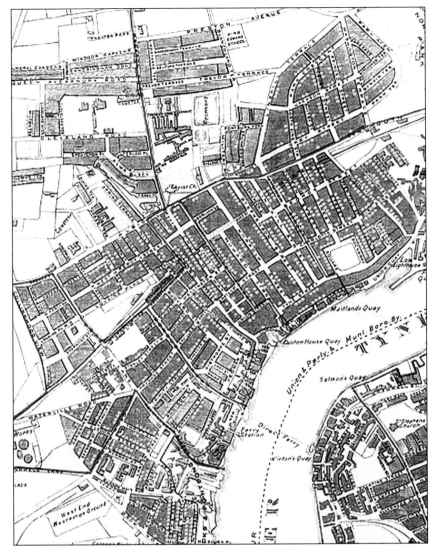

Distribution of First World War fatalities in North Shields. Note the extensive spread of the lives lost in what, understandably, became known as The Great War.

BY COURTESY OF THE TYNEMOUTH WORLD WAR ONE COMMEMO- RATION PROJECT

minimum weekly sum, 'necessary to enable families to secure the necessities of a healthy life', could not be construed as too generous by anyone, yet he still found that 28 per cent of York's population were living below this line. About a third were in what Rowntree called primary poverty because they had insufficient income to avoid poverty no matter how carefully they spent it. Perhaps the most startling figure in his survey was that about 50 per cent of those in primary poverty had a breadwinner in regular employment.

Laslett points to the disturbing personal consequences of these statistics.

More than half of all the children of working men were in this dreadful condition, which meant 40 per cent of children in the country. These were the scrawny, dirty, hungry, ragged, verminous boys and girls who were to grow up into the working class of twentieth century England. This was the generation which was to man the armies of the First World War, although they were inches shorter and pounds lighter than they would have been if they had been properly cared for. Those who were left of them became the fathers and mothers of the working people who endured the Depression of the 1920s and the Great Depression of the 1930s, and who saw their homes luridly lighted up by Hitler's bombs.[86]

My own grandparents belonged to this 'lost' generation. My paternal grandfather was born in Cornwall but, at the age of nine, moved with his family to the North East because there was no work available. He became a coal miner and died in 1908, aged 46, when my father was only four years old. His wife, a domestic servant before their marriage, was left in poverty with a still young family to look after. Later, her home received a direct hit in the bombing of North Shields in 1941 and she lost all her possessions. She died in 1953 while living, with a dependent adult daughter, in a single gas-lit room. My maternal grandfather was orphaned at an early age, wounded at the Somme, and returned to live with his wife and two daughters in a single gas-lit room. Yet he was lucky. Eighty others from North Shields died during the Battle of the Somme and, in total, about 1,700 lost their lives as a result of the war. Research by the Tynemouth World War One Commemoration Project has shown that Tynemouth Borough's war losses were twice the national average. My maternal grandmother, the daughter of an Irish immigrant father forced to leave Ireland because of the potato famine, was brought up in the slums on the riverside and was also an orphan by the time of her marriage. An infant daughter died while my grandfather was at the Front. When he returned, unlike many of his contemporaries, he at least had regular employment and the family could afford to move from their single room in a slum clearance area to a four-roomed rented council flat in the 1930s.

There are no systematic findings comparable to Booth's or Rowntree's for the earnings of those employed in North Shields, but the vagaries of local circumstances would suggest that the situation was unlikely to have been better and would probably have been worse. Some figures are available for the wage *rates* of miners and seamen but they are not the same as *earnings*. Earnings also depended on whether employment was continuous and the number of hours worked. Poverty, in turn, was not just about the level of a wage but the number and needs of the people who had to be supported by it. What would have been an adequate income for a single person might have been a poverty wage for someone with a spouse and family to support. In the nineteenth century, when families were typically larger (an average of 6.2 in the 1860s), this was an obvious problem. When couples began voluntarily to limit the size of their families it was a considerable time before the practice trickled down to the least well off.[87] These several factors mattered a lot in North Shields where the nature of available work often meant there was no such thing as a regular income. In this respect, patterns of employment and earnings in North Shields were significantly different from those in places like the mill towns of Lancashire where, except during cyclical fluctuations, manufacturers were ordinarily able to offer regular employment. In industries such as shipbuilding, even until the late twentieth century, it was normal for workers to be laid off when construction had reached the stage when their particular skills were no longer required, or when a yard was waiting for the next order to be secured. The weather alone could be enough to play havoc with the earnings of those involved directly and indirectly in shipping and in fishing.

Even at the start of the twentieth century, most North Shields fishermen did not receive a basic wage. Their income was determined solely by the value of their catch. The costs of fuel, ice, food, repairs and maintenance were first deducted from the value of the catch. The owner then took 50 per cent of the remainder. Between 10 per cent and 15 per cent went to the skipper. The rest was divided between the crew. While at sea, the wife of a crew member could draw a sub – an advance – on the anticipated earnings of her husband. If the catch was poor, the crew member could end up owing the owner money. The debt was then carried forward until the next catch was brought home to port.[88]

By the end of a working week even careful working-class families could run short of ready cash to buy essentials. Shopkeepers who wanted to keep their regular customers often had little other option than to allow them credit. Many also did the opposite. They collected money from customers in advance, on a weekly basis, so that their 'regulars' could cope with the additional outlay for a special event such as Christmas. Ironically, debt became a growing problem as the standard of living improved in the second half of the nineteenth century. As expectations began to rise, retailers realised that they could make money by stimulating demand and offering interest-bearing credit to those who might not otherwise buy the goods on offer. Walker's, the House of Quality, offered such a service to good customers. In addition, 'ticket agents' provided vouchers to deal with a variety of stores, such as Bell Bros and Howard's Stores, and like the Walker's agents called on customers to collect money on a regular basis.[89] T. Archer Lee and the Provident Clothing and Supply Company Ltd were well-known ticket agents in the area. The latter, founded in Bradford in 1880, with the stated aim of helping 'working-class families provide for themselves through the use of vouchers … exchanged for goods in local shops, and paid for in affordable instalments' is still in operation, with 9,000 agents across the country. In the nineteenth century, only respectable and reliable people were usually offered shop or ticket credit. Others who needed money in a hurry to 'tide them over' had to resort to other sources of support. In many streets, someone with a little capital would lend small sums of money for short periods to neighbours, and receive a small amount in interest in return. Those without access to such support sometimes became the victims of 'loan sharks' who charged much higher rates of interest to those desperate for immediate help. The most vulnerable families in the nineteenth and twentieth centuries then sometimes had to choose which creditor to pay, and by how much, or take a trip to the pawn shop with whatever they had of value that they could afford to do without for a time. It has been estimated that, on average, every working-class family made at least one pledge a fortnight and, unfortunately for the very poorest, interest rates were highest on the lowest value items.[90] There were twelve pawnbrokers in North Shields in the nineteenth century. Monday was the most popular day for business, when Sunday-best clothes went into pawn.[91] This practice continued in North Shields until well into the twentieth century. As an aunt explained to me, she was sent regularly to a pawn shop to redeem my grandfather's suit.

> I couldn't take it in but I could get it out. I used to hate that. I used to get it for him to go out on Friday night or maybe the Saturday. My mother used to take all Sunday night to sponge it up and press it ready to take in again on the Monday.

Fisher's pawn shop, ironically on Thrift Street, about 1940.
BY COURTESY OF DISCOVER NORTH TYNESIDE

| Shiels to Shields

Occupational hazards and individual misfortune

Factors of the third kind, which plunged people either temporarily or permanently into poverty, were related to particular occupational groups or communities. The vagaries and dangers of shipping provide an obvious example. Sailors were paid per voyage or, in the case of fishermen, as a proportion of a catch. They did not receive an upstanding wage when not at sea. So when sailings were greatly reduced in the winter months, and no income was being earned, families could go hungry unless the loss of income could be offset by the earnings of another family member. When sailors were paid reasonably well, for example during the Napoleonic Wars, they might have been in a position to save but when wages were low that was not possible. Families would then become dependent on their extended family, friends or parish relief. In addition to such seasonal factors, structural changes in the local North Shields economy meant that those who had previously enjoyed a regular income could find themselves without work, often for prolonged periods. This was the fate of many of those who had worked in the once profitable salt industry; for the scullermen who lost their livelihoods with the advent of steam ferries, and for the miners who had once earned reasonably good wages in mines that were no longer economically viable.

The fourth and final kind of factor that could plunge a family into poverty was individual in character. Such a fate befell my own father. When my grandfather died in 1908, his mother was left with eight children. Her husband had been in regular employment and earned a reasonable wage as a coal miner, and also had some additional income from the Lawrence Bros small family firm which owned horses, a wagonette and trap, and took passengers to a variety of destinations in the area. However, his unexpected death transformed the family's fortunes. Once an inquest had established that his death could not be attributed directly to his work as a coal hewer, the family's hope of compensation disappeared and they became entirely dependent on their own resources and the help of their extended family.

My grandfather's death may not have been directly related to his work but many families in North Shields did lose their main breadwinner as a result of the many occupational hazards that they confronted on a daily basis. As Haswell put it:

> Sometimes on a dreary afternoon in late November the darkness settled down prematurely. The vane on the old church when last looked at was swirling wildly. ... The roar in the chimney and the whistle through the key-holes and crannies rise now and again to a shriek and the storm cloud blackens every hour. ... The Maister [Master] ... knows that Death is busy this afternoon ... and that – certain as Death itself – at roll call next morning Dixon, or Boyce or little Thomson will be returned absent, and that some small shrill

voice will utter the quite familiar explanation, 'Please sir, his father's droondid'.[92]

It was far from unusual for whole crews to be lost when ships encountered bad weather. In 1800, for example, of the 71 ships that sailed from Shields and Sunderland, 69 were wrecked on their passage to London.[93] Wright has provided some telling figures that illustrate the extent to which such dangerous conditions continued well into the twentieth century. He investigated the fate of the 505 first-class (that is, over 15-ton) fishing vessels registered in North Shields between 1875 and 1976, when safety was given a much higher priority than in earlier periods. Despite that, of these 505 vessels, 27 per cent failed to return to port and were known to have been or were deemed to have been lost.[94] The death of the seamen on such ships would very often mean that their families joined the ranks of the many already poor and destitute.

North Shields seamen and fishermen were such frequent victims of accidents in the course of their work that they, their wives and mothers developed their own peculiar superstitions. Some fishermen even had an agreement written into their conditions of service so that they could refuse to sail if they encountered a bad omen on the day they were to put to sea.[95] On the day of sailing, women did not wash clothes in case their men were 'washed overboard'. In a similar vein, whistling was considered unlucky on board ship because it might 'whistle up a storm'. Sea boots were carried one under each arm with the toes pointing forward because, if a sailor carried his boots with the toes pointing down, it increased the risk that he would be carried home drowned. Many seamen cut off a sliver of the Wooden Dolly on the Custom House Quay in the belief that it would help keep them safe at sea. It was a perverse superstition given the provenance of the Wooden Dolly which had originally been the figurehead of the brig *Alexander and Margaret* on which the owner's son had been killed in 1791.* On the day of sailing, once fishermen had left home, they would not look back towards it, and their womenfolk would not call after them or go to the dock to see them off. It was considered unlucky to meet a clergyman or a nun or, worst of all, a pig – and in the days when North Shields had more than its fair share

---

* When the figurehead of the ship was removed from the *Alexander and Margaret* it was originally positioned as a memorial in the front garden of his parents' home. It was subsequently moved to the Custom House Quay, close to the river's edge in 1814, and became the first 'Wooden Dolly'. It was replaced by a comparable figurehead in 1850. That was replaced by a third Wooden Dolly, another ship's figurehead, in 1864. It had been so disfigured by the end of the century that a stream of letters to the local newspapers demanded a replacement. As a result, a fourth Wooden Dolly was put on the spot in 1902 – but was neither an original ship's figurehead nor even in the likeness of a figurehead. Carved to coincide with the coronation of King Edward VII, it represented an elderly fishwife with a fish basket on her back. That was the Dolly in place during my own early boyhood years in North Shields.

of free range pigs, that was not an unlikely occurrence. The colour green was held to be unlucky (on shore as well as at sea), as was going to sea on a Friday. Once at sea, some words (such as pig, rabbit, monkey, salt and rat) were taboo. Should they be uttered the wrong-doer had to grasp a piece of cold iron or turn his cap a full 360° to mitigate the effect (the equivalent of throwing salt over the shoulder after spilling it).

Serious accidents and loss of life were also common among the coal miners of the area. The biggest disaster took place at the Hartley Pit, just a few miles from North Shields. In January 1862, 204 men and boys lost their lives; 100 wives lost husbands and 250 children were left fatherless when the beam of the pumping engine snapped. Although there were some survivors from the initial accident, because the pit had only a single shaft, it took a long time to reach them and by then no one was left alive. The youngest to die were John Armstrong and John Duffy (both ten). The oldest was William Gledson (aged 71). The scale of the accident made it national news. Queen Victoria, secluded at Osborne Palace, mourning the loss of her husband Prince Albert who had died a month earlier, sent the following telegram: 'The Queen is most anxious to hear that there are hopes of saving the poor people in the colliery for whom her heart bleeds.' The queen sent a second message when she learned that there were no survivors:

> The Queen in the midst of her own overwhelming grief, has taken the deepest interest in the dreadful accident at Hartley, and up to the last had hoped that at least a considerable number of the poor people might have been recovered alive. The appalling news since received has affected the Queen very much. Her Majesty commands me to say that her tenderest sympathy is with the poor widows and mothers, and that her own misery only makes her feel the more for them. Her Majesty hopes that everything will be done, as far as possible, to relieve their distress, and her Majesty will feel a sad satisfaction in assisting in such measures. Pray let me know what is doing.

By early April the relief fund had exceeded £75,000 (equivalent to £47 million in 2014). However, presumably because weekly payments had to be paid from the interest on the invested capital, only 8s. 6d. a week was paid to widows (without children), no more than the amount their husbands would have earned in a couple of days.

Hartley was by no means the only major mining disaster in the area around North Shields. There were at least 30 disasters in Durham and Northumberland in the nineteenth century which together cost more than 1,500 lives. The worst disasters other than Hartley were at Felling in 1812 (92 dead); Wallsend in 1833 (102 dead); Haswell in 1841 (95 dead); Burradon in 1860 (76 dead); Seaham in 1880 (164 dead) and Trimdon in 1882 (74 dead). In contrast, the death of four men following an explosion at North Shields Preston Colliery in 1900 was a small affair but was marked in the town by great solemnity. Two of the dead were from South Shields but made their final journey from their homes to lie alongside their colleagues in Preston cemetery. This added additional poignancy to the occasion as the funeral processions made their way across the river by ferry. The procession from the riverside to the cemetery was led by the Tynemouth Borough Silver Band and *en route* merged with the processions of the two North Shields men who had been killed. In addition to the four hearses, there were twenty carriages and large numbers of friends and workmen who followed the processions on foot. Despite heavy rain, hundreds more were already gathered at the cemetery to pay their last respects. A few days later

The Hartley Pit Disaster Memorial in Earsdon churchyard, photographed in 2014. The 204 people killed ranged in age from 10 to 71.
AUTHOR PHOTOGRAPH

a meeting in the town hall at North Shields established a benevolent fund for the families of the victims. Accidents to single individuals did not receive the same kind of public response. Although a fatal or disabling accident to any breadwinner was likely to prove tragic for the family involved, such personal disasters were often shrugged off with indifference by those in a position to help.*

This chapter has discussed what Beveridge called the five 'giant evils' of squalor, disease, idleness, ignorance and want: evils which were still evident in Britain when he submitted his report in 1942. The chapter ended by outlining the most common sets of circumstances which pushed families into poverty even when overall living standards were improving. Private citizens with income to spare were often sympathetic and put their hands in their pockets in a variety of ways to help those in need but such help often came with strings attached or was patronising and moralising. Those in authority tended to provide only the bare minimum and even that help was often offered in a mean-spirited way. The gross social inequality of the period was regarded as necessary and legitimate. The assumption seemed to be that 'the poor will always be with us'. A redistribution of incomes in favour of the poor was never given serious consideration; nor was the introduction of a national minimum wage – which had to wait until 1999, a century after the research of Booth and Rowntree had demonstrated the need for it. There was relatively little that families on low wages could do for themselves in anticipation of such misfortune but, within those limits, they did try in the ways that will be discussed in the next chapter.

---

* Accidents were not the only perils faced by pitmen, as I became personally aware when I visited the homes of former coal miners to collect rents in a mining community during the summer vacation of 1964. I was distressed at how many of them had severe, chronic breathing problems. Yet it was only in the latter part of the twentieth century that the full extent of the damage caused by coal dust inhalation to the lungs and cardio-vascular systems of coal miners was finally acknowledged. By then, generations of miners had suffered and died from their occupational diseases without compensation.

12

The labouring classes (III)
Responses to poverty

S INCE the advent of the Welfare State in the mid-twentieth century, the relief of what Beveridge called *want* has been the responsibility of central government. That was not the case in earlier centuries. Poor relief was organised locally and raised from parish poor rates which were, in effect, a local property tax. Parish poor relief was supplemented by charitable donations. But these forms of help were only part of the story. Those who could anticipate being in poverty often tried to make preparations for such an eventuality. Both individually and collectively the less well-off tried to reduce the risk that they would become dependent on poor relief or, after 1834, finish up in the parish workhouse. It is these several forms of self-help which will be the focus of the second part of the chapter.

Help from others

Poor relief
Compared to other European countries, England was unusual in having a statutory-based system of poor relief in place as it entered the nineteenth century. However, it was delivered locally and provision varied significantly from parish to parish.[1] Indeed after 1713 in the parish of Tynemouth it varied between its constituent townships. Traditionally, poor relief had been provided by the parish as a whole but, because North Shields had a greater proportion of needy as compared to the other predominantly agricultural parts of the parish, the other townships chose to withdraw their support for riverside paupers. In 1713, during the Christmas season, in a 'charity begins at home' gesture worthy of Dickens' Ebenezer Scrooge, the justices of the peace ordered that each township should accept responsibility for its own poor.[2]

Levels of relief to the poor were changed from time to time, for reasons unrelated to the needs of the individual concerned. The overseers' accounts for the Cornish parish where my fourth great-grandmother Lawrence lived can be used to illustrate this point and what Kidd describes as the 'face to face' nature of the Old Poor Law where the parish overseers usually knew those to whom they were awarding relief. In 1815, Jane Lawrence was a 71-year-old widow dependent on parish relief. In October and November she received 3s. 6d. a week from the overseers. Then, in December, her weekly relief was cut to 3s. It remained at that level until May 1816 when the accounts record that 15 people receiving benefit, including Jane, were to have their poor relief cut by a further 6d. to 2s. 6d. The first overseer to attach his signature to this decision was an unmarried local solicitor who, according to family legend, was the father of Jane's daughter's illegitimate child. In August the accounts recorded, 'Jane Lawrence's pay to be reduced to 2/– [i.e. 2 shillings] per week' but, in September, 'It is ordered that Jane Lawrence do have 6d. per week added to her pay'. In May 1818 her subsidence pay was stopped for a month and she was required to return a blanket loaned to her by the parish. Her subsistence payment returned to 2s. 6d. for a week during June and remained at that level until March 1822. It then fell to 2s. 3d a week until her death in February 1824. When she died, the overseers paid 9s. 8d. for her funeral expenses. There is no evidence that the fall in the level of support she received between 1815 and 1824 was related to her personal circumstances. In all probability it was part of a general attempt to reduce parish spending on poor relief.

Payments to those acknowledged to be genuinely in need seem to have been accepted as legitimate: even the poor had a right to the bare necessities of life.[3] More problematic was how to respond to the able-bodied who sought relief. Of the approximately one million paupers who received help in 1802–03, only eight per cent were resident in England's 2,000 or so workhouses.[4] The vast majority, including the able-bodied, received 'outdoor relief'. To those who subscribed to the new orthodoxy of political economy, that appeared to be an unwarranted intervention in the free play of market forces. A way had to be found to relieve the genuinely destitute without undermining the self-reliance of the able-bodied. The critics of the Old Poor Law became preoccupied, not with the circumstances which made people poor, but the specific form of relief they believed was discouraging the able-bodied from accepting work at the market rate. The Royal Commission on the Poor Law, which reported in 1834, focused on the alleged dangers of out-relief to able-bodied males. It argued it encouraged them to be insolent, lazy, thriftless and immoral: insolent because many seemed to regard relief as a right; lazy because they could receive the same amount of money whether in work or not; thriftless because, in being refused relief if they had savings, they had no incentive to save; and immoral because receiving an allowance for each child encouraged the breeding of illegitimate as well as legitimate children.

These assumptions encouraged the commissioners to draw a clear line between provision for the truly destitute and care for able-bodied males without employment. It recommended that to obtain relief an able-bodied male and his whole family should be required to enter a workhouse. The idea behind this principle of 'less eligibility' was that the experience of any workhouse inmate should be more miserable than that of the poorest paid labourer living outside the workhouse. To ensure that being incarcerated in the workhouse did not produce yet more mouths to feed, there was a further recommendation that men and women and even husbands and wives should be separated and, to make the workhouse even more heartless, parents separated from their children. The two main principles of the new Poor Law are summed up in this hard-hearted quotation from the 1834 report.

> By the workhouse system is meant having all relief through the workhouse, making this workhouse an uninviting place of wholesome restraint, preventing any of its inmates from going out or receiving visitors without a written order to that effect from one of the overseers, disallowing beer and tobacco, and finding them work according to their ability; thus rendering the parish fund the last resource of the pauper, and rendering the person who administers the relief the hardest taskmaster and the worst paymaster that the idle and dissolute can apply.[5]

The division of Northumberland and Durham into poor law unions was not completed until 1836. In the interim, the statistics provided by the old poor law authorities to the new Poor Law Commission demonstrated that:

> The old poor law had not necessarily been administered in a benevolent spirit in North East England. Rather there is clear evidence that both in the growing Tyneside towns and in the neighbouring rural areas there had been in recent years a series of attempts to cut down the expenditure on poor relief.[6]

The guardians elected to run the workhouse in North Shields were not representative of the residents of the area it served. On the contrary, they were 'without exception the most influential persons in their respective parishes'.[7] Public statements by the Assistant Commissioner appointed to administer the new system in Northumberland and Durham suggest that he entirely accepted the spirit of the New Poor Law regime. Despite that, he administered it flexibly. For example, the provision which allowed outdoor relief to be given to the able-bodied poor in times of accident, illness or other urgent situation was sometimes invoked and elderly couples were not always separated on admission.[8] Initially the Tynemouth Union workhouse occupied the existing parish workhouse on Preston Lane (now Preston Road) close to Christ Church. A new enlarged workhouse was built on the same site in 1848. The men's and women's day rooms and yards were separated as were the wards and yard for vagabonds. For some reason, the two wards set aside for 'imbecile women' were much larger than the single area set aside for 'imbecile men'.

Elsewhere in the country, purpose-built workhouses were often impressive structures. That was not the case in North Shields. By the 1860s there was a growing number of complaints about the 'incongruous collection of structures known as the Tynemouth Workhouse'. Complaints about them reached a peak in 1883. Many wanted the workhouse moved from the town into the countryside. In the event, the workhouse was not moved. The adjacent cricket pitch to the north of the workhouse was bought and the whole site redeveloped in 1886. The workhouse subsequently became the responsibility of an elected Board of Guardians until 1930 when it became the responsibility of Tynemouth Council's Public Assistance Committee.[*] After the National Assistance Act of 1948, the workhouse buildings became part of Preston Hospital – although there had already been hospital facilities on the workhouse site before then. Blocks specifically for the infirm had been added in 1903 and 1909, followed by an operating theatre in 1913, a mortuary in 1920 and receiving wards in 1925–26.

In 1851, there were 270 inmates in the workhouse. As Table 12.1 shows, 28 per cent of them were elderly (aged over 65) and an identical proportion young (15 or less). Of the remaining 44 per cent, aged 16–64, women were in the majority. Of the 16 per cent who were males of working age, 11 were described as imbeciles but occupations were still listed alongside most of their names. The most obvious difference thirty years later was that the number of people in the workhouse had risen from 270 to 554 but that was in part the result of a widening of the catchment area. The composition of the inmates was not markedly different. A slightly smaller proportion (23 per cent) was elderly and a slightly higher proportion (35 per cent) in the youngest age group. The proportion aged 16–64 was also down a little (to 38 per cent). Of this 38 per cent of working age, the balance between men and women was slightly changed. Men comprised 36 per cent of the 16–64-year-olds in 1851 and 39 per cent in 1881. So more men of working age, both absolutely and relatively, were in the Tynemouth Union workhouse in 1881 than in 1851. In terms of family composition, there was a significant difference between 1851 and 1881. Of the 20 families headed by females in 1851, 60 per cent

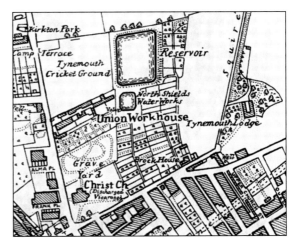

Map 12.1
Tynemouth Union Workhouse, as it was in the mid-nineteenth century before the site was redeveloped in 1886.

---

[*]   After initial meetings at the George Tavern, the guardians met in the Guardians Hall opposite the Police Station on Saville Street until 1904 when they moved to Northumberland Square. The original hall was converted into shops.

were unmarried. Of the 46 comparable families in 1881, 35 per cent were unmarried. Although the number of children living in the workhouse without adults had increased from 54 to 81 between 1851 and 1881, this actually represented a proportionate decline from 20 per cent to 15 per cent.

Table 12.1   Tynemouth Workhouse inmates, 1851 and 1881

	1851		1881	
	Number	%	Number	%
0–15 years	76	28	194	35
16–64 male	43	16	82	15
16–64 female	75	28	130	23
65+ years	76	28	148	27
Total	270	100	554	100
Special cases	21	8	30	5
Widowed	75	28	144	26
FHUM	12	4	16	3
FHMM	3	1	17	3
FHW	5	2	13	2
FHM	0	0	4	1
CWA	54	20	81	15

Source: This analysis is based on census transcriptions from Findmypast, http://findmypast.co.uk (accessed 11 April 2104)

Notes:
SC   = special case (e.g. imbecile)
FHUM   = number of families with children 0–15 headed by unmarried mother
FMMM = number of families with children 0–15 headed by married mother
FHW   = number of families with children 0–15 headed by widow
FHM   = number of families with children 0–15 headed by man
CWA   = children without adults.

Increasingly over the nineteenth century, workhouses catered primarily for those too old, sick or in some other way incapable of taking care of themselves, By the end of the nineteenth century, in the country as a whole, as many as 30 per cent of people over the age of 70 lived in workhouses. In that respect, workhouses had become the functional equivalent of today's old people's homes. Nevertheless, about 20 per cent of workhouse residents were the unemployed able-bodied and their families who had been forced by circumstances largely or entirely out of their control to subject themselves to the indignities of the workhouse.

As a measure for alleviating personal hardship, workhouses did provide minimal support for those admitted. However, as a measure for addressing the problem of poverty, they were a distraction. The principle on which they

Tynemouth Union Workhouse, seen from Military Road. The Brock Farm reservoir can be seen on the upper right of this image.

were based did not take into account the simple fact that many of the poor were in that position simply because their income was too low. That became increasingly difficult to deny after the pioneering social research of Booth and Rowntree. As a result, a 1905 royal commission concluded that formal recognition ought to be given to the fact that there were different types of poverty and that a workhouse based on the principle of deterrence should be retained only for 'incorrigibles' such as chronic drunkards. For the rest, more focused help was recommended.

Charitable help

The limited help provided by central and local government for the poor was, to a degree, offset by a dynamic voluntary sector. How much help was afforded the poor in this way will never be known because casual charitable donations, such as those to beggars, went unrecorded, but some historians have estimated that in total it may have been greater than that offered through the Poor Law.[9] In 1855, Whellan listed a number of specific charities set up to help the poor in the parish of Tynemouth, some of them dating back into the early years of the eighteenth century. The sums involved appear small today but were substantial in real terms at the time. Sir Mark Milbank had directed that after a payment of £2 to the vicar, the residue of a rent charge of £20 per annum should go to the poor of Tynemouth parish. Eleanor Wilson left £25 and William Raper £30 for the same purpose. Other bequests were more specific. George Crawford left the dividends on £700 for the poor of Tynemouth village. George Milburn left ten shillings a year for the poor of Chirton, and Margaret Richardson bequeathed £467 in East India annuities for the poor of North Shields.[10] Thirty years earlier, Thomas Kettlewell had left virtually the whole of his substantial estate to charity with the greater part of it set aside to endow a charity school for orphans and the children of cripples, with preference to be given to the orphans of seamen.

Ordinarily, in the nineteenth century, charity involved more than simple giving. It was widely believed that unconsidered acts of generosity could prove counter-productive. Ideally, charity should be discriminating and have the ultimate aim of fostering self-help on the part of the recipient. However, that aim could not be applied to young children who were considered to be unable to help themselves without adult assistance. Public concern for their moral as well as physical welfare came to the fore in the early nineteenth century when the scale of child destitution was revealed and official enquiries showed that large numbers of children were being employed in appalling working conditions. This growing concern for the welfare of children brought about some improvement in a limited number of industries as well as numerous philanthropic initiatives. For example, the North Shields Holiday Agency provided a week away in Holywell Dene during the summer for a small number of poor children with 'delicate constitutions'. Another local initiative was the society 'formed for the purpose of establishing a school ship on the River Tyne, for the reception of boys who through poverty, parental neglect, or being orphans, or who for any other cause are left destitute and homeless and in danger of contamination from association with vice and crime'. The 1868 meeting to set up this society was called by James Hall, a prominent North Shields business man. His scheme followed an established pattern, begun initially in the middle of the eighteenth century by Jonas Hanway, a governor of the London Foundling Hospital.[11] Similar schemes had also already been set up by the Royal Navy. The first training ship obtained for anchorage at North Shields, from 1868, was the 1812-built, 74-gun HMS *Cornwall*. It was renamed HMS *Wellesley* in honour of the Duke of Wellington (formerly Arthur Wellesley) who led the British army during the Napoleonic Wars and subsequently became prime minister. The ship was broken up in 1874 and replaced in 1875 by the 1844-built HMS *Boscawen*, one of the last of the Royal Navy's wooden battleships. It too was renamed *Wellesley* and provided a home and training for 300 boys from the ages of 12 to 16 (rather than the previous maximum of 200). Hall and his colleagues were insistent that the objective of the training ship was to safeguard young people from crime, rather than reform those who had already committed criminal acts but, in practice, this stipulation was not always observed. Training, in accordance with the Industrial Schools Act of 1866, was designed to encourage the boys to help themselves by equipping them for employment, primarily in either the merchant or Royal Navy. Life on board was disciplined and not especially comfortable. After the second *Wellesley* was destroyed by fire in 1914, the boys were

The training
ship *Wellesley*,
destroyed by a
fire in 1914.

BY COURTESY OF
DISCOVER NORTH
TYNESIDE

housed in Tynemouth Palace (the Plaza) on the sea front, until funds were raised to re-establish the school at the First World War submarine base at Blyth. By this time, there were a number of national charities specifically targeted at children, notably the National Society for the Prevention of Cruelty to Children, National Children's Homes, and those run by Thomas Barnardo.

Not all charitable initiatives incorporated this dimension of an 'investment in the future'. Some were an acknowledgement of a job already well done, based on an understanding that lives had been lived on the straight and narrow until the individuals concerned had been overtaken by old age or adversity to join the ranks of the deserving poor. For example, the town's poor were remembered on the coronation of Queen Victoria. On 28 June 1838 there was a distribution of meat, bread and money to 2,500 poor people in North Shields from a large tent that had been erected for that purpose in Howard Street. Later in the day, a dinner was held, paid for by public subscription, for the seamen of the port, 'many of whom gained a scanty livelihood by acting as watermen'. Around Christmas or the New Year each year, there was an annual dinner for elderly seamen in North Shields.* The venue was usually the grand premises of the Albion Assembly Rooms

---

* They were often described as 'decayed' at the time.

and it is noteworthy that the newspaper report in 1864 emphasised that 'the veterans seemed to thoroughly *appreciate* [my emphasis] and enjoy their annual treat'.[12] The use of the word appreciate was a recognition that those who funded such events liked to know that their generosity had been acknowledged.

> About 900 of these men, whose weather-beaten countenances indicated the pursuit of their early years and some of whose scars evinced the share they had borne in the battles of their country, sat down to dinner in a spacious malting house in George Street, belonging to Mr Richard Robinson, brewer. The place was the centre of attraction during the whole of the morning ... to witness these aged warriors partake of the comfortable fare provided for them. This consisted of barons, round, and sirloins of beef, as such quality as England alone can produce, accompanied by the never-failing plum pudding bountifully supplied by some of the ladies of the Borough: to each man was given as much ale as he chose to drink, but such was the order and decorum influencing the meeting, that not one instance of excess took place. ... On the following day the remains of the viands of this bountiful feast were made into soup, of which 2,000 poor families plentifully partook. The inmates of Tynemouth workhouse had a good substantial dinner, with plenty of ale and tobacco ordered by the Guardians.[13]

Thereafter, of course, the poor returned to their mean dwellings and inadequate diets. There was still widespread ignorance of just how bad those conditions were. Many of those who investigated life in the slums of England in the nineteenth century were like explorers in a foreign land, although Haswell suggests this was less so in North Shields than elsewhere. The dangerous and precarious nature of so many North Shields' occupations produced a 'curious intimacy' between many successful local people and those who through no fault of their own had fallen on hard times.

> The professional man, the lawyer, the magistrate, betrayed in errant locutions the thinness of his educational veneer. The well-to-do ship-owner had hardly cast off the manner and bearing of the skipper and, despite his wide-skirted blue surtout [frock coat], was recognised by the altogether un-awed populace as Captain So-and-so, who had lived not long ago on the banks of the river, or in the long 'narrow street' itself. ... The concentrated life of the Low Street, now passing quickly away, had gone far to produce this curious intimacy, but it was also very much due to the terrible frequency with which the bread-winner was swept away, and his wife and children thus plunged into the depths of poverty and squalor.[14]

This 'curious intimacy' helps to explain the ready charitable response when disaster struck. Two examples of many must suffice. In 1864 the proprietors of a local theatre contributed the takings from a performance to the widows and orphans of the sailors who had lost their lives during a recent bout of severe gales. A similar event took place on 1 July 1869 following another huge storm which had led to yet more loss of life. The families of seamen were not the only beneficiaries of such charitable responses. Miners' families and even individual miners received similar help on occasions.

Another focus for charitable endeavour was the care of the sick and infirm. The Dispensary in Church Street was instituted in 1802, under the patronage of the Duke of Northumberland, and its work continued well into the twentieth century. It was supported by bequests, donations, annual subscriptions and the proceeds from the Tynemouth Dispensary Cup football competition. Mackenzie noted that from April 1823 to the time that he was writing in 1825, 10,303 patients had received treatment, in addition to the 4,594 who had been vaccinated. At times the Dispensary struggled to find sufficient funds. At other times it could afford to employ a full-time doctor. In 1888, for example, the post of house-surgeon and dispenser was advertised in the *British Medical Journal* at a salary of £130 per annum (equivalent to £55,000 in 2014), in addition to a furnished house and

Instituted in 1802, Tynemouth Dispensary continued to provide medical treatment until the advent of the National Health Service in 1948.

BY COURTESY OF DISCOVER NORTH TYNESIDE

unspecified extras. The Indigent Sick Society, set up in 1815 following the end of the Napoleonic Wars, was another local charity aimed at providing comfort and care to a limited number of sick people.[15] North Shields also had a charity for poor *lying-in* married women (that is, for bed rest after giving birth), but the restriction of the service to married women is a further indication of how the Victorians favoured giving help not just on the basis of need but on whether or not someone was 'deserving'.

A particularly striking example of a charitable effort on behalf of the sick is the way in which Tynemouth Jubilee Infirmary came into being. It can be traced back to a St Andrews Congregational church Sunday school teacher and a group of his scholars who, in 1875, formed a flower mission to take flowers (and sometimes food) to those known to be ill. That experience led them to realise that much more help was needed. In 1877 a committee was established to buy medical aids for the sick, such as feeding cups and invalid chairs. They were then lent out free of charge to those in need, irrespective of their religion or social status. At this point, the group's name was changed to The Benevolent and Flower Mission. A permanent visiting nurse to the sick was appointed in 1880 and she was joined the following year by a group of lady volunteers. Their work revealed the need for more organised provision and, in 1884, rooms were opened with six beds in the

To the right of the now demolished Tynemouth Jubilee Infirmary is the memorial erected in 1925 to those from the Borough of Tynemouth who lost their lives in World War One.
BY COURTESY OF DISCOVER NORTH TYNESIDE

north-east corner of Dockwray Square.* At about the same time, a group of North Shields men proposed that the scale of such charitable work should be greatly extended and a subscription infirmary built in the town. The Duke of Northumberland was approached, and he offered a tract of land on Hawkey's Lane as a Queen's Jubilee gift to the town. Appropriately, the foundation stone for the infirmary was laid on Jubilee Day, 21 June 1891. Charitable donations complemented the subscriptions, including those from the Tynemouth Infirmary Cup football competition.

Self-help

Members of the working classes tried in various ways to avoid becoming dependent on charity or going into the workhouse when they fell on unusually hard times. Individually they may have been weak but by cooperating they were able to do more for themselves. Such cooperation ranged from simple exchanges of help between family members, friends and neighbours, right through to attempts to reform the very structure of British society to achieve a more equitable distribution of economic resources. Those who held the reins of power in Britain were ambivalent about these attempts at self-help. When they took the form of friendly societies they were generally applauded. When they took the form of workers combining to try to improve their terms and conditions of employment, they were deprecated and even made illegal for a time.

Family, friends and neighbours
Spreading the notion of self-help was the prime purpose of The Society for the Bettering of the Conditions and Increasing the Comforts of the Poor which was set up at the beginning of the eighteenth century. The underlying assumption was that the poor knew little or nothing about domestic economy and that their ignorance was a prime cause of their poverty.

> *Whatever encourages and promotes habits of* INDUSTRY, PRUDENCE, FORESIGHT, VIRTUE AND CLEANLINESS *among the poor, is beneficial to them and the country; – whatever removes, or diminishes, the incitement to any of these qualities, is detrimental to the* STATE *and pernicious to the* INDIVIDUAL. This is the POLAR STAR of our benevolent affections [original emphasis].[16]

The truth is that through long experience and absolute necessity, most working-class people were only too well versed in how to make their limited resources 'go further' or how to supplement their income, for example by

---

* On a site that was later occupied by Moore's, a firm of printers.

taking in lodgers even when their accommodation was already over-crowded. They were most in danger of falling into debt and poverty when they had no scope for additional economies. It is not possible to provide anything other than anecdotal evidence of the informal ways in which members of families in North Shields coped with adversity, but we do know that they would be astonished at how clothes are now discarded while they still have 'life left in them'. My wife's eldest aunt Alice (born in 1907) recalled that the members of her extended family wore woollen hand-knitted socks and stockings. When they wore thin or developed holes they were not discarded. Holes were darned and when necessary her grandmother (born in 1855) would cut off the old feet and 're-foot' them. Many working-class children never had new clothes. What they wore had been passed down through family and friends or bought second-hand from market stalls or perhaps church sales. When they were no longer capable of being worn further, clothes would be sold to 'the rag man' in the hope of recovering a little of the initial cost. One of my great-grandmothers was forced to earn her living sorting such rags in 1901 after the death of her seaman husband.

Households in need did not exist in isolation. Members of families, friendship groups and local communities provided mutual support for one another.[17] Dupree makes the important point that these groupings should not be regarded as alternative sources of assistance. They were usually complementary: family members, neighbours and institutions typically performed different functions.[18] Census records show that households often contained three generations, or that generations of the same family lived in close proximity to one another. That allowed for mutual support. The middle generation could care for the elderly and, in return, the elderly could help to take care of grandchildren (as they so often do today). Short-term financial support, or gifts of food or clothing, would often be given by friends and neighbours, and could be crucially important when there were no family members in the immediate vicinity. In the over-crowded streets and dwellings of North Shields, there was little scope for a private life style. Neighbours could not but know the business of those who lived alongside them, and help would often be offered without those in need requesting it.[19] An element of reciprocity was invariably implicit when such help was given. Those providing support might have received it in the past or be conscious that they might need it in the future. As Maus maintained, giving of any kind is never truly free. The very act of giving creates a social bond with an obligation of reciprocation on the part of the recipient.[20] Taylor's research on Tyneside provides evidence of this mutuality in working-class communities.[21] However, as traditional working-class areas were torn down and rebuilt or abandoned, existing ties of mutuality were difficult if not impossible to maintain.

The Cooperative movement

In the eighteenth and early decades of the nineteenth century, most working-class people in places like North Shields had no other option but to buy from hawkers, street traders or small local shops.[22] As Fraser puts it:

> The working class, by shopping in the streets or in the corner store, got neither cheapness nor quality. They paid dearly for their small quantities and any credit obtained. The quality was abysmal, with frequent adulteration of the most common products to squeeze a few pence more profit from the poor.[23]

Things improved significantly in the later decades of the century, as shops with multiple branches, such as Home and Colonial Stores and Lipton's, began to spread across the country. With rising incomes and easier access to an improved food supply, it was possible for such chains to develop nationwide reputations for both reasonable quality and prices. Such changes came slowly in North Shields. As Ward's 1897–98 *Trade Directory* shows, of the 121 grocers listed, the vast majority were still small local shops, but there was a branch of the Home and Colonial Tea Stores on Saville Street, and a

The Coop on Camden Street. This photograph was taken shortly before the building was demolished in 1994. The Coop's offices were housed in this building. The Coop grocery shop was opposite on the same section of Camden Street.

BY COURTESY OF THE LATE NORMAN BROOKS

branch of the London and Newcastle Tea Company just a few doors away. Just round the corner from the Home and Colonial on Camden Street was 'The Coop'. Although the Rochdale Cooperative Society is generally credited as being the pioneer of cooperation, it did relatively little that was genuinely innovative. Its real success was fostering the development of the cooperative movement in the nineteenth century.[24] The first known cooperative society in North Shields was formed in 1860 with 40 initial members – three years before the nationally based Cooperative Wholesale Society was established to buy in bulk and manufacture own-brand goods. By the end of the century when, nationally, cooperative stores were responsible for about ten per cent of food sales, there were three more branches in North Shields: on Charlotte Street, Dene Street, and King Street. Others followed in later years. My mother shopped (not exclusively) for groceries at the Camden Street Coop and I can still remember the 16943 membership number she gave after each transaction to ensure that she was credited with the dividend at the end of each financial year – which, during my childhood, was ten per cent of a customer's spending. In 1948, that meant that £75,000 was returned to the 20,000 members of the North Shields Coop in dividends (the equivalent of about £6 million in 2014). According to Kidd, it was this regular 'divi', in addition to the confidence of buying unadulterated food, which best explains the fast growth of the cooperative movement. What made Coop shops less attractive was that initially, they did not give 'tick' (credit), although that rule was relaxed in special circumstances in the later decades of the century.[25]

Friendly and mutual societies

In times of need, limited help sometimes came from workmates, friends and neighbours. In the case of a death, workmates would usually take up a collection to try to mitigate a family's immediate loss of income. But it was to the wider family that people would turn most often for moral as well as financial support during a crisis. For example, after my paternal grandfather died in 1908, his family received help from his extended family. As an elderly relative recalled, 'After that they were very poor. My mother used to help them a lot. My mother and father did a lot for my Aunt Lizzie – bought things and raffled them to get her money. When my Aunt Lizzie came up to the house she never went away empty-handed.'

It was not a huge step to go from informal help of this kind to localised, independent friendly societies. Amongst the earliest I have been able to identify in North Shields are The Provident Association (1790); 'the friendly society who meet at the house of Mr William Foster' (1795); the Good Design Association of Seamen and Landsmen (1799); the Unanimous Association of North Shields (1811); the Friendly Society of Orangemen North Shields (1816); the Friendly Society of Women (1819); the North Shields Friendly Society of the Low Glasshouses Florists (1820); the Loyal

Standard Association (1824) for the mutual relief of sailors and The Aged Seamen's and Scullermen's Society (1842), which met initially in an upturned keelboat near the Low Light. The Shipwrecked Fishermen's and Mariners' Society was singled out by R.M. Ballantyne for a particular mention in his 1883 *Battles with the Sea*. He described it as 'an admirable institution which cannot be too highly commended'. Another, still extant, early society bequeathed a fine building to the area. In 1829, a number of Tyneside master mariners set up a friendly society to provide pensions when they were incapacitated or reached the age of 60. Soon afterwards, they built what are

The Master Mariners' Homes on Tynemouth Road, completed in 1840 and still in use today.
CREATIVE COMMONS, COURTESY OF PHIL SANGWELL

The society was established in 1853. These headquarters, at the junction of Sibthorpe and Waldo streets, were built in Queen Victoria's Diamond Jubilee year of 1897.
AUTHOR PHOTOGRAPH

now known as The Mariners Homes for elderly masters and their wives, on the road between North Shields and Tynemouth. It was completed in 1840 and serves a similar purpose to this day.* The Tyne Steam Packet Provident Society was established in 1853 and its 1897-built headquarters (also known as the Tug-Boatmen's Hall) still exists. This list of local societies is by no means exhaustive. There were, in addition, the North Shields Fishermen's Beneficial Society; North Shields Sailmakers Friendly Society; Tyne and Blyth Trimmers and Teemers Association; Tyne Fishermen's Society; Tyne Foy Boatmen's Provident Society; Tyne Hand-in-Hand Friendly Protecting Society of Journeymen Coopers; Tyne Watermen's Society; Tyne, Wear and Tees Tugboatmen's Federation; Tyneside and District Labourer's Association and the Tyneside and National Labour Union.

Other North Shields friendly societies were local branches or lodges of national institutions, such as the Ancient Order of Foresters and the Manchester Unity of Oddfellows. Initially, local lodges were free to fix their own contributions and benefits, but after 1844 a degree of conformity was required to ensure local societies remained solvent. Each member carried a rule book which specified the contribution to be paid and benefits to which he or she was entitled. Typically, a member unable to work because of illness received a weekly allowance, medical attention and, if necessary, medicine. Members in distressed circumstances received a benefit as, sometimes, did those who needed assistance to travel to seek work. Finally, sums of money were usually paid for the burial of a member (or his or her spouse and children). In the case of the North Shields Friendly Society of Women, £7 (the equivalent of about £5,000 in 2014) was provided on death plus four gallons of ale for the wake.[26]

Many friendly societies held convivial weekly or monthly meetings in pubs to attract new members and help develop a fraternal feeling among existing members. A group of Manchester Methodists, concerned by this close association with pubs, set up the Independent Order of Rechabites in 1835.† Before anyone could join its insurance and saving schemes, they had to be willing to sign 'The Pledge' and commit themselves and the members of their families to becoming total abstainers. An active branch opened in North Shields in 1841 and various groups of teetotallers, including the Rechabites, formed a lengthy procession which walked through the main streets of the town to publicise their cause. The specifically male and initially more exclusive body, The Order of the Sons of Temperance, was set up in the USA in the 1840s and spread quickly in England after it was introduced in 1849. To become a brother, one had to be nominated by an

* Since that time, the Homes have provided 30 flats for retired and needy seafarers and their wives. Few residents today are Master Mariners, but nearly all have been seafarers or have connections with the sea.

† It was named after the Old Testament tribe commanded not to drink wine.

existing brother. Three other existing brothers would then investigate a would-be member to ensure that he was a suitable person for entry to the order. Although its members indulged in secret rituals and used signs, passwords and a particular handshake to identify one another, The Sons of Temperance had a thoroughly practical purpose. It organised insurance and savings plans for its teetotal members, obliged members to visit sick brothers at least once a day, and paid the funeral expenses of any brother who died.

In addition to regular meetings to collect subscriptions, it was common for friendly societies to hold an annual or biannual feast and a club day which might involve an excursion or a procession through the town in which the symbols of membership were put on public display. These were often elaborate and masonic-like in character. Indeed the *Freemason's Pocket Reference Book* for 1883 stressed that the Members of the Garden of Eden Lodge of the Friendly Society, the Ancient Order of Free Gardeners, had no connection with freemasonry but added that it 'presents certain features of masonic interest'. The *Shields Daily News* reported in 1867, that the members of the North Shields Lodge had just taken possession of a grand new silk banner and that its members wore a 'curious blue sash or collar' and a purple and gold apron on which were depicted the four rivers which were believed to have flowed from the Garden of Eden. In these types of societies, officers usually rejoiced in grand titles. To reinforce a sense of shared identity, the rules often specified that members must attend meetings and pay a fine if one was missed. The rules of the Robert Gordon Lodge of the Foresters based in North Shields, for example, specified that members living within two miles of the meeting place (the Clock Vaults pub in Wellington Street) would have to pay a fine unless they gave a satisfactory written apology for their absence.[27] Ordinary (or general) friendly societies were more like commercial insurance companies than the Foresters or Oddfellows. Unlike the affiliated lodges, they did not hold regular meetings. Payments were made impersonally by post rather than in person or collected on a regular basis by paid employees.

Although it is estimated that about 25 per cent of adult males were paying in to some kind of friendly society by the latter half of the nineteenth century, it is reasonable to suppose that more would have done so had they been able to afford the regular contributions.[28] What many of the remainder had to settle for was to join a burial club to make sure that they and the members of their family could at least avoid the indignity of a pauper's funeral. Two such clubs expanded into national institutions: the Liverpool Victoria (which now trades as LV) was set up in 1843.[*] The Royal Liver followed in 1850.[†] Between them, by 1865 they had about 800,000 members

---

[*] LV is still a mutual company owned by its members rather than shareholders.

[†] The Royal Mutual Insurance Society Ltd acquired the business of the Royal Liver Assurance Ltd in 2012.

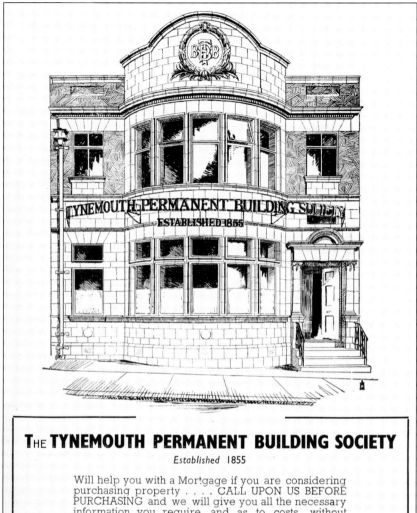

THE TYNEMOUTH PERMANENT BUILDING SOCIETY

Established 1855

Will help you with a Mortgage if you are considering
purchasing property . . . . CALL UPON US BEFORE
PURCHASING and we will give you all the necessary
information you require, and as to costs, without
obligation.

Invest Your Money in our Preference Shares
A Good Investment

53-54 HOWARD STREET - NORTH SHIELDS *Tel. 366*

Chairman : N. G. TATE   *Secretary :* A. H. TITCHENER

paying into their 'penny-policies'.* Despite the growing significance of such national bodies and their profit-making commercial equivalents, trade-specific societies were still being set up. For example, the Federation of Sail

---

* I still hold some of the penny policies which my parents took out on my life when I was born.

Makers of Great Britain and Ireland was formed in 1890 and had eleven branches by the early 1900s, including the North Shields Sail Makers Friendly Society. Others were short-lived. For example, the North Shields Fishermen's Beneficial Society which was established in 1902 closed in 1904.

Friendly societies did not always live up to their name. Membership was sometimes denied to those judged a poor risk because of their character or occupation. The Tyne Iron Society, for example, which despite its name admitted men of most trades, drew the line at coal miners. Rule 1 stated baldly that 'no collier shall be admitted'. The Blaydon Friendly Society used the same phrase in its rules. Faced by such exclusions, some miners chose to establish societies of their own; for example, the Miners' Society of Newcastle which when founded in 1812 welcomed miners from other localities. In marked contrast, some societies were restricted to a single pit and it was not uncommon for them to receive financial support from the mine owners (for example, the Wallsend Colliery Relief which was set up in 1831). In such instances, many miners viewed the society with suspicion. Eventually, these several problems were resolved when Miners Permanent Relief Societies emerged in the 1860s and by the late 1880s almost half of all eligible miners belonged to them.[29]

According to Perkins, friendly societies were generally politically neutral.[30] There were certainly exceptions to this on Tyneside. They were given prominent roles during the Northern Reform League demonstrations in 1867 and a number of friendly society delegates were known radicals. Nor was it unusual for friendly societies to offer financial assistance to members involved in strikes.[31] Indeed, Gosden maintains that, because early one-trade societies did the work of unions as well as friendly societies, this often led to their financial collapse when their accumulated funds were distributed to striking members. He cites as an example the Northumberland and Durham miners' strike of 1844 when societies had to be disbanded because their funds had been divided among their members without an income.

Another important form of mutual society that emerged in the nineteenth was the building society, a financial institution owned by its members with the specific purpose of lending money to enable people to buy their own homes with repayments spread over many years. Several societies were formed in North Shields and Tynemouth though today, after numerous name changes and mergers over the years, they are now part of either the Newcastle or Leeds building societies.

Protest, industrial action and trade unions
The most obvious step for workers to take to try to increase their wages was to come together in trade unions. However, that kind of combination was banned until 1825. As a consequence, to be on a low wage was simply a fact of life. Workers had little other option than to accept their lot with forbearance. However, there were times when those who ordinarily

accepted it with a resigned acceptance used force to seize stocks of food or put pressure on the authorities to lower prices or provide additional relief. Bohstedt has identified more than 700 such incidents and is confident that there were more.[32] To try to explain why people responded in this way during periods of food shortages or unusually high prices, Thompson introduced the concept of the 'moral economy'. People protested in this way because they considered that what had befallen them was beyond the point of what was reasonable.[33] Traditional moral notions had been breached. Rioting was legitimate because the new circumstances were illegitimate. Bohstedt too accepts that need alone does not explain the public disorder. However, he argues that what lay behind rioting was not a breach of shared moral norms but the 'politics of provisions'. Those who rioted most often were the working poor who would ordinarily be able to cope. They reasoned that they would succeed with their just demands because it was easier and cheaper for those in power to appease them than it was to crush them.[34] In their different ways, both Thompson and Bohstedt agree that rioting is best understood as a form of collective bargaining: 'a collective form of self-help that worked.'[35] The rioters were not seeking radical change; all they wanted was a return to normality. The implication is that if the governments of the day had not denied workers the right to combine in trade unions, there would have been fewer disturbances because there would have been then, as there are now, alternative orderly ways to deal with grievances.

Disturbances over the price of food gradually came to end in England as food became more readily available. However, that was not the case in Ireland. There were disturbances during the potato famine of 1845–52, for example in 1846 when outraged Irish men and women tried to prevent the export of grain at a time when some of them were literally starving to death. They were unsuccessful.[36] About a million people died and another million fled from Ireland to seek better lives elsewhere. Among them were three of my great-grandparents who settled in North Shields.

Collective self-help in the form of disorderly behaviour was not restricted to the politics of provisions. It was also provoked by high levels of unemployment. Wellington's final victory over Napoleon in 1815 may now appear to be a national triumph. However, it did little to improve the lot of ordinary people. In many instances, the opposite proved to be the case. England went into a general depression. Industries that had expanded during the war years made large numbers of workers redundant. Demobilised soldiers and sailors added to the ranks of the unemployed. Major social unrest followed. There were widespread mass protest meetings, even hunger marches by coal miners: all intent on persuading the government to do something about the plight of the unemployed. The government of the day was no more persuaded to respond positively than was the government of 1936 when confronted with the plea for help from the unemployed workers who had marched from Jarrow to London after the closure of Palmer's shipyard. Indeed the opposite happened. Measures were taken to make public displays of grievance more difficult.

The most well-known instance of such a repressive reaction is the Peterloo Massacre of 1819. It occurred during a peaceful demonstration in St Peter's Field, Manchester which had been organised to promote voting reform. It left eleven people dead, including two women and a child. Another 400 people are known to have been injured, 113 of them women. A quarter of the injuries of the wounded had been inflicted by the swords of the mounted horsemen let loose on the crowd. The action precipitated public protests throughout the country though, in North Shields, the justices of the peace gave permission for a Peterloo protest meeting only 'upon a pledge being given … that everything should be conducted in the regular and peaceable manner – that [there be] no Music or Banners and no Sticks and Staves – no appearance of marching or arraying themselves in any manner.'[37] Nationally, although the Peterloo massacre was greeted with widespread disapproval, it actually prompted yet more public order measures to stifle protest.

In the absence of trade unions, those who felt that their wage levels had fallen to an illegitimate degree had little other option than to resort to strike action, even though it might drive them into destitution. Desperate circumstances led them to take desperate measures. One of the best documented examples of such action is the seamen's strike of 1815. There had been strikes during the Napoleonic Wars in 1803 and 1812 against impressment into the Royal Navy, but it was unemployment and low pay which prompted the 1815 strike. Following Wellington's victory, most of the merchant vessels hired by the government as troop or supply ships were no longer needed. Unemployment among seamen rose, although that in itself was not enough to provoke the strike. During the wars, when so many seamen had been pressed into the Royal Navy, local merchant ship-owners were obliged to operate with smaller crews. In compensation, sailors were paid higher wages.* After the cessation of hostilities, owners maintained the same manning levels but took advantage of high unemployment to reduce wages. During the wars, North Shields merchant seamen had been paid £8 or £9 (equivalent to about £6,000 in 2014) for a London voyage. Ten years later they were offered only £3 for the same voyage in the summer months and £4 in the winter. As it was against the law for seamen to form a trade union, they had to resort to a subterfuge and set up what was ostensibly a friendly

---

* Interesting corroboration comes from page 85 of Sir William Fairbairn's biography. He had worked as an engineer at Percy Main colliery but when 'Work was difficult to be had … he resolved to try to find his fortune in London. Adopting the cheapest route, he took passage by a Shields collier, in which he sailed for the Thames on the 11th of December 1811. It was then war-time, and the vessel was very short-handed, the crew consisting of three men and three boys, with the skipper and mate; so that the vessel was no sooner fairly at sea than both the passenger youths had to lend a hand in working her, and this continued for the greater part of the voyage [of 14 days].'

society, the Seamen's Loyal Standard Association (SLSA). It was centred in North Shields – although it then spread and operated with independent local control to other ports.[38]

The first indication that local seamen were not going to accept their reduced income without protest came in August 1815. They demanded that no foreign sailors be recruited while indigenous seamen were out of work. The ship-owners refused to yield on that point. Local seamen then pressed for an agreed standard ratio of crew to tonnage, comparable to that in the government's transport service. The owners again refused. The seamen next blocked the entrance to the river with boats. Ordinarily, local magistrates would have appealed for troops to be deployed.[39] On this occasion, both local magistrates and central government were reluctant to intervene on behalf of the ship-owners. There seemed to be a widespread feeling that the seamen's case was just and that it was the owners who were being unreasonable. John Cartwright, representing the Home Secretary, was sent to provide an impartial account of the situation.

> Ships from these ports have gone to sea shamefully deficient in strength to navigate them, and should this subject excite the attention of the legislature, hundreds of cases may be produced, in which avarice has risked at sea a helpless insufficient crew, in a crazy *but highly insured* [his emphasis] ship. ... Your Lordship has too much humanity, to fix an eye exclusively on the crime these poor men are committing in search of redress, without some consideration to the circumstances out of which that crime has arisen. ... I found my way yesterday to a public table at Sunderland, where except myself all were shipowners. They openly, to my deep disgust, avowed the base dissimulation with which they are acting. ... The unprincipled avarice, and want of integrity in this class of men in a body, appears to be one reason for the bias observable in favour of the seamen.[40]

The Home Secretary waited over seven weeks before acting. Eventually, marines seized the boats at the river entrance and the seamen, no doubt conscious of what had happened at Peterloo a month before, called off the strike. The owners tried to renege on the concessions they had already made but, in the face of considerable public outrage, agreed to them – at least for those seamen who returned to work within 48 hours. By 23 October, an observer at North Shields reported that nearly 200 ships had gone to sea that morning.

Open hostilities of this kind between workers and their employers became less common after 1825 when the Combination Act was repealed and trade unions became legal. Initially, their membership was relatively small but by the end of the nineteenth century there were over 2 million registered trade unionists and by the outbreak of war in 1939, they numbered over

6 million.[41] Trade unions provided the equivalent of friendly society services to their members, but their more significant role was that of the collective representation of their members in negotiations over terms and conditions of employment. It is not possible to make definitive statements about how much they were responsible for the improvements in the pay and working conditions that followed, not least because over the same period laissez-faire liberalism ceased to be regarded as sacrosanct and Britain's economy changed in numerous ways. However, trade unions undoubtedly played an important part in the improvement and, although a conservative force in British politics in many ways, helped change the political landscape by lending their support to another example of self-help: the broader, working-class labour movement which found expression in the Labour Party.

Political organisation

It was a sign of changing times that Thomas Burt, born in North Shields in 1837, who was working underground before he was ten years old, went from being secretary of the Northumberland Miners' Association to become not only an MP but a member of Gladstone's 1892 government; a privy councillor in 1906 and Father of the House of Commons from 1910 to 1918. Burt entered Parliament as a Liberal and remained a Liberal throughout his long life. However, later working-class political aspirants had another avenue open to them. In 1900 a meeting attended by a wide range of groups agreed to form a single body, the Labour Representation Committee (LRC), to sponsor parliamentary candidates. Support for it was boosted by a 1901 decision which threatened to return trade unionism to the days before 1825. A dispute, between the Taff Rail Railway and the Amalgamated Society of Railway Servants ended with the union being ordered to pay £23,000 damages (at least £2 million in 2014 prices). The precedent created by this judgement would have effectively rendered strikes impossible since employers would have been able to recoup the cost of any lost business from the trade unions. In the subsequent 1906 general election, the LRC won 29 seats and adopted the name The Labour Party. The Labour and Liberal parties then cooperated in the House of Commons to reverse the Taff Vale judgement and introduce several pieces of legislation of direct benefit to members of the working classes, including the Workmen's Compensation Act (1906), Mines Act (1908) and Old Age Pensions Act (1908).

In the 1910 election, 42 Labour MPs were elected and leading members of the party were invited to join the war-time Liberal government in the hope that this would help secure the cooperation of the trade union movement during a difficult period. From then on, despite splits and other difficulties, representatives of the working class continued to have an influence in the House of Commons. For example, when landlords sought to increase rents during the First World War (which mattered a great deal when 90 per cent of families lived in rented accommodations), this led to numerous extra-parliamentary protests and encouraged the then coalition government to pass legislation to fix wartime rents at pre-war levels to prevent profiteering. The combination of the involvement of the Labour Party in the extra-parliamentary protest and the pressure for action inside Parliament helped to reinforce the image of the Labour Party as representative of working-class interests and was also a clear demonstration of the way in which a government, when it chose to do so, could intervene on behalf of the disadvantaged to protect them against market forces.

Labour Party membership grew after the First World War; an electoral alliance was struck with the political wing of the Cooperative movement and the party firmly dissociated itself from the Communist Party by refusing it affiliate status. The growing strength of the Labour Party coincided with splits within the Liberal Party and with 63 seats in 1918, 142 in 1922 and 191 by 1923; the Labour Party became the second biggest party in the newly elected House of Commons. The 1918 election was the first in which a Labour candidate contested the constituency of Tynemouth. With boundaries which included significant middle-class areas, and the working-class vote split between the Liberal and Labour parties, George Harold Humphrey secured only 15 per cent of the vote (compared to 32 per cent for the Liberal in second place). In 1922, he closed the gap on his Liberal rival but the Conservative candidate left them both trailing. W. Pitt, the Labour candidate in 1923 held on to about 20 per cent of the vote and began to close the gap on the Liberal candidate to such an extent that in 1924 he secured only two more votes than the Labour candidate J. Stuart Barr. However, the Conservative candidate still won easily.

Because of the electoral arithmetic, the Labour leader Ramsay MacDonald became Prime Minister in 1924 and again in 1929 when Labour, with 37 per cent of the popular vote and 287 seats, was the largest party in the House of Commons for the first time. In Tynemouth in 1929, the parties were more evenly split than in earlier elections. Barr secured 30 per cent of the vote, compared to 33 per cent for the Liberal candidate and 37 per cent for the Conservative. Although being in coalition hampered the Labour Party's ambitions, the government still provided half a million homes to rent for working-class families as well as introduce other pieces of legislation relating to social insurance, unemployment and education. Under the 1930 Housing Act, Tynemouth along with other councils was required to draw up slum clearance plans. It was this which led to the clearance of the worst houses on the Bankside, the Low Street and Milburn Place and the building of the Ridges estate.

A period of division followed in the inter-war years after MacDonald agreed to form a National Coalition government. After T.H. Knight, the Labour candidate in Tynemouth in 1931 did less well than his predecessor in 1929; his successor Dr S. Segal took second place for the first time in 1935 (albeit still with only 30 per cent of the vote). Following the Second

World War, the Labour Party was swept to power with an overwhelming majority. As a four-year-old, I can still remember children in the streets singing 'Vote, Vote, Vote for Gracie Colman', the Labour candidate. She was elected both as the Tynemouth constituency's first Labour MP and first woman MP.* She was not, however, North Tyneside's first woman Labour MP. That honour went to the much more influential Margaret Bondfield, MP for Wallsend between 1926 and 1931. She was Britain's first women cabinet minister and privy councillor. A former shop assistant and active full-time trade unionist, she fought hard for women's suffrage, although not on the same terms as militant suffragettes. They favoured extending the vote to women on the same terms that it was available to men. Bondfield wanted it extended to all adults irrespective of whether or not they were property owners.

The Labour Party's landslide victory in 1945 was a pivotal moment in British social policy. Helped by the extent of state control which had been necessary during the war, the new government introduced a raft of measures

---

* The Labour Party did not win the Tynemouth seat again until its second landslide victory in 1997.

designed to make Britain a more fair and open society and introduced the crucial social security reforms which had been recommended by Beveridge in 1942 to try to slay the five giant evils of squalor, disease, idleness, ignorance and want. It was also in 1945 that the Labour Party secured control of Tynemouth Borough Council for the first time.

Whatever the limitations of some social security benefits today, they are a far cry from what was available to those in need in the days of the New Poor Law, or a hundred years later during the depression of the 1930s. But although government social policies may be more enlightened today, it must never be forgotten that politicians had to be persuaded to adopt a more caring approach to those in need. They also took a long time to learn that there were benefits to be derived for society as a whole by turning away from the crude application of market economics to social policy. Yet there are still those who hanker for a return to the days of 1834; who deplore what they call the nanny-state and openly call for benefits to be denied to those who do not, in their opinion, deserve them. Such voices are a reminder that the safeguards provided for those in need today can still not be taken for granted.

13

A final word

T HE many topics covered in *Shiels to Shields* warrant further research. There is much for others to add both by way of elaboration and, no doubt, correction. That is how scholarship progresses and why academics have to accept that their work will one day be superseded as new information becomes available or they are shown to have misunderstood or misinterpreted the data available to them.

Shiels to Shields may represent a significant step forward in our understanding of the development of North Shields, but many local people will ignore it because they have no interest in the past. They are concerned only with the present, in part because the pressure of their daily lives leaves them little time for reflection, and in part because our increasingly consumer-orientated life style encourages self-absorption. Self-absorption is, of course, nothing new. Many Victorians lived their lives unaware of the scale of poverty which surrounded them. Those who did venture into the little-understood districts in which the poor lived saw themselves as explorers in an unknown land.

> Acting as representatives of upper or middle-class life, they cast themselves as 'explorers', entering *for the good of society as a whole*, a world inhabited by the poor and destitute [my emphasis].[1]

In many respects, today's social historians are comparable to those nineteenth-century explorers. They act as representatives of the present population as they explore, *for the good of society as a whole*, the lives of the generations that have gone before. Writing as a retired sociologist, who has had the temerity to stray into the field of social history, that is a key point I wish to emphasise in the closing paragraphs of this book. The research which social historians conduct is *for the good of society as a whole*. They may gain intrinsic satisfaction from their studies and in a small number of cases make a modest living from it but we all benefit from their endeavours.

Ignorance of our past matters – as does ignorance of what is going on in other parts of our own society. We are diminished as human beings if we do not understand who we are and where we have come from. We are also diminished as human beings if we do not appreciate that there are marked differences in the circumstances experienced by other people in our own society. In a world in which pervasive advertising and marketing campaigns encourage instant gratification, it is only too easy to become preoccupied with our immediate self-interest. But, even in terms of our own self-interest, there are risks in living for the present without regard for the past. If we take for granted the rights and opportunities as well as the material benefits we currently enjoy, it increases the possibility that we will let them slip from our grasp. It may seem overly dramatic to suggest that there are real dangers in remaining ignorant of our collective past but I would maintain that this is the case.

It is perhaps because so many of us are now comfortably off that we see no need to know or understand how that degree of comfort was secured or who helped to secure it for us. Yet the assumptions about market forces that so recently resulted in large sections of the British population living in poverty are still with us and are being used as a justification for undermining the achievements of the last century. The worst of our slums have been cleared, but our stock of public housing for the less well-off has been run down. Many people have no prospect of owning their own home and huge numbers rely on housing benefits to keep a roof over their heads. Absolute poverty may be behind us, but income inequality is widening again and opening up divisions in our society that once seemed to be a thing of the past. At the same time that some within the financial sector pay themselves millions of pounds in annual bonuses, numerous food banks have been established by charities to help the growing number of people who are struggling to feed themselves and their children. In 2012, the Institute of Fiscal Studies estimated that there were 3.5 million children in the UK (almost six per cent of the total population) living in poverty. The National Health Service is still available to provide free health care at the point of need but elements within it are now driven by market forces and an increasing number of its services are provided by companies with an obligation to make a profit on behalf of their shareholders. At the time of writing, about 2 million are unemployed. Many more are under-employed (for example working only part-time or in jobs for which they are over-qualified) or working on zero-hours contracts, at the beck and call of their employers, without guaranteed hours or wages to allow them to budget. Social mobility has stalled. Free secondary education is still available to all but to take advantage of higher education students have to enter into levels of debt that we now know many will never be able to repay. But, in addition, as we witnessed in the near melt-down of the world's financial institutions in the opening decade of the twenty-first century, we are all at some risk of losing what we currently enjoy. No one can take it for granted that our comfortable life-styles will continue. We now know that the financial underpinnings of our modern world are inherently unstable and we can no more be sure that we will remain in a good job, with a secure income; than we can be sure that we will continue to enjoy good health.

Yet, despite the many raised voices over who should pay the price for the near collapse of our financial institutions in the opening decade of the twenty-first century, it is remarkable how many people chose not to exercise their right to vote in the subsequent general election. Even more remarkable is the evidence that very few voters took the time to make a serious study of the issues involved. It is this widespread indifference that has allowed much of our political life to degenerate into a mixture of sound-bites, photo-opportunities and preoccupation with personalities. With a better understanding of how long and hard was the battle to secure universal suffrage, and what conditions were like before it was secured, we might not be so complacent. In the same way, with a better understanding of how long and hard was the battle to secure the right to negotiate our own terms and conditions of employment, rather than have them imposed upon us, we might not be so ready to criticise the role of trade unions and professional associations when they cause us inconvenience – and be more inclined to involve ourselves in their work to try to ensure the kind of outcomes we consider preferable.

Many of our elected politicians, and employers, advocate a return to the free markets of the nineteenth century: the very circumstances which created the kind of conditions I described in the previous three chapters of this book. Indeed, the Conservative Party in office as I write is striving to achieve a smaller state with the inevitable implication that more people will have to rely on their own resources when they encounter adverse circumstances. There are obviously arguments for and against the adoption of such policies. But, whatever our personal position and preferences, an understanding of the past is needed so that we can better understand the present and decide what we want for our future. This message applies to all of us and not just our political leaders, although ignorance of our past is particularly dangerous on the part of those determining public policy. In the early 1980s, the then Prime Minister Margaret Thatcher described the disturbances in our inner cities as unprecedented and acted on the basis of that belief. Had she been familiar with our social history and known that the disturbances were far from unprecedented, she might have adopted different policies. Comparable events in the past had been investigated and were well understood by social historians and sociologists and I can claim the dubious honour of predicting the disturbances of the 1980s in a paper to the British Association for the Advancement of Science in 1966.[2] Unfortunately, as the social historian Charles Tilly once remarked, we seem to suffer from collective amnesia when it comes to episodes of collective violence in our own society.[3] That matters because as George Santayana warned us in *A Life of Reason*: 'Those who cannot remember the past are condemned to repeat it.'

Thomas Gray may have suggested that 'where ignorance is bliss, 'tis folly to be wise', but that recommendation ought not to be taken seriously. What we do not know can hurt us. Ignorance of our past is potentially dangerous. Only by understanding how our present comfortable situation has come about can we appreciate how little change is needed to undermine it. As the dynamic driving the world's economy shifts from Europe and North America towards countries like China, India and Brazil, we obviously need more than an understanding of our own past to appreciate what the future may have in store. But knowing what was once normal in this country will help us form more intelligent judgements about some of the things that are now happening in the world's developing societies.

Many people, consciously or otherwise, believe that they subscribe to the sentiment Henry Ford expressed in 1916: 'History is more or less bunk. It's tradition. We don't want tradition. We want to live in the present, and the only history that is worth a tinker's dam is the history we make today.' The truth is that Ford has been misunderstood, as he pointed out later in 1935.

> As a young man, I was very interested in how people lived in earlier times; how they got from place to place, lighted their homes, cooked their meals and so on. So I went to the history books. Well, I could find out all about kings and presidents; but I could learn nothing of everyday lives. So I decided that history is bunk.*

In short, the kind of history Ford regarded as bunk was the kind of history I was taught at school: a history preoccupied with monarchs and statesmen. He dismissed it because what interested him was how ordinary people lived their lives in the past. Hopefully *Shiels to Shields* would have met with Ford's approval not only because it attempts to describe how ordinary people lived in the past but also because it shows how their ways of life evolved, dynamically, over many centuries. There may be much more to the life story of North Shields than I have been able to capture in these pages but my hope is that *Shiels to Shields* represents a reasonable start and will encourage other scholars to give the town the attention it deserves.

---

* I am grateful to Prof. Alan Armstrong for drawing this clarification of Ford's views to my attention.

Notes and references

Notes to Preface and Acknowledgements

1 R. Finnegan in M. Drake, R. Finnegan and J. Eustace, *Sources and Methods for Family and Community Historians: a Handbook* (Cambridge: Cambridge University Press in association with the Open University, 1994), p. 13.

2 N. Christenson, *North Shield: Plodgin' Through the Clarts* (Seaham: The People's History, 1999), pp. 8–9.

3 H.H.E. Craster, *Northumberland County History, Volume VIII: Tynemouth* (Newcastle: A. Reid, 1907).

4 P.D. Stearns, *European Society in Upheaval: Social History since 1880* (London: Macmillan, 1967), p. vii.

5 http://www.measuringworth.com/ukcompare (accessed 24 April 2014).

Notes to Chapter 1: The early history of Tynemouth

1 W. Camden, *Britain: or a Chorographicall Description of the most Flourishing Kingdoms, England, Scotland and Ireland* (London: George Bishop and John Norton, 1586), para. 17 of the Northumberland section of the online version: http://www.visionofbritain.org.uk/text/chap_page.jsp;jsessionid=D57F9C2B6A8E9EA1CE6B79773CC60FA3?t_id=Camden&c_id=29 (accessed 24 April 2014).

2 G. Reed, 'Tynemouth During Roman Times', *The Beacon* 112 (July–Aug. 1990), pp. 8–9.

3 *Northumberland County Handbook* (London: Wargrave Press, undated), p. 41.

4 R.N. Hadcock, *Tynemouth Priory and Castle, Northumberland* (London: HMSO, Ministry of Works, 1959), p. 3.

5 Tynemouth County Borough, *County Borough of Tynemouth, 1849–1949* (North Shields: J.W. Moore, 1949), p. 9.

6 G.H. Haswell, *The Maister: A Century of Tyneside Life, being some account of the life and work and times of Thomas Haswell* (London: Walter Scott, 1895), p. 17.

7 S. Laycock, *Warlords: The Struggle for Power in Post-Roman Britain* (London The History Press, 2009).

8 S. Elmes, *Talking for Britain: A Journey Through the Nation's Dialects* (London: Penguin, 2005), p. 243.

9 P.H. Blair, *Northumbria in the Days of Bede* (London: Gollancz, 1976), p. 40.

10 J. Marsden, *Northanhymbre Saga: the History of the Anglo-Saxon Kings of Northumbria* (London: Kyle Cathie, 1992), pp. 51–103.

11 Ibid., pp. 86–7.

12 W.S. Gibson, *The History of the Monastery Founded at Tynemouth, in the Diocese of Durham, to the Honour of God, under the Invocation of the Blessed Virgin Mary and S. Oswin, King & Martyr* (London: William Pickering, 1847), p. 95.

13 Ibid., pp. 11–12.

14 Marsden, *Northanhymbre Saga*, p. 149.

15 Ibid., pp. 140–1.

16 N.J. Higham, *The Kingdom of Northumbria, AD 350–1100* (Stroud: A. Sutton, 1993), p. 130.

17 Blair, *Northumbria in the Days of Bede*, p. 51.

18 Ibid., p. 129.

19 Hadcock, *Tynemouth Priory and Castle*, pp. 3–5.

20 Higham, *The Kingdom of Northumbria*, p. 178.

21 Ibid., p. 179.

22 Ibid., p. 181.

23 Elmes, *Talking for Britain*, p. 245.

24 W.E. Kapelle, *The Norman Conquest of the North: The Region and Its Transformation, 1100–1135* (London: Croom Helm, 1979), p. 12.

25 Higham, *The Kingdom of Northumbria*, pp. 242–7.

26 Craster, *Northumberland County History*, pp. 43–4.

27 Ibid., p. 47

28 Ibid., pp. 48–50.

29 Hadcock, *Tynemouth Priory and Castle*, p. 6.

30 Craster, *Northumberland County History*, pp. 72–3.

31 J. Bradford, *Tynemouth Christian Chronology: A Year-by-Year Record of Christianity within the Ancient Parish of Tynemouth Linked to Simultaneous Historical Events* (Tynemouth: 'Tynemouth 2000', 2001), p. 47.

32 Craster, *Northumberland County History*, p. 83.

33 Ibid., p. 156.

34 Ibid., p. 157.

35 Ibid., pp. 162–3.

36 Ibid., p. 163.

37 Ibid., p. 164.

38 Ibid., pp. 165–6.

39 Ibid., p. 176.

40 Ibid., p. 181.

41 R. Howell, *Newcastle upon Tyne and the Puritan Revolution: A Study of the Civil War in North England* (Oxford: Clarendon, 1967), p. 73.

42 Craster, *Northumberland County History*, p. 183.

43 Haswell, *The Maister*, p. 22.

44 Howell, *Newcastle upon Tyne and the Puritan Revolution*, pp. 146–57.

45 Craster, *Northumberland County History*, p. 185.

46 Ibid., p. 187.

47 Ibid., p. 191.

48 Ibid., p. 192 and Howell, *Newcastle upon Tyne and the Puritan Revolution*, p. 201.

49 Craster, *Northumberland County History*, p. 196.

50 Ibid., p. 193.

51 Ibid., p. 199.

52 Ibid., p. 199.

53 Ibid., p. 201.

54 Ibid., p. 203.

Notes to Chapter 2: North Shields *v.* Newcastle: a struggle for survival

1 M.N. Coates, *The Pow Burn North Shields* (Newcastle: Summerhill Books, 2014), p. 12.

2 Craster, *Northumberland County History*, p. 285.

3 Ibid., pp. 285–8; Tynemouth, *County Borough of Tynemouth*, pp. 18–19, and W. Garson, *The Origin of North Shields and Its Growth* (North Shields: Fish Quay Festival, 1992: a reprint of a 1926 publication), p. 7.

4 Craster, *Northumberland County History*, p. 286.

5 Haswell, *The Maister*, pp. 18–19.

6 Craster, *Northumberland County History*, p. 67.

7 Ibid., p. 288.

8 Haswell, *The Maister*, pp. 19–20.

9 J. Hatcher, *The History of the British Coal Industry, Volume 1: Before 1700: Towards the Age of Coal* (Oxford: Clarendon Press, 1993), p. 511.

10 Craster, *Northumberland County History*, p. 289.

11 Ibid., p. 290.

12 Tynemouth, *County Borough of Tynemouth*, p. 20.

13 Craster, *Northumberland County History*, p. 292.

14 Coates, *The Pow Burn*, p. 6.

15 G.B. Hodgson, *The Borough of South Shields: from the earliest period to the close of the nineteenth century* (Newcastle: A. Reid, 1903 reprinted 1996), pp. 89–94.

16 Craster, *Northumberland County History*, p. 299.

17 Haswell, *The Maister*, p. 28.

18 Howell, *Newcastle upon Tyne and the Puritan Revolution*, p. 302.

19 Haswell, *The Maister*, p. 23.

20 Hodgson, *The Borough of South Shields*, pp. 89–94.

21 Haswell, *The Maister*, p. 25.

22 Howell, *Newcastle upon Tyne and the Puritan Revolution*, p. 304.

23 Haswell, *The Maister*, pp. 25–9.

24 Hodgson, *The Borough of South Shields*, pp. 89–94.

25 Craster, *Northumberland County History*, p. 303.

26 Ibid., p. 308.

27 E.A. Wrigley, 'The Process of Modernization and the Industrial Revolution in England', *The Journal of Interdisciplinary History* 3:2 (1972), p. 232.

28 N. McCord, *North East England: an Economic and Social History* (London: Batsford, 1979), p. 51.

Notes to Chapter 3: It's like taking coals to Shields

1 Craster, *Northumberland County History*, p. 309.

2 Howell, *Newcastle upon Tyne and the Puritan Revolution*, p. 2.

3 R.L. Galloway, *Annals of Coal Mining and the Coal Trade: the invention of the steam engine and the origin of the railway* (London: Galloway, 1898), p. 5, and A.V.H. Smith, 'Provenance of Coals from Roman Sites in England and Wales', *Britannia* 28 (1997), pp. 297–324.

4 B. Lewis, *Coal mining in the Eighteenth and Nineteenth Centuries* (London: Longman, 1971), p. 3.

5 Galloway, *Annals of Coal Mining*, p. 20.

6 Hatcher, *The History of the British Coal Industry*, chapter 5.

7 Lewis, *Coal Mining*, p. 4.

8 Galloway, *Annals of Coal Mining*, p. 5.

9 Ibid., pp. 10, 31.

10 R. Finch, *Coals from Newcastle: the story of the north-east coal trade in the days of sail* (Lavenham: T. Dalton, 1973), p. 21.

11 Galloway, *Annals of Coal Mining*, p. 80.

12 Finch, *Coals from Newcastle*, p. 28.

13 Galloway, *Annals of Coal Mining*, p. 68.

14 Ibid., p. 98.

15 Ibid., p. 99.

16 Ibid., pp. 101, 138.

17 Ibid., p. 95.

18 Hatcher, *The History of the British Coal Industry*, p. 78.

19 Finch, *Coals from Newcastle*, p. 35.

20 Hatcher, *The History of the British Coal Industry*, p. 78.

21 Galloway, *Annals of Coal Mining*, p. 149.

22 Finch, *Coals from Newcastle*, p. 44.

23 Ibid., p. 49.

24 Ibid., p. 41.

25 Galloway, *Annals of Coal Mining*, p. 361.

26 Flinn, *The History of the British Coal Industry*, p. 168.

27 Finch, *Coals from Newcastle*, p. 31.

28 Flinn, *The History of the British Coal Industry*, p. 170.

Notes to Chapter 4: Free at last: economic change since the eighteenth century

1 P.N. Stearns, *European Society in Upheaval: Social History since 1800* (New York, Macmillan, 1967), p. vii.

2 Pigot, *National Commercial Directory* (London: J. Pigot & Co., 1829), p. 616.

3 W.S. Gibson, *A Descriptive and Historical Guide to Tynemouth* (North Shields: Philipson & Hare, 1849), pp. 150–1.

4 Tynemouth, *County Borough of Tynemouth*, p. 122.

5 Ibid., pp. 22–5.

6 McCord, *North East England*, p. 37.

7 Flinn, *The History of the British Coal Industry*, p. 21.

8 Finch, *Coals from Newcastle*, p. 169.

9 McCord, *North East England*, pp. 113–14.

10 Finch, *Coals from Newcastle*, p. 170.

11 Craster, *Northumberland County History*, p. 29.

12 Tynemouth, *County Borough of Tynemouth*, p. 126.

13 B. Harrison and P. Hollis, *Robert Lowery: Radical and Chartist* (London: Europa Publications, 1979), pp. 53–4.

14 R. Wright, *North Shields: Memories of Fish 'n Chips* (Seaham: The People's History, 2001), p. 17.

15 Craster, *Northumberland County History*, p. 205.

16 Finch, *Coals from Newcastle*, p. 182.

17 R. Wright, *Beyond the Piers* (Seaham: The People's History, 2002), p. 18.

18 Craster, *Northumberland County History*, p. 312.

19 T.F. Dibdin, *A Bibliographical Antiquarian and Picturesque Tour in the Northern Counties of England and in Scotland* (London: T.F. Dibdin, 1838), pp. 318–19.

20 W. Ranger, *Report to the General Board of Health on a Preliminary Inquiry into the Sewerage, Drainage, and Supply of Water, and the Sanitary Condition of the Inhabitants of the Borough of Tynemouth* (London: HMSO, General Board of Health, 1851), p. 15.

21 Craster, *Northumberland County History,* p. 353.

22 F. Manders and R. Potts, *Crossing the Tyne* (Newcastle upon Tyne: Tyne Bridge Publishing, 2001), p. 9.

23 J.J. Cowen, *Speech delivered by Joseph Cowen Jun., at a special meeting of the*

Newcastle Town Council held on Monday, February 19, 1872 (reprinted from the Official Report of the Newcastle Town Hall Proceedings, Newcastle, River Tyne Improvement Commission, 1872).

24 This account draws heavily on a talk given by Mr John Dobson in the Knott Memorial Hall, Heddon on the Wall, 24 February 2001.

25 This account is based on *Stag Line and Joseph Robinson and Sons* by Nicholas J. Robinson

26 Wright, *Beyond the Piers*, p. 18.

27 Ibid., pp. 38–9.

28 McCord, *North East England*, p. 34.

29 Tynemouth, *County Borough of Tynemouth*, p. 29.

30 Wright, *Beyond the Piers*, p. 15.

31 Craster, *Northumberland County History*, p. 380.

32 Ibid., pp. 384, 304; Wright, *Beyond the Piers*, pp. 14–18.

33 W.H. Fraser, *The Coming of the Mass Market* (London: Macmillan, 1981), p. 160.

34 Wright, *Beyond the Piers*, pp. 36–8.

35 Craster, *Northumberland County History*, pp. 385–7.

36 M. Phillips, *A History of Banks, Bankers and Banking in Northumberland, Durham and North Yorkshire* (London: Effingham Wilson & Co., 1894), pp. 221–5.

37 Gibson, *A Descriptive and Historical Guide to Tynemouth*, p. 154.

38 E. Mackenzie, *An Historical, Topographical, and Descriptive View of the County of Northumberland* (Newcastle upon Tyne: Mackenzie and Dent, 1825), p. 452.

39 S. Ville, 'The Growth of Specialization in English Ship Owning, 1750–1850', *Economic History Review* new series 46:4 (1993), p. 719.

40 Craster, *Northumberland County History*, p. 310.

41 Tynemouth, *Tynemouth County Borough*, p. 29.

42 Craster, *Northumberland County History*, p. 313.

Notes to Chapter 5: Transformation of the built environment

1 R. Woods, *The Population History of Britain in the Nineteenth Century* (Cambridge: Cambridge University Press, 1992), p. 10.

2 F.M.L. Thompson, *The Cambridge Social History of Britain, 1750–1950* (Cambridge: Cambridge University Press, 1990), p. 33.

3 D. Hey, *The Oxford Companion to Local and Family History* (Oxford: Oxford University Press, 1996), pp. 72, 448.

4 Ranger, *Report to the General Board of Health*, p. 68.

5 Haswell, *The Maister*, p. 33.

6 M. Turner, *Enclosures in Britain, 1750–1830* (London: Macmillan, 1984).

7 A.O. Boyce, *Records of a Quaker family: the Richardsons of Cleveland* (London: West, Newman and Co., 1889). p. 119.

8 Ibid., pp. 66, 71.

9 M.N. Coates, *The Story of Northumberland Park* (Newcastle: Summerhill Books, 2012).

10 Fraser, *The Coming of the Mass Market*, p. 85.

11 Phillips, *A History of Banks*, p. 170.

12 J. Shotton, *Stepping Back in Time* (Newcastle: Summerhill Books, 2011).

13 *Shields Evening News*, 13 October 1944.

14 Tynemouth, *County Borough of Tynemouth*, p. 108.

Notes to Chapter 6: Beyond Shields

1 Phillips, *A History of Banks*, p. 25.
2 Manders and Potts, *Crossing the Tyne*, p. 100.
3 M. Lambert, *Handbook to Tynemouth and Guide to the Blyth and Tyne Railway* (Newcastle: M. and M.W. Lambert, 1864), p. 37.
4 Tynemouth, *County Borough of Tynemouth*, p. 26.
5 J. Thompson, *Observations on the most advantageous line of country through which a canal navigation may be carried from Newcastle or North Shields towards Cumberland* (Newcastle: R. Sands, 1795).
6 W.W. Tomlinson, *The North Eastern Railway: Its Rise and Development* (London: Longmans and Green, 1914), pp. 209, 326, 356.
7 Gibson, *A Descriptive and Historical Guide to Tynemouth*, p. 151.
8 Manders and Potts, *Crossing the Tyne*, p. 102.
9 Kearney's advocacy of a monorail system is discussed in detail by A. Badsey-Ellis in *London's Lost Tube Schemes* (London: Capital Transport Publishing, 2005), pp. 257–63.
10 P. Trimmer, *personal communication*.
11 G.S. Hearse, *Remember the Trams? Tyneside* (Isle of Man: George S. Hearse, 1972), pp. 7–10.
12 Ibid., pp. 33–4.
13 P. Trimmer, *personal communication*.

Notes to Chapter 7: Civic pride and independence

1 Craster, *Northumberland County History*, p. 351.
2 Tynemouth, *County Borough of Tynemouth*, p. 39.
3 Craster, *Northumberland County History*, p. 352.
4 Ibid., p. 314.
5 Ibid., pp. 284, 342, 389, 409, 402, 247, 315 and 280.
6 W. Hughes and S. Maunders, *The Treasury of Geography, 1860* (London: Longman, 1860), p. 87.
7 Lambert, *Handbook to Tynemouth*, p. 3.
8 G. Storey, *The Letters of Charles Dickens, Volume 11: 1865–1867* (Oxford: Clarendon, 1999), p. 327.
9 H. Pearson, *Dickens: His Character, Comedy and Career* (New York: Harper, 1949), p. 305.
10 H. Spencer, *An Autobiography* (New York: Appleton, 1904), p. 147.
11 Lambert, *Handbook to Tynemouth*, p. 31.
12 W.W. Tomlinson, *Historical Notes on Cullercoats, Whitley and Monkseaton* (London: Walter Scott, 1893), p. 20.
13 Lambert, *Handbook to Tynemouth*, p. 39
14 Craster, *Northumberland County History*, p. 315.
15 Ibid., p. 42.
16 Ibid., pp. 332–3.
17 Ibid., p. 341.
18 Ibid., p. 354.
19 Tynemouth County Borough, *County Borough of Tynemouth Police, 1850-1969* (North Shields: County Borough of Tynemouth, 1969), p. 14.
20 Ibid., p. 8.
21 M. Scott, *The History of Christ Church, North Shields* (North Shields: Christ Church, 1996), p. 14.

22 E.H. Peel, *The Victorian Institution for the Prosecution of Felons and Study of Crime in the Town of North Shields in the years 1800–1870* (North Shields: Local Studies Library, undated dissertation), p. 25.

23 Tynemouth, *County Borough of Tynemouth*, p. 57.

24 Ibid., p. 56.

25 R. King, *North Shields Theatres* (Gateshead: Northumberland Press, 1948), p. 82.

26 Ranger, *Report to the General Board of Health*, p. 52.

27 Tynemouth, *County Borough of Tynemouth*, p. 76.

28 A.S. Wohl, *Endangered Lives. Public Health in Victorian Britain* (London: J.M. Dent & Sons, 1983), pp. 101–11.

29 R. Rawlinson, 'Sewerage and Drainage of Tynemouth', *The Civil Engineer and Architect's Journal* 18 (1855), pp. 9-10.

30 Tynemouth, *County Borough of Tynemouth*, p. 84.

31 Ibid., p. 85

32 Wohl, *Endangered Lives*, p. 111.

33 Tynemouth, *County Borough of Tynemouth*, pp. 85–6.

34 Wohl, *Endangered Lives*, p. 112.

35 E. Lobina and D. Hall, *UK Water Privatisation* (University of Greenwich, Public Services International Research Unit, 2001).

36 M.E. Falkus, 'The British Gas Industry Before 1850', *The Economic History Review* 20:3 (1967), p. 498.

37 Boyce, *Records of a Quaker family*, p. 119.

38 Tynemouth, *Tynemouth County Borough*, p. 72.

Notes to Chapter 8: Religious institutions

1 B. Wilson, *Religion in a Secular Society* (London: Penguin, 1966), p. ix.

2 J. Stark, *St Cuthbert's Church, North Shields: some account of its foundation and early history* (North Shields: St Cuthbert's, 1902), pp. 6, 5.

3 Ibid., p. 6.

4 Dolman's Magazine, 'Remarks on Religious Houses, and a Glance at the Present State of Catholicity in the North. North Shields in the Parish of Tynemouth', *Dolman's Magazine* new series 1 (Jan.–June 1849), p. 387.

5 J.W. Fawcett, 'Refugees of the French Revolution', *Notes and Queries* (1934), p. 447.

6 Stark, *St Cuthbert's Church*, pp. 8–10.

7 Ibid., p. 14.

8 Ibid., p. 10.

9 Ibid., p. 26.

10 Ibid., pp. 16–17.

11 Ibid., p. 50.

12 J. Wolffe, *God and Greater Britain. Religion and National Life in Britain and Ireland, 1843–1945* (London: Routledge, 1994), p. 34.

13 Stark, *St Cuthbert's Church*, p. 76.

14 Ibid., p. 44.

15 Ibid., p. 53.

16 Bradford, *Tynemouth Christian Chronology*, p. 64.

17 Scott, *The History of Christ Church*, p. 2.

18 Ibid., p. 3.

19 Ibid., p. 3.

20 Ibid., p. 11.

21 Bradford, *Tynemouth Christian Chronology*, p. 27.

22 Gibson, *A Descriptive and Historical Guide to Tynemouth*, pp. 132–3.

23 Scott, *The History of Christ Church*, p. 18.

24 Haswell, *The Maister*, p. 189.

25 Scott, *The History of Christ Church*, p. 38.

26 A.D. Gilbert, *Religion and Society in Industrial England: Church, Chapel and Social Change, 1740–1914* (London: Longman, 1976), pp. 27–8.

27 Scott, *The History of Christ Church*, p. 17.

28 Gilbert, *Religion and Society* (1976), p. 16.

29 Presbyterianism in North Shields, St Columba's Church, 1999, online at http://northshields.urc.org.uk/?page_id=29 (accessed 7 April 2014).

30 Craster, *Northumberland County History*, p. 372.

31 E. Mackenzie, *The Descriptive and Historical Account of the Town and County of Newcastle upon Tyne, 1585–1676* (Newcastle: Mackenzie and Dent, 1827), pp. 367–70.

32 Craster, *Northumberland County History*, p. 373.

33 Ibid., p. 373.

34 A. Lloyd, *Quaker Social History, 1669–1738* (London: Longmans, 1950), p. 18.

35 Craster, *Northumberland County History*, pp. 371–2.

36 D. Butler, *The Quaker Meeting Houses of Britain* (London: Friends Historical Society, 2000), p. 481.

37 Boyce, *Records of a Quaker family*, p. 119.

38 Craster, *Northumberland County History*, p. 375.

39 V.A. Shepherd, 'From New Connexion Methodist to William Booth', *Papers of the Canadian Methodist Historical Society* 9 (1993), pp. 91–107.

40 R. Currie, *Methodism Divided* (London: Faber, 1968), p. 22.

41 D. Hempton, *The Religion of the People: Methodism and Popular Religion c.1750–1900* (London: Routledge, 1996), p. 73.

42 Ibid., pp. 73–90.

43 Craster, *Northumberland County History*, p. 375.

44 Currie, *Methodism Divided*, p. 43.

45 Hempton, *The Religion of the People*, pp. 91, 96.

46 C.C. Short, *Durham Colliers and West Country Methodists: the story of the Bible Christian Mission in County Durham, 1874–1910* (Kidderminster: C.C. Short, 1995).

47 R. Colls, *The Pitmen of the Northern Coalfield: Work, Culture and Protest, 1790–1850* (Manchester: Manchester University Press, 1977), p. 175.

48 W.M. Patterson, *Northern Primitive Methodism* (London: Dalton, 1909), p. 333.

49 Colls, *Pitmen of the Northern Coalfield*, p. 154.

50 Currie, *Methodism Divided*, p. 65.

51 Ibid., p. 72.

52 Currie, *Methodism Divided*, p. 75.

53 *The United Free Churches Magazine for 1859* (1859), p. 227.

54 H. Mann, *Religious Worship in England and Wales* (London: Registrar General, 1854), p. 93.

55 F.M.L. Thompson, *The Rise of Respectable Society: A Social History of Victorian Britain, 1830–1900* (London: Fontana, 1988), p. 251.

56 H. McLeod, *Religion and the Working Class in Nineteenth-Century Britain* (London: Macmillan, 1984), p. 10.

57 Mann, *Religious Worship in England and Wales*, p. 93.

58 McLeod, *Religion and the Working Class*, p. 58.

59 Haswell, *The Maister*, p. 189.

60 Scott, *The History of Christ Church*, p. 17.

61 Bradford, *Tynemouth Christian Chronology*, pp. 95–6.

62 Mann, *Religious Worship in England and Wales*, p. 94.

63 Ibid., p. 95.
64 Ibid., p. 97.
65 Bradford, *Tynemouth Christian Chronology*, p. 92.
66 McLeod, *Religion and the Working Class*, p. 33.
67 Ibid., p. 66.
68 T. Chambers MP, House of Commons Debate, 23 July 1869, vol. 198 cc620-33, p. 626.
69 T.E. Smith MP, House of Commons Debate, 23 July 1869, vol. 198 cc620-33, p. 627.
70 Gilbert, *Religion and Society*, pp. 27–9.
71 Scott, *The History of Christ Church*, pp. 93–4.
72 Currie, *Methodism Divided*, p. 87.
73 Gilbert, *Religion and Society*, pp. 30–2.
74 Currie, *Methodism Divided*, p. 90.
75 Ibid., p. 306.
76 Patterson, *Northern Primitive Methodism*, p. 336.
77 N.H. Murdoch, 'Female Ministry in the Thought and Work of Catherine Booth', *Church History* 53:3 (1984), pp. 351, 361.
78 H. Pollins, 'The Jewish Community of North Shields', *Jewish Journal of Sociology* 49:1 and 2 (2007), p. 51.
79 L. Olsover, *The Jewish Communities of North-East England, 1755–1980* (London: Ashley Mark, 1981), p. 251.
80 Ibid., p. 251; Craster, *Northumberland County History*, p. 378; Pollins, 'The Jewish Community of North Shields', p. 51; and B. Kyanski, 'An Old Jewish Cemetery', *Jewish Chronicle*, 15 August 1924.
81 *Jewish Chronicle*, 1 November 1864, p. 1.
82 *Shields Daily News*, 23 March 1876.
83 *Jewish Chronicle*, 18 September 1874.
84 Olsover, *The Jewish Community of North-East England*, p. 252.
85 *Jewish Chronicle*, 24 March 1876, p. 835.
86 Craster, *Northumberland County History*, p. 378.
87 Pollins, 'The Jewish Community of North Shields', p. 47.
88 Olsover, *The Jewish Community of North-East England*, p. 254.
89 Ibid., p. 255.
90 M. Banton, 'Kingsley's Racial Philosophy', *Theology* 78 (1975), pp. 22–30.

Notes to Chapter 9: Leisure time

1 G.M. Young, *Victorian England: Portrait of an Age* (Oxford: Oxford University Press, 1936), p. 2.
2 Ibid.
3 Wright, *Beyond the Piers*, p. 28.
4 T.B. Macaulay, *History of England, Volume 1* (London: Longman, Brown, Green and Longmans, 1848), p. 425.
5 Haswell, *The Maister*, p. 5.
6 L. Pearson, *Played in Tyne and Wear: Charting the Heritage of a City at Play* (London: English Heritage, 2010), p. 11.
7 A. Metcalfe, *Leisure and Recreation in a Victorian Mining Community: The Social Economy of Leisure in North-East England, 1820–1914* (Oxford: Routledge, 2006), p. 68.
8 Pearson, *Played in Tyne and Wear*, pp. 128–31.
9 J.S. Shaw, 'Campbell, Archibald, first Duke of Argyll (d.1703)', *Oxford Dictionary of National Biography*, online edition http://www.oxforddnb.com/view/article/4474 (accessed 15 October 2012).

10 Thompson, *The Rise of Respectable Society*, p. 247 and B.R. Mitchell and P. Deane *Abstract of British Historical Statistics* (Cambridge: Cambridge University Press, 1962), p. 12.

11 Thompson, *The Rise of Respectable Society*, p. 249.

12 Ibid., pp. 251, 254.

13 J.M. Black, *Development of the Shields Daily News, 1864–1984* (Newcastle: History of the Book Trade in the North, 1986), p. 6.

14 M. and R.D. King, *Street games of North Shields Children* (North Shields: Priory Press, 1926).

15 Thompson, *The Rise of Respectable Society*, p. 252.

16 Northern Union of Mechanics' Institutions, 'The Forty-Sixth Annual Report' (Morpeth: G. Flint, 1894), pp. 15, 21.

17 For a detailed description of the development of Northumberland Park see M.N. Coates, *The Story of Northumberland Park* and *The Pow Burn*.

18 H. Cunningham, 'Leisure and Culture', in Thompson, *The Cambridge Social History of Britain*, p. 297.

19 Metcalfe, *Leisure and Recreation,* pp. 76–86.

20 Pearson, *Played in Tyne and Wear*, p. 134.

21 C.E. Mountford, *Tynemouth Cricket Club, 1847–1996, and its Place in the History of Cricket in Northumberland* (Newcastle: Sovereign Press, 1997).

22 *Shields Daily Gazette*, 13 May 1897.

23 Cunningham, *Leisure and Change*, p. 309 and Metcalfe, *Leisure and Recreation*, pp. 96–103.

24 *Tyne Mercury*, 19 July 1842.

25 *Shields Daily Gazette*, 30 August 1889; 10 September 1889 and 15 November 1889.

26 King, *North Shields Theatres*, pp. 12, 96, 103.

27 Ibid., pp. 34–6.

28 Ibid., p. 88.

29 Ibid., p. 95.

30 Ibid., p. 102.

31 Ibid., p. 106.

32 Ibid., p. 114.

33 *Shields Daily News*, 17 August 1895.

34 Lawrence, *The Making of Stan Laurel*, pp. 36, 37.

35 King, *North Shields Theatres*, p. 120.

36 Ibid., p. 120.

37 Ibid., pp. 107, 120, 142.

38 Ibid., p. 612.

39 Ibid., p. 613.

40 Fraser, *The Coming of the Mass Market*, p. 209.

41 C. Steel, *Inns and Taverns of North Shields* (London: Tempus, 2007), p. 10.

42 W. Foster, *Pages from a Worker's Life* (New York: International Publishers, 1939), p. 101.

43 Wright, *Beyond the Piers*, p. 27.

44 Union Association, *Deed made by the Union Association for the Mutual Insurance of Their Ships* (North Shields: Union Association, 1786).

45 Mackenzie, *A Historical, Topographical and Descriptive View*, p. 455.

46 B. Harrison, *Drink and the Victorian* (London: Faber & Faber, 1971), p. 55.

47 *The Friendly Societies' Journal*, 1856, p. 87.

48 J. Shotton, *Pubs of North Shields* (North Shields: North Tyneside Libraries, 2006) and Steel, *Inns and Taverns of North Shields*.

Notes to Chapter 10: The labouring classes (I):
barriers to progress

1 Haswell, *The Maister*, p. 9.
2 P. Gregg, *A Social and Economic History of Britain, 1760–1955* (London: Harrap, 1961), pp. 149–50.
3 W.H. Maehl, 'Chartist Disturbances in North-Eastern England, 1839', *International Review of Social History* 8:3 (1963), pp. 389–414; D.J. Rowe, 'Some Aspects of Chartism on Tyneside', *International Review of Social History* 16:1 (1971), pp. 17–39.
4 T.J. Nossiter, 'Voting Behaviour, 1832–1872', *Political Studies* 18:3 (1970), pp. 380–9; J. Allen, *Joseph Cowen and Popular Radicalism on Tyneside, 1829–1900* (Monmouth: Merlin Press, 2007).
5 Maehl, 'Chartist Disturbances', p. 404.
6 Rowe, 'Some Aspects of Chartism', p. 28.
7 T.M. Kemnitz, 'Approaches to the Chartist Movement', *Albion* Violence and Social Control issue 5:1 (1973), pp. 67–73; T.M. Kemnitz, 'The Chartist Convention of 1839', *Albion* 10:2 (1978), pp. 152–70.
8 W.H. Maehl, 'The Dynamics of Violence in Chartism: A Case Study in North-eastern England', *Albion* 7:2 (1975), pp. 101–19.
9 Ibid., p. 108.
10 R.E. Swift, 'Policing Chartism, 1839-1848: The role of the "Specials" reconsidered', *English Historical Review* 122 (2007), p. 693.
11 Harrison and Hollis, *Robert Lowery*, p. 222.
12 Ibid., pp. 225–6.
13 Maehl, *The Dynamics of Violence*, p. 107.
14 Allen, *Joseph Cowen*, p. 28.
15 M.P. Sutcliffe, 'Negotiating the "Garibaldi Moment" in Newcastle-upon-Tyne, 1854–1861', *Modern Italy* 15:2 (2010), pp. 129–44.
16 Colls, *Pitmen of the Northern Coalfield*, p. 246.
17 Ibid., p. 247.
18 B. Disraeli, *Sybil, or The Two Nations* (London: Colburn, 1845), book 2, chapter 5, p. 68.
19 J.A. Jaffe, 'The State, Capital, and Workers' Control during the Industrial Revolution: the rise and fall of the North-East Pitmen's Union, 1831–32', *Journal of Social History* 21:4 (1988), p. 720.
20 Ibid., pp. 728–30.
21 R.S. Watson, *Joseph Skipsey: his life and work* (London: Fisher Unwin, 1908), p. 519.
22 T. Kelly, *Gibbeting of Wm. Jobling* (Jarrow: Bede Gallery Press, 1972), p. 12.
23 Colls, *Pitmen of the Northern Coalfield*, p. 252.
24 N. McCord, 'The Government of Tyneside, 1800–1850', *Transactions of the Royal Historical Society* 20 (1970), pp. 5–30.
25 G. Morgan and P. Ruston, *Rogues, Thieves and the Rule of Law: The problem of law enforcement in North-East England, 1718–1800* (London: UCL Press, 1998), p. 210.
26 Phillips, *A History of Banks*, pp. 33, 272.
27 N. Green, *Tough Times and Grisly Crimes: A history of crime in Northumberland and County Durham* (Newcastle: Nigel Green Media, 2005), p. 7.
28 Ibid., p. 8.
29 H. Askew, 'Certificate of Protection Against Press-Gangs', *Notes and Queries*, December 1925, p. 410.
30 King, *North Shields Theatres*, p. 18.
31 Ibid., p. 19.
32 Haswell, *The Maister*, p. 84.

33 Ibid., pp. 82–9.

34 Ibid., p. 132.

35 E.A. Wrigley, 'The Process of Modernization and the Industrial Revolution in England', *The Journal of Interdisciplinary History* 3:2 (1972), p. 232.

36 T.H. Marshall, *Citizenship and Social Class: and other essays* (Cambridge: Cambridge University Press, 1950).

Notes to Chapter 11: The labouring classes (II): social and economic conditions

1 Haswell, *The Maister*, p. 33.

2 Dibdin, *A Bibliographical Antiquarian and Picturesque Tour*, p. 320.

3 Tynemouth, *Borough of Tynemouth*, p. 23.

4 Haswell, *The Maister*, p. 35.

5 Craster, *Northumberland County History*, p. 307.

6 Tynemouth, *Borough of Tynemouth*, p. 24.

7 Ibid., p. 28.

8 Ranger, *Report to the General Board of Health*, pp. 76, 15.

9 Wohl, *Endangered Lives*, p. 206.

10 Ibid., p. 207.

11 Boyce, *Records of a Quaker family*, p. 122.

12 Ranger, *Report to the General Board of Health*, pp. 28, 72.

13 Quoted by Craster, *Northumberland County History*, p. 307.

14 Ranger, *Report to the General Board of Health*, p. 65.

15 Tynemouth, *Borough of Tynemouth*, pp. 74–5.

16 Ranger, *Report to the General Board of Health*, p. 47.

17 Tynemouth, *Borough of Tynemouth*, p. 89.

18 Ibid., p. 88.

19 Cholera Inquiry Commission, *Report of the Commissioners ...* (London: HMSO, 1854), para. 135.

20 Ranger, *Report to the General Board of Health*, p. 52.

21 Ibid., p. 68.

22 Ibid., p. 69.

23 Tynemouth, *Borough of Tynemouth*, p. 89.

24 M. Barker and G.M. Turnbull, *Meadowell: The Biography of an 'Estate with Problems'* (Newcastle: Avebury, 1993), p. 21.

25 N. Price, *Housing Access and the Marginal Poor: Housing in North Shields, 1850–1940* (unpublished MA thesis, Newcastle Polytechnic, 1988), p. 20.

26 Barker and Turnbull, *Meadowell*, p. 29.

27 Ibid., pp. 34–5.

28 P. Jalland, *Death in the Victorian Family* (Oxford: Oxford University Press, 1996), p. 142.

29 Ranger, *Report to the General Board of Health*, p. 20.

30 J. Sykes, *Local Records; Or, Historical Register on Remarkable Events, ...* (Newcastle: J. Sykes, 1833).

31 Woods, *The Population History of Britain in the Nineteenth Century*, p. 42.

32 L. Rose, *The Massacre of the Innocents: Infanticide in Britain, 1800–1939* (London: Routledge & Kegan Paul, 1986), p. 6.

33 Ibid., p. 11.

34 N. Williams and C. Galley. 'Urban–Rural Differentials in Infant Mortality in Victorian England', *Population Studies* 49:3 (1995), pp. 401–20.

35 S. Szreter. 'Debating mortality trends in nineteenth-century Britain', *International Journal of Epidemiology* 33:4 (2004), pp. 705–9.

36 Williams and Galley, 'Urban–Rural Differentials', pp. 401–20.

37 Ranger, *Report to the General Board of Health*, p. 23.

38 Fenwick, quoted by Ranger, *Report to the General Board of Health*, pp. 24–5.

39 E.M. Gould, and D.B. Chappel, 'Graveyard gleanings: socio-economic, geographical and gender inequalities in health at Tynemouth, UK, 1833–1853', *Journal of Public Health Medicine* 22:3 (2000), p. 284.

40 Howell, *Newcastle upon Tyne and the Puritan Revolution*, p. 7 and Sykes, *Local Records*, p. 89.

41 Tynemouth, *Borough of Tynemouth*, p. 76.

42 Barker and Turnbull, *Meadowell*, p. 34.

43 A. Meiklejohn, 'The Origin of the Term Anthracosis', *British Journal of Industrial Medicine* 16 (1959), pp. 324–5.

44 Colls, *Pitmen of the Northern Coalfield*, p. 21.

45 T.G. Wright, *Diary of a Doctor: Surgeon's Assistant in Newcastle upon Tyne, 1826–1829* (Newcastle upon Tyne: Newcastle Libraries, 1998), p. 7.

46 Ibid.

47 Haswell, *The Maister*, pp. 154–5.

48 J.M. Winter, 'Military Fitness and Civilian Health in Britain during the First World War', *Journal of Contemporary History* 15:2 (1980), p. 211; Wohl, *Endangered Lives*, pp. 331–3.

49 Mitchell and Deane, *Abstract of British Historical Statistics*.

50 J. Burnett, *The Experience of Unemployment, 1790–1990* (London: Routledge, 1994), p. 147.

51 Ibid., p. 92.

52 Ibid., p. 147.

53 Ibid., pp. 153–6.

54 Ibid., p. 157.

55 Ibid., p. 158.

56 Tynemouth, *Borough of Tynemouth*, p. 132.

57 Parliamentary Papers, Reports from Commissioners: Children's Employment (Mines) Session 3 February–12 August 1842, vol. xv, pp. 36, 40, 57, 109, 121, 124, 133, 148, 178.

58 C.M. Cipolla, *Literacy and Development in the West* (London: Penguin, 1969), pp. 21–5.

59 Committee of Council of Education, Minutes of the Committee of Council of Education 1846. *Parliamentary Papers*, vol. xlv (London: HMSO, 1847), p. 134.

60 Haswell, *The Maister*, pp. 71-3.

61 W.B. Stephens, *Minutes and Reports of the Committee of Council on Education, 1839–1899* (Microform Academic Publishers, 1985), pp. 1-3.

62 Haswell, *The Maister*, p. 79.

63 Ibid., pp. 79–80.

64 Ibid., p. 78.

65 Ibid., p. 228.

66 Ibid., pp. 156–7.

67 Ibid., p. 160.

68 E.G. West, 'Resource Allocation and Growth in Early Nineteenth-century Education', pp. 53 92 and 'The Interpretation of Early Nineteenth-century British Education', pp. 107–20, in M. Drake, *Applied Historical Studies* (Milton Keynes: Open University, 1973); E.G. West, *Education and the Industrial Revolution* (London: Batsford, 1975); J.S. Hurt, *Education in Evolution: Church, State, Society and Popular Education, 1800–1870* (London: Hart-Davis, 1971); J.S. Hurt, 'Professor West on early nineteenth-century education', in Drake, *Applied Historical Studies*,

pp. 93–106; M. Sanderson, 'Review of education and the Industrial Revolution', *Economic History Review* 24:2 (1976), pp. 323–4.

69 Committee of Council of Education, Minutes of the Committee of Council of Education 1840–41, *Parliamentary Papers* (London: HMSO, 1941), p. 134.

70 Craster, *Northumberland County History*, p. 312.

71 Committee of Council of Education, Minutes, 1840–41, p. 135.

72 Boyce, *Records of a Quaker family*, pp. 117, 129–32.

73 Gregg, *A Social and Economic History of Britain*, pp. 506–7.

74 E.J. Evans, ed., *Social Policy, 1830–1914: Individualism, Collectivism and the Origins of the Welfare State* (London: Routledge, 1978), p. 87.

75 G. Pugh, *London's Forgotten Children: Thomas Coram and the Foundling Hospital* (Brimscombe Port: The History Press, 2007), p. 40.

76 R. Lowe, *Hansard* 3rd series, vol. clxv, (London: HMSO, 1862).

77 D. Wardle, *English Popular Education, 1780–1975* (Cambridge: Cambridge University Press, 1970), p. 69.

78 Stephens, *Minutes and Reports*, p. 4 and *Shields Daily Gazette*, 21 February 1901.

79 Fraser, *The Coming of the Mass Market*.

80 Ibid., p. 27.

81 Craster, *Northumberland County History*, p. 2.

82 Ibid., p. 5.

83 Ibid., pp. 230–2.

84 J. Benson, *The Working Class in Britain, 1850–1939* (London: I.B. Tauris, 2003), pp. 54–5.

85 Mitchell and Deane, *Abstract of British Historical Statistics*, pp. 343–4.

86 P. Laslett, *The World We Have Lost* (London: Methuen, 1965), p. 201.

87 J. and O. Banks. *Prosperity and Parenthood: A Study of Family Planning among the Victorian Middle Classes* (London: Routledge and Kegan Paul, 1954).

88 Wright, *Beyond the Piers*, pp. 22–3.

89 A. Taylor, 'Working-class credit on Tyneside since 1918' (Ph.D. thesis, University of Durham, 1996), pp. 271–3.

90 A. Kidd, *State, Society and the Poor in Nineteenth-century England* (London: Macmillan, 1999), p. 151.

91 Fraser, *The Coming of the Mass Market*, p. 90.

92 Craster, *Northumberland County History*, pp. 235, 232.

93 Sykes, *Local Records*, p. 1.

94 Wright, *Beyond the Piers*, p. 87.

95 Ibid., pp. 30–1.

Notes to Chapter 12: The labouring classes (III): responses to poverty

1 Kidd, *State, Society and the Poor*, pp. 17–19.

2 Craster, *Northumberland County History*, p. 308.

3 Kidd, *State, Society and the Poor*, p. 13.

4 Ibid., p. 16.

5 Gregg, *A Social and Economic History*, p. 183.

6 N. McCord, 'The Implementation of the 1834 Poor Law Amendment Act on Tyneside', *International Review of Social History* 14 (1969), p. 91.

7 Ibid., p. 97.

8 Ibid., pp. 95–6, 102.

9 Kidd, *State, Society and the Poor*, p. 67.

10 W. Whellan, *Whellan's History, Topography and Directory of Northumberland* (London: W. Whellan, 1855), pp. 475–6.

11 Pugh, *London's Forgotten Children*.

12 W. Fordyce, *History of Tynemouth: Its Priory & Castle, and Stranger's guide to places of interest in the vicinity of this justly celebrated bathing place* (Newcastle upon Tyne: W. & T. Fordyce, 1837), p. 423.

13 M.A. Richardson, *The Local Historian's Table Book of Remarkable Occurrences: Historical Division, Volume 5* (Newcastle upon Tyne: M.A. Richardson, 1846), pp. 29–30.

14 Haswell, *The Maister*, pp. 137–8.

15 Tynemouth, *Borough of Tynemouth*, p. 76.

16 Society for Bettering the Condition and Increasing the Comforts of the Poor. *Reports 1800–1802* (London: 1802), p. 10.

17 M. Anderson, *Family Structure in Nineteenth-century Lancashire* (Cambridge: Cambridge University Press, 1971) and M.W. Dupree, *Family Structure in the Staffordshire Potteries, 1840–1880* (Oxford: Clarendon Press, 1995).

18 Dupree, *Family Structure in the Staffordshire Potteries*, p. 273.

19 Taylor, 'Working-class credit', p. 30.

20 M. Maus, *The Gift*, translated by Ian Cunnison from the original 1925 edition (London: Cohen and West, 1966).

21 Taylor, 'Working-class credit'.

22 R. King and J.G. Jewels, *Old Tyneside Street Cries* [with melodies], collected by Robert King, standardised by J.G. Jewels and drawn by F. Austin Child (North Shields: Priory Press, 1924).

23 Fraser, *The Coming of the Mass Market*, p. 110.

24 Ibid., p. 122.

25 Kidd, *State, Society and the Poor*, p. 133.

26 Allen, *Joseph Cowen*, p. 71.

27 D.G. Green, *Reinventing Civil Society: The Rediscovery of Welfare Without Politics* (London: Institute of Economic Affairs, 1993), p. 30.

28 Kidd, *State, Society and the Poor*, p. 122.

29 P. Gosden, *The Friendly Societies in England, 1815–1875* (Aldershot: Gregg Revivals, 1961), pp. 85–6.

30 H. Perkins, *The Origins of Modern English Society, 1780–1880* (London: Routledge & Kegan Paul, 1967), pp. 381–3.

31 Allen, *Joseph Cowen*, p. 72.

32 J. Bohstedt, *The Politics of Provisions: Food Riots, Moral Economy and Market Transition in England, c.1550–1850* (London: Ashgate, 2010).

33 E.P. Thompson, 'The Moral Economy of the English Crowd in the Eighteenth Century', *Past and Present* 50 (1971), p. 79.

34 Bohstedt, *The Politics of Provisions*, p. 266.

35 Ibid., p. 270.

36 Ibid., pp. 271–3.

37 Colls, *Pitmen of the Northern Coalfield*, p. 220.

38 D. Rowe, 'A Trade Union of the North-East Coast Seamen in 1825', *The Economic History Review* 25:1 (1972), p. 82.

39 G. Morgan and P. Ruston, *Rogues, Thieves and the Rule of Law: The Problem of Law Enforcement in North-East England, 1718–1800* (London: UCL Press, 1998), p. 201.

40 N. McCord, 'The Seamen's Strike of 1815 in North-East England', *The Economic History Review* 21:1 (1968), p. 137.

41 Mitchell and Deane, *Abstract of British Historical Statistics*, p. 68.

Notes to Chapter 13: A Final Word

1 P.E. Keating, ed., *Into Unknown England, 1866–1913: Selection from the Social Explorers* (Glasgow: Fontana/Collins, 1976), p. 9.

2 D. Lawrence, 'Racial Violence or Harmony: The Prospect for Britain' (unpublished lecture, British Association for the Advancement of Science, University of Nottingham, 1966).

3 C. Tilly, 'Collective Violence in European Perspective', in H. Graham and T. Gurr, eds, *Violence in America: Historical and Comparative Perspectives* (New York: Bantam, 1969).

Bibliography

Adamson, H.A., *The Villiers Family as Governors of Tynemouth Castle and Owners of the Lighthouse* (London: A. Reid, 1898).

Alexander, J., *Tynemouth and Cullercoats* (Brimscombe Port: Tempus, 1999).

Alexander, J., *Memory Lane North Shields* (Derby: Breedon, 2002).

Allen, J., *Joseph Cowen and Popular Radicalism on Tyneside 1829-1900* (Monmouth: Merlin Press, 2007).

Anderson, M., *Family Structure in Nineteenth-century Lancashire* (Cambridge: Cambridge University Press, 1971).

Angus, G., *The Square, 1779–1929: being the history of the congregation of Northumberland Square Presbyterian Church, North Shields: from its foundation until the present day* (Newcastle: A. Reid, 1929).

Anonymous, *The Cause of Truth Defended being a plain statement of the fact connected with the two trials of the Rev. T. Hill, Methodist Preacher, for defamation of the character of Miss Bell of North Shields, containing a correct report of the trial at York and other matters relative thereto* (London: 1827).

Anonymous, 'The Fast Age', *The Friendly Societies' Journal* 1:3 (1856), p. 87.

Anonymous, *Liberal and Radical Yearbook* (London: Harvester Press, 1887).

Armstrong, A., *Stability and Change in an English County Town: A Social Study of York, 1850–51* (Cambridge: Cambridge University Press, 1974).

Armstrong, K. and P. Dixon, *North Tyneside Steam* (Whitley Bay: Northern Voices Community Projects, 2014).

Askew, H., 'Certificate of Protection Against Press-Gangs', *Notes and Queries* (1925).

Askew, H., 'Martineau', *Notes and Queries* (1934).

Atkinson, F., *The Great Northern Coalfield, 1700-1900: Illustrated Notes on the Durham and Northumberland Coalfield* (London: University Tutorial Press, new edn, 1968).

Badsey-Ellis, A., *London's Lost Tube Schemes* (London: Capital Transport Publishing, 2005).

Banks, J. and O. Banks, *Prosperity and Parenthood: A Study of Family Planning among the Victorian Middle Classes* (London: Routledge & Kegan Paul, 1954).

Banton, M., 'Kingsley's Racial Philosophy', *Theology* 78:655 (1975), pp. 22–30.

Barke, M., 'The "New" Town of North Shields in the Early Nineteenth Century: From Georgian Elegance to Incipient Slums? Population and Housing Relationships 1811–1851', *The Journal of Regional and Local Studies* 22:1 (2002), pp. 3–19.

Barker, M. and G.M. Turnbull, *Meadowell: The Biography of an 'Estate with Problems'* (Newcastle: Avebury, 1993).

Barrow, T., *Trafalgar Geordies and North Country Seamen of Nelson's Navy, 1793–1815* (Sunderland: North East England Press, 2005).

Bell, R.C., *Maling and Other Tyneside Pottery* (Risborough: Shire, 2010).

Benevolent Association, *Copy of the articles of the Benevolent Association established the first day of April 1796, at Mr. Smith's … North Shields, for mutual relief and also for the relief of their widows and children* (North Shields: W. Kelley, 1796).

Benson, J., *The Working Class in Britain, 1850–1939* (London: I.B. Tauris, 2003).

Bewick, T., *A Memoir of Thomas Bewick written by himself* (Newcastle: Printed by Robert Ward for Jane Bewick, 1862).

Black, J.M., *Development of the Shields Daily News, 1864–1984* (Newcastle upon Tyne: History of the Book Trade in the North, 1986).

Black, J.W. and F.W. Corner, *Wor Canny Toon: a potted history of North Shields* (South Shields: Jennings and Son, 1925).

Blair, P.H., *Northumbria in the Days of Bede* (London: Gollancz, 1976).

Bohstedt, J., *The Politics of Provisions: Food Riots, Moral Economy and Market Transition in England, c.1550–1850* (London: Ashgate, 2010).

Boyce, A.O., *Records of a Quaker family: the Richardsons of Cleveland* (London: Samuel Harris and Co., 1889).

Bradford, J., *Tynemouth Christian Chronology: A Year-by-Year Record of Christianity within the Ancient Parish of Tynemouth Linked to Simultaneous Historical Events* (Tynemouth: 'Tynemouth 2000', 2001).

Briggs, A., *The History of Broadcasting in the United Kingdom, Volume II: The Golden Age of Wireless* (Oxford: Oxford University Press, 1995).

Brison, P.F., *Garibaldi: Sul Fiume Tyne* (Newcastle: Davide Ghaleb Editore, 2014).

British Association for the Advancement of Science, *Excursions* (Newcastle upon Tyne: Tyne Printing Works Co., 1889).

Brockie, W., *History of the Town, Trade, and Port of Shields and the surrounding District* ([South] Shields: Gazette Offices, 1851).

Brockie, W., *The family names of the folks of Shields traced to their origin: with brief notices of distinguished persons. To which is appended a dissertation on the origin of the Britannic race* (Cambridge: Chadwyck-Healey, 1990).

Brookfield, K., T.S. Gray and J.L. Hatchard, 'The Concept of the Fisheries-Dependent Communities – A Comparative Analysis of Four UK Case Studies', *Fisheries Research* 72:1 (2005), pp. 55–69.

Brooks, W.A., *Reprint of a Report Dated 1845* (London: Saunders and Stanford, 1853).

Brown, C., 'Religion', in R. Pope, ed., *Atlas of British Social and Economic History* (London: Routledge, 1989), pp. 211–23.

Burkhardt, F., ed., *Charles Darwin: The Beagle Letters* (Cambridge: Cambridge University Press, 2008).

Burnett, J., *The Experience of Unemployment, 1790–1990* (London and New York: Routledge, 1994).

Butler, D., *The Quaker Meeting Houses of Britain: An Account of the Some 1,300 Meeting Houses and 900 Burial Grounds in England, Wales and Scotland* (London: Friends Historical Society, 2000).

Byrne, D.S., 'The Standard of Council Housing in Inter-War North Shields – a case study in the politics of reproduction', in J. Melling, *Housing, Social Policy and the State* (London: Croom Helm, 1980), pp. 168–93.

Byrne, D.S., *Beyond the Inner City* (Milton Keynes: Open University Press, 1989).

Camden, W., *Britain: or a Chorographicall Description of the most Flourishing Kingdoms, England, Scotland and Ireland* (London: George Bishop and John Norton, 1586). Online version https://archive.org/details/gri_britanniaora02camd (accessed 15 July 2016).

Carr, S.S., *The Early Monumental Remains of Tynemouth* (Newcastle upon Tyne: Newcastle Society of Antiquaries, 1904).

Chittenden, R. and A. Fidler, *The Response: The North East and the Great War, 1914–1918* (North Tyneside Council and Tynemouth World War One Commemoration Project in association with the North East Chamber of Commerce, 2014).

Cholera Inquiry Commission, *Report of the Commissioners appointed to inquire into the causes which have led to, or have aggravated the late outbreak of cholera in the towns of Newcastle-upon-Tyne, Gateshead, and Tynemouth* (London: HMSO, 1854).

Christenson, N., *North Shield: Plodgin' Through the Clarts* (Seaham: The People's History, 1999).

Church, R., *The History of the British Coal Industry, Volume 3: 1830–1913: Victorian Pre-eminence* (Oxford: Clarendon Press, 1986).

Cipolla, C.M., *Literacy and Development in the West* (London: Penguin, 1969).

Clark, J.C.D., *English Society, 1688–1832: Ideology, Social Structure and Political Practice during the Ancien Regime* (Cambridge: Cambridge University Press, 1985).

Clarke, T.T., *Ralph Gardner and the Tyne: a chapter of local history* (North Shields: W.J. Potts & Co., 1881).

Coates, M.N., *The Story of Northumberland Park* (Newcastle: Summerhill Books, 2012).

Coates, M.N., *The Pow Burn North Shields: Once An Important Tributary of the River Tyne* (Newcastle: Summerhill Books, 2014)

Coe, D., *Variety Certainly Adds Spice: A Memoir of My Life in Education, Politics and the Arts* (Sussex: Book Guild Publishing, 2008).

Cole, G.D.H. and R.W. Postgate, *The Common People, 1746–1946* (London: Methuen & Co., 1956).

Colls, R., *The Pitmen of the Northern Coalfield: Work, Culture and Protest 1790–1850* (Manchester: Manchester University Press, 1987).

Committee of Council of Education Minutes of the Committee of Council of Education 1840–41, *Parliamentary Papers* (London: HMSO, 1841).

Committee of Council of Education Minutes of the Committee of Council of Education 1846, *Parliamentary Papers*, vol. xlv (London: HMSO, 1847).

Cooter, R.J., 'The Irish in County Durham and Newcastle *c.*1840–1880' (unpublished MA thesis, University of Durham, 1972).

Cowen, J.J., Speech delivered by Joseph Cowen Jun., at a special meeting of the Newcastle Town Council held on Monday, 19 February 1872. *Reprinted from the Official Report of the Newcastle Town Hall Proceedings* (Newcastle: River Tyne Improvement Commission, 1872).

Craster, H.H.E., *Northumberland County History, Volume VIII: Tynemouth* (Newcastle: A. Reid, 1907).

Craster, H.H.E. and R.N. Hadcock, *Tynemouth Priory* (Newcastle upon Tyne: Northumberland Press, 1937).

Cunningham, H., 'Leisure and Culture', in F.M.L. Thompson, *The Cambridge Social History of Britain, 1750–1950* (Cambridge: Cambridge University Press, 1990), pp. 279–339.

Currie, R., *Methodism Divided* (London: Faber, 1968).

Davies, R.E., A.R. George and G. Rupp, *A History of the Methodist Church in Great Britain* (London: Epworth Press, 1988).

Dibdin, T.F., *A Bibliographical Antiquarian and Picturesque Tour in the Northern Counties of England and in Scotland* (London: T.F. Dibdin, 1838).

Dinning, A., *The Custom house branch; or, Shields disappointed* (Newcastle: Printed for A. Dinning, by J. Marshall, 1816).

Dingle, A.E., 'Drink and Working-Class Living Standards in Britain, 1870–1914', *The Economic History Review* 25:4 (1972), pp. 608–22.

Disraeli, B., *Sybil, or The Two Nations* (London: Colburn, 1845).

Dodds, M.H. and V.N. Rainbird, *The North Shields lighthouses* (Tynemouth: Priory Press, 1928).

Dolman, 'Remarks on Religious Houses, and a Glance at the Present State of Catholicity in the North: Chapter II – North Shields in the Parish of Tynemouth', *Dolman's Magazine* new series 1 (1849), pp. 387–96.

Drake, M., *Applied Historical Studies* (Milton Keynes: Open University, 1973).

Drake, M., R. Finnegan and J. Eustace, *Sources and Methods for Family and Community Historians: a handbook* (Cambridge: Cambridge University Press in association with the Open University, 1997).

Dupree, M.W., *Family Structure in the Staffordshire Potteries, 1840–1880* (Oxford: Clarendon Press, 1995).

Egner, F.G., *Town and Country Planning Act 1947: County Borough of Tynemouth development plan: first review: written statement: amendment no. 1 (1959)* (Tynemouth: County Borough of Tynemouth, 1959).

Elmes, S., *Talking for Britain: A journey Through the Nation's Dialects* (London: Penguin, 2005).

Ensor, R.C.K., *England, 1870–1914* (Oxford: Clarendon Press, 1936).

Evans, E.J., ed., *Social Policy, 1830–1914: Individualism, Collectivism and the Origins of the Welfare State* (London: Routledge, 1978).

Fairbairn, W., *The Life of Sir William Fairbairn* (originally published 1877, London: David and Charles, 1970).

Falkus, M.E., 'The British Gas Industry Before 1850', *The Economic History Review* 20:3 (1967), pp. 494–508.

Fawcett, J.W., 'Refugees of the French Revolution', *Notes and Queries* (1934).

Finch, R., *Coals from Newcastle: the story of the North East coal trade in the days of sail* (Lavenham: T. Dalton, 1973).

Flagg, A.C., *Notes on the History of Shipbuilding in South Shields, 1746–1946* (South Tyneside: South Tyneside Borough Council Library Service, 1979).

Flinn, M.W., *The History of the British Coal Industry, Volume 2: 1700–1830: The Industrial Revolution* (Oxford: Clarendon Press, 1984).

Fordyce, W., *History of Tynemouth: Its Priory & Castle, and Stranger's guide to places of interest in the vicinity of this justly celebrated bathing place* (Newcastle upon Tyne: W. & T. Fordyce, 1837).

Foster, J., *Class Struggle and the Industrial Revolution: Early Industrial Capitalism in Three English Towns* (London: Routledge, 1977).

Foster, W.Z., *Pages from a Worker's Life* (New York: International Publishers, 1939).

Fraser, W.H., *The Coming of the Mass Market, 1889–1914* (London: Macmillan, 1981).

French, R. and K. Smith, *Lost Shipyards of the Tyne* (Newcastle: Tyne Bridge Publishing, 2007).

Fynes, R., *The Miners of Northumberland and Durham: a history of their social and political progress* (East Ardsley: Wakefield, S.R. Publishers, 1971).

Gair, R., *St Augustin, Tynemouth: 1884–1984: The First Hundred Years* (North Shields: St Augustin's Church, 1986).

Gale, A., *Wrecks and Rescues: shelter from the storm: a history of maritime disasters and heroism in Tyne & Wear* (Newcastle upon Tyne: Keepdate, 1993).

Galloway, R.L., *Annals of Coal Mining and the Coal Trade: the invention of the steam engine and the origin of the railway* (London, Galloway, 1898).

Galloway, R.L., *A History of Coal Mining in Great Britain* (Newton Abbot: David & Charles, 1969).

Gardner, R., *England's Grievances Discovered in Relation to the Coal Trade* (London: Ibbotson and Street, 1655).

Garson, W.S., *The Origin of North Shields and Its Growth* (North Shields: 1926, re-issued by Fish Quay Festival, 1992).

Garson, W.S., *The Romance of old Tynemouth* (North Shields: The Northern Press, 1932).

Gibson, W.S., *Tynemouth Priory: an historical lecture* (North Shields: J. Philipson, 1870).

Gibson, W.S., *The History of the Monastery Founded at Tynemouth, in the Diocese of Durham, to the Honour of God, under the Invocation of the Blessed Virgin Mary and S. Oswin, King & Martyr* (London: William Pickering, 1847).

Gibson, W.S., *A Descriptive and Historical Guide to Tynemouth: comprising a popular sketch of the history of the monastery, the church and the castle: with notices of North Shields, Seaton Delaval, and neighbouring antiquities* (North Shields: Philipson & Hare, 1849).

Gilbert, A.D., *Religion and Society in Industrial England: Church, Chapel and Social Change, 1740–1914* (London: Longman, 1976).

Gillow, T., *A Sermon, preached at the opening of the Catholic Chapel, in the town of North Shields, on Thursday the 14th June, 1821* (Newcastle: Preston & Heaton, 1821).

Godfrey, B., *The Tyne Training Ship Wellesley Remembered* (Newcastle: Summerhill Books, 2014).

Goodfellow, D.M., *Tyneside: the social facts* (Newcastle upon Tyne: Newcastle Cooperative Society, 1942).

Gosden, P., *The Friendly Societies in England, 1815–1875* (Aldershot: Gregg Revivals, 1961).

Gould, E.M. and D.B. Chappel, 'Graveyard gleanings: socio-economic, geographical and gender inequalities in health at Tynemouth, UK, 1833–1853', *Journal of Public Health Medicine* 22:3 (2000), pp. 280–6.

Gowans, W., *Address delivered before the British Medical Association (North of England branch) assembled at South Shields, June 29th 1886* (South Shields: Shields Gazette, 1886).

Graham, F., *Tynemouth, Cullercoats, Whitley Bay, Seaton Delaval: a short history and guide* (Newcastle upon Tyne: Graham, 1973).

Green, D.G., *Reinventing Civil Society: The Rediscovery of Welfare Without Politics* (London: Institute of Economic Affairs, 1993).

Green, J., B. Green, *et al.*, *On the Timber Viaducts of the Newcastle and North Shields Railway* (Newcastle: T. and J. Hodgson, 1839).

Green, N., *Tough Times and Grisly Crimes: A History of Crime in Northumberland and County Durham* (Newcastle: Nigel Green Media, 2005)

Greenhow, E.H., *Papers Relating to the Sanitary State of the People of England* (London: General Board of Health 1858; re-issued by Gregg Revivals, 1973).

Greenhow, E.H. and the Epidemiological Society of London, *Cholera in Tynemouth in 1831–2, 1848–9, and 1853* (London: T. Richards, 1855, reprinted from the *Journal of Public Health*).

Gregg, P., *A Social and Economic History of Britain, 1760–1955* (London: G.C. Harrap, 1961).

Gregory, J.V., H.A. Adamson and A. Hesilrige, *The Mayor and the Monks of Tynemouth* (Newcastle upon Tyne: Richardson, 1843).

Griffin, A., *Cuthbert Collingwood: The Northumbrian Who Saved the Nation* (Alston: Mouth of Tyne Publications, 2004).

Hadcock, R.N., *Tynemouth Priory and Castle, Northumberland* (London: HMSO, Ministry of Works, 1959).

Hamer, L., *The Cullercoats Fishwife* (Sunderland: Tyne and Wear County Council Museums, 1984).

Harrison, A.H.W., *The Methodist Church: its origins, divisions, and reunion* (London: Methodist Publishing House, 1932).

Harrison, B. and P. Hollis, *Robert Lowery: Radical and Chartist* (London: Europa Publications Limited, 1979).

Harrison, B. and P. Hollis, 'Chartism, Liberalism and the Life of Robert Lowery', *The English Historical Review* 82:324 (1967), pp. 503–35.

Harrison, B., *Drink and the Victorians* (London: Faber & Faber, 1971).

Harrison, T., *Winslow Homer in England* (Maine USA: Hornby Publications, 2004).

Harvey, J., *The Castle at Tynemouth: A Tale* (London: Longman, Hurst, Rees and Orme, 1806).

Haswell, G.H., *The Maister: A Century of Tyneside life, being some account of the life and work and times of Thomas Haswell* (London: Walter Scott, 1895).

Hatcher, J., *The History of the British Coal Industry, Volume 1: Before 1700: Towards the Age of Coal* (Oxford: Clarendon Press, 1993).

Hearse, G.S., *Remember the Trams? Tyneside* (Isle of Man: George S. Hearse, 1972).

Hempton, D., *The Religion of the People: Methodism and Popular Religion, c.1750–1900* (London: Routledge, 1996).

Hey, D., *The Oxford Companion to Local and Family History* (Oxford: Oxford University Press, 1996).

Higham, N.J., *The Kingdom of Northumbria, AD 350–1100* (Stroud: A. Sutton, 1993).

Hill, A.G., ed., *The Letters of William and Dorothy Wordsworth VI: The Later Years Part III, 1835–1839* (Oxford: Clarendon Press, 2000).

Hodgson, G.B., *The Borough of South Shields: from the earliest period to the close of the nineteenth century* (Newcastle: A. Reid, 1903, reprinted 1996).

Hodgson, J., *A History of Northumberland* (Newcastle: A. Reid, 1940).

Hollerton, E., *North Shields* (Stroud: Chalford, 1997).

Hollerton, E.J., *Tynemouth in Old Picture Postcards* (Zaltbommel: European Library, 1988).

Hope, P., *Chirton and Percy Main* (Seaham: The People's Press, 2001).

Howell, R., *Newcastle upon Tyne and the Puritan Revolution: A Study of the Civil War in North England* (Oxford: Clarendon, 1967).

Hurt, J.S., 'Professor West on Early Nineteenth-Century Education', in M. Drake, *Applied Historical Studies* (Milton Keynes: Open University, 1973), pp. 93–106.

Hurt, J.S., *Education in Evolution: Church, State, Society and Popular Education 1800–1870* (London: Hart-Davis, 1971).

Inglis, K.S., *Church and the Working Classes in Industrial England* (London: Routledge & Kegan Paul, 1963).

Jaffe, J.A., 'The State, Capital, and Workers' Control during the Industrial Revolution: The Rise and Fall of the North-East Pitmen's Union, 1831–2', *Journal of Social History* 21:4 (1988), pp. 717–34.

Jalland, P., *Death in the Victorian Family* (Oxford: Oxford University Press, 1996).

Jobey, G., *Excavation at Tynemouth Priory and Castle* (Gateshead: Northumberland Press, 1967).

Kapelle, W.E., *The Norman Conquest of the North: The Region and Its Transformation, 1100–1135* (London: Croom Helm, 1979).

Keating, P.E., ed., *Into Unknown England, 1866–1913: Selection from the Social Explorers* (Glasgow: Fontana/Collins, 1976).

Kelly, T., *Gibbeting of Wm Jobling* (Jarrow: Bede Gallery Press, 1972).

Kemnitz, T.M., 'Approaches to the Chartist Movement: Feargus O'Connor and Chartist Strategy', *Albion: A Quarterly Journal Concerned with British Studies* Violence and Social Control issue 5:1 (1973), pp. 67–73.

Kemnitz, T.M., 'The Chartist Convention of 1839', *Albion: A Quarterly Journal Concerned with British Studies* 10:2 (1978), pp. 152–70.

Kidd, A., *State, Society and the Poor in Nineteenth-century England* (London: Macmillan, 1999).

King, M. and R.D. King, *Street Games of North Shields Children* (North Shields: Priory Press, 1926).

King, R., *Old North Shields Stairs* (North Shields: Priory Press, 1941).

King, R., *North Shields Theatres* (Gateshead: Northumberland Press, 1948).

King, R. and J.G. Jewels, *Old Tyneside Street Cries* [with melodies], collected by Robert King, standardised by J.G. Jewels and drawn by F. Austin Child (North Shields: Priory Press, 1924).

Lambert, M., *Handbook to Tynemouth and Guide to the Blyth and Tyne Railway* (Newcastle: M. and M.W. Lambert, 1864).

Laslett, P., *The World We Have Lost* (London: Methuen, 1965).

Lawrence, D., 'Racial Violence or Harmony: The Prospect for Britain' (unpublished lecture, British Association for the Advancement of Science, University of Nottingham, 1966).

Lawrence, D., *Black Migrants, White Natives: a Study of Race Relations in Nottingham* (Cambridge: Cambridge University Press, 1974, reprinted 1992 by Gregg Revivals).

Lawrence, D., *The Making of Stan Laurel: Echoes of a British Boyhood* (Jefferson, NC: McFarland, 2011).

Lawson, J.J., *A Man's Life* (London: Hodder & Stoughton, 1944).

Laycock, S., *Warlords: The Struggle for Power in Post-Roman Britain* (London: The History Press, 2009).

Lewis, B., *Coal Mining in the Eighteenth and Nineteenth Centuries* (London: Longman, 1971).

Lloyd, A., *Quaker Social History, 1669–1738* (London, New York: Longmans, Green & Co., 1950).

Lobina, E. and D. Hall, *UK Water Privatisation* (Public Services International Research Unit, University of Greenwich, 2001).

Louvish, S., *Stan and Ollie: The Double Life of Laurel and Hardy* (London: Faber & Faber, 2001).

Lowe, R., *Hansard* 3rd series vol. clxv (London: HMSO, 1862).

Lubi, K., *Tyne Pilots, 1865–2008* (Tyne Area Shipping Club, 2008). http://tyneareasc. org.uk/category/tyne-pilots (accessed 15 July 2016).

Lumley, D., *The Story of Tynemouth Priory and Castle* (Newcastle upon Tyne, Northumberland Press, 1934).

Mackenzie, E., *An Historical, Topographical, and Descriptive View of the County of Northumberland* (Newcastle upon Tyne: Mackenzie and Dent, 1825).

Mackenzie, E., *The Descriptive and Historical Account of the Town and County of Newcastle upon Tyne, 1585–1676* (Newcastle upon Tyne: Mackenzie and Dent, 1827).

Macaulay, T.B., *History of England, Volume 1* (London: Longman, Brown, Green and Longmans, 1849).

Maehl, W.H., 'Chartist Disturbances in North-Eastern England 1839', *International Review of Social History* 8:3 (1963), pp. 389–414.

Maehl, W.H., 'The Dynamics of Violence in Chartism: A Case Study in North-eastern England', *Albion: A Quarterly Journal Concerned with British Studies* 7:2 (1975), pp. 101–19.

Manders, F. and R. Potts, *Crossing the Tyne* (Newcastle upon Tyne: Tyne Bridge Publishing, 2001).

Mann, H., *Religious Worship in England and Wales* (London: Registrar General, 1854).

Marsden, J., *Northanhymbre Saga: the history of the Anglo-Saxon kings of Northumbria* (London: Kyle Cathie, 1992).

Marsden, W., 'Certificate of Protection Against Press-Gangs', in W. Sabine, *Notes and Queries* (1803), p. 410.

Marshall, T.H., *Citizenship and Social Class: and other essays* (Cambridge: Cambridge University Press, 1950).

Maus, M., *The Gift* (London: Cohen & West, 1966; translated by Ian Cunnison from the original 1925 edition).

McCord, N., 'The Seamen's Strike of 1815 in North-East England', *The Economic History Review* 21:1 (1968), pp. 127–43.

McCord, N., 'The Implementation of the 1834 Poor Law Amendment Act on Tyneside', *International Review of Social History* 14 (1969), pp. 90–108.

McCord, N., 'The Government of Tyneside, 1800–1850', *Transactions of the Royal Historical Society* 20 (1970), pp. 5–30.

McCord, N., *North East England: an Economic and Social History* (London, Batsford Academic, 1979).

McLeod, H., *Religion and the Working Class in Nineteenth-century Britain* (London, Macmillan, 1984).

McLeod, H., *Religion and Irreligion in Victorian England: How Secular Was the Working Class?* (Bangor: Headstart Press, 1993).

Meiklejohn, A., 'The Origin of the Term Anthracosis', *British Journal of Industrial Medicine* 16 (1959), pp. 324–35.

Meller, H.E., *Leisure and the Changing City, 1870–1914* (London: Routledge & Kegan Paul, 1976).

Mellor, G.J., *Picture Pioneers: The Story of the Northern Cinemas, 1896–1971* (Newcastle upon Tyne: Frank Graham, 1971).

Metcalfe, A., *Leisure and Recreation in a Victorian Mining Community: The Social Economy of Leisure in North-East England, 1820–1914* (Oxford: Routledge, 2006).

Ministry of Labour, *Local Unemployment Index, 1927–1939* (London: HMSO, 1939).

Mitchell, B.R. and P. Deane, *Abstract of British Historical Statistics* (Cambridge: Cambridge University Press, 1962).

Morgan, G. and P. Ruston, *Rogues, Thieves and the Rule of Law: The Problem of Law Enforcement in North-East England, 1718–1800* (London: UCL Press, 1998).

Morris, J., *The History of the Tynemouth Lifeboats* (Coventry: J. Morris, 1995).

Morton Edward, F., *An Adventure in Co-operation among the Working Classes in North Shields* (North Shields: North Shields Co-operative Society, 1925).

Mountford, C.E., *Tynemouth Cricket Club, 1847–1996, and its place in the history of cricket in Northumberland and in the development of education in North Shields* (Newcastle: Sovereign Press,1997).

Murdoch, N.H., 'Female Ministry in the Thought and Work of Catherine Booth', *Church History* 53:3 (1984), pp. 348–62.

Newton, L. and A.B. Gerdts, *Cullercoats: A North-East Colony of Artists* (Bristol: Sansom, 2003).

North Shields, *An Archeological Assessment and Strategy*, Tyne and Wear Historical Towns Survey, March 2004.

North Shields Gas, *A Copy of the Deeds Relating to the North Shields Gas Company, in the Custody of Mr John Tinley* (North Shields: Printed by J.K. Pollock, 1821).

North Shields and Tynemouth Auxiliary Bible Society, *Proceedings at the second anniversary meeting of the North Shields and Tynemouth Auxiliary Bible Society: Instituted 4th June, 1812* (North Shields: Printed by T. Appleby, 1814).

North Tyneside Community Development Project, *Community Profile* (Newcastle: North Tyneside CDP, 1973).

North Tyneside Community Development Project, *Some Housing and Town Planning Issues in North Tyneside: an Overview* (Newcastle: North Tyneside CDP, 1976).

Northern Union of Mechanics' Institutions, 'The Forty-Sixth Annual Report' (Morpeth: G. Flint, 1894).

Northumberland County Handbook (London: Wargrave Press, undated).

Nossiter, T.J., 'Voting Behaviour, 1832–1872', *Political Studies* 18:3 (1970), pp. 380–9.

Oliver, C. and C. Fairclough, *Rescue at Sea* (London: Watts, 2002).

Olsover, L., *The Jewish Communities of North-East England, 1755–1980* (London: Ashley Mark, 1981).

Parliamentary Papers, *Report from Commissioners: Children's Employment (Mines), Session 3 February–12 August 1842*, vol. xv (London: HMSO, 1842).

Patterson, W.M., *Northern Primitive Methodism* (London: E. Dalton, 1909).

Pearson, H., *Dickens: His Character, Comedy and Career* (New York: Harper, 1949).

Pearson, L., *Played in Tyne and Wear: Charting the heritage of a city at play* (London: English Heritage, 2010).

Peel, E.H., 'The Victorian Institution for the Prosecution of Felons and Study of Crime in the Town of North Shields in the years 1800–1870' (undated, unpublished dissertation).

Perkin, H., *The Origins of Modern English Society, 1780–1880* (London: Routledge & Kegan Paul, 1969).

Phillips, M., *A History of Banks, Bankers and Banking in Northumberland, Durham and North Yorkshire* (London: Effingham Wilson & Co., 1894).

Pigot, *National Commercial Directory* (London: J. Pigot & Co., 1829).

Poll-Book of the Contested Election for the County of Northumberland from June 20th to July 6th 1826 (Alnwick: W. Davison, 1827).

Pollins, H., 'The Jewish Community of North Shields', *Jewish Journal of Sociology* 49:1 and 2 (2007), pp. 47–70.

Pope, R., ed., *Atlas of British Social and Economic History* (London: Routledge, 1989).

Price, H., *A Collection of Original Newcastle Songs: illustrative of the language and manners of the common people on the banks of the Tyne and neighbourhood* (Newcastle upon Tyne: Printed by John Marshall, in the Old Flesh-Market, 1823).

Price, N., 'Housing Access and the Marginal Poor: Housing in North Shields, 1850–1940' (unpublished MA thesis, Newcastle Polytechnic, 1988).

Procter, H.R. *et al.*, 'Experiments in tanning conducted June 1877–October 1887 at Lowlights Tannery, North Shields, by Henry Richardson Procter' (GB 206 MS 290 University of Leeds Library).

Pugh, G., *London's Forgotten Children: Thomas Coram and the Foundling Hospital* (Brimscombe Port: The History Press, 2007).

Ranger, W., *Report to the General Board of Health on a Preliminary Inquiry into the Sewerage, Drainage, and Supply of Water, and the Sanitary Condition of the Inhabitants of the Borough of Tynemouth*, General Board of Health (London: W. Clowes & Sons for HMSO, 1851).

Rawlinson, R., 'Sewerage and Drainage of Tynemouth', *The Civil Engineer and Architect's Journal* 18 (1855), pp. 9–10.

Reed, G., 'Tynemouth During Roman Times' *The Beacon* 112 (July–Aug. 1990), pp. 8–9.

Richardson, J., *Observations on the Proposed Railway from Newcastle upon Tyne to North Shields and Tynemouth* (Newcastle upon Tyne: Empson, 1831).

Richardson, M.A., *The Local Historian's Table Book of Remarkable Occurrences: Historical Division, Volume 5* (Newcastle upon Tyne: M.A. Richardson, 1846).

Robinson N.J., *Stag Line and Joseph Robinson and Sons* (Kendal: World Ship Society, 1984).

Roddam, H.R., 'Tyneside Theatres', *The Era*, 29 August 1896, p. 20.

Rose, L., *The Massacre of the Innocents: Infanticide in Britain, 1800–1939* (London, Boston and Henley: Routledge & Kegan Paul 1986).

Rowe, D., 'A Trade Union of the North-East Coast Seamen in 1825' *The Economic History Review* 25:1 (1972), pp. 81–98.

Rowe, D.J., 'Some Aspects of Chartism on Tyneside', *International Review of Social History* 16 (1971), pp. 17–39.

Rowe, D.J., 'Occupations in Northumberland and Durham 1851–1911', *Northern History* 8 (1973), pp. 119–31.

Rowe, D.J., 'The North-East', in F.M.L. Thompson, *The Cambridge Social History of Britain 1750–1950, Volume 1: Regions and Communities* (Cambridge: Cambridge University Press, 1990), pp. 415–70.

Rupp, E.G. and R.E. Davies, *A History of the Methodist Church in Great Britain* (London: Epworth Press, 1965).

Sanderson, M., 'Review of Education and the Industrial Revolution', *Economic History Review* 24:2 (1976), pp. 323–4.

Saunders, A.D., *Tynemouth Priory, Castle and Twentieth-century Fortifications, Tyne and Wear* (London: English Heritage, 1993).

School of Industry, *Twenty-sixth annual report of the School of Industry established by voluntary contributions in the parish of Tynemouth: for the instruction of poor girls in reading, sewing, knitting, &c.* (North Shields, Barnes and Co., 1834).

Scott, M., *The History of Christ Church, North Shields* (North Shields: Christ Church, 1996).

Shepherd, V.A., 'From New Connexion Methodist to William Booth', *Papers of the Canadian Methodist Historical Society* 9 (1993), pp. 91–107.

Short, C.C., *Durham Colliers and West Country Methodists: the story of the Bible Christian Mission in County Durham, 1874–1910* (Kidderminster: C.C. Short, 1995).

Shaw, J.S., 'Campbell, Archibald, first Duke of Argyll (d. 1703)', *Oxford Dictionary of National Biography*, edited by Lawrence Goldman (Oxford: Oxford University Press, 2004), online edn, http://www.oxforddnb.com/view/article/4474 (accessed 15 July 2016).

Shotton, J., *Pubs of North Shields* (North Shields: North Tyneside Library and Museums, 2006).

Shotton, J., *Stepping Back in Time* (Newcastle: Summerhill Books, 2011).

Simpson, R., *North Shields and Tynemouth: a pictorial history* (Chichester: Phillimore, 1988).

Smith, A.H.V., 'Provenance of Coals from Roman Sites in England and Wales', *Britannia* 28 (1997), pp. 297–324.

Smith, G.D. and J. Lynch, 'Commentary: Social capital, social epidemiology and disease aetiology', *International Journal of Epidemiology* 33:4 (2004), pp. 691–700.

Smith's Dock Company, *The Evolution of our North Shields Dockyard* (North Shields: Smith's Dock Company, 1930).

Smurthwaite, W.H., *Notes on the History of North Shields*, available in the North Tyneside Local Studies Library (handwritten, undated, un-numbered).

Smurthwaite, W.H., *Our Heritage: Preston Township and Preston Village* (North Shields: W.H. Smurthwaite, 1992).

Society for Bettering the Condition and Increasing the Comforts of the Poor, *Reports, 1800–1802* (London).

Spencer, H., *An Autobiography* (New York: Appleton, 1904).

St Columba's United Reform Church, *St Columba's: Fifty Years and More, 1949–1999* (North Shields: St Columba's United Reform Church, 1999).

Stark, J., *St Cuthbert's Church, North Shields: some account of its foundation and early history* (North Shields: St Cuthbert's, 1902).

Stearns, P.N., *European Society in Upheaval: social history since 1800* (New York, London: Macmillan, Collier-Macmillan, 1967).

Steel, C., *Inns and Taverns of North Shields* (London: Tempus, 2007).

Steel, C., *Monkseaton Village, Volume One* (Newcastle: Summerhill Books, 2012).

Stephens, W.B., *Minutes and Reports of the Committee of Council on Education 1839–1899* (Microform Academic Publishers, 1985).

Stevenson, J., *Popular Disturbances in England, 1700–1870* (London: Allen & Unwin, 1974).

Storey, G., ed., *The Letters of Charles Dickens, Volume 11: 1865–1867* (Oxford: Clarendon Press, 1999).

Supple, B., *The History of the British Coal Industry, Volume 4: 1913–1946: The Political Economy of Decline* (Oxford: Clarendon Press, 1987).

Sutcliffe, M.P., 'Negotiating the "Garibaldi moment" in Newcastle upon Tyne 1854–1861', *Modern Italy* 15:2 (2010), pp. 129–44.

Sweezy, P.M., *Monopoly and Competition in the English Coal Trade, 1550–1850* (Westport, CT: Greenwood Press, 1938 and 1972).

Swift, R.E., 'Policing Chartism, 1839–1848: The Role of the "Specials" Reconsidered', *English Historical Review* 122 (2007), pp. 669–99.

Sykes, J., *Local Records; Or, Historical Register on Remarkable Events: Which Have Occurred in Northumberland and Durham, Newcastle upon Tyne and Berwick upon Tweed, from the Earliest Times of Authentic Record to the Present Time, with Biographical Notices of Deceased Persons of Talent, Eccentricity and Longevity* (Newcastle: J. Sykes, 1833).

Szreter, S., 'Debating mortality trends in nineteenth-century Britain', *International Journal of Epidemiology* 33:4 (2004), pp. 705–9.

Taggart, J., *Records of Tynemouth, Volumes 1–3* (1957; unpublished document available in the North Tyneside Local Studies Library).

Taylor, A., 'Working-class credit on Tyneside since 1918' (Ph.D. thesis, University of Durham, 1996).

Taylor, M., 'Rethinking the Chartists: Searching for Synthesis in the Historiography of Chartism', *The Historical Journal* 39:2 (1996), pp. 479–95.

The History of Parliament website http://www.historyofparliamentonline.org/volume/1820–1832/constituencies/northumberland (accessed 8 July 2014).

Thompson, E.P., 'The Moral Economy of the English Crowd in the Eighteenth Century', *Past and Present* 50 (1971), pp. 76–136.

Thompson, F.M.L., *The Rise of Respectable Society: A Social History of Victorian Britain, 1830–1900* (London: Fontana Press, 1988).

Thompson, F.M.L., ed., *The Cambridge Social History of Britain, 1750–1950* (Cambridge: Cambridge University Press, 1990).

Thompson, J., *Observations on the most advantageous line of country through which a canal navigation may be carried from Newcastle or North Shields towards Cumberland with a proposal to extend collateral branches by the Pont and Blyth rivers to Morpeth and the Port of Blyth and pointing out the practicability of carrying a line of canal through the middle of Northumberland to Berwick upon Tweed* (Newcastle: R. Sands, 1795).

Tilly, C., 'Collective Violence in European Perspective', in H. Graham and T. Gurr, eds, *Violence in America: Historical and Comparative Perspectives, a report to the National Commission on the Causes and Prevention of Violence, Volume 1* (New York: Bantam, 1969), pp. 4–45.

Tomlinson, W.W., *Historical Notes on Cullercoats, Whitley and Monkseaton, with a descriptive memoir of the coast from Tynemouth to St. Mary's Island* (London: Walter Scott, 1893).

Tomlinson, W.W., *The North Eastern Railway: Its Rise and Development* (London: Longmans and Green, 1914).

Trimmer, P., *Tyneside Trams* (2008) *personal communication.*

Turner, M., *Enclosures in Britain, 1750–1830* (London: Macmillan, 1984).

Tyne Built Ships: A History of Tyne Shipbuilders, http://www.tynebuiltships.co.uk/NorthShields.html (accessed 15 July 2016)

Tynemouth County Borough, Education Committee, *Young Tynemouth: Response to the 1944 Education Act* (North Shields: County Borough of Tynemouth, 1944).

Tynemouth County Borough, *County Borough of Tynemouth, 1849–1949* (North Shields: J.W. Moore, 1949).

Tynemouth County Borough, *County Borough of Tynemouth Police, 1850–1969* (North Shields: County Borough of Tynemouth, 1969).

Tynemouth County Borough, *Tynemouth: Official Industrial Handbook* (North Shields: County Borough of Tynemouth Council, 1970).

Tynemouth Photographic Society and North Tyneside Libraries *Photographs of the Borough of Tynemouth past and present: a celebration of the centenary of Tynemouth Photographic Society* (North Shields: North Tyneside Libraries, 2002).

The United Free Churches Magazine for 1859 (1859), pp. 226–7.

Union Association, *Deed made by the Union Association for the Mutual Insurance of Their Ships (and subsequent by-laws)* (North Shields: Union Association, 1786).

Ville, S., 'Total Factor Productivity in the English Shipping Industry: The North-East Coal Trade, 1700–1850', *The Economic History Review* new series 39:3 (1986), pp. 355–70.

Ville, S., 'The Growth of Specialization in English Ship Owning, 1750–1850', *The Economic History Review* new series 46:4 (1993), pp. 702–22.

Waller, D., *personal communication,* 6 April 2014.

Ward, Dame I., River Tyne (Pollution), House of Commons Oral Questions, *Hansard* 11 February 1958 (London: HMSO, 1958).

Wardle, D., *English Popular Education, 1780–1975* (Cambridge: Cambridge University Press, 1970).

Watson, I., *The Fire Worm* (London: Gollancz, 1988).

Watson, R.S., *Joseph Skipsey: His Life and Work* (London: Fisher Unwin, 1908).

Webb, S., *The Story of the Durham Miners (1662–1921)* (London: The Fabian Society, The Labour Publishing Company, 1921).

West, E.G., 'Resource Allocation and Growth in Early Nineteenth-century Education', in M. Drake, *Applied Historical Studies* (Milton Keynes: Open University, 1973), pp. 53-92.

West, E.G., 'The Interpretation of Early Nineteenth-century Education British Education', in M. Drake, *Applied Historical Studies* (Milton Keynes, Open University, 1973), pp. 107–20.

West, E.G., *Education and the Industrial Revolution* (London: Batsford, 1975).

Whellan, W., *Whellan's History, Topography and Directory of Northumberland* (London: William Whellan, 1855).

Wickham, E.R., *Church and People in an Industrial City* (London: Lutterworth Press, 1957).

Williams, N. and C. Galley, 'Urban–Rural Differentials in Infant Mortality in Victorian England', *Population Studies* 49:3 (1995), pp. 401–20.

Wilson, B., *Religion in a Secular Society* (London: Penguin, 1969).

Winifred, C., *Down the Lonely Stairs* (Oxford: Oxford University Press, 1964).

Winter, J.M., 'Military Fitness and Civilian Health in Britain during the First World War', *Journal of Contemporary History* 15:2 (1980), pp. 211–44.

Wohl, A.S., *Endangered Lives: Public Health in Victorian Britain* (London: J.M. Dent & Sons, 1983).

Wolffe, J., *God and Greater Britain: Religion and National Life in Britain and Ireland, 1843–1945* (London: Routledge, 1994).

Woods, R., *The Population History of Britain in the Nineteenth Century* (Cambridge: Cambridge University Press, 1992).

Wright, R., *North Shields: Memories of Fish 'n Chips* (Seaham: The People's History, 2001).

Wright, R., *Beyond the Piers* (Seaham: The People's History, 2002).

Wright, T.G., *Diary of a Doctor: Surgeon's Assistant in Newcastle upon Tyne 1826–1829* (Newcastle upon Tyne: Newcastle Libraries, 1998).

Wrigley, E.A., 'The Process of Modernization and the Industrial Revolution in England', *The Journal of Interdisciplinary History* 3:2 (1972), pp. 225–59.

Young, G.F., *Free-Trade Fallacies Refuted* (London: James Madden, 1852).

Index

abstain, abstainers, abstinence (see temperance)

Acknowledgements xvii–xix, 307

actors (see theatre)

Adams, Gladstone 64

Adamson, H.A. 137, 225, 323, 327

Adelfotis 64

Admiralty 38

Aelia Classica 1

Aelius Hadrianus (see Hadrian)

Æthelbert 5, 7

Æthelburh 5

Æthelfrith 4, 7

Aetheling, Edgar 10

Aged Seamen's and Scullermen's Society 291

air raid shelters 94–6

airport, proposed for Tynemouth Borough 94

Alam Penting 50

Alam Pesona 50

Albert Edward Dock 63–4, 94, 115

Albion Assembly Rooms 90–1, 120, 180, 190, 198–9, 283

Albion Cinema 199

Albion Road 73–4, 96, 134, 137, 157, 162, 165, 257, 317, 328–9

alcohol (see drinking of alcohol and pubs)

ale-houses (see drinking of alcohol and pubs)

Alexander Scott Park 96, 143

Algernon Pit 58

Allen, J. 212, 215, 317, 321, 323, 333

Alnmouth 210

Alnwick 11, 19, 185, 210–11, 331

Alvo, Henry 197

Amateur Athletics Club 184

amateur, amateurism 183–4, 186–7, 189, 198, 203

Amble 13

ambulance service 118, 121

America, Americans 58, 61, 70, 112, 144, 161, 188, 206, 208, 214, 223, 225, 306, 322, 333

American War of Independence 70, 208, 223

Ancient Order of Foresters 292

Angles 3–4, 9

Anglesey 4

Anglican, Anglicanism 20, 26, 114, 131, 133, 138–40, 144–5, 148–9, 152, 155, 157–8, 165, 255–6

angling 188, 190

Anglo-Saxons 1, 3–4, 9–11, 66, 307, 329

anthracosis (see also inhalation of coal dust and pneumoconiosis) 244, 319, 330

anti-Catholicism 19–26, 131, 134–5, 155–6

apartheid 153, 259

apothecaries 140, 245

Appleby Park 185–6

apprentices 245

Arbeia 2

archaeological excavations 5, 88, 90, 328

Argyll, Duke of 114, 174, 315, 332

Arkwright, Richard 250

Arminian Methodists 147

armonica 175

Armstrong, Prof. Alan xix, 306, 323

Ashkenazi Jews 169–70

Astley Arms 184

astronomy 256

Asylum for Betrayed Shareholders in Joint Stock Banks 77

Athenaeum 179–80
athletes, athletics 184–5, 187–8
Atkinson, F. 323
Augustine, Paulinus 6
Augustine, Yorke 178
Australia, transportation to 223

Backworth 13, 49, 55, 57–8, 135, 164, 212
Bailey, E. McDonald 185
bakeries, bake-houses 30, 32
Balkwell 114–15, 157–9, 199, 220, 238
Ballantyne, R.M. 291
ballast 35–6, 38, 60, 92
Baltic 61, 72, 228, 242
Bamburgh 9, 11–12
Bandman-Palmer's Theatrical Company 196
Bank Top (Bankhead) ix, xiv–xv, 86–96, 234, 241
bank, banking 77–8, 154
bankers 77, 311, 331
Banton, Michael 170, 315, 323
Bantu Education Act 259
Baptists 139–40, 142, 149–50, 152, 154, 160–1, 179, 256
Barebones Parliament 38
barque 46, 68, 70, 228
Barr, J. Stuart 300
bear-baiting 173
Beaumont, Alma 191–2
Beaumont, T. Wentworth 209–11
Bebside 13, 109
Bede, the Venerable 5–6, 8
Bedford Street 74, 90, 92–3, 104, 133–4, 195
Bedford Terrace 96
beer (see also drinking of alcohol and pubs) 121, 199–200, 206, 278
Benebalcrag 4–7, 9, 11–13, 16, 32, 60
Benedictine 11, 90
Benevolent and Flower Mission 286
Benevolent Association 323
Benton 104, 109
Benwell 13
Bernicia 3–8
Berwick 25, 27, 34, 185
Beveridge, William xvi, 204, 228, 247, 249, 275–6, 302
Bewick 13
Bewick, Thomas 30, 324
bicycle (see cycling)
billiards 190, 195

bingo halls 199
Bird-in-Hand Quay 200
Bird Street 235
Bishop of Durham 11, 32
bishops 6, 20, 129, 132, 135, 138–9, 148
Bishops' War 20
Black Cock Quay 200
Blackburn's Quay 200
Blaydon Friendly Society 295
Blondin 185, 190–1
Blue Bell Pit 58
Blyth 104, 198, 283, 292, 312, 329, 333
boats (see also ships) 30, 44, 61, 72, 74, 97–8, 100, 182, 188–9, 298
Boer Wars 216, 246
Bohstedt, J. 296, 321, 324
Bolam 13
bombing 94–6, 120, 165–6, 181, 261, 267
Bondfield, Margaret M.P. 301
Booth, Catherine 167, 315, 330
Booth, Charles 266
Boro' Theatre and Cinema 197–9
Borough Bank (see Borough Road)
Borough of Tynemouth (Rugby) Football Club (BTRFC) 186
Borough of Tynemouth viii–ix, 2, 24, 51–2, 58, 62–3, 74, 79, 83, 88, 90–1, 94, 105, 109–10, 112, 114–16, 120–3, 125–7, 138, 143, 148–50, 152, 160, 165, 177–8, 180, 182, 185–6, 189, 197, 200, 213, 225, 231, 233, 235, 237–43, 248, 260, 267, 279, 286, 302, 307, 334
Borough Road 74, 84, 92, 94, 96, 105–6, 154, 157–8, 192, 195, 249, 258
Boscawen, HMS 282
Bothal 13
Bothwell, Earl of 17
Bourne, Hugh 146
Bouverie, General 220
bowls 182–3
boxing 155, 172, 190
Boyce, A.O. 144, 271, 311, 313–14, 318, 320, 324
Boyce, Herbert W. 102
Bradford, J. 308, 313–15, 324
Bramwell, Sir Byrom 121
bread (see corn)
breweries, brewers 30, 32–3, 35, 37, 40, 43, 53, 78, 93, 113, 121, 164, 203, 231, 284
bridges 98, 101–2
brigantines 228

brigs 57–8, 61, 66, 68, 70, 228, 246, 272

brine (see also salt) 34

British Association for the Advancement of Science 305, 324, 329

British Medical Association 327

British Women's Temperance Association 203

Brittany 4

Broadbent, John 159

Broadway 112, 164

Broadway Methodist Church 164

Brock Farm 123–4, 136, 185, 281

Brock Farm Reservoir 281

brothels (see also prostitution) 174

Brotherhood (miners) 218–19

Brown, Samuel 98

Brutton, Rev. Thomas 157

Bull Ring 84, 100, 114, 118, 143, 154, 162, 168, 172

bull-baiting and bulldogs 172–3

bulls 84, 100, 114, 118, 143, 154, 162, 168, 172–3

bulwarks 44

Bunting, Jarez 146–7

Bunyan, John 139

Burdon Main Colliery 252

Burdon Row 163, 165

burgesses of Newcastle 19, 25, 28–31, 35–6, 41, 44–5

burials 7–8, 11, 52, 88, 90, 110, 143, 168–9, 187, 202, 242, 292–3, 324

Burradon 58, 274

Burt, Thomas 299

buses ix, 107

butchers 32, 234–5

by-election 212–13

Byker 102

Byker Mission 165

Bywell 13

Camden Lane 154

Camden Street 90, 104–5, 121, 129, 141, 159, 289–90

Camden, William 1, 307, 324

Camp Terrace 185

Campbell, Archibald (see Argyll, Duke of)

Camperdown 109

canals, proposed network 101, 312, 333

Cardonnel, Col. Lawson de 192

Carlisle 27, 41, 214

Carlton cinema 165

Carmichael, James Wilson 27, 232

Carr pottery 5, 54

Carr, Thomas 202

Carruth, John 86

Carter, President Jimmy 72

Cartwright, John 298

Catholicism 15–20, 24–6, 114, 130–5, 138–9, 147, 149–50, 152, 155–7, 169, 208, 210, 255–6, 259, 261, 313, 326–7

causeway, to the Bank Top 113

Cavendish, William (Earl of Newcastle) 21

Cecil Street 93

celibacy 130

Celts 2, 6

cemeteries 114, 143, 168–9, 242, 274, 315

Central Palace of Varieties (see Comedy Palace of Varieties)

Chadwick, Sir Edwin 241

chaldron (coal measure) 43–5

chapels: in Allotment 164, 166; in Backworth 164; in Bell Street 140; on Benebalcrag 5; in Chirton 162, 166; on Church Way 142; in Cullercoats 163–4; on Dene Street 163; in Earsdon 164; on Hudson Street 154; in Milburn Place (Catholic) 132–4; in Milburn Place (Methodist) 145–7; on Percy Main 163; in Shiremoor 164; on Union Street 132

Chapman, William and Edward 77

charcoal 42

charities 77, 98, 133, 151, 179, 192–3, 198, 245–6, 254, 258, 276, 281–2, 283, 285–7, 304

Charles I, King 19–26, 131

Charles II, King 25–6, 131, 137

Charles, Earl of Westmorland 17

Charleton, Captain William 224

Charlotte Street ix, 73, 91, 120, 159, 213, 235, 290

charters, royal 10, 29, 31–2, 38, 42, 109, 212, 215

Chartism 58, 212–15, 310, 317, 328–9, 332–3

child labour 176, 218, 245, 250–4

children's toys 177–9

chimneys 43, 46, 232–3

Chirton 13, 24, 37, 39, 49, 55, 74, 79, 81–3, 92, 94, 101, 108–10, 113–15, 162, 165–6, 168, 174, 211, 238, 241, 261–2, 281, 328

Chirton Dene 114

Chirton Grange Methodist Church 165–6, 168, 188

Chisholm, Samuel 195

choke damp 244

cholera 122, 147, 220, 235, 241–3, 318, 325, 327

Christ Church 86, 109, 113, 116, 133, 135–40, 151, 154, 157–8, 194, 256, 261, 278, 312–15, 332

Christenson, Norman viii, 307, 325

Christianity 5–6, 9, 129–30, 138, 140, 144, 146, 154, 161–2, 167–8, 171, 203, 308, 313–15, 324, 332

Church of England 15, 25, 130–1, 135, 138–9, 144–5, 155, 157, 169, 255–6, 261

Church of Scotland 140–1

church on Benebalcrag (see Tynemouth Priory)

Church Road 169

Church Street 73, 235, 245, 285

Church Way 96, 113, 125, 142

cinemas 146, 165, 197–9, 330

Cipolla, C.M. 319, 325

circus 185, 195, 197

civil wars 19–25, 46, 63, 131, 308, 328

Clasper, Harry 189

clergy 53, 132–3, 137, 139, 145–6, 153, 157, 272

Cliffe, Thomas 35–7

Clifford's Fort 20, 23, 26, 47, 97–8

Clinton, President Bill 72

Clive Street 195, 200–1

Clock Vaults pub (Wellington Street) 293

Clowes, William 146–7, 331

clubs 78, 144, 178–80, 182, 184–90, 192, 199, 202–3, 258, 293, 316, 329–30

Coach Lane 74, 93–4, 100–1, 114, 143, 157, 162, 165–6, 168

coaches 77, 98, 101

coal xiv, 20–1, 23–5, 30–6, 38, 40–50, 52–8, 60, 63, 72, 78, 91, 111–13, 115, 126, 147, 174–7, 187, 191–2, 212, 215, 218–21, 231, 233, 242, 244–5, 250–3, 258, 266–7, 271, 273, 275, 295–6, 309–10, 314, 317, 319, 321, 323, 325–6, 328–9, 333–4

Coast Road (A1058 dual-carriageway) 101

Cobalt Business Park 96

Coble Dene 63, 70–1, 114–15

cobles 33, 58, 70, 112

cock-boats 62

Cockermouth 19

cock-fighting 172–3

collieries 35, 38, 45, 49, 56–8, 63, 113, 115, 121–2, 164, 185, 187, 220, 248, 251–3, 274, 295, 297

colliers (ships) 41, 44, 46–9, 55, 57–8, 61–2, 66, 70, 219, 228, 244–6, 295, 297

Collingwood School 262

Collingwood Street 162, 168

Collingwood, Admiral Lord 114, 327

Collingwood's Monument ix–x, 60

Collinson, William 90

Colls, R. 217, 314, 317, 319, 321, 325

Colman, Grace M.P. 301

Combination Acts 217–18, 296

Comedy Palace of Varieties 198

comfortables 97

Commines, Robert 10

Committee of Council of Education 254–6, 319–20, 325, 333

Commonwealth Commissioners 135–6

communion 18, 130–3, 135, 145, 157, 161

Communist Party 300

Congregational churches 139–42, 148–50, 152, 159–60, 163, 165, 256, 258, 286

congregations 132–3, 135, 139–42, 146, 151, 153, 157–60, 162–6, 168, 323

Constituency of Northumberland 298

Constituency of Tynemouth (and North Shields) 81, 212, 216–17, 300–1

Constituency of Tyneside 66

Conventicle Act 139–40

convict ship 212

Cooperative movement and shops 215, 289–90, 300, 327, 330

Copsig 10

Coquet Island 13

Coquet, Sir Henry 8

Coram, Thomas 320, 331

Corbridge 13

corf and corves 251–2

corn (and bread) 32–3, 53, 208, 263–5, 283

Corn Laws 208–9, 264

Cornish miners 146

Cornwall 4, 49, 58, 74, 212, 220, 243, 267, 282

Council of Whitby 6

County Borough of Tynemouth (see Borough of Tynemouth)

Courtauld, Samuel 250

courthouse 116

Covenanters 20–1

Cowen, Joseph 310, 317, 321, 323, 325

Cowpen 13, 109, 135
Cramlington 109
Cranmer, Thomas 17, 130
Craster 13
Craster, H.H.E. xiii, 11, 22, 30, 52, 58,
    61, 74, 86, 115, 168–9, 261, 307–12,
    314–15, 318, 320, 325
Crawford, George 281
cricket 155, 183–7, 190, 279, 316, 330
crimes and criminals 6, 17–18, 31, 116–17,
    130, 217, 221–3, 282, 298, 313, 317,
    327, 331
Cromwell, Thomas 24–5, 38, 135, 139
croquet 185
Cullercoats 55, 66, 77, 79, 94, 101, 104–5,
    109–13, 121, 135, 143, 157, 163–6, 182,
    211, 262, 312, 323, 327, 330, 333
Cumberland 312, 333
Cumbria 4
Cunningham, H. 316, 325
Currie, R. 145, 162–4, 314–15, 325
Custom House Quay 272
customs (powers) 31, 44, 48, 62, 65, 224
cycling 55, 105, 185, 187–8, 191, 203

Daiches, Rabbi Salis 168–9
Danes 1, 8–11
Davy, Humphrey 244, 247
death penalty 221–3
death rates 79, 239–45, 263, 271–4, 288,
    290, 292, 296, 318, 328
debt 37, 174, 269, 288, 304
Declaration of Independence 206–7
Declaration of Liberty of Conscience 26
decline (in North Shields) 51–2, 96
decline in religious observance 129,
    155–66
defence of the area (see also Tynemouth
    Castle and Clifford's Fort) 4, 8–9, 11,
    16–18, 20, 31, 214
Defoe, Daniel 231
Deira 3–8
Delaval family 11, 37, 174, 192, 327
democracy 146, 206, 211
demonstrations (protest) 247, 297
Dene Street 163, 290
Denmark 24
deodands 33
department stores 91–2, 127
depressions in trade 68–9, 90, 102, 226,
    246–8, 264, 267, 296, 302
Derbyshire miners 220

desk (see Resolute)
dialects 307, 326
Dianunti family and café 106
Diary of a Doctor 245, 319, 335
Dibdin, Thomas 61, 229–30, 310, 318, 325
Dickens, Charles 111, 206, 276, 312, 331,
    333
diets 208, 242, 263, 264, 284
Dingle, A.E. 199, 200, 325
diphtheria 243
disasters in coal mines 57, 273–5
disease(s) 23, 25, 121–2, 133, 136, 147, 204,
    228, 233–4, 236, 239–46, 262, 264, 275,
    278, 292, 302, 332, 325
dispensary (see North Shields and
    Tynemouth Dispensary)
Disraeli, Benjamin 218, 317, 325
dissent (see old dissent and new dissent)
Dissington 13
disturbances (public order) 131, 156, 211,
    217, 220, 250, 296, 305, 317, 321, 324,
    329, 333
Dixon, George 127
Dobson, John ix, xi, 93, 109, 141, 142,
    220, 311
dockers 246
Dockwray family 86–8, 96, 137–8
Dockwray Square 86, 88, 93, 96, 144, 189,
    233, 235, 259, 287
doctors (medical) 121, 137, 202, 243, 265,
    285, 319, 335
Dodd, Ralph 97–8
dodgers (see ha'penny dodger ferries)
dog-fighting 172–3
Dogger Letch 113
dole 249
dolly tub (see poss tub)
Dolman's Magazine 313, 326
Domesday Book 10
Donkin Rig 13
Donkin, Richard Sims M.P. 216
Dotwick Sands 63
Dove family 88, 90, 143
drains and sewers 30, 88, 122, 189, 231–6,
    240, 310, 313, 331
Drake, M. 307, 319–20, 326, 328, 334
drama (see theatres)
dredging (the Tyne) 40, 49–50, 61, 63
drinking of alcohol (see also pubs) 118,
    121, 174, 199–204, 209, 236, 282, 284,
    292, 316, 325, 328
Drummond Terrace 123

Drury Lane Theatre 174
Dudley, John 130
Duke of Northumberland (see also Earl of
    Northumberland) 84, 88, 90, 182, 187,
    285, 287
Dunfermline 8
dung heaps 122, 234
Dupree M.W. 288, 321, 326
Durham 10–11, 13, 43, 49, 58, 77, 97, 99,
    132, 141, 231, 244, 248, 274, 278, 295
Dutch 24–6, 137, 228
Dutch Wars 24–6, 137
dwellings (see housing)
dyers 43

Earl of Northumberland (see also Duke of
    Northumberland) 9–12, 18–19, 86, 136
earnings 188, 211, 249, 268, 269, 271
Earsdon 13, 57, 58, 79, 81, 109, 115, 135,
    140, 164, 212, 275
East Anglia 4–5, 8, 10
East Percy Street 96
economic exploitation 217–22
economics 40–1, 51–2, 57, 67, 74, 77–8,
    96, 102, 107, 112, 115, 124, 128, 170,
    204–5, 208, 213, 216–17, 228, 231,
    246–7, 249–50, 271, 277, 287–8, 296,
    299, 302, 305, 309–10, 311, 315, 324,
    330, 333
Edinburgh 17, 121, 185
Edington, J.S. 127
Edlingham 13
education 66, 180, 192, 194, 198, 203, 212,
    215, 240, 250, 253–62, 284, 300, 304,
    319–20, 325, 328, 330, 332–4
Edwin 4–6, 15
eels 123
Eglingham 13
Egner, F.G. 326
elderly 157, 174, 239, 272–3, 278–9, 283,
    288, 290, 292
elections and the electorate 66, 109, 115,
    134, 206–8, 210–12, 216–17, 243,
    278–9, 299–301, 305, 311
electricity and electrification ix, 48–9, 78,
    88, 104–5, 107, 126–7, 176, 178, 198
Elementary Education Act 1870 and
    North Shields Elementary Schools
    260–1
Elizabeth I, Queen 16–18, 44–5, 130–1
Ellington 13
Elmes, S. 9, 307, 308, 326

Elswick 13
emergency services 116–19
Emperor of Variety 1, 198
emphysema 244
employment 36, 43, 46, 52–3, 88, 100,
    116–17, 123, 143, 176, 179, 184, 189,
    196, 204, 217–22, 227, 242, 246–51,
    261, 263, 267–71, 277, 282, 285, 287,
    293, 298–9, 304–5, 319, 331
enclosure 86, 182, 311, 334
enemy action 69, 94, 129
engineering and engineers 48–9, 55–6, 58,
    66, 70, 76, 94, 97, 101, 104, 115, 119,
    120, 122, 174, 187, 205, 244, 273, 297,
    309, 326
entertainment 94, 178, 191–2, 194–5,
    198–9
entrepreneurs 29, 51, 65, 75, 196, 208
epidemics 122, 220, 235, 242–3, 327
episcopacy 20, 135
equality 207, 227, 266
estates 11, 18, 29, 68, 90, 94, 104, 115, 157,
    158, 165, 168, 174, 206, 238, 239, 282,
    300, 318, 323
estuary 17, 20
Etal Villa 74
ethnic groups, distribution 3
Eton 212
Europe 17, 33, 51, 77, 207, 264, 276,
    306–7, 310, 322
European Amateur Cup 186
European Hotel 103
evangelicalism 6, 144, 154, 157, 159,
    167–8, 171, 203
evolution 111, 129
excise authority 200
excommunication 15, 130
excursions (trips) 154, 324, 293
executions 11, 18, 25, 130, 221–5
exploitation 45, 217–22
explosion 274
exports 43, 48, 50, 54–5, 63, 76, 296
extremists 19, 131
eyes 14, 172, 244, 265

factionalism 16, 129, 145, 153
factories 48, 73–4, 76, 96, 115, 192, 231–3,
    250
Fairbairn, Sir William 297, 326
Fairles, Nicholas 220–1
Falklands 76
Falkus, M.E. 326

famine 156, 267, 296
faults (see Tynemouth Dyke)
Fawcus (see Pow and Fawcus)
Fawkes, Guy 19–20
Federation of Sail Makers of Great
    Britain and Ireland 294–5
felons 116, 313, 331
Fenwick, Dr 241, 319
ferreting 172
ferries 61, 97–101, 105, 114, 156, 169, 192,
    271, 274
fertilizer 76
feudal system 29
fever 133, 234
films 72, 77, 93, 196–8, 243
filtration of sewage 236
fin keel 189
finance 13, 18, 20, 33, 75, 122, 140, 174,
    185–6, 122, 213, 220, 258, 260, 288,
    290, 295, 304–5
Finch, R. 45–6, 309–10, 326
Findmypast 280
Finnegan, Ruth vii, 307, 326
fire and fires 10–11, 25, 31, 42, 60, 111,
    118–20, 137–8, 163, 166, 176–7, 193–4,
    198, 244, 282–3, 334
fire damp 244
fire service 119–20
firearms (see also guns) 214, 220
fire-ships 25
fireworks 191, 210
First World War 43, 65–7, 69, 94, 104,
    178, 199, 217, 266–8, 283, 286,
    299–300, 319, 334
Fish Quay ix, 26, 30, 71, 74–8, 94, 141,
    179, 209, 235, 248, 309, 326
fish and fishing 12, 26, 30–4, 43, 52–3, 61,
    70–2, 74–8, 97, 112, 163, 175, 185, 190,
    230, 235, 263, 269, 271–3, 291, 295,
    309–10, 324, 326–7, 335
Fisher Chapel and Choir (Cullercoats)
    163–4, 189, 317, 334
Fisher's pawn shop 270
Flatworth 13, 49, 55, 63, 114–15
Flinn, M.W. 310, 326
flint 92
flogging 226
flooding in mines 56
floral displays in parks 182
Floral Society 185
flotation of early lifeboats 61
flotsam 33

flour (see corn)
flour-mill 231
flushing the streets 189
fodder 11
Fontburn 123
food 8, 11, 24, 52, 90, 182–3, 199, 219,
    243, 252, 264–6, 269, 286, 288–90,
    296, 304, 321, 324
football (soccer) 28, 155, 184–6, 223, 258,
    285, 287
Football Association 184
Ford, Henry 306
Fordyce, W. 321, 326
Forster's 1870 Education Act 260
fortifications 1–2, 8–9, 15–16, 20–1, 24–5,
    332
fossil fuel dependency 49
Foster, Miles Birket 258
Foster, W. 200, 316, 326
foundries 72, 88
Four and Twenty (see vestry)
Fox Hunter's Inn 58
Fox, George 139, 142–3
foy boats 189, 292
fractures 245
France (and the French) 4, 11, 18–19,
    23–4, 43, 68, 131–3, 185, 206–8, 213,
    217, 225, 228, 313, 326
Franklin, Benjamin 175, 218
Franklin, Sir John 72
Fraser, W.H. 263, 289, 311, 316, 320–1,
    326
freemen (of Newcastle) 36
freemasonry 293
free-trade 335
French Revolutions 132, 151, 207–8, 217,
    313, 326
fridges 176
friendly societies 78, 202, 287, 290–5, 316,
    321, 323, 327
Friendly Society of Orangemen North
    Shields 290
Friendly Society of Women 290
frigates 70
Fryer's map of North Shields 84, 86
funerals 189, 274, 277, 293
furnaces 34, 43, 46, 126, 245
Fynes, R. 326

Gagging Acts 208
Gaiety Theatre and Picture Hall 198
Gale, A. 326

Galley, C. 240, 318–19, 334
Galloway, R.I. 45, 309–10, 326
Gallowgate 223
Gambia 223
gambling 171, 173, 184
games 178, 183–4, 188, 199, 214, 316, 329
Garden of Eden Lodge of the Friendly
    Society, the Ancient Order of Free
    Gardeners 293
gardens and gardening 88, 93, 182, 186,
    190, 239, 262
Gardner, Ralph 24, 35, 37–9, 63, 71, 84,
    114, 136, 262, 325–6
Garibaldi, Giuseppe 215–16, 317, 324,
    333
Garson W. 309, 326–7
gas (coal) and gasworks 48, 78, 91, 126–8,
    191–2, 221, 231, 267, 313, 326, 330
Gateshead 13, 21, 101, 122, 167, 235–6,
    242–3, 313, 325, 328–9
Gaumont Theatre and Cinema 198–9
Gentlemen of the Friendly Club 192
Gentlemen v Players (cricket match) 183
gentry 15, 53, 172, 254
Geordies 323
George Black 198
George III, King 255
George Street 258, 284
George Tavern 159, 202, 209, 279
Georgia 76
Georgian North Shields 90, 323
Gerdts, A.B. 330
Germanus, Prior 30
gibbeting 221, 317, 328
Gibson, W.S. 5, 14, 53, 77, 104, 137, 307,
    310–13, 327
Gilbert, A.D. 138–9, 161, 314–15, 327
Giles, Robert 134
Gilling 6
Gillow, Rev. 135, 327
gladiators 172
Gladstone, William Ewart 111, 216, 299
Glasgow 192, 198, 322, 328
glass and glassworks 45–6, 88, 115, 174–5,
    180, 244
Glorious Revolution 131
Good Design Association of Seamen and
    Landsmen 290
Gosden, P. 295, 321, 327
Gosforth 104, 106–7
Gould, E.M. 242, 319, 327
Graham, H. 322, 333

grain 33, 38, 263–5, 296
Greathead, Henry 60–1
Greek Orthodox Church 157
Greenhow, Dr, Edward Headlam and
    family 111, 121–2, 243, 327
Gregg, P. 317, 320–1, 327, 329
groceries and grocers 289–90
Guardians (Poor Law) 138, 180, 202, 265,
    278–9, 284
guard-ships 25
gun-brigs 70
gunnel 44
Gunpowder Plot 19
guns (see also firearms) 21–2, 26, 92, 144,
    173, 188, 194, 209, 282
gunwhales 61
Gurr, T. 322, 333

ha'penny dodger ferries 99
habeus corpus 37
Hadcock, R.N. 13, 307–8, 325, 327
haddock 74, 76
Hadrian's Wall 1, 4, 30, 42
Half Moon Inn 202
Hallelujah lasses 167
Haltwhistle 13
handball 184
handbooks 2, 110, 113–14, 307, 312, 326,
    329, 331, 334
handcuffs 117
hanging (execution) 221–2
harbours 25, 35–6, 55, 58–9, 62, 74, 76,
    84, 112, 174, 188, 228, 235
hard-labour 217
Hardrada 9
Harehope 13
Harford 13
Harold (Goodwinson), King 9–10, 300
Harrison, B. 310, 316–17, 327–8
Harrison, Ralph 188
Hartburn 13
Hartford (East and West) 109
Hartley 13
Hartley Pans 55
Hartley Pit disaster 273–5
harvests 263–5
Harvey, J. 328
Hastings, Battle of 9–11
Haswell, G.H. 3, 32, 38, 137, 151, 172,
    205, 225–6, 256, 258, 261, 264–5, 271,
    274, 284, 307–9, 311, 314–15, 317–19,
    321, 328

Hatchard, J.L. 324
Hatcher, J. 45, 309–10, 328
Hauxley 13
havens (including Tynemouth Haven) 21, 29, 34, 41, 54, 99, 182, 189
hawkers 202, 289
Hawkey's Hall Quoits Club 184
Hawkey's Lane 110, 164, 166, 184, 187, 189–91, 262, 287
Hawkey's Lane cycling ground and track 187
Hawkey's Lane Methodist Church 164, 166
Hawkey's Lane swimming pool 189–90
Hayter, Sir George 212
Healfdene 8
health 43, 66, 111, 113, 121–4, 166, 181, 203, 209, 231–5, 241, 243–6, 250, 253, 263, 266–7, 285, 304, 310–11, 313, 318–19, 327, 331, 334–5
Heath, Sir Robin 36
heathen 5
Hebburn 62, 198
Hedwin Streams 32, 34, 45
Hempton, D. 314, 328
Hemy, T.M.M. 229
Henderson, William 140
Henley Regatta 189
Henry I, King 12, 31, 113
Henry II, King 38
Henry VI, King 33
Henry VIII, King 1, 15–18, 33–4, 130, 138
Henry, of Coquet 8
Hepburn, Thomas 219
Hereward 11
herrings 32–3, 72, 74, 76, 231
Hertford, Earl of 16
hewers 175, 244, 251–2, 271
Hey, David 311, 328
High Light (see Low and High Lights)
Higham, N.J. 6, 308, 328
Hill-Carter's department store 91–2, 127
Hobbes, Thomas 245
hobbies 177
Hodgson G.B. 309, 327–8
Hogarth, Georgina 111
Hogarth, William 173
Hogg, Mr 203
Holland 24–7, 131
Hollerton, Eric 328
Hollis, P. 310, 317, 328

Holy Club (see Methodists) 143–4
Holy Saviour's Church (of England), Tynemouth 157
Holy Trinity Church (of England), Coach Lane 157–8
Holywell 13, 58, 115, 164, 282
Holywell Dene 282
Home and Colonial shops 289–90
home-crafts 177
Homer, Winslow 112, 163, 328
horseplay 245
horses 8, 17, 44, 55–6, 97–9, 100–1, 105, 119–20, 133, 179, 209, 225, 252, 271, 297
Horton 109
hose (leather) 119
hospitals 49, 88, 90, 96, 122, 243, 245, 259, 279, 282, 320, 331
hostmen 45, 49
hotels 90–1, 94, 103, 200, 209–10
Hotspur locomotive 103
household means test (see means test)
housework 176
housing 30–4, 37, 43, 63, 82–4, 86, 88, 92–6, 110, 114–15, 118–25, 153, 157–8, 168, 176–7, 186, 219, 229–30, 234, 236–9, 241, 262, 284, 283, 288, 300, 304, 318, 323–4, 330–1
Howard Hall Theatre and Cinema 146, 167, 198, 203
Howard Stores 269
Howard Street 32, 66, 70, 90–3, 96, 109, 119, 127, 141–2, 146–8, 159–63, 165, 167, 180–1, 186, 192, 198, 203, 209, 234, 261, 283
Howard, Lord 90
Howdon 49, 56, 65, 94, 96, 102, 114–15, 135, 183, 248, 252
Howdon Pit 252
Howell, R. 242, 308–9, 319, 328
Howick, Viscount 209–11
hoy boats 45
Hudson Street 154, 235
Humber River 4, 102, 188
Hume, James 135
Humphrey, George Harold 300
hunger march (see Jarrow)
Huntingdon, Earl of 18
husband-killing 222
hustings 211
hydrants 119
Hylton Street 74

Ibbotson, Derek 185, 326
ice 76, 269
idleness 204, 228, 246–50, 266–75, 302
igneous dyke 54
ignorance 204, 207, 218, 228, 240, 245,
    250–62, 264, 275, 284, 287, 302–6
illegitimate 9, 17, 240, 259, 277, 296–7
illiteracy 202, 212, 221, 254
illness (see disease)
immersion of adults (baptism) 142
immigration 135, 156–7, 169, 267
imports 49, 63, 264–5
impressment (see Press Gangs)
imprisonment 17–18, 36–7, 67, 140, 143,
    217, 223
incendiary bombs 94, 120
income 12–13, 31, 44, 55, 115, 243, 263,
    265–9, 271, 275, 281, 287, 289–90, 295,
    298, 304
independence 20, 37, 40, 62–3, 108, 141,
    145, 147, 164, 205–6, 208, 215, 223,
    298, 312
independent (non-denominational)
    churches 129
Independent (see Congregational)
    churches
Independent Order of Rechabites 292
India 226, 242, 282, 306
Indigent Sick Society 286
Industrial Revolution 110, 317–18, 320,
    326, 328, 332, 334–5
industrialisation 260, 266
industry (commercial) 41, 43, 47–8, 52–3,
    55, 57–8, 70, 72, 74, 88, 94, 110–12, 115,
    121, 126, 128, 166, 169, 177, 198, 202,
    205–6, 208, 211, 215, 217, 219–21, 232–3,
    247–8, 266, 269, 271, 282, 295–6, 309–10,
    313–14, 317–20, 325–8, 330, 332–5
industry (personal) 192, 227, 255–8, 260,
    287
inequalities 205–306, 304, 319, 327
infant mortality (see also death rates)
    240–1, 243, 267, 318, 334
infanticide 240–1, 318, 332
infections (see disease)
Infirmary, Tynemouth Jubilee 185–7, 245,
    286–7
Inglis, K.S. 328
Ingram, Alice (née Duncan) 124
inhabitants (of North Shields) 16, 39, 51,
    84, 156, 188, 197, 218, 231, 234–6, 310,
    331

inhalation of coal dust (see also
    anthracosis and pneumoconiosis) 253,
    275
injustice 222–7
inns (see pubs)
inspection of schools 255–9
insurance 68, 78, 119, 137, 197, 202, 228,
    249, 292–3, 298, 300, 316, 334
international 41, 66, 76, 121, 130, 178–9,
    215, 233, 313, 316–18, 320, 326,
    329–30, 332–3
internet 214
internment 169
interregnum 136
inter-war years 94, 102, 228, 248, 262,
    300, 324
Iona 6
Iowa 200–1
Ireland and Irish 4, 6, 20, 24, 131, 135,
    156–7, 224, 256, 267, 295–6, 307, 313,
    324–5, 335
iron (and steel) 34, 44, 53, 55, 72–3, 77,
    88, 98, 104, 175, 177, 180, 189, 204,
    221, 273, 295, 316, 333
Irvin, Richard 75–6
Isle of Man 4, 226
Isle of Wight 22
isolation hospitals 90, 243
itinerant preacher 142, 166

Jackson, Thomas 147
Jaffe, J.A. 317, 328
Jalland, P. 318, 328
James I, King of England (and VI of
    Scotland) 18, 130
James II, King 26–7
Jarrow 11, 40, 135, 189, 191, 248, 296, 317,
    328
Jefferson, Arthur and Stanley (Stan
    Laurel) 196–8, 282, 329
Jefferson, Thomas 206–7
Jehovah's Witnesses 129
Jesmond 33
jetsam 33
Jews 14, 149–50, 152, 168–9, 256, 187,
    315, 331
Jobey, G. 328
Jobling, William 220–1, 317, 328
Johannesburg 76
John Street, Cullercoats 105, 143
John Street, Percy Main 162, 165
John, King 31, 38

Johnson, Humphrey 35
Jorgensen 201
Jubilee School 255–8, 261–2
judges 212, 221
judgements (court) 31–2, 36, 195, 260,
    299, 306
Jupiter Optimus Maximus altar 2
justices of the peace 202, 276, 297
Jutes 3–5

Kapelle, W.E. 10, 308, 328
Kean, Edmund 194
Kearney E.W.C. 104–5, 312
Keating, P.E. 322, 328
keel boats and keel men 44–5, 48–9, 59,
    61, 70, 75, 98, 189, 230, 247, 291
Keith, Lord 17
Kelly, T. 317, 328
Kelso 185
Kemnitz, T.M. 213, 317, 328
Kennedy, President John F. 72
Kent 5–6
Kerr, Sir Andrew 17, 71, 225
Kettlewell School 255, 258, 261, 282
Kettlewell, Thomas 258, 282
Keynes, John Maynard 249
Kidd, A. 276, 290, 320–1, 329
Kilham, Alexander 145
Killingworth 56
King Edward Primary School xvii–xviii,
    182, 62
King Street 195, 198, 209, 235, 290
King, R. 225, 313, 316–17, 321, 329
Kingsley, Charles, 315, 323
Knott, James 65–8, 74, 239, 311
Knowles, Robert 223
Kyanski, B. 315

Labour Exchanges 248
labour market 263
Labour Party ix, 249, 299–302
labouring classes 205–302, 317–20
labouring classes and religion 150–5
labour-intensive housework 176
labour-saving device 176
laissez-faire 115, 124, 128, 247, 250, 254,
    299
Lamberts' Handbook 110, 113–14, 312,
    329
Lambton & C. Bank 140
Langton, Prior 33
Laslett, P. 267, 320, 329

Latvia 225
Laurel, Stan (and Oliver Hardy) xvii, 93,
    196, 198, 316, 329
Lawrence, Danny vii–xiii, xvii, 113, 305,
    329, 336, 342
Lawson Street 96
Laycock, S. 307, 329
Leeds Building Society 295
leisure xv, 52, 155, 171–204, 315–16, 325,
    330
Leland 1
Leno, Dan 120
lepers 88–90
less eligibility (see Poor Law)
Leviathan 245
Lewis, B 309, 329
Liberal Party 156, 178, 188, 212, 216, 246,
    299–300, 323
libraries 69, 91, 96, 127–8, 179–81
licenced premises for the consumption of
    alcohol (see pubs)
Licenced Victuallers' Association 202
Liddell Street 234, 238
Liddell, Henry Thomas 209–11
lifeboats 60–1, 330
lighthouses 1–2, 15, 22, 27, 60, 63–5, 323,
    325
Lilburn 13
Lilburn, Col. Henry 24
Lime and limestone 1, 16, 53, 55, 112–13,
    123
lime-burners 43
Limekiln Shore 92
limestone 1, 55, 112–13, 123
Lindisfarne 5–7
Lindsay, W.S. 61, 212
ling 33
Lingone Celts 2
linguistic record 9
Linskill Estate 157
Linskill School 262
Linskill Street 90, 146, 163, 169–70
Linskill Terrace 90
Linskill, William 90, 192, 262
Linskill's Ropery 73
Lipton's grocery shops 289
Lishman's Quay 200
Lisle, John 163–4
literacy 177–8, 202, 194, 212, 254, 319,
    325
Liverpool Victoria insurance 293
Lizard, HMS 225–6

Lloyd, A. 314, 329
Lloyd's insurance 57
Lloyd-George, David 94
loaf (see corn)
Lobina, E. 313, 329
locomotives 48, 56, 103
lodging-houses 117
Lomax, John 140
Lombard Arms 200
Lord Clifford 19
Lord Collingwood 114
Lord George Gordon 131
Lord Grey 209
Lord Howard 90
Lord Keith 17
Lord Protector 38
Lords of Coal 45
Louvish, S. 329
Lovaine Place 262
Low and High Lights 21–2, 55, 60, 62, 78, 88, 98, 159, 291
Lowe, Robert 259, 320, 329
Lowery, Robert 58, 214–15, 310, 317, 328
Loyal Standard Association 290–1
Luftwaffe 94, 120, 181
luggers 74, 228
Lukin, Lionel 61
luminism 47
Lumley, D. 329
Luther, Martin 144
Lutheran (also known as the Scandinavian or Norwegian) Church 154, 168
Lynch, J. 240, 332
Lynn Road Estate 94

Macaulay, T.B. 172, 216, 315, 329
Macdonald, Ramsay 300
Mackenzie, E. 285, 311, 314, 316, 329
mackerel 74, 190
Maehl, W.H. 212–13, 317, 329
magistrates 116, 173, 200, 218, 220–2, 284, 298
Magnesia Bank 121, 140
magnesian limestone 112
Maister 38, 265, 271, 307–9, 311, 314–15, 317–19, 321, 328
Malcolm III, King of Scotland 8, 11
malting house 135, 284
Manchester Unity of Oddfellows 292
Manders, F. 310, 312, 329
mangles 125, 177

Mann, Horace 150–4, 314, 329
Mansell, Robert 46
manslaughter 220, 240
manufacturing industries 34, 41, 45–6, 48, 52–4, 72–3, 91, 100, 103, 189, 214, 217, 269, 231, 290
manure 235, 122
maps 28, 79, 81–4, 86–9, 93–6, 168, 187, 200–1, 212, 279
Marden Burn 121
Marden Estate 30, 94, 104, 158
mariners (see seamen)
market forces (see also laissez-faire) 40, 48, 94, 115, 122, 124, 127–8, 138, 204, 218, 228, 263–4, 277, 300, 302, 304, 311, 316, 320–1, 324, 326
markets (physical) 32, 36–40, 52, 74, 76–7, 84, 97–8, 100, 235, 288
Marsden, J. 6, 307–8, 329–30
Marshall, T.H. 227, 318, 330
Marston Moor 23
Martineau, Harriet 111, 323
Marx, Karl and Marxism 128, 151, 205, 218
Mary I, Queen 26–7, 130–1
Mary, Queen of Scots 17–18
masonic lodges 192, 293
mass (see communion)
Master Mariners Homes 292
masters (ship's) 35–6, 38, 47, 57, 67, 101, 291–2
mate (ship's) 68, 297
Maude Pit 57
Maunders, S. 312
Maus, M. 288, 321, 330
Mayhew, Henry 76, 172
Mayor of London 45
Mayor of North Tyneside 243
Mayors of Newcastle 30, 35–7, 219
Mayors of Tynemouth 88, 90, 109, 156, 235, 327
McCombies (bomb shelter) 96
McCord, N. 221, 309–11, 317, 320–1, 330
McLeod, H. 151, 154, 314–15, 330
Meadowell (formerly the Ridges) Estate 238–9, 318–19, 323
medicine 90. 121, 245, 292, 319, 327, 330
medieval era 15, 17, 29–30, 33, 38, 115, 263
meeting-house 138, 140, 161, 214

Meiklejohn, A. 319, 330
Meller, H.E. 330
Mellor, G.J. 330
Menzies, Dr S.M. 168
mercantilism 40
Merchant Navy (see navy)
Mercia 4, 6, 8–9
Mersey 104
Mersfen 13
Messis Ab Altis 51–2
Metcalfe, A. 315–16, 330
Methodism 138, 142, 144–50, 152–4,
    158, 161–8, 198, 219, 252, 255–6, 293,
    314–15, 323, 325, 327–8, 331–2
midden-heaps 59–60, 65, 122, 237
Middle Chirton Farm 115
middle-class 153, 171–2, 176, 178–9, 194,
    300, 303
middle-men (see hostmen)
Middlesbrough 28, 102
Milbank, Sir Mark 281
Milbourne family of Chirton House 92
Milburn Place 110, 132, 145–6, 154, 233,
    300
Milburn, George 281
mine-owners 219, 244
miners 41, 52, 54–6, 58, 72, 94, 117,
    146–7, 164, 212, 218–21, 230, 242,
    244, 267–8, 250, 253, 271, 273, 275,
    285, 295–6, 299, 314, 317, 319, 321,
    325–6, 328, 334
Miners' Permanent Relief Societies 295
mines 32, 42–5, 48–9, 52, 54–8, 91, 100,
    111–13, 115, 121–3, 147, 184, 187,
    219–20, 242, 244–5, 248, 251–3, 254,
    267, 271, 273–5, 295, 299, 309–10, 315,
    319, 326, 329–31
Minton Lane 126, 182
minyan 169
Mitcalf's Ropery 73
Mitcalfe, Henry 212
Mitchell, B.R. 246, 266, 316, 319–21,
    330
Mitchell, Robert 117
Moffat, Edith 154
monarchy 20–1, 25, 40, 131, 136, 139, 206,
    208
monasteries 7–10, 12, 13–16, 28, 30–1, 34,
    307, 327
Monck, General 25
Monkchester (later Newcastle upon Tyne)
    11

monks (of Tynemouth Priory) 1, 5, 8,
    10–11, 13, 15–16, 29, 31–3, 113, 327
Monkseaton 8, 13, 55, 104, 110, 112–13,
    115, 157, 312, 333
monopolistic 37, 41, 44, 51, 138
monorail 104, 312
Montreal 189
Moravians 144
Morgan, G. 221, 317, 321, 330
Morpeth 77, 101, 115–16, 135–6, 316, 331,
    333
Morris, J. 330
mortality 236, 239–41, 243, 318, 333–4
Morton, E. 330
mortuary 126, 279
Mountford, C.E. 185, 316, 330
mourning 274
Mowbray, Robert de 11–12, 15
murders 6, 18, 221–3, 240
Murdoch, N.H. 167, 315, 330
Murphy, William 156
Murton 13, 55, 110, 114–15
museums 56, 127, 179–80, 244, 248, 327,
    332
Music Box (The) 93
music halls 175, 192, 194, 196, 198
music of the Salvation Army 167
muskets 215
mussel-scalps 33
mutiny (at Spithead) 223

Napoleonic wars 68, 92, 132, 207–8,
    225–6, 247, 264, 271, 282, 286,
    296–7
Narrows (the) 26
Naseby 23
Nater's House, Cullercoats 164
nationalisation 120, 126
navigation (of the River Tyne) 29, 32, 35,
    37, 44, 58, 60–2, 98, 298, 312, 333
navy (merchant and Royal) 61, 70, 82,
    223–5, 282, 297, 323
Neal, Daniel 139–40
Netherlands (see Holland)
nets (fishing) 74
Neville, Ralph de 16
new dissent 114, 144–8, 161–7
New Quay 84, 98, 104–6, 119, 141, 179,
    195, 209, 235
Newark 22
Newbiggin 13
Newburn 13, 20

Newcastle upon Tyne vii, xiv, 1, 11–13, 17,
    19–26, 28–41, 34, 36–8, 40–1, 43–51,
    55, 62–3, 65–6, 70, 74, 77, 82, 84, 90,
    94, 96–9, 101–4, 106–8, 110–11, 114,
    121–2, 127, 132–3, 135–6, 142, 145,
    169, 173, 178, 180–1, 189, 200, 203,
    205, 208–10, 214–15, 219, 223, 232, 235,
    239, 242–3, 245, 258, 261, 290, 295,
    307–12, 314, 316–19, 321, 323–3, 335
newspapers 76, 116, 173, 177–8, 180–1,
    184, 191–2, 202, 212, 215, 254, 272, 284
New York (in North Tyneside) 163–4
night-soil 234
Nile Street 65, 103
Ninnius 1
non-conformists 129, 138–40, 151, 255
non-denominational 165, 255, 260
Norfolk Street 73, 90, 105, 109, 119–20,
    129, 132, 142, 147, 179, 203
Norham 231
Norman Conquest 1, 9–11, 308, 328
North and South Shields Gazette 178, 327
North Shields Amateur Bicycle Club 203
North Shields and Tynemouth
    Dispensary 245, 285
North Shields Association Football Club
    185
North Shields Bicycle Club 187
North Shields Fishermen's Beneficial
    Society 292, 295
North Shields Friendly Society of the
    Low Glasshouses Florists 290
North Shields Friendly Society of Women
    292
North Shields Gentlemen's Club 179–80
North Shields Improvement
    Commissioners 108–09, 126
North Shields Sailmakers Friendly
    Society 292, 295
North Shields shipbuilders 70–4
North Shields Union Association 334
North Tyneside Metropolitan Borough
    Council viii, 55, 96
north-east (of England) 20, 49, 61, 101–2,
    108, 169, 202, 248, 266, 309, 315, 317,
    321, 328–32, 334
North-Eastern Football League 28, 329
Northern Press Association 178
Northumberland Arms 84, 209–10
Northumberland Dock 55, 63, 94, 115, 185
Northumberland Fusiliers 66
Northumberland Miners' Association 299

Northumberland Music Hall 195
Northumberland Park 29–30, 84, 88, 90,
    182, 311, 316, 325
Northumberland Shipbuilding Company
    248
Northumberland Square ix, 94, 96, 127,
    142, 159–60, 180–1, 186, 239, 279
Northumberland Street 154, 159–60, 235
Northumbria and Northumberland 4–6,
    8–13, 16–19, 30, 37, 42–3, 49, 54, 70,
    77, 86, 109, 133, 136, 141, 147, 173,
    192, 250–1, 253, 261, 274, 278, 285,
    287, 295, 307–18, 320, 323–4, 325–34
Norway 59
Norwegian Church (see Lutheran)
Nottingham 21, 322, 329
nuns and nunnery 8, 90, 132
nurses 133, 286
nystagmus 244

Obama, President Barack 70, 72
occupations 34–5, 43, 52–3, 77–8, 98, 103,
    127–8, 179, 197, 217, 241–4, 246, 263,
    271, 275, 279, 284, 294–5, 332
Oddfellows, Manchester Unity of 195,
    197, 292–3
odour (see smells)
offal 235
old dissent 26, 60, 114, 138–44, 159–61
Olsover, L. 169, 315, 331
Olympics (1908) 188
omnibuses (horse-drawn) 98, 101
OPEC 219
open-cast mining 43, 58
opera 194
opiates 151, 240
oppression 206–17, 222, 233
Orange, Prince of 24, 26
Orange-men 290
Order of the Sons of Temperance 292
ordination 144–5, 157
Oregis 59–60, 65
orphans 192, 196, 267, 282, 285
Orthodox Ashkenazi Jews 169–70
Orthodox churches 157
Osred 8
Ostia Verdre (South Shields) 1
Oswald 5–6
Oswin 6–8, 12–13, 15, 31, 157, 307, 327
Oswy 6
Othello 174
otter trawl net 75

Otterburn 16

Ouseburn 102

outbreaks (see disease)

outcrops of coal 43

out-relief of the poor 277

overcrowding 177–8, 181, 199, 234, 236, 237, 243, 238, 288

over-fishing 77

Overing, John 40

overseers (of the Poor Law) 276–8

Ovington 13

Oxford Movement 157

Oxford Street, Tynemouth 104, 164

paddle steamers 74, 99

pagans 5–6

Palladium (London) 198

Palmer's shipyard in Jarrow 248, 296

parachutist 94, 191

Parke, Willie 190, 221

Parliamentarians 19–26, 37–8, 46

Parliamentary Borough of Tynemouth (and North Shields) 79, 81, 108–9, 211

Parsons, Charles 66

Pasteur, Louis 245

pastimes (see leisure)

Paulinus (see Augustine)

paupers 144, 151, 241, 250, 265, 276–8, 293

pawnbrokers and pawn shops 270

Payne, Tom 188

Pearson's Ropery 73, 86, 106

Pearson, Anthony 90, 106

Pearson, H. 73, 111, 312, 331

Pearson, L. 315–16, 331

Peart, Joseph 146

pedestrian (and cyclist) tunnel (under the Tyne) 98, 105

pedestrianism 188

Peel, E.H. 116, 313, 331

Peel, Sir Robert 117

Peggy, HMS 223

Peggy's Hole 223

penal code 140, 217, 222–7

penalty (death) 222–3, 243

penalties (financial) 33

pen-hal-crag (see Benebalcrag)

Penman Street 96

penny-policies (insurance) 294

pensions 265, 291, 299

Pentecostal Assemblies of God 168

Percy Main 49, 56, 94, 101, 115, 135, 157–8, 220, 251–2, 261, 297, 328

Percy Main Pit 252

Percy Main Primitive Methodist Church 162–3, 165

Percy Park 186

Percy Park Rugby Football Club 186–7

Percy, Henry 17–19

Percy, Thomas 17–19

Perkin, H. 295, 321, 331

Peterloo 297–8

pews 151–2

philanthropy 68, 179, 239, 282

Phillips, M. 311–12, 317, 331

physicians 245

pianos 93, 177

Pickering, Father 118

Pickwick Papers 206

Picts 4, 8

pier (see Tynemouth Pier)

Pigot's Directory 52–3, 101, 200, 254, 310, 331

pigs 233, 235, 272–3

Pilgrim Fathers 139

Pilgrim's Progress 139

pilgrims 7–8

pilots (Tyne) 36, 38, 58–9, 60, 189, 230, 329

Pinder, Richard 143

piped water supply 121–6, 239–40

pitmen (see miners)

pits (see mines)

Pitt, W. 300

plague 23, 25, 136, 145, 233, 242

planning (town) 68, 94, 105, 199, 238–9, 300, 326, 330

Players (professionals) 183–5

Plaza (The) 107, 190, 197–8, 274, 283

plumbed-in (water, toilet and bathroom facilities) 124–5, 176

Plymouth Brethren 168

pneumoconiosis (see also anthracosis and inhalation of coal dust) 242, 244

Poland 242

police and policing 96, 116–19, 121, 156, 172, 180, 202, 214–15, 220, 234–5, 247, 279, 312, 317, 333–4

Police Quay 234

political issues 4, 6–7, 9, 20, 31, 38, 49, 51, 66, 123, 128, 139, 145–6, 170, 182, 202, 204–17, 222, 228, 247, 277, 295–6, 299–02, 305, 317, 321, 331, 324–7, 331, 333

Pollins, H. 169, 315, 331

pollution (of air and water) 122, 199, 233, 236, 334
Pons Alius 1
Poor Law Commissioners 241, 277
Pope (The) and 'popery' 17, 131, 133, 135, 138, 155, 210
Pope, R. 324, 331
Popplewell's Ropery 74
population (counts and composition) 9, 20, 30, 32, 52, 63, 79, 82–4, 94, 111, 121–2, 125, 133, 135, 139, 148–9, 155, 157–8, 161–2, 169, 176, 178, 181, 192, 200, 204, 223, 229, 233, 235, 241, 243, 246, 263–4, 266–7, 303–4, 311, 318, 323, 334–5
porpoises 30
port(s) 31, 33–4, 36, 40, 45, 47, 49, 51, 53, 55, 61–3, 72, 74, 76, 78, 82, 84, 91, 98, 108, 154, 172, 204, 208, 235, 242, 246, 269, 272, 283, 298, 323–4, 333
Portsmouth 226
Portuguese West Africa 76
poss stick and tub 176
Post Office ix
Postgate, R.W. 325
postman (executed) 223
postmaster (North Shields) 97
potato famine 156, 267, 296
potshare bowling 184
Potter, Emmanuel 86
pottery 53–4, 231, 323
Potts, R. 310, 312, 325, 329
poverty 76, 167, 238, 240–1, 246–7, 249, 254, 263–304, 320
Pow and Fawcus 72, 189
Pow Burn 29, 55, 60, 84, 88, 110, 223, 308–9, 316, 325
power (social, economic and political) 7, 14–15, 25, 31, 41, 45, 99, 116, 121, 123, 129, 139, 204, 206–7, 210–11, 216–17, 219, 222, 227, 246, 264–5, 287, 296, 301, 307, 329
power station (electricity) 48, 127
Presbyterian Churches 21, 24, 139–41, 149–50, 152, 154, 159–60, 163, 167, 239, 256, 314, 323
presentism 170
press gangs 222–5, 297–8, 317, 323, 330
Preston (township and village) 13, 30, 55, 79, 81–3, 101, 108–10, 113–14, 136–7, 143, 158, 168–9, 185, 190, 211, 245, 261, 274, 278–9, 332

Preston Avenue 185–7
Preston Cemetery 143, 169
Preston Colliery 49, 58, 185, 187, 248, 274
Preston Grange 30, 129, 158, 164
Preston Hospital 245, 279
Preston Park 96
Preston Road (formerly Preston Lane) 109, 123, 136–7, 185, 187, 190, 257, 278
Preston School 261
price levels 23, 43, 45, 48, 98, 186, 192, 195, 199, 206, 208, 219, 263–6, 289, 296, 299, 305, 318, 331
Price, H. 331
Price, N. 82, 318, 331
priests 130–3, 135, 138, 145
primary poverty (see also poverty) 267
primary schools 262
Primitive Methodism 146–7, 149–50, 152–3, 162–6, 252, 256, 314–15, 331
Prince Albert 115, 274
prince bishops 6
Prince Line 65–8
Prince of Orange 22
Prince Rupert 21
Prince's Theatre and Cinema (later the Gaumont) 198
Prior Germanus (of Tynemouth) 30
Prior Langton (of Tynemouth) 33
Priors of Tynemouth 15–16, 29–33
Prior of Winchcombe 11
Prior's Haven 99, 182
Priory Cycling Club 188
Priory School 261
prisons and prisoners 17, 24, 35, 37, 39, 116, 133, 139, 144, 221
private (as distinct from public) provision and initiatives 29, 78, 86, 96, 101, 103, 115–17, 119, 121–9, 138, 155, 162, 202, 205, 228, 238–9, 242, 275, 288, 313, 329
privies (lavatories) 18, 212, 233, 235, 238, 254, 299, 301
prizes 177, 183, 188–9, 226
Procter, H.R. 331
promontory (see also Benebalcrag) 1–4, 8, 11, 16, 19, 60, 182
propellers 74
Prosperous Pit 57
prostitution (see also brothels) 116, 118, 154, 172, 201
protectionism 207, 212

Protestantism 17–20, 131, 135, 133, 135, 138–40, 147, 149, 155–6, 210
prototype underground carriage 104–5
Provident Association 290
Provident Clothing and Supply Company (T. Archer Lee) 269
Prudhoe Castle 19
Prudhoe Street 94, 96, 105, 107, 195–6
Ptarmigan 72
public health legislation 231, 235, 245, 313, 335
public utilities and services 115–28
pubs 32, 53, 58, 65, 110, 112–13, 118, 121, 131, 140, 159, 178, 184, 195, 198–204, 209, 220, 230–1, 240, 279, 292–3, 316, 332–3
Pugh G. 259, 320–1, 331
pumps (water) 122–3
Punjab 242
Purdy, William 74, 76
puritanism 19–25, 131, 136, 139, 308–9, 319, 328
pursuits (see pastimes)
Purvis, Billy 195
putters 251–3
puys 44

Quakers 77, 88, 92, 110, 138–40, 142–4, 255, 259, 311, 313–14, 318, 320, 324, 329
quarries 42, 55, 112–13, 123
Quebec 228
Queen Alexandra Sixth Form College 262
Queen Street 142, 235
Queen Victoria 70, 72, 109, 218, 247, 274, 283, 291
Queen Victoria School 261–2
quoits 184–5

Rabbi Salis Daiches 168–9
radicalism 146, 208, 212, 215, 295–6, 310, 317, 323, 328
Rædwald 4
ragged churches 153
rag-man 288
railways and railway stations ix–xi, 48, 55–6, 74, 93–4, 100, 102–4, 108, 111, 115, 191, 235, 299, 309, 312, 326–7, 329, 331, 334
Rainbird, V.N. 325
Ralph Gardner (see Gardner, Ralph)
Ramsay, John 239

Randvoll projector 197
Ranger Report (Ranger, William) 62, 84, 122, 181, 231, 233–7, 310–11, 313, 318–19, 331
Ranters and Ranters' Chapel (see also Primitive Methodism) 146–7, 252
Raper, William 281
rationing 58
rattle (policemen's) 117
Rawlinson, R, 122, 313, 331
Reagan, President Ronald 72
Rechabites 292
re-creation 177
recreation/re-creation (see also leisure) 84, 182, 315–16, 330
Redistribution Act (1885) 215–16
Reed Street 235
Reed, Christopher 138
Reed, G. 1, 307
Reed, John 138
reflectors, revolving in the lighthouse 60
Reform Acts, 1832, 1867 and 1884 108–9, 207–8, 211–16
Reformation 19–20, 138–9, 157, 160
refrigeration 266
Regent Street 229
religion xv, 5–6, 9, 15, 17–18, 20, 129–73, 177–9, 210, 255–6, 286, 313–15, 324, 326–30, 334–5
Religious census (1851) 148–55
Renforth. James 189
rents (during the First World War) 299–300
reservoirs 123–4, 185, 187, 189, 199, 281
residential developments 73, 81, 83, 90, 93–4, 104, 112–13, 157, 160, 164, 180, 182
Resolute, HMS 70, 72
respectability 146, 166, 171, 177, 179, 183–4, 199, 227, 269, 314, 316, 333
restaurants (on the Fish Quay) 76–7
restoration (of the monarchy) 25, 40, 131, 139, 206, 208
retailing (see also shops) 90–1, 96, 204, 269
revivalism (religious) 145–7, 161, 165, 167
Rex Cinema 199
rhetoric (violent in Chartism) 213
ribboner (see white ribboners)
Richard I, King 31
Richard II, King 32, 43
Richardson M.A. 321

Richardson, Elizabeth 259
Richardson, John 78, 88, 144, 311, 324
Richardson, Margaret 281
Richardson's Tannery 78, 127, 144, 259, 311, 324
Richardsons of Cleveland 311, 324
Ridges housing estate (see also Meadow Well) 165, 238–9, 262, 300
Ridges Mission 165
Ridges School 262
riff-raff (and William Booth) 152
riots (see disturbances)
Rippon, George 93
River Humber 4
River Tees 10
River Tyne 1–4, 13, 8, 10–14, 17–27, 29–38, 40–1, 43–6, 48–52, 55, 57–63, 65, 70, 73–4, 76, 79, 81–4, 86, 88, 94, 96–102, 104, 106, 110, 113–15, 123, 154–5, 167–9, 179, 181, 188–9, 191–2, 200–1, 205, 216, 219, 221, 229–31, 235–6, 242, 246, 248, 272, 274, 282, 284, 292, 295, 298, 308–12, 314–16, 319, 321, 324–35, 334
River Wear 34, 46, 219
riverside 40, 44, 52–3, 83–4, 88, 90, 94, 96, 100, 104, 109, 115, 200, 205, 214, 229–30, 233, 238–9, 241, 243, 267, 274, 276
roads 30, 49, 55, 57, 73–4, 84, 88, 90, 92–4, 96, 98, 100–2, 104–10, 113–16, 123, 134, 136–8, 154, 157–9, 162, 165, 168–9, 183, 185, 190, 192, 195, 249, 257, 278, 281, 291–2
Robert Gordon Lodge of the Foresters 293
Robinson, Elizabeth Amy 162
Robinson, James 68–9, 311, 331
Robinson, John 68–9
Robinson, Joseph 68–9, 162
Robinson, Nicholas J. 311, 331
Robinson, Richard 284
Rochdale Cooperative Society 290
Roddam, H.R. 331
Roman Catholicism (see Catholicism)
Romans 1–6, 30, 42, 101, 307, 309, 331–2
roperies 47, 53, 73–4, 77, 86, 90, 93, 104, 115, 141–2, 177
Ropery Banks 104, 141–2
Rosella (Edwin's daughter) 5, 96
Rothbury 13
rotten-borough 211

Rowe, D. 212, 317, 321, 332
rowing 61, 97, 182, 188–9
rowlock 189
Rowntree, Seebohm 266–7, 275, 281
Roxby-Beverley partnership 193
Royal Liver insurance 293
Royal Mutual Insurance Society 293
Royal Navy (see navy)
Royal Northumberland Glassworks 174
Royal Quays 103
RSPCA 173
Rudyerd Street 154, 168, 197
Rufus (see William II)
rugby football 184–6
Rupp, G. 325, 332
Russell Street 198
Russia 242
Russian Orthodox Church 157
Russian revolution 94
Ruston P. 221, 317, 321, 330
Ryton 32

safety lamps (for coal miners) 244
sailing ships 30, 44, 46, 48, 52–3, 57–9, 61–3, 66, 68, 70, 74, 82, 188–9, 225, 271–2, 294–5, 297, 309, 326
sail-makers 47, 53, 258, 292
sailors (see seamen)
Salem Methodist Church 146, 163, 165, 256
salmon 30, 33, 47, 236
salt (see also brine) 14, 33–6, 38, 52–3, 55, 57, 72, 76, 112, 115, 123, 125, 136, 174, 187, 192, 231, 271, 273
Saltburn 42
Salvation Army 141, 152, 166–7, 195
sandbanks 32, 59–60, 63–4
Sanderson, M. 320, 332
Sanger's Circus 185
sanitation 84, 121, 199, 231, 234–5, 243, 310, 327, 331
Sankey, David 161
Santayana, George 305
Saville Street viii–ix, 73, 90–2, 94, 96, 106, 109, 116, 118, 120, 125, 127, 129, 163–4, 179–80, 195, 197, 213, 279, 289
saving and savings (money) 78, 154, 213, 249, 277, 292–3
Saxons (see Anglo-Saxons)
Scandinavia 9, 11, 154, 168
Scarth, John (Tynemouth's last town-crier) 177

scavenging 233

schools 37, 66, 94, 119, 142, 146, 151, 154–5, 162–3, 169, 184, 215, 205, 223, 239, 251–2, 254–62, 265, 282–3, 286, 306, 332

schooners 228

Scot, Nicholas (Mayor of Newcastle) 30

Scotch Church 6, 135, 141, 147–8, 256, 259, 261

Scotland 4, 6, 8, 10–11, 13, 16–25, 32, 37, 41, 74, 77, 111, 130–1, 140–2, 190, 307, 310, 324–5

Scott, Alexander 93–4, 96, 143

Scott, Michael 137, 313–15, 332

Scott, Robert 75

screw-driven boats 57, 61

sculler-boats and scullermen 97–8, 189, 226, 230, 271, 291

sea coal (see also coal) 42–3

sea-air 15

sea-bathing 110

seafarers (see seamen)

sea-frets 14

Seaham 274, 307, 310, 325, 328, 335

seams (see coal)

seamen (including mariners, sailors and seafarers) 24, 37, 52, 58, 60, 63, 82, 84, 144, 154, 168, 172, 175, 200–1, 209–10, 220–47, 269, 271–2, 282–3, 285, 288, 290–2, 296–8, 321, 323, 330, 332

Seamen's Loyal Standard Association 154

seaside 113, 164, 182

Seaton Delaval 37, 174, 326–7

seaweed 14

Second World War xi, 58, 69, 94, 105, 120, 126, 166, 183, 217, 228, 249, 258, 262, 266, 298, 301

secular 15, 29, 128–9, 138, 151, 170, 255, 313, 330, 334

Segal, Dr S. 300

Segedunum 1–2, 4

Seghill 13, 58

self-improvement 177–9

self-sufficiency 29

sentences (court) 116, 220–1, 223

servant 222, 267

servants 37, 151, 175–6, 222, 257, 267, 299

Seven Years War 247

Severus 1

sewers (see drains and sewers)

Shakespeare 194–6, 198

Shanghai 201

Shaw, J.S. 315, 332

Shaw, William 212

shawl (worn in Cullercoats) 163

sheep 235

shellfish 77

shelters (see air raid shelters)

Shepherd, V.A. 314, 332

Shetlands 33

Shield(s) alternative meaning 30

Shields and Tynemouth Argos 178

Shields Bar 59–60, 63, 111

Shields Engineering and Dry Dock 76

Shields Daily News 178, 293, 316, 324

shiels (also known as sheales and sheeles) 21, 29–31

shingle 42, 59

shipbrokers 66

shipbuilders and shipyards 47, 53, 68, 70–3, 90, 97, 115, 212, 216, 248, 269, 326, 334

shipbuilding and shipyards (specifically in North Shields) 70–2, 94, 326

ship-owners 33, 47, 66, 68–9, 76–7, 143–4, 162, 225, 254, 284, 297–8

shipping 40, 43–4, 53, 58, 61, 63, 65–8, 98, 102, 269, 271, 329, 334

ship-repairing 72

ships (in the Tyne) 14, 22–3, 25, 31–6, 38, 40–1, 43–8, 57–64, 66–72, 74–6, 78, 82, 92, 98–101, 103, 111, 175, 188, 216, 221, 222–4, 228, 235, 242, 246, 248, 272, 297–8, 316, 334

Shipwrecked Fishermen's and Mariners' Society 291

shipwrecks 12, 57, 59–60, 66, 272, 292, 326

shipwrights 35–6, 209

Shiremoor 49, 55–6, 58, 114–15, 122–3, 164

shops 38, 90–2, 96, 109, 117, 127, 160, 176, 179, 188, 195, 199, 219, 224, 234–5, 239, 269, 279, 289–90

Shotton, Jack 204, 311, 316, 332

shrine (on Benebalcrag) 7, 13, 15

Sibthorpe Street 291

Silkey's Lane 115

Simpson Street, Cullercoats 163

Simpson, R. 332

skating (roller) 190

Skipsey, Cuthbert 220, 317, 334

slaughterhouses 235

slauk 14

sloops 228

slums and slum clearance 158, 237–9, 243, 267, 284, 300, 304, 323

smack (fishing) 74

smallpox 243, 265

smells 76, 232, 237

smelting 115

Smith, A.V.H. 309, 332

Smith, G.D. 240, 332

Smith, K. 326

Smith, Adam 227

Smith, Thomas 67, 247

Smith, Thomas Eustace 72, 216, 315

Smith, William Thomas 70–2

Smith's Dock x, 70–3, 118, 332

smoke (from coal) 43, 126, 231–2

smoked fish 33, 76

Smurthwaite, Harold 114, 332

Smyth, John 19

snooker 190

snow 14, 133, 195, 265

Snowdon, L.M. 197

societies (leisure) 178–9

soldiers 17, 21, 24, 27, 38, 98, 132, 136, 213, 215, 221, 226, 247, 296

Somme, Battle of 67, 268

Souter Point 60

Southampton 34

South Shields 1–2, 22, 30, 34–5, 40, 52, 55, 59–65, 68, 77–8, 84, 97–102, 104–5, 119, 135, 142, 169, 178, 180, 185, 189, 197, 213, 274, 309, 326–8, 350, 356

Southwold, Battle of 137

Spain 16, 18–20, 21, 230

Sparhawk sandbank 32, 34, 45

Spence, Ald. J.F. 90, 239

Spence, Robert 77, 230

Spencer, Herbert 111, 312, 332

spiritists and spiritualists 129, 168

Spital Dene 88

Spithead Mutiny 223

sports 155, 172–3, 183–5, 188–90

squalor 204, 225–9, 231, 233, 275, 284, 302

St Aidan 5–6, 158

St Aidan's Church (of England), Billy Mill 158

St Aidan's Church on Lindisfarne 5

St Andrew's Congregational Church 141

St Albans Abbey 5, 11, 13, 31

St Augustin Church (of England) 152, 157–8, 326

St Columba 6

St Columba's Presbyterian Church 159–60, 314, 332

St Cuthbert's Roman Catholic Church 133–5, 149, 157, 169, 255, 313, 332

St Hilda's Church (of England), South Shields 28, 157, 178

St John's Ambulance Certificate 121

St John's Church (of England), Percy Main 158, 165

St Joseph's Roman Catholic Church 157, 261–2

St Leonard's hospital 88

St Luke's Mission 158

St Margaret's Methodist Church 163, 166

St Mary's Roman Catholic Church, Cullercoats 157

St Oswin's Church (of Our Lady and St. Oswin) 12

St Oswin's School 262

St Paul's Church (of England), Whitley Bay 157, 247

St Peter's Church (of England) 157–8, 261, 297

St Peter's School 261

stables 32, 120

staithes 33, 44, 48–9, 53, 55, 57, 113, 115

Stamford 9–10

Stamfordham, Vicar of 86

Stanley Street West 93, 129

Stanley, Emma 198

Star and Garter Quay 195

steam-driven 48–9, 53, 55–9, 62, 66, 68, 70, 74–7, 88, 98–9, 105, 117, 120, 188, 210, 231, 248, 271, 292, 309, 323, 326

Stearns, P. xiv, 51, 307, 310, 333

steel (see iron)

Stephen, King 31

Stephens, W.B. 319–20, 333

Stephenson, George 56, 244

Stephenson Railway Museum 56

Stephenson Street 73, 96, 142–3, 159–62, 234

Stephenson Street Congregational Church 159–60

Stephenson, Robert 215, 193

Stephenson's Ropery 73, 86, 90

steps (from the riverside to Bank Top) 93, 96, 192, 230

Stevenson, J. 333

Stockholm 228

stocks (parish) 116

stores (see shops)
Storey, G. 312, 333
Storey, John 14
Storey, W.H. 76
storms 14, 30, 60, 63–4, 111, 244, 271–2, 285, 326
Strathclyde 8
Stratton, Dr Thomas 244
street cleaning 123, 189, 233–7, 241
street lamps and lighting 48, 108, 126–7
strikes 44, 211, 218–21, 295, 297–9, 321, 330
submarine base (Blyth) 283
Suez Canal 68
Suez Street 105
suffrage 185, 203, 209, 301, 305
Sunday Schools 252, 259
Sunderland 23, 28, 46, 66, 77, 135, 169, 212, 242, 272, 298
superstitions 143, 272
surgeons 121, 140, 236, 245, 319, 335
suspension bridge proposal 98
Sutcliffe, M.P. 317, 333
Sutton United 186
Swan, Hunter and Wigham Richardson shipyard xii, 66, 73
swape 44
Swarthmoor Hall 143
Sweezy, P.M. 333
swimming 30, 96, 188–90
swinging sixties (1860s) 163–4
Sybil 218, 317, 325
Sykes, J. 239, 318–20, 333
synagogue 168–70
Szreter, R. 240, 318, 333

Taggart, J. 30, 333
tallow candles 60
tallymen 202
Tanner's Bank 88, 116, 127
tanneries 30, 53, 78, 88, 127, 144, 231, 331
taverns (see pubs)
tax (on coal) 45, 276
Taylor, A. 288, 320–1
Taylor, Hugh 212
Taylor, M. 333
teachers and teaching 140, 142, 255–6, 259–60, 286
Tearle, Osmond 195–6
teetotal (see temperance)
telephones 118–20, 197
telescope (present to Garibaldi) 215

television 178, 199
Telford, Thomas 98, 101
temperance 58, 78, 147, 159, 171, 179–80, 200, 202–3, 292–3
tennis 182, 185, 190
Thames (River) 57, 97, 189, 297
Thatcher, Margaret 249, 305
theatres 25, 96, 119, 142, 146, 174, 192–9, 225, 279, 285, 313, 316–17, 329, 331
thieves 116–18, 317, 321, 330
thirties (see inter-war years)
Thompson, F.M.L. 150, 177, 311, 314, 316, 325, 332, 333
Thompson, E.P. 296, 321, 333
Thompson, J. 312, 333
Thorburn and Grant 216
Thorne's theatrical booth 195
Thorpe, Henry Alvo 197
thrift 154, 270, 277
tides 33–4, 44, 55, 60, 112, 234
Tilbury 97
Tilly, Charles 305, 322, 333
timber 5, 14, 19, 57–8, 72, 104, 160, 228, 327
Tinmouth (see Tynemouth)
tinned fish 76
tithes 13, 18
tobacco 53, 278, 284
toilets (indoor) 124, 239
Toll Square 235
Toll, Edward 86
Tomlinson, W.W. 102, 113, 312, 333–4
tommy shops 219
Tostig 9–10
Tower of London 18–19
Town Hall ix
town-crier 177
townships 13, 24, 30–1, 35, 37, 49, 54, 79, 81–3, 97, 107–11, 114, 233, 236–7, 241, 276, 332
toys 177–8
track (cycling) 185–8
tracks (railway and tram) 104–7
trade 20–2, 29–34, 36–8, 40–6, 48–9, 52–5, 58, 61, 66, 68–70, 72, 84, 92, 94, 100–1, 103, 105, 140, 168, 208–9, 212, 217–19, 221, 231–3, 242–3, 246, 250, 289, 295–9, 301, 305, 309, 316, 321, 324, 326, 332–4
trade disputes 218, 202, 218, 220–1, 299
trade(s) unions 202, 217–21, 246, 292, 295–9, 301, 305, 317, 321, 328, 332

trades (see occupations)

Trafalgar, Battle of ix, 247, 323

traffic (river) 61, 99, 102

training ship 282–3, 327

trains (see railways)

traitors (see treason)

trams 100, 102, 105–7, 251, 312, 328, 334

transportation (as a punishment) 48, 222–3

transporter bridge 102

transubstantiation 131, 157

trapdoors 117

trappers 250

trawl net and trawlers 70, 74–7

treason 17, 19, 29, 208, 222

Trevelyan, George Otto 216

Trimdon Grange mining disaster 274

Trimmer, P. 107, 312, 334

Trinity Church (of England), Coach Lane 157–8

Trinity House 36, 224, 261

Trinity Methodist Church, Chirton Grange 164–6, 168

Trinity School 261

truncheon (police) 117

tube train (proposed for Tyne) 104, 312, 323

tuberculosis 243

tugs and tug boatmen 61, 74, 76, 216. 292

tunnels (under the Tyne) 97–8, 104–5, 221

Tunnocellum 1–2

turbines (steam) 66

Turnbull, G.M. 318–19, 323

Turner, George Grey 121

Turner, M. 311, 334

turnpikes 101, 110

Tweed (River) 98, 333

Tyne (see River Tyne)

Tyne and Blyth Trimmers and Teemers Association 292

Tyne Brand trademark 76, 146

Tyne Commissioners 37–8, 40, 63, 99–100, 102

Tyne Dock 57, 72

Tyne Fishermen's Society 292

Tyne Foy Boatmen's Provident Society 292

Tyne Hand-in-Hand Friendly Protecting Society of Journeymen Coopers 202

Tyne Iron Society 295

Tyne pilots 329

Tyne Steam Packet Provident Society 292

Tyne Watermen's Society 292

Tyne, Wear and Tees Tugboatmen's Federation 292

Tynemouth 1–33, 35, 38, 51–2, 54–6, 58–9, 65, 79, 81–2, 86, 88, 90, 99, 101–5, 107–16, 118–23, 130, 132–2, 135–6, 138, 143, 147, 151–2, 157–8, 160, 162, 173, 181, 189–90, 195, 198, 215, 233, 242, 276, 281, 283, 291–2, 307–16, 318–19, 321–34

Tynemouth Amateur Operatic Society 198

Tynemouth Aquarium and Water Garden (see Plaza)

Tynemouth Association for the Prosecution of Felons 116

Tynemouth Borough Council (see Borough of Tynemouth)

Tynemouth Borough Silver Band 274

Tynemouth Castle xiii–xiv, 14–28, 35, 54, 59, 60, 119, 132, 135–6, 143, 147, 323, 326–9, 332

Tynemouth dyke 54

Tynemouth Golf Club 30, 184, 190

Tynemouth Literary and Philosophical Society 69–70, 127–8, 179

Tynemouth Municipal High School xii, xviii, 262

Tynemouth Palace (see Plaza)

Tynemouth Park 182

Tynemouth Photographic Society 334

Tynemouth Pier 54, 59–60, 63–5

Tynemouth Priory viii, xiv, 1–5, 10–15, 23–4, 26–7, 30–4, 52, 54–5, 86, 90, 99, 112–13, 115, 130, 132, 182, 307–8, 316, 321, 325–9, 332

Tynemouth south field 86

Tynemouth World War One Commemoration Project 267, 268

Tyneside 9, 21, 25, 28, 36, 39–41, 43, 46, 48–9, 55–6, 58, 66, 70, 96, 106–7, 109–10, 167, 173, 188–9, 212–13, 215–16, 243, 278, 288, 291–2, 295, 301, 307, 312, 316–17, 320–1, 323–4, 326–34

Tyneside and District Labourer's Association 292

Tyneside and National Labour Union 292

Ulgham Grange 211

Unanimous Association of North Shields 290

under-employment 249, 304

unemployment 90, 175, 226, 246–50, 266, 280, 296–7, 300, 304, 319, 324, 330
Union Association 202
Union Bank 78
Union Quay 74
Union School for Girls 258
Union Ship Insurance 78
Union Stairs 154, 238
Union Street 32, 92, 119, 127, 132–3, 147, 163, 192–3
unions (see trade(s) unions)
unitarianism 140
United Association of Colliers 219
urban-sanitary-diarrhoea 240
USA 153, 175, 292, 328
utilitarian 137
utilities 52, 77, 115, 128

vaccinations 285
Veblen, Thorstein 174
velocipedes 185
ventilation 90–1, 198, 237, 244, 250
Verne Road 159
vessels (see ships)
vestry (Four and Twenty) 108, 157
viaducts 102, 327
vicars 19, 86, 135, 137–8, 140, 157, 191–2, 281
Victorian Association for the Prosecution of Felons 116
Victorian period 117–18, 166, 176–9, 183, 204–5, 239–40, 246–7, 286, 291, 303, 313–16, 318, 320, 323, 325, 328, 330–1, 333–5
victuallers (licensed) 201–2, 224
Villiers, Col. 25–7, 323
Vinci (da Vinci code) 72
voting 109, 117, 206, 208–12, 216–17, 227, 297, 300–1, 305, 317, 331

wages 117, 175, 201, 217, 222, 249, 263, 265–6, 268–9, 271, 275, 295, 297, 304
wagons (coal) 47, 49, 55–6, 97, 104, 112, 115, 252
Waldo Street 291
Walker Place 88
Walker, John 88, 91–2
Walker's (The House of Quality) 91–2, 269
Wallace, William 16
Waller, David 70–1, 334
Wallis, Robert 97

Wallsend 1, 3, 49, 66, 70, 94, 102, 106–7, 109, 135, 198, 274, 295, 301
Wallsend Colliery Relief 295
want 263–75
Wappat, Frank 165
Ward's Trade Directories 78, 289
Wardle, D. 320, 334
Warkworth 13
warlords 307, 329
wars (see also individual conflicts) 13, 17, 20–2, 24–6, 43, 46, 58, 63, 65–70, 76, 92, 94, 104–5, 120, 126, 131–2, 135, 166, 178, 183, 199, 207–8, 215–17, 223, 225–6, 228, 246–9, 258, 262, 264, 266–8, 271, 282–3, 286, 296–301, 308, 319, 324, 328, 334
washing clothes 125, 176, 237
Washington Terrace 90, 96, 157
watchmen 116
water (drinking) 78, 119–28, 137, 176, 185, 199–200, 231, 235–7, 239–42, 310, 313, 329, 331
Waterloo (Battle of) 208
watermen 283, 292
Waters, Matthew 74, 86, 93, 209
Waterville 93–4, 129
Waterville Road 168
waterworks 78, 123
Watson, R.S. 317, 334
Watt, Mrs Patrick 231
Webb, Sidney 334
Weetslade 109
Weir's, Miss (school) 259
welfare state 204, 263, 266, 276, 320–1, 326–7
Wellesley training ship 282–3, 327
Wellington locomotive 103, 282, 293
Wellington Street 293
Wellington, Duke of 282, 296–7
wells 121–2, 151
Welton 13
Wembley 186
Wentzel, Chuck xvii
Wesley Coach Lane Methodist Church 166
Wesley, John and Charles 144–5, 167
Wesleyan Methodist Association 147
Wesleyan Methodists 146–7, 149–50, 152–4, 159, 161–2, 168, 219, 255–6, 258
West Chirton farm 94
West End Park 182–3
West Percy Street 96

Westbrook, Emma 167
Western Board School 261
Westgate 13
Westminster Abbey 247
Westmorland, Earl of 17–18
whaling 76
Whalton 13
wharves 30–1, 36, 226, 230–1
Whellan, W. 281, 320–1, 334
wherries 62
whistle (police) 117
whistling superstition 272
Whitby 6, 47, 68, 77, 88, 112, 143
white ribboners 203
Whitehead, James 61
Whitehill Point 40, 63, 99
Whitley (Bay) 13, 55, 60, 104–5, 107, 110,
    112–13, 115, 123, 135, 143, 157, 163–4,
    166, 188, 197, 199, 312, 323, 327, 333
Wickham, E.R. 334
Wilkinson's Factory 96
Williams, James 214
William (of Orange) and Mary 15, 26–7,
    131, 140, 143
William, the Conqueror 9–11
William II, King (Rufus) 10–11, 15
Williams, N. 240, 318–19, 334
Willington 109, 115, 135
Willington Dene 63
Willington Quay 94, 109, 115, 164, 248
Willington Quay Primitive Methodist
    Church 164
Wilson, B. 313, 334
Wilson, Eleanor 281
Wilton, Rob 120
Winchcombe, Prior of 11
Winchelsea (rotten borough) 211
windlasses 53
winds 14, 44, 58–9, 74, 111, 231
Windsor Castle 72
Winifred, C. 334
Witan 10
Wohl, A.S. 124, 232, 313, 318–19, 335
Wolffe, J. 313, 335
Wolsington 13

Wombwell Menagerie 195
Wood, Willie 188
Wooden Bridge Bank 154
wooden chapel on Benebalcrag 5–6
wooden dollies 272–3
wooden-railed wagonways 55
Woodhorn 13
Woods, R. 311, 318, 335
Wooler 13, 140
Woolworth's 164
Wooperton 13
Wordsworth, William 111, 328
workhouse 109, 114, 123, 133, 151, 168,
    185, 244–5, 250, 265, 276–81, 284,
    287
working conditions 57, 175, 177, 199–200,
    217–21, 232–3, 244–53, 266–7, 269,
    282, 287, 295–9, 304, 317, 328
Workmen's Compensation Act 299
workmen's trains 100, 104, 210, 274
workshop of the world (Britain) 41, 48,
    250
World War One (see First World War)
World War Two (see Second World War)
Worswick, Rev. James 132–3, 135
Wouldhave, William 60–1, 71
Wright, John 90–1, 192, 234
Wright, Ron 201, 272, 310–11, 315–16,
    320, 335
Wright, Thomas Giodarni 245, 319, 335
Wrigley, E.A. 309, 318, 335
wringer (see mangle)
writer 1, 111, 132
Wylam 13

Yarmouth 46, 226
YMCA (Young Men's Christian
    Association) 168, 203
York 5, 8, 10, 27, 266–7, 323
Yorke, Auguste 178
Young, Frederick M.P. 212
Ypres 66

Zenith (fishing boat) 74–5
zero-hours contracts 304